Logic and Contemporary Rhetoric

The Use of Reason in Everyday Life

ELEVENTH EDITION

9780495804116 0019

Logic and Contemporary Rhetoric

The Use of Reason in Everyday Life

ELEVENTH EDITION

Nancy Cavender

Professor Emeritus
College of Marin

Howard Kahane

Late of
University of Maryland
Baltimore County

WADSWORTH
CENGAGE Learning

Australia • Brazil • Japan • Korea • Mexico • Singapore • Spain • United Kingdom • United States

WADSWORTH
CENGAGE Learning™

Logic and Contemporary Rhetoric: The Use of Reason in Everyday Life, **Eleventh Edition**
Nancy M. Cavender and
Howard Kahane

Senior Sponsoring Editor:
Joann Kozyrev

Assistant Editor:
Nathan Gamache

Editorial Assistant:
Michaela Henry

Media Editor: Diane Akerman

Marketing Manager:
Mark Haynes

Marketing Assistant:
Josh Hendrick

Marketing Communications
Manager: Elizabeth Rodio

Project Manager, Editorial
Production: Matt Ballantyne

Creative Director: Bruce Bond

Art Director: Faith Brosnan

Print Buyer: Marcia Locke

Permissions Editor:
Timothy Sisler

Production Service:
Robin Calkins

Copy Editor: Jennifer Gordon

Cover Designer: RHDG

Cover Image:
© images.com/Veer

Compositor: Macmillan
Publishing Solutions

For product information and technology assistance,
contact us
at **Cengage Learning Customer & Sales Support,**
1-800-354-9706
For permission to use material from this text or product,
submit all requests online at **www.cengage.com/permissions**
Further permissions questions can be e-mailed to
permissionrequest@cengage.com

Library of Congress Control Number: 2008911155

Student Edition:
ISBN-13: 978-0-495-80411-6
ISBN-10: 0-495-80411-8

Wadsworth
10 Davis Drive
Belmont, CA 94002-3098
USA

Cengage Learning is a leading provider of customized learning solutions with office locations around the globe, including Singapore, the United Kingdom, Australia, Mexico, Brazil, and Japan. Locate your local office at **www.cengage.com/international**

Cengage Learning products are represented in Canada by Nelson Education, Ltd.

To learn more about Wadsworth, visit
www.cengage.com/wadsworth

Purchase any of our products at your local college store or at our preferred online store **www.ichapters.com**

Printed in Canada
3 4 5 6 7 13 12 11 10 09

In memory of Virginia Pittenger Tulenko

CONTENTS

I do not pretend to know what many ignorant men are sure of.

      —Clarence Darrow

To know that we know what we know, and that we do not know what we do not know. That is true knowledge.

      —Henry David Thoreau

We have met the enemy and he is us.

      —Walt Kelly's "Pogo"

Education is not simply the work of abstract verbalized knowledge.

      —Aldous Huxley

Many people would sooner die than think. In fact, they do.

      —Bertrand Russell

You can fool too many of the people too much of the time.

      —James Thurber

PREFACE

The purpose of this eleventh edition of *Logic and Contemporary Rhetoric,* as of the previous ten, is to help students improve their ability to reason well about problems they encounter in everyday life and about issues that are debated in the social/political arena. (The intent certainly is not to move students to the right or left on the political spectrum but rather to help them move up on the scale measuring rational sophistication.)

The text contains examples and exercise items drawn from a broad range of sources—television programs, advertisements, literary works, political speeches, newspaper columns, the Internet, and so on.

Students get to sharpen their ability to think critically by reasoning about important topics and issues—Internet ethics, astrology, sexism in politics, economic downturns, steroid abuse, government doublespeak—instead of examples concerning sophomores dating seniors or all Greeks being mortal.

It quotes from or refers to writings and comments of Aristotle, Bertrand Russell, Barack Obama, Jerry Seinfeld, Maya Angelou, Winston Churchill, Ann Coulter, Jane Austen, Rush Limbaugh, Mohammed el-Nawawy, Alice Walker, Dostoevsky, Pliny the Elder, Sarah Palin, William Shakespeare, Charles Darwin, David Halberstam, and a host of others.

Examples are drawn from astrological predictions, celebrity ads, Obama and McCain political doings, syndicated columnists, works of literature, and hundreds of other sources.

Instead of the made-to-order cartoons that appear in some other texts, *Logic and Contemporary Rhetoric* contains drawings by the likes of David Levine, Edward Sorel, Tom Toles, George Booth, Jack Ziegler, and many others, and comic strips featuring *Calvin & Hobbes, Andy Capp, Doonesbury, Boondocks, Peanuts,* and *Dennis the Menace,* and others to illustrate points in a lively and interesting manner. The trademark of *Logic and Contemporary Rhetoric* always has been, and still is, ease of comprehension and the presentation of up-to- date and interesting material. Textbooks need not be dull!

NEW TO THE ELEVENTH EDITION

The principal changes in this edition are these:

1. Hundreds of old examples have been replaced by more up to date items culled from the (sadly) thousands of new candidates. For example, political items drawn from the Obama and McCain campaigns have replaced outdated ones about the Bush administration. (It is unnerving, though, that examples culled over the years from the Iraq/Afghanistan wars are all too current as the wars continue to drag on.)
2. Dozens of old exercise items have been replaced by new ones.
3. Although some of the text again has been rewritten to improve organization, style, and flow, the general subject matter covered by this new edition has not changed. But several changes have been made.

   Because of the historic nature of the 2008 presidential election, many political examples have been woven into the text reflecting attitudes toward gender and race, campaign strategies, and the usual fallacious reasoning that muddies the waters in every election. The text also includes examples and exercise items about the current economic crisis (that the author hopes will be outdated long before the next edition).

   Chapter 7 includes a new section on the languages used to frame public policy (along with a wicked cartoon). Based on George Lakoff's theories about the science and art of framing, it discusses the way politicians used loaded language to tap into world views that persuade people to adopt policies. The chapter also includes an exercise in evaluating the use of language in a section of Barack Obama's now-famous speech on race, "A More Perfect Union."

   The updates in Chapter 10 reflect a barrage of advertising ploys designed to manipulate consumers. Examples include gambits like whitewashing corporate imagery, using the shopping mall as a marketing tool, hyping ordinary products with inflated language that gives them luxury status, and a host of others. Political ads continue to come under special scrutiny because of the profound effect they have on voters. Particular attention is paid to the distortions in the overwhelming number of negative ads unleashed by both sides during the 2008 election.

   Chapter 11 has been revised to reflect the huge transformation that the news media is going through—comparable to what it experienced in the early days of television. The chapter discusses the problems involved as traditional news outlets shrink, but also the benefits that evolve as more and more people access news on the Internet.

ORGANIZATION OF THE TEXT

The thought that sparked the original organization of material in *Logic and Contemporary Rhetoric* way back in 1969–1970 was that student reasoning about everyday topics could be improved by acquainting them with a few basic principles of good reasoning and, in particular, by enlightening them concerning common ways in which people are taken in by fallacious arguments and reasoning in everyday life. But a close examination of the ways in which reasoning, in fact, goes wrong in everyday life shows that it does so in a majority of cases first because of a lack of sufficient (or sufficiently accurate) background information; second, because of the psychological impediments (wishful thinking, rationalization, prejudice, superstition, provincialism, and so on) that stand in the way of cogent reasoning; and third, because of a poor understanding of the nature and quality of the various information sources.

Taking account of this insight has resulted in a book that divides into eight parts, as follows:

1. *Good and Bad Reasoning:* Chapter 1 introduces students to some basic ideas about good and bad reasoning, the importance of having good background beliefs, in particular of having well-pruned worldviews, as well as some very rudimentary remarks about deduction and induction and the three overarching fallacy categories employed in chapters 3, 4, and 5.

2. *Deduction and Induction:* Chapter 2 contains more detailed material on deductive and inductive validity and invalidity.

3. *Fallacious Reasoning:* Chapters 3, 4, and 5 discuss fallacious reasoning, concentrating on how to avoid fallacies by becoming familiar with the types most frequently encountered in everyday life. The point is to help students increase their ability to spot fallacious reasoning by discussing the most common types of fallacious argument and by providing students with everyday life examples on which to practice.

4. *Impediments to Cogent Reasoning:* Chapter 6 discusses wishful thinking, rationalization, provincialism, denial, and so on, and how to overcome them. It explains the attractiveness and mistaken nature of belief in the paranormal and other pseudosciences. In some ways, this is the most important chapter in the book, because these skewers of rational thought so severely infect the thinking of all of us. (Some instructors pass over this chapter on the grounds that the topic is more appropriately taught in psychology classes, not in classes primarily concerned with critical reasoning. But the reality here is that many students do not take the relevant psychology classes and that those who do often are provided with a purely theoretical account divorced from the students' own reasoning in everyday life, not with a "how-to" discussion designed to help them overcome these obstacles to rational thought.)

5. *Language:* Chapter 7 discusses the ways in which language itself can be used to manipulate meaning, for instance, via doubletalk and long-winded locutions. (This chapter also contains a section, not common in critical-thinking texts, on the linguistic revolution that has tremendously reduced the use of sexist, racist, and other pejorative locutions in everyday discourse; and it also has a few things to say about the use of politically correct [PC] locutions.)

6. *Evaluating and Writing Cogent Essays:* Chapter 8 deals with the evaluation of extended argumentative passages—essays, editorials, political speeches, and so on. Chapter 9 addresses the writing of these kinds of argumentative passages. (Instructors are urged not to pass over Chapter 9 and urged to have students write *at least* two argumentative papers during the semester. Writing is very likely the

best way in which we all can learn to sharpen our ability to reason well. Writing is indeed nature's way of letting us know how sloppy our thinking often is. But it also is the best way to learn how to sharpen our ability to think straight.)

7. *Important Sources of Information:* Chapter 10 discusses advertising as an information source (singling out political ads for special scrutiny); Chapter 11, the media (television, newspapers, radio, books, and magazines), in particular, the mass media; and Chapter 12, public school textbooks. (For many people, these are the most important sources of information about how the world works. Instructors are urged not to pass over the chapter on the media too quickly: In this day and age, so much that happens in our lives depends on our being able to assess accurately what the media—in particular, the mass media—tell us.)

8. *More on Cogent Reasoning:* The Appendix provides additional material on deduction and induction (including a few words about syllogisms); cause and effect; scientific method; and so on.

Note also that a section at the back of the book provides answers to selected exercise items. It should be remembered, however, that most of the exercise items in this text are drawn from everyday life, where shades of gray outnumber blacks and whites. The answers provided thus constitute author responses rather than definitive pronouncements. Similar remarks apply to the answers to the remaining exercise items provided in the *Instructor's Manual* designed to accompany *Logic and Contemporary Rhetoric.*

THE UNIQUE NATURE OF LOGIC AND CONTEMPORARY RHETORIC

This book is unique among critical reasoning texts in bringing together all of these apparently diverse elements, in particular, in stressing the importance of overcoming natural impediments to cogent reasoning; in bringing to bear good background information when dealing with everyday problems; and in so extensively discussing the most important information sources. In this complicated modern world, all of us are laypersons most of the time with respect to most topics; the ability to deal effectively with the "expert" information available to us via the media, textbooks and periodicals—to separate wheat from chaff—thus is crucial to our ability to reason well about everyday problems, whether of a personal or of a social/political nature.

Although the text contains much discussion of theory, this is *not* a treatise on the theory of cogent and fallacious reasoning. Rather, it is designed to help students learn *how* to reason well and *how* to avoid fallacious reasoning. That is why so many examples and exercise items have been included—arranged so as to increase student sophistication as they progress through the book—and why exercises and examples have been drawn primarily from everyday life. Learning how to reason well and how to evaluate the rhetoric of others is a skill that, like most others, requires practice, in this case practice on the genuine article—actual examples drawn from everyday life.

This text provides students with a good deal more than the usual supply of exercise items, but perhaps the most important are those requiring them to do things on their own: find examples from the mass media, write letters to elected officials, do research on specified topics. (The *Instructor's Manual,* available to adopters of the text, suggests several other kinds of student activities—for example, classroom debates on issues of the day—that dovetail nicely with the spirit of the text.)

A true critical reasoning course, or textbook, is unthinkable in a closed or authoritarian society and antithetical to the indoctrination practiced in that kind of culture. The authors of this text take very seriously the admonition that eternal vigilance is the price of liberty. Citizens who think for themselves, rather than uncritically ingesting what their leaders and others with power tell them, are the absolutely necessary ingredient of a society that is to remain free.

ACKNOWLEDGMENTS

Many thanks to the publisher's reviewers for this eleventh edition: Jonathan Gainor, Harrisburg Area Community College; Lori Hoffman, Moravian College; Sughra Hussain, Harrisburg Area Community College; Kate McCorkle, Butte College; Robert Covert, Coastline Community College; and Carlotta Campbell, College of Alameda.

Thanks also to the others who have aided in the preparation of this and previous editions, including Professors Thomas Allen, California Polytechnic University, San Luis Obispo; Don Anderson, Pierce College; Anatole Anton, San Francisco State University; Gary L. Baran, Los Angeles City College; Lawrence Beloof, West Hills Community College; William Bonis, California State University, Long Beach; Gene Booth, University of New Mexico; Donald Burrell, California State University, Los Angeles; Henry C. Byerly, University of Arizona; Joseph Campbell, Washington State University; Alice Cleveland, College of Marin; Monte Cook, University of Oklahoma; Rosemary Cook, Saybrook Institute; Wally Cox, Regent University; Leland Creer, Central Connecticut State University; Robert Cogan, Edinboro University; David Detmer, Purdue University, Calumet Campus; R. V. Dusek, University of New Hampshire; Frank Fair, Sam Houston State University; Dana R. Flint, Lincoln University; Marilyn M. Fry, Coastline Community College; Sidney Gendin, Eastern Michigan University; Norman L. Geisler, Liberty University; James A. Gould, University of South Florida; J. Anthony Greybasch, Central State University; Paul J. Haanstad, University of Utah; Max O. Hallman, Merced College; Alan Hausman, Hunter College; James Heffernan, University of the Pacific; John Hernandez, Palo Alto College; Mark Herron, National University; J. Thomas Howald, Franklin College; John L. King, University of North Carolina; Charles Landesman, Hunter College and CUNY Graduate Center; Donald Lazere, California Polytechnic State University; Herschel Mack, Humbolt State University; Patrick Maher, University of Pittsburgh; Reed Markham, California Polytechnic University, Pomona; Judith McBride, somewhere in Arizona; Thomas McKay, Syracuse University; Donna Monahan, College of Marin; David Morgan, University of Northern Iowa; Clayton Morgareidge, Lewis and Clark College; Gonzalo T. Palacios, University of the District of Columbia; Ray Perkins, Jr., Plymouth State University; Linda Plackowski, Delta College; Nelson Pole, Cleveland State University; Merrill Proudfoot, Park College; Malcolm Reid, Gordon College; Vincent Riccardi, Orange Coast College; Paul O. Ricci, Cypress College; Paul A. Roth, University of Missouri; Arent H. Schuyler, Jr., University of California, Santa Barbara; Robert Schwartz, University of Wisconsin—Milwaukee; Roger Seanom, University of British Columbia; S. Samuel Shermis, Purdue University; Pamela Spoto, California State University, Chico; Douglas Stalker, University of Delaware; Ben Starr, Modesto Junior College; Joan Straumanis, Kenyon College;

John Stroupe, Western Michigan University; Gregory P. Swartzentruber, Villanova University; Roye Templeton, University of Maryland, Baltimore County; John Titchener, University of Maryland, Baltimore County; and Perry Weddle, California State University, Sacramento.

Finally, our very special thanks to the students of Whitman College, the University of Kansas, Bernard Baruch College of CUNY, the University of Maryland Baltimore County, and the College of Marin.

NANCY CAVENDER
Mill Valley, California

What is the use of philosophy, if all it does is enable you to talk . . . about some abstruse questions of logic, etc., and if it does not improve your thinking about the important questions of everyday life?

—Ludwig Wittgenstein

"Congratulations, Dave! I don't think I've read a more beautifully evasive and subtly misleading public statement in all my years in government."

Cartoon commentary on the state of contemporary rhetoric.

It's much easier to do and die than it is to reason why.

—H. A. Studdert Kennedy

Read not to contradict and confute, nor to believe and take for granted . . . but to weigh and consider.

—Francis Bacon

You can lead a man up to the university, but you can't make him think.

—Finley Peter Dunne

You can lead me to college . . . but you can't make me think.

—Sweatshirt update seen at Duke University

Ignorance of reality provides no protection from it.

—Harold Gordon

Reason is logic, or reason is motive, or reason is a way of life.

—John Le Carré

Chapter

1

GOOD AND BAD REASONING

There is much truth to the old saying that life is just one problem after another. That's why problem solving is one of life's major preoccupations. **Reasoning** is the essential ingredient in problem solving. When confronted with a problem, those of us who are rational reason from what we already know, or have good reason to believe, or can find out, to new beliefs useful in solving that problem. The trick, of course, is to reason well. This book is about good reasoning—about how to reason well in everyday life—whether dealing with personal problems or those of a social or political nature.

Fortunately, no one is an island. We all have available to us a great deal of knowledge others have gained through experience and good reasoning—accurate information and well-intended advice available to anyone who reaches out for it. Unfortunately, not all information is created equal. Charlatans and fools can speak as loudly as saints or Nobel Prize winners. Self-interest often clouds the thinking of even the brightest individuals. The trick when evaluating the mountain of verbiage we all are exposed to is to separate the nourishing wheat from the expendable chaff. One way to become good at doing this is to think a bit about what makes reasoning good (cogent), as opposed to bad (fallacious).

1. REASONING AND ARGUMENTS

Here is a simple example of reasoning about the nature/nurture issue:

> Identical twins sometimes have different IQ test scores. Yet these twins inherit exactly the same genes. So environment must play some part in determining a person's IQ.

Logicians call this kind of reasoning an **argument.** In this case, the argument consists of three statements:

1. Identical twins often have different IQ test scores.
2. Identical twins inherit the same genes.
3. So environment must play some part in determining IQ.

The first two statements in this argument give reasons for accepting the third. In logic talk, they are said to be **premises** of the argument; and the third statement, which asserts the **claim** made by the argument, is called the argument's **conclusion.**

In everyday life, few of us bother to label premises or conclusions. We usually don't even bother to distinguish one argument from another. But we do sometimes give clues. Words such as *because, since,* and *for* usually indicate that what follows is a premise of an argument. *Therefore, thus, consequently,* and *so* generally signal conclusions. Similarly, expressions such as "It has been observed that . . . ," "In support of this . . . ," and "The relevant data are . . . " are used to introduce premises, while expressions such as "The point of all of this is . . . ," "The implication is . . . ," and "It follows that . . . " are used to signal conclusions. Here is a simple example:

> *Since* it's always wrong to kill a human being [premise], it *follows* that capital punishment is wrong [conclusion], *because* capital punishment takes the life of [kills] a human being [premise].

Put into textbook form, the argument looks like this:

1. It's always wrong to kill a human being.
2. Capital punishment takes the life of (kills) a human being.
∴3. Capital punishment is wrong.[1]

Of course, an argument may have any number of premises and may be surrounded by or embedded in other arguments or extraneous material.

In addition to using transitional words such as *since, because,* and *therefore,* we sometimes employ sentence order—the last sentence in a series stating an argument's conclusion—and occasionally even express a conclusion in the form of a question. When the Los Angeles Galaxy signed David Beckham, international soccer star, in 2007, an enthusiastic fan gave reasons that hiring him was the right thing to do—not just for the team but for Major League Soccer as well (which isn't nearly as popular in the United States as in other countries). Claiming that Beckham was one of the best players in the world and had star power to popularize the sport, she stated her conclusion in the form of a question: "Doesn't it make sense that he will be a major force in popularizing soccer in this country?"

---

[1]The symbol ∴ often is used as shorthand for the word *therefore* and thus indicates that a conclusion follows.

We should also note that, in daily life, premises and even the conclusions of arguments sometimes are omitted as understood. Life is short, and we don't always bother to spell out matters that are obvious or not at issue or can be taken for granted. In the IQ example given earlier, for instance, the premise that IQ differences must be due either to genetic or to environmental factors was omitted as generally understood. When assessing arguments, we should by all means add omitted premises of this kind when they are relevant.

EXERCISE 1-1

Identify the premises and conclusions in the following arguments. (A few are from student exams—modestly edited.)[2] Remember, sometimes a premise or conclusion may be implied.

Example
Argument
The barometer is falling sharply, so the weather is going to change.
Argument Structure
Premise: The barometer is falling sharply.
Implied premise: Whenever the barometer falls sharply, the weather changes.
Conclusion: The weather is going to change.

1. Since everyone deserves health care, and more than 40 million Americans don't have medical insurance, the United States should institute national insurance.

2. Barry Bonds will never be the hero that Hank Aaron or Babe Ruth was, even though he set a new home run record. Everyone says he pumped himself up with steroids and tarnished his image forever. Aaron and Ruth got there on their own steam, without any boost from drugs.

3. *The Economist:* "It is difficult to gauge the pain felt by animals because pain is subjective and animals cannot talk."

*4. William Shakespeare: "Forbear to judge, for we are sinners all."

5. Aristotle: "The Earth has a spherical shape. For the night sky looks different in the northern and the southern parts of the Earth, and that would be the case if the Earth were spherical in shape."

*6. The government thinks 18-year-olds are responsible enough to vote and mature enough to fight a war, so why can't they drink alcohol?

7. Human activities have become the major source of global warming. Over the past 200 years, they have been responsible for the rising carbon dioxide levels from burning fossil fuels and for increased concentrations of other greenhouse gases like methane and nitrous oxide.

8. America is a society that values its freedoms. Censorship clearly has no place in a society that values its freedoms. It curtails independent thought, and it discourages people from examining societal problems.

---

[2] Starred (*) items are answered in a section at the back of the book.

9. College costs big bucks. When you put out that kind of money, you should be able to decide where your money goes. Students shouldn't have to take introductory courses if they don't want to. Besides, you don't need those basic courses for lots of careers.

10. Giving illegal aliens driver's licenses would undermine our immigration laws. After all, they are here illegally to begin with. Besides, there is the security issue. If anyone can get a license, so can terrorists, and that means they can fly anywhere in the country with just a license for an ID. Who knows how many planes they might blow up?

2. EXPOSITION AND ARGUMENT

Of course, only those groups of statements that provide reasons for believing something form arguments. Thus, anecdotes are not usually arguments, nor are most other forms of **exposition.** But even in these cases, arguments often are implied. Here is a sales clerk talking about the difference between two digital cameras, an Olympus and a Kodak. "Well, the Olympus has 4.1 megapixels and the Kodak has only 2.2. They both have terrific image quality, but the Olympus is better for cropping and enlarging your prints. The Kodak is $300 less, but it's not as high-powered." Although the clerk's remarks contain no specific argument because no conclusion is drawn, a conclusion is definitely implied. You should choose the Olympus if you want a more high-powered camera; otherwise you should choose the Kodak.

The point is that talk generally is not aimless. A good deal of everyday talk, even gossip, is intended to influence the beliefs and actions of others and thus constitutes a kind of argument. In the camera example, the clerk provided information intended to convince the customer to draw either the conclusion, "I'll buy the Olympus because the range of options is worth the extra $300 to me," or the conclusion, "I'll buy the Kodak because high-powered options aren't worth $300 more to me." In other words, the point of the clerk's chatter was to sell a camera. Similarly, advertisements often just provide product information rather than advance explicit arguments, yet clearly every such ad has an implied conclusion—that you should buy the advertised product.

Nevertheless, it is important to understand the difference between rhetoric that is primarily expository and discourse that is basically argumentative. An argument makes the claim, explicit or implicit, that one of its statements follows from some of its other statements. It at least implies that acceptance of its conclusion is justified if one accepts its premises. A passage that is purely expository gives us no reason to accept any "facts" it may contain (other than the implied authority of the writer or speaker, as, for example, when a friend tells us that she had a good time at the beach).

EXERCISE 1-2

Here are several passages. (Some are from student papers—again, modestly edited.) Indicate which contain arguments and which do not, label the premises and conclusions of those passages that do (as you did in the previous exercise), and explain why you think the other passages do not contain arguments.

Example

Passage from an Agatha Christie novel: "M. Hercule Poirot, having nothing better to do, amused himself by studying her without appearing to do so. She was, he judged, the kind of young woman who could take care of herself with perfect ease wherever she went. . . . He rather liked the severe regularity of her features and the delicate pallor of her skin. He liked the burnished black head with its neat waves of hair, and her eyes—cool, impersonal and gray."

Evaluation: This is not an argument. The author says Poirot judged (reasoned) that the woman could take care of herself but does not describe his reasoning. And the rest of the passage simply says that Poirot liked certain features of the young woman.

*1. If we keep burning so much coal and oil, the greenhouse effect will continue to get worse. But it will be a disaster if that happens. So we've got to reduce dependency on these fossil fuels.

2. We are never going to find a cure for diabetes, cancer, Alzheimer's and a lot of other diseases unless we use the most promising research available. Stem cell research is the way to go.

3. Tuition for state colleges should be lowered. Lots of students drop out of school because they can't afford it and there's not enough financial aid to go around. If they go to school and work, it takes them forever to get their degrees.

*4. My summer vacation was spent working in Las Vegas. I worked as a waitress at the Desert Inn and made tons of money. But I guess I got addicted to the slots and didn't save too much. Next summer my friend Hal and I are going to work in Reno, if we can find jobs there.

5. Legalizing prostitution is bound to increase sexually transmitted diseases. And look what it would do to women. It can't help but lead to their degradation. Besides, most people don't like the idea, anyway.

6. The U.S. Census Bureau estimated that 18 million students were enrolled in the nation's 4,300 institutions of higher learning in fall 2007. The average cost of tuition, room, and board for in-state students at four-year public colleges and universities was $13,425 and at private schools, $36,510. Half the full-time college students were employed.

7. Some people in the field of medicine are keen on embedding computer chips inside the body, but I've got a problem with that. True, the chips could provide helpful medical information if I'm unconscious or something, which I guess is the main reason for doing it, but I don't want to make that kind of information available to the government or anyone else, for that matter, who might want to invade my privacy.

8. Why is there so much opposition to using animals for medical research? We know medical research saves the lives of humans. True, some animals suffer in the process, but it's worth it in the long run. After all, most people value the lives of humans more than animals.

*9. Descartes: "Good sense is of all things in the world the most equally distributed, for everybody thinks himself so abundantly provided with it, that even those most difficult to please in all other matters do not commonly desire more of it than they already possess."

10. Quarterback Michael Vick shouldn't have been sentenced for running a dog-fighting operation from his property. It's punishment enough that the Atlanta Falcons suspended him indefinitely. True, he did admit to financing the operation and being involved in killing the dogs that didn't perform well, but the felony charges were trumped up against him. No other first-time offender has been convicted on the charge of sponsoring a dog in a fight or on the conspiracy charges brought against him. Besides, he admitted he made a mistake and said he was sorry.

11. Why shouldn't public schools take donations from private business? The government doesn't expend enough money to repair the buildings, let alone pay teachers a decent salary. Besides, big business would demand more for its money—like higher standards and better discipline.

12. Alexis de Tocqueville, *Democracy in America:* "Men will never establish any equality with which they will be contented. . . . When equality of condition is the common law of society, the most marked inequalities do not strike the eye: when everything is nearly on the same level, the slightest are marked enough to hurt it.

    Hence the desire for equality always becomes more insatiable in proportion as equality is more complete."

3. COGENT REASONING

Reasoning can be either **cogent** (good) or **fallacious** (bad). We reason cogently when we satisfy the following conditions:

1. The premises of our reasoning are believable (**warranted,** justified), given what we already know or believe.
2. We consider all likely relevant information.[3]
3. Our reasoning is **valid,** or **correct,** which means that the premises we employ provide good grounds for accepting the conclusion we draw.[4]

When all three of these conditions of cogent reasoning are not satisfied, reasoning is said to be *fallacious.* Note, by the way, that in daily life, we often speak of arguments as being

---

[3]Satisfying this extremely stringent requirement is usually beyond the ability of most of us most of the time. The point is that good reasoners try to come as close as possible to satisfying it, taking into account the importance of drawing the right conclusion and the cost (in time, effort, or money) of obtaining or recalling relevant information. (One of the marks of genius is the ability to recognize that information is relevant when the rest of us fail to notice.)

[4]Provided we know nothing else relevant to the conclusion. Note that reasoning from an unjustified premise may still be cogent if it also employs justified premises that sufficiently support its conclusion. Note also that the term *valid* sometimes is used more broadly than we have used it here.

fallacious or cogent, even though, strictly speaking, it is reasoners—individuals—who reason either fallaciously or cogently. Life is short, and we often speak imprecisely when context makes clear what is intended.

Believable Premises

The first condition of cogent reasoning requires that we bring to bear whatever we already know or believe—our relevant **background beliefs** and information—to determine whether we should or shouldn't accept the premises of an argument being evaluated. Take, for instance, the first premise of the capital punishment argument discussed earlier—the premise making the claim that taking the life of a human being always is wrong. Most of us are not pacifists—we don't believe that it always is wrong to take a human life. Bringing that background belief to bear thus should make us see the first premise of the capital punishment argument as questionable. So we should not accept the conclusion of that argument unless further reasons are presented in its support. (On the other hand, those of us who *are* pacifists obviously should reason differently.)

By way of contrast, consider the stated premise of the following argument:

> Venus Williams must be a terrific tennis player. She won the Wimbledon championship in 2008. (The implied premise is that anyone who took a first at Wimbledon must be an outstanding athlete.)

Tennis fans know that the Wimbledon grand slam championship is one of the most demanding tennis competitions in the world, and acceptance of the stated premise (that Williams won the tournament) was warranted by plenty of background information.

It's interesting to notice that, in effect, evaluating a premise of an argument by bringing background beliefs to bear entails constructing another argument whose conclusion is either that the premise in question is believable or that it isn't. For example, when evaluating the capital punishment argument discussed before, someone who is not a pacifist might construct the following argument: "I believe that it isn't wrong to kill in self-defense, or in wartime, or to kill those guilty of murder. So I should reject the premise that taking a human life always is wrong."

This brings to mind the fact that in daily life we often are exposed to assertions, or claims, that are not supported by reasons or arguments. Clearly, it is not rational to accept these assertions without evaluating them for believability, and, obviously, their correct evaluation requires us to do exactly what we do when evaluating the believability of the premises of an argument—namely, bring to bear what we already know or believe. Evaluating unsupported assertions thus involves just part of what is done when we evaluate arguments.

No Relevant Information Passed Over

The second criterion of cogent reasoning requires that we not pass over relevant information. In particular, it tells us to resist the temptation to neglect evidence contrary to what we want to believe.

Here, for instance, is the substance of remarks made in fall 2006, by a young woman who just bought a condo with a subprime loan.

Now is the time to buy a condo. I got a loan without even making a down payment. And interest rates are so cheap. A two-year loan goes for under 5 percent, and I can refinance it later for even less. Besides, I was tired of renting an apartment and wanted a place of my own. It's just money down the drain to rent. The price of condos has really gone up the past few years, so I'm bound to make a profit when I sell. I may be scraping by now, but I can always run up a few credit cards to get along.

Here is the implied argument.

1. This is a good time to buy a condo.
2. Financially it's a good deal since I don't have to make a down payment, and interest rates on short-term loans are low.
3. Real estate will continue to appreciate, and I'll make a profit when I sell.

Alas, this home buyer and thousands like her went into bankruptcy when the housing bubble burst, real estate prices fell, and short-term loans could only be refinanced at higher interest rates than many buyers could afford. Her reasoning neglected to consider her own financial situation and evidence that a little research might have unearthed.

1. The housing market was at an all-time high, and there was bound to be a correction in the market. Past experience shows that housing booms end and prices decline.
2. Short-term loans at very low introductory rates (known as *subprimes* because they are below the prime rate) are just teasers that loan sharks use to lure consumers into taking out mortgages. Subprimes are hyped to people with sketchy credit histories and low incomes, in other words, people without the usual qualifications for buying real estate. When the time comes to refinance, usually two years later, the rates shoot up as much as 3 percentage points.
3. Buyers with sufficient incomes who make down payments and qualify for conventional prime rate loans can usually ride out a dip in the market, but not lower income buyers who finance everything on credit. When money is tight, as it began to be in 2007, loan companies refuse to lend to high-risk buyers, who may have to resort to selling at a loss or face foreclosure and possibly bankruptcy.

Hindsight is certainly better than foresight, but with a realistic understanding of one's own financial situation, a little research into the nature of housing markets in general and the shady practices of loan sharks in particular, these points can be figured out by an intelligent person who thinks carefully about the matter. While it is understandable that the young woman wanted a home of her own, too often common sense gives way to magical thinking.

Valid Reasoning

The third criterion of cogent reasoning requires that the premises of an argument genuinely support its conclusion; or, as logicians like to say, it requires that an argument be valid, or correct. It is vitally important to understand that the validity of an argument has nothing whatever to do with the truth of its premises or conclusion. Validity concerns the nature of the *connection* between the premises and conclusion of an argument, not the truth or believability of its premises. Determining that an argument is valid tells us that *if* we are justified in believing in its premises, *then* we also are justified in believing in the truth of its conclusion. It doesn't tell us *whether* its premises are true. An argument thus can be perfectly valid and have completely false premises, and even have a false conclusion. Here is an example:

1. The Cleveland Indians have won more World Series games than any other major league team. (false premise, alas!)
∴2. They have won more World Series games than the New York Yankees. (false conclusion)

The argument is valid because if the beloved Indians *had* won more World Series games than any other Major League team, then, obviously (well, it's obvious to baseball fans), they would have won more World Series games than the Yankees. The argument is valid, even though its premise and conclusion both are false. It's valid because anyone who is justified in believing its premise is justified in believing its conclusion.

4. Two Basic Kinds of Valid Arguments

Premises may correctly support conclusions in two fundamentally different ways. The first way yields *deductively valid* arguments; the second, *inductively valid* (or inductively strong) arguments.[5]

Deductive Validity

The fundamental property of a **deductively valid** argument is this: If all of its premises are true, then its conclusion must be true also, because the claim asserted by its conclusion already has been stated in its premises, although usually only implicitly.

Here is an example of a very simple deductively valid argument:

1. If this wire is made of copper, then it will conduct electricity. (premise)
2. This wire is made of copper. (premise)
∴3. This wire will conduct electricity. (conclusion)

Taken alone, neither premise makes the claim that the wire will conduct electricity; but taken together, they do. We cannot imagine what it would be like for both premises of this argument to be true, yet its conclusion turn out to be false. Indeed, it would be contradictory to assert both of its premises and then to deny its conclusion.

It is important to see that it is the **form** of this argument—namely:

1. If <u>some sentence, then a second sentence</u>.
2. <u>The first sentence</u>.
∴3. <u>The second sentence</u>.

---

[5] Some authorities believe that there is at least one other kind of legitimate argument—namely, the kind in which various alternatives are evaluated. The authors of this text incline to the view that evaluative arguments fall into one or the other of the two basic kinds about to be mentioned. Note also that some authorities restrict the use of the term *valid* so that it refers only to deductively good arguments, even though in everyday life inductively strong arguments generally are said to be valid. In addition, note that the reasoning process called "mathematical induction" happens to be a kind of deductive reasoning. (Terminology sometimes is misleading.)

that makes it deductively valid, not the truth values of its statements. Letting the capital letter *A* stand for the first sentence and *B* for the second sentence, the *form* of the argument can be stated this way:

1. If *A* then *B*.
2. *A*.
∴3. *B*.

Clearly, every argument having this form is deductively valid, another example being this argument:

1. If Sonia reads *Vogue* magazine, then she's up on the latest fashions.
2. Sonia reads *Vogue* magazine.
3. She's up on the latest fashions.

Logicians, by the way, call the form of this argument, and every argument having this form, ***modus ponens.***

It's very important to clearly understand that the deductive validity of an argument guarantees that its conclusion is true *only if* its premises are true. Determining that an argument is deductively valid thus tells us just that *if* its premises are true, *then* its conclusion must be true also; it doesn't tell us *whether* its premises are true and thus doesn't tell us *whether* its conclusion is true.

Here, for instance, is a deductively valid argument having the form *modus ponens* that contains one true and one very likely false premise and thus does not guarantee the truth of its conclusion:

1. If more people read Agatha Christie's mystery novels than read Shakespeare's plays, then her novels must be better than his plays. (false premise?)
2. Her novels have been read by more people than have Shakespeare's plays. (true premise)
∴3. Her novels must be better than his plays. (false conclusion?)

Of course, a deductively valid argument that contains a false premise may, luckily, have a true conclusion. But that would be a matter of luck, not of good reasoning.

The fact that a deductively valid argument cannot move from true premises to a false conclusion constitutes its chief characteristic and great virtue. But deductive arguments are limited. They cannot yield conclusions that are not at least implicit in the premises from which they are derived. **Induction** is needed to perform this task.

Inductive Validity

Inductively valid (inductively strong) arguments, unlike deductively valid ones, have conclusions that go beyond what is contained in their premises. The idea behind valid induction is that of *learning from experience.* We often observe patterns, resemblances, and other kinds of regularities in our experiences, some quite simple (sugar sweetening coffee), some very complicated (objects moving according to Newton's laws—well, Newton noticed this, anyway). Valid inductions simply project regularities of this kind observed in our experiences so far onto other possible experiences.[6]

---

[6]This includes those experiences we can't have but might have if we had lived millions of years ago or if, say, we could go into the interior of the sun without being incinerated.

Here is a simple example of an inductively valid argument, of the kind sometimes called *induction by enumeration,* expressed by a rather smart child in Jacksonville, Florida, explaining why he is doubtful about the existence of Santa Claus:

> The tooth fairy turned out not to be real. The Easter Bunny turned out not to be real. So I'm beginning to wonder about Santa.

Admittedly this is a small sample, but perhaps not for a 4-year-old with a limited range of experience.

We use inductive reasoning so frequently in everyday life that its nature generally goes unnoticed. Being informed about induction is a bit like being told that we've been speaking prose all our lives. We start drawing perfectly good inferences of this kind (and some klinkers) at a very early age. By age 5 or 6, the use of induction has taught us a great many of the basic truths that guide everyday behavior—for instance, that some foods taste good and some don't, the sun rises every morning and sets every evening, very hot things burn the skin, some people are trustworthy and some aren't (something most of us seem to need to relearn over and over), and so on.

The great virtue of inductive reasoning is that it provides us with a way of reasoning to genuinely new beliefs, not just to psychologically new ones that are implicit in what we already know, as in the case of valid deductions. However, this benefit is purchased at the cost of an increase in the possibility of error. As remarked before, the truth of the premises of a deductively valid argument guarantees the truth of its conclusion; but the premises of a perfectly good induction may all be true and yet its conclusion be false. Even the best "inductive leap" may lead us astray, because the patterns noticed in our experiences up to a given point may not turn out to be the exact patterns of the whole universe. This happens all too often in daily life—for example, when a restaurant that has served excellent food many times in the past fails us on a special occasion. But it sometimes happens even in the lofty realm of theoretical science. Physicists, for instance, believed for a long time that asbestos does not conduct electricity—a belief supported by very good, very strong inductive reasoning—but then discovered that all substances, including asbestos, conduct electricity when cooled down close to absolute zero.

Nevertheless, rational people use induction in formulating their ideas about how things are going to turn out, whether in ordinary, everyday circumstances or in the rather special ones scientists bring about in the laboratory. Induction, thinking of Winston Churchill's famous remark about democracy, is the worst way to expand one's knowledge except for all of the other ways (guessing, wishful thinking, astrology, and so on).

EXERCISE 1-3

Which of the following passages (modestly edited to make them more straightforward than arguments often are in daily life) do you think are deductively valid? Inductively valid? Defend your answers, showing the structure of those you believe to be valid.

1. My doctor told me to take Tylenol (actually, acetaminophen, the active ingredient in Tylenol) when I get a headache, and I've done that. Well, the stuff has cured my headaches, but it also has made me feel drugged. I've apparently just been trading a headache for a drugged feeling. So I figure that if I take it again

*Calvin is no match for Miss Wormwood, who easily reads between the lines of Calvin's
attempts at ingratiation.*

to cure this headache, the result will be the same. I'm switching back to
aspirin.

2. If I buy these potato chips, I know I'm going to eat the whole bagful at one sitting. But if I do that, I'll upset my stomach. Well, then, if I buy this tempting
item, my guts are going to get upset again. Satan, get thee behind me!

3. My father has always voted for Republican candidates, and my mother has also.
Hah! Now that I'm old enough to vote, I'm going to vote Democratic. That'll
show them.

4. According to statistics released by the U.S. Census Bureau for 2005, workers
without high school degrees earned $19,915 a year; high school graduates,
$24,448; college graduates with bachelor's degrees, $54,689; college graduates
with advanced degrees, $79,946. Is college worth it? Absolutely.

5. SOME WRONG IDEAS ABOUT COGENT REASONING

Having just presented three standards of cogent reasoning and having explained the nature of valid deduction and induction, perhaps we need to mention several recently
voiced ideas about logic and good reasoning. According to these modestly trendy ways
of looking at the topic, what counts as good reasoning is "culturally relative," or
"gender-relative," or even (popular among students) "individually relative." We hear talk
of "feminine logic," supposedly different from the "male logic" taught in logic classes
(often by female logicians, but let that pass), and of "black intelligence," different from
the "Eurocentric" variety foisted on us by white males, as though what makes reasoning

A wise person hears one word and understands two.

—Jewish proverb

Reading Between the Lines

The expression "reading between the lines" has several meanings. One captures the idea of grasping an intended thought that is not expressed, another of getting more information from a statement or argument than it explicitly—or even implicitly—contains, still another of noticing what rhetoric either deliberately or accidentally hides. Reading between the lines often is the essential ingredient in assessing a good deal of the everyday talk we all encounter, in particular political rhetoric and (interestingly) advertisements.

Take the Bufferin ad that states, "No regular aspirin product reduces fever better." Reading between the lines of this ad, we should conclude that Bufferin does *not* reduce fever better than some competing products, because if it did, the ad would make that stronger claim ("Bufferin reduces fever better than any other aspirin product") rather than the weaker one that none reduces fever better. The point is that our own background beliefs should lead us to expect an advertisement to make the strongest claim possible and thus lead us to at least tentatively conclude that a less strong claim is made because stronger claims would be false.

Reading between the lines is the linguistic equivalent of "sizing up" other people—for example, of gleaning information about their beliefs or likely actions from their overt behavior or way of saying something. A good poker player, for instance, looks for signs of bluffing—some players often unwittingly signal a bluff by increasing chatter or by nervous behavior; others do so by feigning lack of concern. Similarly, intelligent voters try to size up political candidates by looking for nonverbal clues and by reading between the lines of campaign rhetoric. (More will be said about campaign rhetoric in Chapters 7 and 10.)

---

good differs from group to group, race to race, or one sex to the other. We all too often hear students say things such as "That may well be true for you, but it isn't true for me" and listen to academics talk disparagingly of "Aristotelian linear reasoning," as opposed to a more "intuitive" type of reasoning, and so on.

But there is no truth to these ideas about what constitutes good reasoning. It is the height of folly to conclude, say, that an argument having the form *modus ponens* is not valid. Think, for example, what it means to assert seriously that all human beings have a right to life and then in the next breath to claim, equally seriously, that a particular human being, Smith, has no right to life. What sense is there in first saying that if Jones has been to China, then he's been to Asia, and then asserting that he has indeed been to China but not to Asia? Yet accepting reasonings that violate the standards of deductive logic means precisely accepting some sorts of contradictory assertions or other, because the point of the principles of valid deduction (including the valid principles of mathematics) is to assure that we do not contradict ourselves when we reason from one thing to another. (That's why, to take just one of a thousand examples, double-entry bookkeeping works.)

Similarly, what reason could there be for violating the standards of good inductive reasoning—for denying what experience teaches us? That a large majority of the

scientists who laid the groundwork in physics, chemistry, and biology were white males
is totally irrelevant to the truth of their basic ideas and theories. *The way the world works
does not differ depending on the race or sex of those trying to discover the way the world
works!* That is why, to take an everyday example, it is foolish to toss away money on
homeopathic medicines: Medical science has shown, over and over again, by means of
inductive reasoning, to say nothing of very highly confirmed general biological principles, that homeopathy does not work. The point cannot be stressed too heavily. There
simply is no truth whatsoever to the idea that standards of good reasoning differ from
group to group, male to female, or person to person.

There is, however, a good deal of truth to three much different ideas. One is that self-
interest, prejudice, and/or narrowmindedness do in fact often lead people to reason
invalidly. Bigotry has a bad name for good reason. Another is that self-interest often motivates us to neglect the values or interests of others, even when we share those values,
so that some groups or individuals find their interests frequently neglected. For instance,
rich people who believe fairness requires that everyone ought to have an equal chance
when starting out in life often forget about equality of opportunity when they argue for
the elimination of all inheritance taxes; in families in which both parents work, husbands
notoriously tend to paper over their failure to share household and child-rearing duties;
in the business world, high executives, while asserting their belief in equal rights for all,
frequently overlook the ways in which women, Latinos, and blacks are often passed over
for corporate advancement. In all of these cases, the problem is not with the principles
of good reasoning. It is with the fallacious nature of the ways in which these principles
sometimes are employed.

Those who champion other sorts of "logics" than the standard variety thus may well
be mistaken in their target. They attack the principles of good reasoning rather than
the failure of their opponents to employ these perfectly good (indeed the *only* good)
standards of reasoning correctly or to reason from acceptable moral or other kinds of
values.

A good deal more will be said in later chapters on these matters, in particular about
moral and other value claims. For now, the point is just that we must distinguish the principles of good reasoning, which are the same for all, from the ways in which these principles are employed (sometimes fallaciously), and from the differing values that enter
into the premises of different reasonings.

6. BACKGROUND BELIEFS

Earlier, we characterized cogent reasoning in terms of three conditions: the validity of connections between premises and conclusions, the believability of premises, and the discovery and use of relevant information. Clearly, satisfaction of the last two of these three conditions requires the employment of background beliefs. That is why bringing one's background beliefs to bear often is the most important task in evaluating an argument for cogency.

Consider, for example, the argument frequently heard in the early 1980s that AIDS is essentially a gay plague inflicted on homosexuals as punishment for their perverse sexual conduct (a claim still occasionally heard). The key premise of this argument was that AIDS can be transmitted sexually only via homosexual conduct, a premise that was supported by the evidence that in the United States a large majority of those reported early on to have the disease were indeed homosexuals. But people with good background information did not accept this argument. For one thing, they knew that in other places around the world—for instance, in Haiti and parts of Africa—large numbers of heterosexuals also had contracted AIDS via sexual behavior. And for another, those familiar with some of the basic scientific ideas concerning disease had theoretical (which means higher-level inductive) reasons for believing that AIDS could be transmitted via heterosexual behavior, as are syphilis, hepatitis B, herpes, and so on.

Today most Americans know that AIDs is transmitted by both heterosexuals and homosexuals, but many people wrongly think that the disease is curable because they have heard about drugs used to treat HIV. In fact, these drugs suppress the viral infection but do not cure it, and no vaccine has been successfully developed to date. Unfortunately, many young people believe they can be cured if they become infected and thus fail to take adequate precautions. This mistaken belief in part accounts for the steep increase in HIV patients over the past decade in the United States.

The point is that contrary to the old saying, ignorance is *not* bliss. It just renders us incapable of intelligently evaluating claims, premises, arguments, and other sorts of rhetoric we all are subject to every day. When evaluating arguments and issues, we can't bring relevant beliefs to bear if we don't have them, and we cannot make good judgments if what we believe is off the mark.

7. KINDS OF BACKGROUND BELIEFS

Background beliefs can be divided up in many different ways, an important one being a separation into beliefs about *matters of fact* and beliefs about values. It is a factual question, for example, whether capital punishment is practiced in every society (it isn't); it is a question of values whether capital punishment is morally justified (is it?). In dealing with most social or political issues, we need to separate claims that are about matters of fact from those concerning values, because these two different sorts of claims are defended, or justified, in different ways. The statement, for example, that a given state

---

Knowledge not renewed quickly becomes ignorance.

—Peter Drucker

> Those who do not remember the past are condemned to relive it.
>
> — George Santayana

has a death penalty is proved true, or false, by an examination of relevant government records; the judgment that capital punishment is, or isn't, morally justified as the punishment for heinous crimes is determined by bringing to bear an accepted moral code, or subjective intuitions.[7]

Background beliefs also can be divided into those that are *true* and (unfortunately) those that are *false*. Someone who believes, for example, that capital punishment exists as a practice in every society has a false belief; those who believe that every society punishes murderers in one way or another has a belief that is true. An important reason for regularly testing our background beliefs in terms of our experiences and of what we learn from others is precisely to weed out background beliefs that are false. Education consists in a lot more than simply learning a mountain of facts; it also has to do with weeding out beliefs that turn out to be false (or unjustified).

Beliefs also differ as to how firmly they are or should be held. We feel completely sure, completely confident, of some beliefs (for example, that the sun will rise tomorrow); less sure, but still quite confident, of others (for example, that the United States will still be in existence in the year 2050); and a good deal less sure, but still mildly confident, of others (for example, that we won't get killed some day in an auto accident). The trick is to believe firmly what should be believed, given the evidence, and believe less firmly, or not at all, what is less well supported by evidence.

All of this relates directly to decisions we have to make in everyday life. Wise individuals take into account the probability of one thing or another happening and thus of the confidence they should place in their beliefs about what to do. That's a large part of the truth behind familiar sayings such as "A bird in the hand is worth two in the bush."

8. WORLDVIEWS OR PHILOSOPHIES

As we grow up from childhood into adults, we tend to absorb the beliefs and standards of those in the world around us—our families, friends, and culture. It is no accident that so many of us have the same religious affiliation, or lack of same, as do our parents, that we accept the principles and standards of our own society, and so on.

These beliefs constitute an important part of our **worldviews** or **philosophies**.[8] They tend to be the most deeply ingrained and most resistant to amendment of all of our background beliefs. They become so much a part of us that we often appeal to them without consciously realizing we have done so. They are so intricately woven into the fabric of our belief systems that we often find it hard to isolate and examine individual strands.

---

[7] Philosophers and others disagree seriously concerning the question whether there are such things as objective moral principles that all clear-minded, rational individuals are bound to see as correct, or whether moral right and wrong is a matter of subjective opinion—of feelings that can, and perhaps do, differ from person to person.

[8] This includes religious beliefs in the case of those who have religious convictions.

And when we do examine them, our natural tendency is to reaffirm them without thought and to disparage conflicting claims and evidence, quickly dismissing evidence that might count against them.

Most of these beliefs are general—for example, that killing always is morally wrong, that there is some good in virtually all human beings, or that we all die sooner or later. But not all are. Belief in a monotheistic deity, for instance, or rejection of such a belief, is a particular belief.

But in spite of the example just cited, more general beliefs usually (that is, generally!) are more important than beliefs that are particular, or less general, because they tell us about a wider range of cases and thus tend to be more useful in everyday life. Believing that it rarely rains in July in Los Angeles, for instance, clearly is more useful than believing merely that it won't rain there, say, on July 16, 2010. That is why most of the important beliefs in one's worldview are general and also why most important scientific pronouncements are general—indeed, often extremely general. (Newton's laws, for example, don't just tell us about apples falling from trees or even just about items of all kinds falling toward the Earth. They also tell us about the motion of the Earth around the sun, about the motion of all planets around the sun, about how tides rise and fall, and, in fact, about the motions of all objects whatsoever.) It also is why it is so important, and useful, to expand our worldviews to contain at least a few modestly well-founded beliefs about important scientific theories—for example, about the theory of the evolution of all life on Earth.

The worldviews of political parties are implied in the words and phrases they use repeatedly in their discourse. University of California linguist George Lakoff came up with a list of words used over and over in the speeches and writings of conservatives and liberals. It's worth examining them to figure out the dominant worldviews reflected in the language.*

Conservatives: "character, virtue, discipline, tough it out, get tough, tough love, strong, self-reliance, individual responsibility, backbone, standards, authority, heritage, competition, earn, hard work, enterprise, property rights, reward, freedom, intrusion, interference, meddling, punishment, human nature, traditional, common sense, dependency, self-indulgent, elite, quotas, breakdown, corrupt, decay, rot, degenerate, deviant, lifestyle."

Liberals: "social forces, social responsibility, free expression, human rights, equal rights, concern, care, help, health, safety, nutrition, basic human dignity, oppression, diversity, deprivation, alienation, big corporations, corporate welfare, ecology, ecosystem, biodiversity, pollution, and so on."

What worldviews did you come up with?

*Taken from Lakoff's book Moral Politics: How Liberals and Conservatives Think, University of Chicago Press, 2002.

Compare the worldview reflected in this gem, excerpted from a 1950s women's magazine, to your worldview.

The Good Wife's Guide

- Prepare yourself. Take 15 minutes to rest so you'll be refreshed when he arrives. Touch up your make-up, put a ribbon in your hair and be fresh-looking. He has just been with a lot of work-weary people. . . .
- Listen to him. You may have a dozen important things to tell him, but the moment of his arrival is not the time. Let him talk first—remember, his topics of conversation are more important than yours. . . .
- Make the evening his. Never complain if he comes home late or goes out to dinner, or other places of entertainment without you. Instead, try to understand his world of strains and pressure and his very real need to be at home and relax. . . .
- Don't complain if he's late home for dinner or even if he stays out all night. Count this as minor compared to what he might have gone through that day. . . .
- Don't ask him questions about his actions or question his judgment or integrity. Remember, he is the master of the house and as such will always exercise his will with fairness and truthfulness. You have no right to question him. . . .
- A good wife always knows her place.

—Housekeeping Monthly, May 13, 1955

An astute reader noted that he couldn't find a history of this magazine and suspected it was a put-on. He may be right, but anyone raised in the 1950s will recognize the all-too-familiar worldview it reflects.

---

9. INSUFFICIENTLY GROUNDED BELIEFS

Most of us have strongly held beliefs about a great many controversial issues, and so we tend to respond automatically to arguments about these matters. We feel confident that we know whether marijuana or cocaine should be legalized, whether we should privatize Social Security, whether this candidate or that is more likely to serve all of the people equally if elected to office, and so on. We hold these beliefs, often very strongly, even though a good deal of the time we have insufficient justifying background knowledge and have engaged in too little thought to be able to support our beliefs intelligently or defend them against informed objections. What, for example, do we usually know about candidates running for seats in the U.S. House of Representatives? (In 2008, a significant number of voters did not even know the names of both major party candidates for congressional seats in their districts; fewer still could name both candidates for state legislatures in their districts. Could you?) Too often we base our vote on our party affiliation (that is, our political beliefs) not on the merit of individual candidates. Clearly,

It is worth noting here that widespread failure to revise worldviews often results in serious political and social unrest and injustice. E. M. Forster captures this poignantly in his novel *A Passage to India,* in which he depicts intense conflicts in colonial India between English masters and their conquered Indian subjects. Believing themselves socially and racially superior, the English relegate the Indians to subordinate positions, never allowing them equality under the British raj. The insensitivity of the British to the plight of their subjects is met with resentment, distrust, anger, and threats of violent retaliation by the Indians. (To make matters worse, the Indians are divided from one another by differing religious and cultural beliefs.) Very few of the British or Indians Forster depicts ever revise their biases and prejudices in the light of new information—for instance, in the light of obvious evidence about the competence of individual Indians or the glaring prejudice of English officials. The novel makes a compelling case for a widespread reexamination of worldviews and other background beliefs if human beings are to arrive at a peaceful, nonexploitative coexistence on planet Earth.

then, weeding out insufficiently grounded background information is vital if we are to improve our reasoning about important, to say nothing of relatively trivial, matters. (It also might be a good idea to find out something about candidates for various offices before stepping into a booth and casting our ballots.)

Having well-supported background beliefs is particularly important with respect to those basic background beliefs that make up our worldviews. Worldviews are like lenses that cause us to see the world in a particular way or filters through which we process all new ideas and information. Reasoning based on a grossly inaccurate or shallow worldview tends to yield grossly inaccurate, inappropriate, or self-defeating conclusions (except when we're just plain lucky), no matter how smart we otherwise may be. Sometimes the harm is relatively minor (gamblers who waste a few bucks playing "lucky" lottery numbers; astrology column readers who arrange vacation times to fit their sign), but at other times the harm can be more serious (people with an overly rosy view of human nature who get taken by sharp operators; misanthropes who miss out on the benefits and joys of trusting relationships).

Obviously, then, we need to examine our background beliefs, in particular, those that make up our worldviews, for consistency and believability, and we need to amend them so as to square with newly acquired information. The point is that having a good supply of background beliefs is not just a matter of filling up one's "tank" with gallons of facts. It is at least equally important to improve one's existing stock of beliefs by weeding out those that experience proves to be false, to sharpen vague beliefs, and to replace crude beliefs with those that are more sophisticated—beliefs that penetrate more deeply into the complexities of life and the world.

People who hold different worldviews often clash on a personal level, but when cultures or nations have conflicting worldviews, they can create tension and spark antagonism internationally. One recent example involved a controversy over whether an Afghan should be sentenced to death because he converted from Islam to Christianity. Under Sharia law, a Muslim who rejects Islam may be tried and executed. So when it became known that the man had converted to Christianity, he was put on trial by the

Afghan government, whose constitution allows prosecution under Sharia law. When Muslim clerics demanded that he be sentenced to death, prominent leaders in the Western world urged the government to honor human rights principles and free him. The conflicting worldviews caused an uproar on both sides. When the Afghan government looked for ways to drop the case in order to comply with international pressure, the clerics warned that if the man were freed, the people of Afghanistan would kill him. (The government resolved this dilemma by declaring him mentally unfit and citing "investigative gaps" in the case.) When clashes like this multiply and escalate, they may give rise to violence on a large scale. It is probably no exaggeration to say that major conflicts in worldviews are at the heart of most wars.

Socrates is said to have claimed that the unexamined life is not worth living. While clearly an exaggeration, there surely is a great deal of truth in this idea. By the same token, there is a large dose of truth in the idea that an unexamined worldview is not likely to be worth holding, in particular because it will contain little more than an accumulation of the ideas and prejudices of others. Examining worldviews allows us to take control of our lives by actively sorting out our fundamental beliefs, testing them against ideas and information that point to conclusions contrary to what we already believe, and making whatever revisions are indicated in the light of what we have learned. *Doing this helps us to become our own person rather than just a passive follower of others!*

Unfortunately it is no easy matter for us to examine our worldviews objectively. Psychological studies show that people hold on to their beliefs for dear life, ignoring evidence that undermines them and dredging up weak evidence to support them. This obstacle to rational thought is compounded by our natural tendency to take short-cuts in reasoning that reduce our mental effort, allowing us to slide past unwelcome evidence and leap to hasty conclusions that support our existing beliefs. All this makes rational self-analysis difficult to say the least—but not impossible. To reason cogently we need to fight this human tendency (discussed further in Chapter 6).

EXERCISE 1-4

1. Using the Internet, go to Google and search for "I have a dream" under the exact phrase option. Figure out which parts of the speech state or imply Martin Luther King's philosophy and explain his worldview.

2. Here is a Japanese bar association official, Koji Yanase (quoted in *Newsweek*, February 26, 1996), explaining why there are only half as many lawyers in his country as there are in the greater Washington, D.C., area alone: "If an American is hit on the head by a ball at the ballpark, he sues. If a Japanese person is hit on the head he says, 'It's my honor. It's my fault. I shouldn't have been standing there.'" Explain the two different worldviews implied in Yanase's observation.

3. Find at least one item on the Internet or in the mass media (a newspaper or magazine article or a television program) that seems to be based on a worldview contrary to the one you yourself hold. Explain your choice.

4. Find at least one item on the Internet or in the mass media that reflects a typically American point of view you happen to share, and explain what makes it typically American. (This is not as easy to do as it sounds. Recalling the content of the box on E. M. Forster's novel may help prod your memory.)

5. Describe a situation in which you changed your mind on some more or less fundamental belief, and explain what convinced you to do so. (This is a very difficult question for many people to answer, another bit of evidence for the fact that much of what goes on in the accumulation and emendation of important background beliefs happens only on the edge of consciousness.)

EXERCISE 1-5

1. When Barack Obama and Hillary Rodham Clinton ran for the Democratic presidential nomination in 2008, many people thought that the time had come to elect an African American or a woman as president. Never in our history had two candidates from these politically underrepresented groups come so close to leading the nation. What changes in worldviews are reflected in voters' willingness to elect a woman or an African American to the highest position in the country? Compare the worldviews voters might have held before this historic shift to those they hold now.

2. The tax bill passed by Congress in the spring of 2003 was the second large tax break in three years. The Bush administration claimed that the average tax cut would be $1,000, but that was because tax breaks to the rich were so large. As Laura Tyson, dean of the London Business School, pointed out (in *Business Week,* August 11, 2003), "Payroll taxes that pose the heaviest burden for most American families have been left untouched while the top marginal income tax rate, the capital-gains tax, and the dividend tax [all of which benefit the wealthy] have been reduced." Nevertheless, the bill was popular with lots of lower-income taxpayers who liked it because they thought it would probably cut their own tax bills. Bring your background beliefs to bear and reason about whether these people were right in thinking the bill benefited them. Did you modify your beliefs in 2008 when the country slid into a major recession?

*3. A *Time* magazine story headlined "China's Arms Race: The World's Most Populous Country Wants the World's Best Military" claimed that "Beijing [China's capital, for those whose grasp of geography is not up to snuff] is buying and spying its way to superpower status." It listed China's annual military budget as $10.9 billion. What figures do you need to know, even if just approximately, to evaluate *Time*'s spin on the story? If you have this knowledge, what is your judgment? If you don't, a tiny bit of research will be in order here.

EXERCISE 1-6

Sex scandals involving politicians have hit the media with increasing frequency in recent years. The most famous, of course, was Bill Clinton's extramarital affairs that eventually led to his impeachment. Then there was the governor of New Jersey, James McGreevey, who came out as a gay man and admitted to having an affair with a male employee, and Eliot Spitzer, who resigned as governor of New York when he was nailed for patronizing a high-priced prostitution service. These are but a few of the many sex scandals involving politicians, and in each case the wives stood by them in front of the cameras as they made their excruciating public confession and apologized. Inevitably, now that women feel increasingly liberated, these wives have drawn fire for standing by their men, following what some critics call an outmoded tradition. But others argue that wives are part of the political team and should provide support no matter how devastating the ordeal. Still others think that the men should make the decision themselves and refuse to implicate their wives. (As one writer put it: "You want to be an alpha male with extra helpings of testosterone and appetites that can't be denied? Fine, but if you get caught, Be. A. Man. Don't drag your wife in front of the cameras to prove how strong your marriage is.[9])

This is obviously a personal decision, but given your worldview, do you think that the men should take the responsibility to got it alone and not involve their wives? If they are reluctant to do so, should the wives stand by them, or should they refuse and let their husbands hang out to dry? (The answer is more complex than it seems when you consider, for instance, the effect on the couples' children.)

EXERCISE 1-7

How do the ideas expressed in the following excerpt from an essay by British philosopher Bertrand Russell compare with those in your own worldview and other background beliefs?

> The aesthetic indictment of industrialism is perhaps the least serious. A much more serious feature is the way in which it forces men, women, and children to live a life against instinct, unnatural, unspontaneous, artificial. Where industry is thoroughly developed, men are deprived of the sight of green fields and the smell of earth after rain; they are cooped together in irksome proximity, surrounded by noise and dirt, compelled to spend many hours a day performing some utterly uninteresting and monotonous mechanical task. Women are, for the most part, obliged to work in factories, and to leave to others the care of their children. The children themselves, if they are preserved from work in the factories, are kept at work in school, with an intensity that is especially damaging to the best brains. The result of this life against instinct is that industrial populations tend to be listless and trivial, in constant search of excitement, delighted by a murder, and still more delighted by a war.

Russell's essay, by the way, appeared in the June 1921 issue of the *Atlantic Monthly.* (The more things change, the more they remain the same?)

EXERCISE 1-8

Here is an excerpt from a speech delivered to the Utah chapter of NOW in May 1997 by Elizabeth Joseph in which she argues that polygamy is beneficial to women in the modern world:

> I've often said that if polygamy didn't exist the modern American career woman would have invented it. Because, despite its reputation, polygamy is the one lifestyle that offers an independent woman a real chance to "have it all." . . .

---

[9]Katha Pollitt, "Eliot Spitzer: John Q. Public," *The Nation,* March 31, 2008.

As a journalist, I work many unpredictable hours in a fast-paced environment. The news determines my schedule. . . . Because of my plural marriage arrangement, I don't have to worry [about coming home late]. I know that when I have to work late my daughter will be surrounded by loving adults with whom she is comfortable and who know her schedule without my telling them. My eight-year-old has never seen the inside of a day-care center, and my husband has never eaten a TV dinner. And I know that when I get home from work, if I'm dog-tired and stressed-out, I can be alone and guilt free. It's a rare day when all eight of my husband's wives are tired and stressed at the same time.

It's helpful to think of polygamy in terms of a free-market approach to marriage. Why shouldn't you or your daughters have the opportunity to marry the best man available, regardless of his marital status? . . .

Polygamy is an empowering lifestyle for women. It provides me the environment and opportunity to maximize my female potential without all the trade-offs and compromises that attend monogamy. The women in my family are friends. You don't share two decades of experience, and a man, without those friendships becoming very special. . . . [P]olygamy [is] the ultimate feminist lifestyle.

Compare Joseph's view to your own on marital arrangements. Do you find her ideas persuasive? Does your worldview jibe with hers? Why or why not? Most of us think of monogamy as "natural," yet polygamy has been common throughout the world at different times in history. (Although Utah outlawed the practice in the nineteenth century as a condition of statehood, the antibigamist law is rarely enforced in that state. Estimates put the number of polygamists in Utah in the tens of thousands, even though it's impossible to verify the statistics, given the illegal nature of the activity.) Portions of Joseph's speech were reprinted in the February 1998 issue of *Harper's*.

10. Two Vital Kinds of Background Beliefs

Background beliefs obviously differ greatly in their importance. Two kinds that are extremely important concern the *nature of human nature* and the *reliability of information sources*.

The Nature of Human Nature

Good beliefs about what we ourselves and other people are like constitute a vital part of everyone's worldview. They are crucial in applying what we know to the problems encountered in everyday life, whether of a personal or a social nature. When can we trust our friends? Is an instructor to be believed who says that students are graded solely on the quality of their exams and not on agreement with the instructor's personal opinions? Will people be sufficiently motivated to work diligently under a socialistic system? Are large numbers of elected officials motivated by selfish interests that frequently override their sense of duty to those who have elected them?

Fortunately, we don't have to start constructing theories about human nature from scratch, since other people, including some of the great writers (Shakespeare, Aristotle, Darwin, Freud) have been at the task for some time now. (Of course, tapping these sources has its risks. Freud, for instance, had some way-off-target ideas on the subject to go along with some extremely penetrating ones.) But even common everyday sayings contain a mother lode of wisdom. Blood *is* thicker than water, and power *does* tend to corrupt, even if it is doubtful that the female of the species is any more vain than the male.

The Reliability of Information Sources

Thoughts about the accuracy, sufficiency, and truthfulness of information sources constitute another vital kind of background belief. As with computers, so also with the human mind: "Garbage in, garbage out." We therefore need constantly to reassess the reliability of important information sources—television, newspapers, magazines, friends, the Internet, teachers, textbooks, and so on. Under what conditions are these sources likely to provide truthful or, at least, sensible information or opinions? When are alleged experts likely even to possess the truth, much less be motivated to tell it to us straight? When are they likely to be prejudiced in ways that may cloud their judgment? We can't assume automatically that a source is reliable without some *reason* for believing this. As lamented a while back, many people seem to think that if they read it in print or hear it on the TV evening news, then it must be true. Sophisticated reasoners, however, realize that these information sources do not always furnish "the truth, the whole truth, and nothing but the truth"; they don't necessarily provide us with "All the news that's fit to print" (the *New York Times* motto), instead sometimes shaving matters either out of ignorance or from self-serving motives. Intelligent viewers of the scene thus try to determine when these sources are likely to be reliable and when not. That is why a whole chapter in this text, Chapter 10, deals with advertising as an information source; Chapter 11 with the reliability of the media; and another chapter, Chapter 12, with public school textbooks as information sources.

11. SCIENCE TO THE RESCUE

The mention of Darwin and Freud a while back brings to mind the central place that science plays in modern life and in the construction of accurate stocks of background beliefs—in particular, in the formulation of sensible worldviews. Although no information source is absolutely reliable and no theory exempt from at least a small measure of doubt, the most reliable, the most accurate information comes from the well-established sciences of physics, chemistry, biology, and, to a lesser extent, psychology, the social sciences, and the applied sciences such as engineering. The scientific enterprise is an organized, ongoing, worldwide activity that builds and corrects from generation to generation. The method of science is just the rigorous, systematic, dogged application of cogent inductive reasoning, mixed with all sorts of deductive— including mathematical—reasoning from what has so far been observed over many centuries to theories about how the universe and the many things in it have functioned and are likely to function. Theories falsified by experience are tossed out, no matter whose pet ideas happen to get stepped on. Absolutely no one, starting from scratch, could hope to obtain in one lifetime anything remotely resembling the sophisticated and accurate conclusions of any of the sciences, even if that person were a Galileo, Newton, Darwin, and Einstein all rolled into one. *It is foolish indeed to dismiss what science has to say on any topic without very careful thought and without having extremely important reasons for doing so!*[10]

Indeed, one justification for requiring all high school students to take at least one course in a physical or biological science is to allow them to gain an understanding of the great rigor with which scientific principles are tested and proved. But another, easier way to come to understand the power of science as compared to other ways of finding about the world is to think carefully about the thousands of everyday items available to us today that did not exist 300 years ago, products that owe their existence to the tremendous advances in scientific theory that have been made since the days of Galileo and Newton. Without science, there would be no automobiles, no airplanes (not to mention spacecraft), no telephones, electric lightbulbs, air conditioning, or other electric devices of any kind (certainly no computers!), no batteries, no aspirin or other common painkillers, no anesthetics (alcohol used to be the painkiller used during amputations), no antibiotics (or even knowledge of the existence of microbes and thus the extreme importance of cleanliness), no ways to purify drinking water, no indoor plumbing, no eyeglasses, no insulin for diabetics, . . . the list goes on and on. Instead there were plenty of mosquitoes and flies (and fly paper) everywhere on summer days, and people made do with commodes, outhouses, and well-drawn drinking and washing water. In those days, doctors could cure only a handful of ailments, horse dung and its foul smell were everywhere in every city and town, lighting after dark was furnished by candles or oil lamps, and so on. Before the existence of the scientific, modern, industrial world, the average life span almost everywhere was less than 50 years, much less in most societies.

Of course, to avoid having beliefs contradicted by scientific theory or to successfully apply scientific principles in dealing with everyday problems, one does have to have at least a casual acquaintance with what science has to say on various topics. The problem is that large numbers of people have no idea what science is up to and have only the tiniest stock of scientific facts about the nature of the world.

Unfortunately, it isn't just the average person (or average college graduate?) who is more or less illiterate when it comes to science. Even those who need to know about specific scientific results in order to do their jobs adequately are frequently remiss in this way. During a quite severe drought in California, one government official defended his inaction by stating that "One problem [in deciding whether to enact water rationing measures] is that we have only 110 years of [precipitation] records. Our statistics [on California droughts] aren't very good." Yet, just prior to that time, a U.S. Geological Survey study of giant sequoia tree rings had yielded a record going back more than 2,000 years.

Students sometimes defend their ignorance of science by arguing that they only need to know the science, if any, that is relevant to the job they will perform after graduation from college. But this is a serious mistake. For one thing, it isn't possible to know now what basic scientific ideas will be relevant to a job held several years down the pike. (It isn't really possible, except in unusual cases, to know what sort of job it will *be,* much less what kinds of knowledge are going to be relevant to it.) In this

---

[10]Note, however, that psychology has just recently come out of its infancy. Note also that there is more chicanery in medical research (because of the profit motive?) than in most other areas of science.

Here is Isaac Asimov, one of the best-known popularizers of science (also famous for his science fiction), explaining why cheating in science is so rare, why getting caught is almost inevitable sooner or later, and thus why scientists on the whole are so much more trustworthy (when they're doing science!) than, say, politicians and other public servants.

Self-Correction

Every once in a while—not often—scientists discover that one of their number has published false data or has plagiarized someone else's work.

This is always deeply embarrassing, especially since these days such news usually receives wide publicity in the nonscientific world.

In some ways, however, these scandals actually reflect credit upon the world of science. Consider:

1. Scientists are, after all, human. There is enormous pressure and competition in the world of science. Promotion and status depend on how much you publish and how soon you publish, for the lion's share of credit comes if you are first with an important theory or observation. Under these circumstances, there is great temptation to rush things; to make up some data you are sure you will eventually find anyway that will support your theory; or to help yourself to someone else's work. The surprise, really, is not that it sometimes happens, but that it doesn't happen much more often. Scientists resist the pressure marvelously well.

2. When it does happen, the mere fact that it is so publicized is a tribute to scientists. If it were a common event, or if people expected scientists to be corrupt, it would make smaller headlines and drop out of sight sooner. Single cases of scientific corruption, however, will be talked about for years and inspire articles and books by the score. It's really a compliment.

3. Cases of scientific misbehavior point out how difficult it actually is to carry them out successfully, or even for very long. . . . [A] vital principle in scientific research is that nothing counts until observations can be repeated independently and there, almost inevitably, anything peculiar is uncovered. Science is self-correcting in a way that no other field of intellectual endeavor can match.

4. It is scientists themselves who catch the frauds; no one else is equipped to do so. The point is that scientists do catch them. There is never any cover-up on the grounds that science itself must not be disgraced. However embarrassing the facts may be, the culprit is exposed pitilessly and publicly. Science is self-policing in a way that no other field is.

5. Finally, the punishment is absolute. Anyone who proves to have violated the ethics of scientific endeavor is ruined for life. There is no second chance, no vestige of status. He or she must drop out, forever disgraced.

Add to all this the fact that scientific ethics requires all scientists to labor to find flaws in their own observations and theories—and to publicize these flaws when they find them—and you will understand how stern the requirements are and how astonishing it is that scandal is so infrequent.

—From *SciQuest* (February 1982).
Reprinted by permission of the author.

increasingly technological age, more and more jobs require at least a general idea of what science has to say about various topics.

More to the point, a rudimentary understanding of science also is of immeasurable value when dealing with all sorts of everyday problems that aren't related to earning a living. Consumers spend millions of dollars every year on over-the-counter nostrums that don't work, or may even be harmful, because they don't know simple scientific facts—for instance, that no remedies they can buy will cure the flulike infections common in winter. (A friend of ours who had a hearing problem wasted six months having his back manipulated by a chiropractor before going to a physician who removed wax from his ear and restored normal hearing.[11]) Every day, people throw their money away on get-rich-quick schemes that defy the most basic principles of economics. Large sums are wasted on fortune tellers, mediums, and other charlatans who science has proved over and over again cannot deliver the promised goods. (This point is discussed a bit more in Chapter 6.)

Students often are put off science by the sheer complexity of the subject matter. Biology, for example, has to be an extremely complicated science, given that the human body contains trillions of cells, each one of which contains millions of atoms and subatomic particles (did you know this?). So the bad news is that every science quickly gets over the heads of almost all laypeople. But the good news is that with only modest perseverance, people who are reasonably intelligent can learn enough about science to greatly improve their everyday reasoning and thus their chances of success in everyday life. (Clearly, similar remarks apply to mathematics, particularly to arithmetic and simple algebra—note the confusion that occasionally results in supermarkets when the power goes out and clerks need to actually add and subtract to figure out what is owed.)

EXERCISE 1-9

A quiz was given to determine how much American adults know about the nature of the world. Answer the following true/false questions that were part of this quiz.

1. Lasers work by focusing sound waves.
2. Antibiotics kill viruses as well as bacteria.
3. The earliest human beings lived at the same time as the dinosaurs.
4. Human beings developed from earlier species of animals.

If some of these are a bit difficult for you to answer, you might take comfort in the fact that only the following percentages of the adult Americans answered the questions correctly:

1. 45	3. 48
2. 51	4. 53

SUMMARY OF CHAPTER 1

Reasoning is the essential ingredient in solving life's problems. This chapter discusses some of the fundamentals of good reasoning and presents an overview of the material to be covered later on the topic of reasoning well in everyday life.

---

[11]The point is not to knock all chiropractors but to stress the need for care when consulting experts of any kind.

1. *Reasoning* can be cast into *arguments,* which consist of one or more *premises* (reasons) offered in support of a *conclusion.* In real life (as opposed to in textbooks), arguments usually are not labeled and divided from surrounding rhetoric, nor are their premises and conclusions neatly specified. But clues generally are given. Words such as *because, since,* and *for* usually signal premises; *hence, therefore,* and *so,* conclusions.

2. Not all groups of sentences form arguments. They may be anecdotes or other types of *exposition* or *explanation.*

3. Reasoning is either *cogent* (good) or *fallacious* (bad). Cogent reasoning must satisfy three criteria: It must (1) start with justified (warranted, believable) premises, (2) include all likely relevant information, and (3) be *valid* (correct).

4. There are two basic kinds of valid reasoning: *deductive* and *inductive.* The fundamental property of a *deductively valid* argument is this: If its premises are true, then its conclusion must be true also. This is so because the conclusion of a deductively valid argument already is contained in its premises, although usually implicitly, not explicitly. (Note that a deductively valid argument may have false premises. What makes it valid is that *if* its premises are true, then its conclusion must be also.) Unlike deductively valid arguments, those that are *inductively valid* (correct, strong) have conclusions that go beyond the claims made by their premises, projecting patterns stated in the premises onto additional cases.

5. There is no truth to claims about there being such things as "feminine logic," different from "male logic." Logic is not "gender-relative." Similarly, there is no truth to the idea that something exists called "black logic," different from the "Eurocentric" variety espoused by white male teachers. Good reasoning does not differ from sex to sex or race to race; it is not in any way tied to ethnicity. Furthermore, with respect to facts, at any rate, the idea embodied in the idea that "It may well be true for you, but it isn't true for me" is without merit, as is the academic talk of there being something called "Aristotelian linear reasoning," different from a more "intuitive" type of reasoning. (But more needs to be said, and will be, about beliefs concerning values. The point made in this chapter is that, however we may arrive at value beliefs, reasoning from those beliefs must employ the same principles of logic as does reasoning about purely factual matters.)

6. Background beliefs can be divided in many ways, one being into beliefs about *matters of fact* (snow is white) and beliefs about *values* (Jane Austen's novels are better than those of Stephen King). (Note that when speaking of beliefs here, we have in mind a broad sense covering everything accepted as true, or very likely true, and all value judgments and convictions.)

7. Beliefs also, of course, can be divided into those that happen to be true and those that are false. They also can be differentiated in terms of how firmly they are or should be held, and with respect to whether they concern particular events (Jones went to the show last Wednesday) or those that are general (Copper conducts electricity).

8. Our most important beliefs, taken together, make up our *worldviews* or *philosophies*. They are particularly important because they enter into decisions of all kinds—about what to do or what to believe—that we need to make in everyday life. *Examples:* We all die sooner or later; it's always wrong to betray a friend; the best way to find out about how things work is to use induction and deduction. Note that, although most beliefs in our worldviews are general—even extremely general—a few are not. *Example:* We don't know whether there is or isn't a God (part of the worldviews of agnostics).

9. Unfortunately, we all tend at least sometimes to hold a belief without sufficient reason for doing so—for example, when complicated social or political issues are discussed. This is true even with respect to some of the beliefs that make up our worldviews. But worldviews, just as any beliefs, need to be carefully examined: Does evidence support them? Do we really value this more than that? Having an accurate supply of background beliefs is not just a matter of regularly acquiring more beliefs but also of pruning those we already have.

   We tend to absorb the beliefs of those around us as we mature from children into adults. Our worldviews, in particular, tend to grow out of family values, religious training, peer group attitudes, cultural heritages, and so on. We often hold these vital beliefs uncritically—indeed, often without realizing that we hold them. Good critical reasoners, on the contrary, try to become aware of and to critically evaluate their background beliefs, especially those making up their worldviews.

10. Beliefs about human nature are of vital importance when reasoning in daily life, because the success or failure of everyday interactions depends on them. Whether we can trust this sort of person or that is an example. That is one reason why reading the writings of great literary and scientific figures is so useful (in addition to being entertaining).

    Beliefs about the accuracy and truthfulness of information sources also are of great importance, because, as the saying goes, "Garbage in, garbage out." We can't reason well from poor or false information. That is why later chapters in this book deal with several important information sources.

11. Because science plays such an important part in everyone's life these days, it behooves us to become as well acquainted as we can, and as time permits, with the scientific view of the world and with the ways in which scientists come to their conclusions. No one on their own could possibly discover even a tiny fraction of what scientists have learned over hundreds of years about the way the world works. (Those who don't see the importance of science in their own lives should reflect on how much we depend, every day, on the fruits of scientific investigations. *Examples:* Electrical devices, painkillers and other modern medicines, toilet paper.) Unfortunately, most people do not have even a reasonably good grasp of what science is up to.

Peanuts by Charles Schulz. ©1999 United Feature Syndicate, Inc.
Reprinted by permission of United Feature Syndicate, Inc.

A canine induction by enumeration.

Truth is more of a stranger than fiction.
—Mark Twain

The pure and the simple truth is rarely pure and never simple.
—Oscar Wilde

Man has such a predilection for systems and abstract deductions that he is ready to distort the truth intentionally; he is ready to deny the evidence of his senses in order to justify his logic.
—Fyodor Dostoevsky

Every man is encompassed by a cloud of comforting convictions, which move with him like flies on a summer day.
—Bertrand Russell

Chapter

2

MORE ON DEDUCTION AND INDUCTION

1. DEDUCTIVE VALIDITY

In Chapter 1, we distinguished between deductively valid and inductively valid arguments. Here now is a discussion of some of the basic principles of deductive reasoning, which, by the way, the vast majority of people find quite intuitive.

As pointed out in Chapter 1, different arguments may have the same *form,* or *structure.* Here are two arguments that have the same form—namely, *modus ponens:*

(1) 1. If it's spring, then the birds are chirping.
     2. It is spring.
  ∴3. The birds are chirping.
(2) 1. If a world government doesn't evolve soon, then wars will continue to occur.
     2. A world government isn't going to evolve soon.
  ∴3. Wars will continue to occur.

In Chapter 1, we noted that the form of *modus ponens* can be indicated this way:

  1. If *A* then *B.*
  2. *A.*
∴3. *B.*

Now, here is another commonly occurring deductively valid form, called ***modus tollens:***

> *Form:*   1. If *A* then *B*.
>   2. Not *B*.
>   ∴3. Not *A*.
> *Example:*   1. If it's spring, then the birds are chirping.
>   2. The birds aren't chirping.
>   ∴3. It isn't spring.

Here is still another commonly occurring deductively valid argument form, usually called **hypothetical syllogism:**

> *Form:*   1. If *A* then *B*.
>   2. If *B* then *C*.
>   ∴3. If *A* then *C*.
> *Example:*   1. If we successfully develop nuclear fusion power, then power will become cheap and plentiful.
>   2. If power becomes cheap and plentiful, then the economy will flourish.
>   ∴3. If we successfully develop nuclear fusion power, then the economy will flourish.

And here is the deductively valid form called **disjunctive syllogism:** [1]

> *Form:*   1. *A* or *B*.
>   2. Not *A*.
>   ∴3. *B*.
> *Example:*   1. Either McCain won in 2008 or Obama did.
>   2. McCain didn't win.
>   ∴3. Obama did.

Note that, while the first premise is true, the second, unfortunately for Obama, is false, as is the conclusion. Nevertheless, the validity of this argument guarantees that *if* both its premises had been true, *then* so would its conclusion have been true.

Finally, here are several argument forms of a different kind (all but the first two are called *syllogisms*): [2]

> *Form:*   1. No *F*s are *G*s.
>   ∴2. It's false that some *F*s are *G*s.
> *Example:*   1. No police officers accept bribes.
>   ∴2. It's false that some police officers accept bribes. (uh, huh)
> *Form:*   1. All *F*s are *G*s.
>   ∴2. If this is an *F*, then this is a *G*.
> *Example:*   1. All salamis are tasty.
>   ∴2. If this is a salami, then it is tasty. (no dispute on this one)

---

[1] Strictly speaking, in spite of their names, *disjunctive syllogism* and *hypothetical syllogism* are not syllogisms.
[2] See the appendix and also Alan Hausman, Howard Kahane, and Paul Tidman, *Logic and Philosophy,* 10th edition (Belmont, Calif.: Wadsworth, 2006), for additional material on deduction and induction.

Form: 1. All *F*s are *G*s.
            2. All *G*s are *H*s.
       ∴3. All *F*s are *H*s.
Example: 1. All TV evangelists have high moral standards.
            2. All who have high moral standards live up to those standards.
       ∴3. All TV evangelists live up to high moral standards. (proven by history)

Form: 1. All *F*s are *G*s.
            2. This is an *F*.
       ∴3. This is a *G*. (note that this is *not* the form called *modus ponens!*)
Example: 1. All elected officials always tell the truth.
            2. George Bush (the younger) is an elected official.
       ∴3. George Bush (the younger) always tells the truth. (ho, ho, ho!)

Form: 1. All *F*s are *G*s.
            2. No *G*s are *H*s.
       ∴3. No *F*s are *H*s.
Example: 1. All males are chauvinist pigs.
            2. No chauvinist pigs are likeable.
       ∴3. No males are likeable.

Form: 1. No *F*s are *G*s.
            2. Some *H*s are *F*s.
       ∴3. Some *H*s are not *G*s.
Example: 1. No foreigners can be trusted.
            2. Some newborn babies are foreigners.
       ∴3. Some newborn babies cannot be trusted. (obviously)

In daily life, arguments tend to get strung together into larger arguments leading up to a point, a grand conclusion or **thesis.** Here is an example (with logical structure exhibited to the left) in which the conclusion of the first argument is used as a premise in the second, and the conclusion of the second is used as a premise in the third, and final, argument:

1. If *A* then *B*.	1. If a world government doesn't evolve soon, then wars will continue to occur.
2. If *B* then *C*.	2. But if they continue to occur, then nuclear weapons will proliferate.
∴3. If *A* then *C*.	3. So if a world government doesn't evolve soon, then nuclear weapons will proliferate.
4. If *C* then *D*.	4. But if they proliferate, then a nuclear war will be inevitable, sooner or later.
∴5. If *A* then *D*.	5. Which proves that if a world government doesn't evolve soon, we'll end up fighting a nuclear war sooner or later.
6. Not *D*.	6. But it's ridiculous to think we'll actually have a nuclear war (that is, it's false that we'll have such a war).
∴7. Not *A*.	7. So a world government is going to evolve soon (that is, it's false that a world government won't evolve soon).

Humorous use of disjunctive syllogism. General Halftrack's reasoning is this: Either the box is too small, or we're not running this camp right. But it's false that we're not running this camp right. So the box is too small. Build a bigger one. Just as we often do in daily life, Halftrack omits a premise as understood—namely, the premise that it's false that the camp is not being run right.

Exercise 2-1

1. Invent deductively valid arguments having the forms *modus ponens, modus tollens,* disjunctive syllogism, and hypothetical syllogism.

2. Use the conclusion of one of the arguments you have just constructed as a premise in another argument that is deductively valid.

2. Deductive Invalidity

Any argument that doesn't have a deductively valid form is said to be *deductively invalid.*[3] The number of deductively invalid argument forms is legion, but a few occur so frequently that they've been given names. Here are two examples (to give the flavor):

Fallacy of **denying the antecedent:**
Form: 1. If *A* then *B.*
             2. Not *A.*
          ∴3. Not *B.*
Example: 1. If abortion is murder, then it's wrong.
             2. But abortion isn't murder.
          ∴3. Abortion isn't wrong.

The conclusion doesn't follow: Even supposing abortion isn't murder, it may be wrong for other reasons.

Fallacy of **affirming the consequent:**
Form: 1. If *A* then *B.*
             2. *B.*
          ∴3. *A.*

---

[3]A deductively invalid argument may still be a good argument if it is inductively correct. Arguments that have the forms about to be discussed are bad because they are neither deductively valid nor inductively correct.

Example: 1. If Obama is president, then a liberal is now president.
               2. A liberal is now president.
           ∴ 3. Obama is president.

The conclusion doesn't follow: Some other conservative may now be president.

EXERCISE 2-2

1. Invent an argument having the form of the fallacy *denying the antecedent,* and then show that it is deductively invalid by explaining how its premises might be true when its conclusion is false.

2. Do the same with an argument having the form *affirming the consequent.*

3. SYLLOGISMS

A lot more needs to be said about invalid reasoning and will be in later chapters, in particular, Chapters 3, 4, and 5, where various other kinds of fallacious reasoning are discussed. But let's now discuss a few more matters concerning the deductively valid reasonings called **syllogisms.**

We said before that arguments having the form called *hypothetical syllogism,*

     1. If *A* then *B.*
     2. If *B* then *C.*
   ∴ 3. If *A* then *C.*

are not true syllogisms (at least not in the sense intended by Aristotle, the inventor of syllogistic logic[4]), while those having the form

     1. All *A*s are *B*s.
     2. All *B*s are *C*s.
     3. All *A*s are *C*s.

are the genuine article. What makes one the real thing and the other not? The difference between these two kinds of arguments that makes the difference should become clear in the following little exposition as to the nature of syllogisms in traditional syllogistic logic.[5]

In traditional syllogistic logic, a **categorical proposition** is a subject-predicate proposition that asserts or denies a relationship between a **subject class** and a **predicate class.** There are exactly four kinds of categorical propositions (with one variation): **universal affirmative** (A propositions), having the form "All *S* are *P*" (*Example:* "All sinners are betrayers."); **universal negative** (E propositions), having the form "No *S* are *P*"

---

[4]Obviously, something has changed since days of old, and that is why, for example, argument forms such as *hypothetical syllogism* now sometimes are thought of as the genuine article. The point is that Aristotle and Aristotelians, until recently, would not have considered these other forms to be syllogisms.

[5]For now, let's just note that we replace the *A*s, *B*s, and *C*s in the form of *hypothetical syllogism* by whole sentences, as in "If Art goes to the show, then Betsy will stay home, but the *A*s and *B*s in "All *A* are *B*" are replaced by subjects of sentences, or predicates, as in "All women are fickle."

(*Example:* "No chess players are imbeciles."); **particular affirmative** (I propositions), having the form "Some *S* are *P*" (*Example:* "Some men are chauvinists."); and **particular negative** (O propositions), having the form "Some *S* are not *P*" (*Example:* "Some logicians are not nitpickers."). The one common variation is that statements such as "Socrates is a man," having as their subject a particular item rather than a class of items, are often honorifically considered to be A propositions.

A *syllogism* is an argument containing three categorical propositions, two of them premises, one a conclusion. Here is one of the original examples (dechauvinized):

Syllogism	Traditional Symbolization
All humans are mortal.	MAP
All Greeks are human.	SAM
∴All Greeks are mortal.	∴SAP

The term *P,* the predicate of the conclusion, is said to be the syllogism's **major term;** the term *S,* the subject of the conclusion, its **minor term;** and the term *M,* which occurs once in each premise but not in the conclusion, its **middle term.** Every syllogism has exactly three terms (none used equivocally), each one repeated twice but not in the same proposition. There are hundreds of different syllogistic forms (figure out how many), but, of course, only some are valid. The one given above is valid, whereas the syllogism "All Greeks are human; all humans are mortal; therefore, all mortals are Greek" is not.

The valid syllogism about Greeks being mortal is said to be in the **mood** AAA (for obvious reasons). (In this case, the syllogism is said to be in the *first figure,* and its *form* is said to be AAA-I, but let's pass over this complication.) There are, of course, other moods (and figures). Here, for instance, is a syllogism in the mood AII (it happens to be in the third figure):[6]

Syllogism	Traditional Symbolization
All things made out of grass are green.	MAG
Some things made out of grass are cigarettes.	MIC
∴Some cigarettes are green.	∴CIG

EXERCISE 2-3

1. Invent a deductively valid syllogism that has the same form as the valid syllogism about Greeks being mortal just mentioned.

2. Invent another deductively valid syllogism in some other mood (but not the mood AII).

3. Now invent a deductively invalid syllogism, and explain why you think that it is not valid.

*4. Explain why *disjunctive syllogisms* are not true syllogisms in the sense intended by Aristotle. (Try to do this before looking at the answer in the back of the book.)

---

[6]In the Middle Ages, students determined the validity of syllogistic forms by reciting a chant containing a name for each of the valid cases in each figure. For example, the name "bArbArA" occurs in the chant for the first figure, indicating that the form AAA-1 is valid.

4. Indirect Proofs

Another common everyday kind of reasoning is called an **indirect** or a **reductio ad absurdum** (reduce to an absurdity) **proof.** We reason in this way when we assume the opposite of what we wish to prove and then deductively derive a conclusion claimed to be false, indeed, often contradictory or otherwise absurd. The point is that if we validly reason to an obviously false conclusion, then our original assumption must be false and hence its negation—the thing we wish to prove—must be true. Here is an example:

> Assume for the moment that when Bill Clinton was president, he offered a night's stay in the Lincoln Room in the White House in return for campaign contributions. Then, since doing so would definitely be at least shady, if not illegal, Clinton would have done something shady if not illegal. But Clinton is an honorable man, so we can be sure that he did not do anything shady or illegal. Therefore, the assumption that Clinton offered a stay in the Lincoln room in return for money must be false. (Notice that the fact that Clinton did, according to most viewers of the scene, rent out the Lincoln bedroom does not detract from the fact that the reasoning in this indirect argument is deductively valid. It just means that one of the premises of this argument must be false.

An indirect proof can be defeated in either of two ways. One is by showing that there is a mistake in reasoning. (In our example, there is no mistake in reasoning. The argument is deductively valid, which just means that if its premises are true, then its conclusion must be true). The other way is to show that at least one of its premises (other than the assumed premise) is false. (In our example, the likely premise would be . . . ?)

5. Tautologies, Contradictions, and Contingent Statements

A **tautology** is a statement that is *logically,* or *necessarily,* true or is so devoid of content as to be practically empty (and thus true because completely empty statements, making no claim, cannot be false).[7] *Example:* "Barry Bonds did take steroids, or he didn't." A **contradiction** is a statement that is necessarily false (because it contradicts itself). *Example:* "Barry Bonds did take steroids, and he didn't take them." All other statements are said to be **contingent.** *Example:* "Barry Bonds didn't take them."

We can determine the truth value of a contradiction or of a tautology by logical—deductive—means alone, without the need for any empirical investigation or inductive reasoning. But determining the truth or falsity of a contingent statement requires observation by ourselves or others and, usually, the employment of inductive reasoning. *Example:* Tasting and disliking cooked vegetables several times has led many people to conclude inductively that in general they will dislike cooked vegetables. (Note that there is no contradiction between always disliking cooked vegetables in the past and liking them sometime in the future. Nor does this past dislike guarantee that they always will be disliked in the future.)

---

[7] Note that logicians often use the term *tautology* in a more restricted manner, so as to cover only the logical truths provable by means of what is called *sentential logic.*

EXERCISE 2-4

Which of the following are tautologies, which contradictions, and which contingent statements? Defend your answers. (Be careful; at least one of these is sneaky.)

1. Either Ralph Nader ran for president of the United States in 2008, or a lot of newspapers were mistaken.

2. Either Ralph Nader was on the ballot in Georgia in 2008, or he wasn't.

*3. Nader didn't campaign both for the presidency and for the vice presidency.

4. Snow is always white, except, of course, when it isn't.

5. The media always report the news accurately.

6. No politicians ever keep any of their campaign promises.

7. Those who laugh last, laugh best.

8. I learned in school that 2 + 2 always equals 4, but I don't believe it.

9. Either you're in favor of an equal rights amendment to the Constitution, or you're against it.

10. Trespassers will be shot and then they'll never trespass again.

11. If you don't play the state lottery, you can't win it.

12. If I didn't get all of the first ten questions here right, then I did get them all right.

6. INDUCTIVE VALIDITY (CORRECTNESS) AND INVALIDITY (INCORRECTNESS)

As indicated before, we can think of induction as a kind of *patterning*. Perhaps the simplest form of induction is the one called **induction by enumeration,** mentioned in Chapter 1. In this kind of inductive reasoning, we reason from the fact that all As observed so far are Bs to the conclusion that all As whatsoever are Bs. For example, a study of 100 members of Congress no doubt would show that they all accept campaign contributions from lobbyists intent on influencing legislation, and finding this out would count as good evidence for the inductive conclusion that all 535 members of Congress accept funds of this kind.

Obviously, some inductions of this kind are better than others and make their conclusions more probable. While there are several modestly different theories about how to determine the probability of the conclusions of enumerative inductions, almost all agree on a few points.

Greater sample size yields greater probability. The more instances in a sample (the instances observed so far), the greater the probability of a conclusion based on that sample. A sample of 100 members of Congress who accept campaign contributions from lobbyists provides a higher degree of probability that all do than a smaller sample, say, of 50 members. The point is that more of the same sort of evidence doesn't change the conclusion of an induction; rather, it changes the degree of probability of that conclusion and thus changes the strength of belief a rational person should have in it.

More representative samples yield higher probabilities than those that are less representative. The quality of a sample is even more important than its size. (Indeed, the higher its quality, the smaller a sample needs to be to yield a given degree of probability.) When sampling apples in a barrel, for instance, it won't do just to sample a few from the top (the classic case); after all, rotten apples are more likely to be at the bottom than at the top of a barrel. Samples that neglect possible rotten apples at the bottom of metaphorical barrels are said to be *biased* or *unrepresentative*. Obviously, the less biased, more representative a sample, the higher the degree of probability of an inference based on that sample.

One definite counterexample shoots down an enumerative induction. The most important reason that inductive reasoning is superior to many other kinds (for example, of the superstitious or the pseudoscientific variety to be discussed later) is that it does not allow us to pass over evidence that indicates a pet theory is false. For example, if one woman who takes a birth control pill as directed gets pregnant, then no valid enumerative induction about the pill's effectiveness can be drawn. (Note that it still may be possible to draw other kinds of valid inductive inferences, including the statistical kind to be discussed shortly.)

However, it often is hard to be sure that what looks like a counterexample really is one. A woman on birth control pills who becomes pregnant, for instance, may have accidentally neglected to take the pills properly, and we may not be aware of that fact. The moral is that it is risky to reject an enumerative induction on the basis of one counterexample, or even two, unless we are very sure that at least one is a genuine counterexample. But when we are sure, then an enumerative induction in question must be rejected.

Reasoning by Analogy

Several other kinds of inductive reasoning are very similar to enumerative induction, including reasoning by **analogy.** In one version of this kind of inductive reasoning, we reason from the similarity of two things in several relevant respects to their similarity in another. Thus, if we know that two people have similar tastes in books, art, food, music, and TV programs and find out that one likes to watch *Masterpiece Theater!* on public television (PBS), then we're justified in concluding by analogy that the other probably does also.

The trouble is that every two things resemble each other in an indefinitely large number of ways. Only *relevant* resemblances count in drawing correct analogies. But what makes a resemblance relevant? The answer is background beliefs about how, in general, things hang together. For example, if the stock market rises and falls in concert with ups and downs in the Olympic elk population over several years, only fools are likely to conclude that the two will fluctuate together in the future, because so much background information contradicts this idea. On the other hand, if stocks were to rise and fall over several years in concert with ups and downs in retail sales, we could reason by analogy that the next change in one will produce a similar change in the other. (Of course, given all of the other factors relevant to stock market prices, an induction of the kind just described would have to be assigned a very modest degree of probability.)

In another version of analogical induction, we reason from the fact that all examined items of a certain kind have a particular property to the conclusion that a particular as yet unexamined item of that kind will be found to have that property. Finding out that, say, 100 members of Congress accept money from lobbyists, we can conclude by this kind of analogy that a certain other member probably also does so.

As this last example shows, analogical inductions are much safer, and thus have a higher degree of probability, than their enumerative counterparts, because they have much weaker conclusions. Concluding, for example, that a particular member of Congress accepts money from lobbyists is a much weaker, hence safer, prediction than that all members of Congress do so.

Statistical Induction

When drawing a sample from a population, we often find that not all of the examined As are Bs, so that we cannot draw a valid enumerative induction. But having found that a certain percentage of the As have the property in question, we can conclude by a **statistical induction** that the same percentage of the total population of As have that property. Having found, say, that 480 of the first 1,000 observed tosses of a given coin land face up, we can conclude that 48 percent of all of the tosses with that coin will land face up (thus learning, incidentally, that the coin probably is slightly biased in favor of tails, as many coins are).

Of course, what was said about the quality and, hence, the degree of probability of enumerative inductions also applies to the statistical variety. The larger the sample employed and the more representative it is, the higher the degree of probability of a statistical induction based on that sample.

Higher-Level Inductions

More general, **higher-level inductions** can be used to evaluate those that are less general. For example, we use higher-level induction when we conclude that an automobile engine eventually will wear out or need to be repaired, even though it has run perfectly for 100,000 miles. We overrule a low-level conclusion telling us that because the car has run perfectly so far, it will do so forever, by appeal to a higher-level, more general induction such as this one: All mechanical devices with moving parts checked up on so far have eventually worn out or needed to be repaired, so very probably this particular mechanical device (the engine in question) also eventually will wear out or need to be repaired.

More general inferences, based on larger samples about more kinds of items, usually have higher degrees of probability than do those that are less general. That is why an enumerative induction about a particular automobile is overruled by a more general one about many mechanical devices. (There are, in fact, even higher-level reasons for tossing out this low-level induction by enumeration—for example, scientific inductions concerning basic principles of physics and chemistry having to do with the effects of friction.)

Reasoning to Causal Connections

When we reason inductively, we often are looking for explanations, or **causes.** For instance, early investigators of the connection between cigarette smoking and lung cancer, emphysema, and heart disease wanted to determine by means of statistical inductions whether smoking *causes* these death-dealing diseases. They found that smokers contract these diseases much more frequently than nonsmokers, and heavy smokers more than light. That is, they discovered a statistical link between smoking cigarettes and contracting these diseases. Finding no higher-level evidence to the contrary, they concluded that cigarette smoking does indeed cause these life-threatening illnesses. (That some people smoke like chimneys and never come down with these illnesses doesn't prove the contrary, but it does suggest that part of the cause of these diseases must be some other, very likely genetic, factor.[8])

The inductive patterns discussed in this chapter are relatively neat and simple. Enumerative induction is an example. But in daily life, and in particular in scientific theorizing, inductive reasoning often is much more complicated and may involve mathematical reasoning (a kind of deductive reasoning) as well. We believe cigarette smoking causes lung cancer, for example, not just because a certain percentage of those who smoke get that deadly disease but also because the percentage of those who do not smoke and get lung cancer is much lower than for those who do smoke. It is the comparison of the two groups that proves the point. (In fact, the reasoning linking smoking and lung cancer is even more complicated than we have indicated here. For instance, we haven't mentioned how theorists ruled out certain other causal possibilities by carefully selecting the individuals in their samples to rule out the effects of other likely carcinogens.)

Concatenated Inductions

The cigarette/cancer example just discussed brings to mind the fact that in the vast majority of scientific cases, the reasoning employed is of the kind that can be called **concatenated**—a joining together of inductions and deductions in the discovery of a *pattern* that fits what has been observed or previously reasoned to. In scientific reasoning, inductively confirmed theories of several disciplines typically are brought to bear to reach a conclusion. This is done, for example, in determining the types and significance of the food our ancestors ate before the time of recorded history. Carbon 14 dating is used to determine the approximate date at which, say, animal feces, now fossilized, were deposited at an archeological dig; chemical analysis to reveal what kind of food it was (grain, meat, and so on) and that it was eaten by human beings and not other animals—all of this coupled with anthropological theories about how this sort of food fit into the everyday diet of people in those days. Knowledge of this kind may then be used as part of the evidence in theories about the migrations of ancient peoples and the dispersal of and changes in various kinds of grains, fruits, and domesticated animals.

EXERCISE 2-5

1. What is the difference between an induction by enumeration and analogical reasoning? Provide an example (not mentioned in the text) of each.

2. Explain in your own words what the difference is between an induction by enumeration and a statistical induction. Provide an example (not mentioned in the text) of a valid statistical induction.

3. What is meant by saying that an inference is a higher-level induction? Provide an example (not mentioned in the text).

---

[8] See the section in the appendix concerning necessary and sufficient conditions.

7. A MISCONCEPTION ABOUT DEDUCTION AND INDUCTION

There is a widespread but erroneous idea about the difference between deductive and inductive validity. This is the idea that in deductively valid reasoning, we go from the general to the particular, while in inductively valid reasoning, we move from the particular to the general. But little can be said in support of this idea. For instance, the deductively valid argument

    1. All Republican politicians are to the right of Barack Obama.
∴ 2. All who are not to the right of Barack Obama are not Republican politicians.

moves from the general to the equally general, while the inductively valid argument

    1. Bill Clinton made promises during the 1996 campaign that he didn't keep.
    2. George Bush (the younger) made promises during the 2000 campaign that he didn't keep.
    3. George Bush made promises during the 2004 campaign that he didn't keep.
∴ 4. Barack Obama very likely won't keep all the promises he made during the 2008 campaign.

moves from the particular to the equally particular. And the inductively valid argument

    1. So far, all presidential candidates of the Republican Party have been male.
∴ 2. The next Republican Party presidential candidate will be male.

moves from the general to the particular, not the other way around.

So there isn't much truth to the old idea that deductive reasoning moves from the general to the particular, while inductive reasoning moves from the particular to the general. More accurately, when we reason deductively, we reason to conclusions already contained (implicitly or explicitly) in our premises; when we reason inductively, we move to conclusions by extending patterns or resemblances from one set of events to another set.

Some of those who argue otherwise claim that the idea of deduction moving from the general to the particular is intended to be true only for syllogistic reasoning. Thus, the valid syllogism "All humans are mortal; Socrates is human; therefore, Socrates is mortal," does indeed move from the general to the particular. The trouble, of course, is that this is not true for the vast majority of other valid syllogisms, including the one mentioned a while back, whose conclusion is that all Greeks are mortal.

8. REASONING COGENTLY VERSUS BEING RIGHT IN FACT

Reasoning correctly and getting a true conclusion are unfortunately not the same thing. We can reason correctly and get a false conclusion, and we can reason fallaciously and get a true conclusion.[9] *Examples:* Scientists in times past reasoned correctly from what was known then to the conclusion that superconductivity occurs only at temperatures very close to absolute zero, but we now know that this conclusion is false. Astrology buffs reason incorrectly that they will have a good day from the fact that a newspaper

---

[9] In philosophical jargon, we can be *epistemologically right* although *ontologically wrong,* and we can be *epistemologically wrong* but *ontologically right.*

column says they will or that the stars are in a certain position in the sky, and then luck-ily they do have a good day (for completely different reasons having nothing whatever to do with astrology or where the stars happen to be).

On the whole, it's a lot better to reason incorrectly to true—right—conclusions than it is to reason well to false ones.[10] *But the most likely way to be right, in the long run, is to reason correctly!* When people who follow astrology columns thereby do better than they otherwise would have, they're just extremely lucky, not smart. (They're also an ex-tremely rare species of speculator.) In daily life, however, people often equate being smart with being successful, as though success proves reasoning has been cogent. It doesn't, nor does failure prove reasoning fallacious. That's life. Smart people, as they say, "play the odds"—they try to reason well and take their chances in this not quite best of all possible worlds, and *in the long run in most cases, they do a lot better than those whose reasoning is excessively fallacious.*

SUMMARY OF CHAPTER 2

1. Different arguments may have the same form, or structure. *Modus ponens, modus tollens, hypothetical syllogism,* and so on, are deductively valid argument forms. Note that in everyday life, arguments frequently get strung together, lead-ing to a grand conclusion, a *thesis.*

2. But lots of other forms are deductively invalid. *Affirming the consequent* and *denying the antecedent* are examples of deductively invalid argument forms.

3. A *categorical proposition* asserts or denies a relationship between a *subject class* and a *predicate class.* There are four kinds of categorical propositions: *uni-versal affirmative* (A propositions), having the form "All *S* are *P*"; *universal negative* (E propositions), having the form "No *S* are *P*"; *particular affirmative* (I propositions), having the form "Some *S* are *P*"; and *particular negative* (O propositions), having the form "Some *S* are not *P*." Statements such as "Socrates is a man," having as their subject a particular item rather than a class of items, are often honorifically considered to be A propositions.

   A *syllogism* is an argument containing three categorical propositions, two of them premises, one a conclusion. *Example:* "No foreigners are trustable. Some newborn babies are foreigners. Therefore, some newborn babies cannot be trusted." The predicate of the conclusion of a syllogism is said to be its *major term;* the subject of the conclusion, its *minor term;* and the term that occurs once in each premise but not in the conclusion, its *middle term.* Every syllogism has exactly three terms (none used equivocally), each one repeated twice but not in the same proposition. There are hundreds of different syllogistic forms (figure out how many), but, of course, only some are valid. *Example:* The syllogism "All Greeks are humans; all humans are mortals; therefore, all mortals are Greek" is not valid.

---

[10]Philosophical slogan: "I'd rather be epistemologically wrong and ontologically right than vice versa, but the best way to be ontologically right is to be epistemologically right." (Philosophical jargon can be just as opaque as that of every other discipline.)

The *mood* of a syllogism is determined by the kinds of propositions it contains. Thus the syllogism just mentioned is in the mood AAA.

4. In an *indirect* or *reductio ad absurdum proof,* we assume the opposite of what we wish to prove and then deductively derive a conclusion claimed to be false, contradictory, or otherwise absurd. The point is that if we reason validly to a false, or absurd, conclusion, then our original assumption must be false and hence its negation—the thing we wish to prove—must be true.

5. A *tautology* is a statement that is *logically,* or *necessarily,* true or is so devoid of content as to be practically empty. *Example:* "Madonna is world-famous, or she isn't." A *contradiction* is a statement that is necessarily false (because it contradicts itself). *Example:* "Madonna is world-famous and she isn't." All other statements are said to be contingent. *Example:* "Madonna is talented and world-famous."

    The truth values of contradictions and tautologies can be determined by logical—deductive—means alone, but the truth or falsity of contingent statements cannot. They are justified by observation or by reasoning, part of which must be inductive, from what we and/or other people have observed.

6. There are several kinds of valid, or correct, inductions. One is *induction by enumeration,* in which we infer from the fact that all *A*s observed so far are *B*s to the conclusion that all *A*s whatsoever are *B*s.

    In general, the larger or the more representative a sample, the greater the probability of an induction based on it. Note that one definite counterexample invalidates an induction. (But we have to be sure that it really is a counterexample.)

    Analogical reasoning is very much like induction by enumeration, the chief difference being that analogies yield conclusions about just one case (which is why they have higher degrees of probability than corresponding enumerative inductions), whereas enumerative inductions typically concern a great many.

    Statistical inductions also are similar to the enumerative variety, but they move from the fact that a certain percentage of a sample has a given property to the conclusion that the same percentage in the population at large has that property.

    We can use more general, *higher-level* inductions to correct, or overrule, lower-level ones. If experience shows that all mechanical devices eventually wear out or need to be repaired, then it isn't reasonable to conclude that a particular auto engine will not, even though it has run perfectly for 100,000 miles.

    Inductive reasoning often is used to discover *causes,* as in the case of the statistical induction linking cigarette smoking and various life-threatening diseases.

    Reasoning called *concatenated* often brings new evidence together with several already inductively established conclusions, combined with deductive reasoning, to obtain a further conclusion. This is especially true in the sciences. *Example:* Anthropologists or evolutionary theorists reason from principles of physics and chemistry in reaching conclusions from newly discovered evidence.

7. It often is said that deductively valid reasonings move from general premises to particular conclusions, while inductively valid reasoning moves from particular premises to general conclusions. But this is not correct. *Examples:* The deductively valid argument "If you jump off the Brooklyn Bridge, then you'll be killed.

So if you aren't killed, you haven't jumped off the Brooklyn Bridge," moves from the particular to the particular. (By the way, the form of this inference—"If *A* then *B*; therefore, if not-*B* then not-*A*—is sometimes called *contraposition.*) The inductively valid reasoning "If Dan Rather has obtained power, then he has been corrupted by it. He has obtained power. Hence, he has been corrupted by it," moves from the particular to the equally particular (employing *modus ponens,* by the way).

8. Life being what it is, reasoning correctly sometimes results in drawing false conclusions, even from a true premise. *Example:* The person who, having loaned a friend money many times before and having always been repaid, loans the friend money again and gets stiffed. Furthermore, again life being what it is, reasoning fallaciously sometimes results in drawing true conclusions, even sometimes from false premises. *Example:* risking one's life savings at a dice table in Las Vegas employing the "double the bet" method (discussed in the appendix) and winning a small fortune.

But, still again, life being what it is, *in a large majority of cases,* those who reason cogently do better, often a great deal better, than those who reason fallaciously.

"Having concluded, Your Highness, an exhaustive study of this nation's political, social and economic history, and after examining, Sire, the unfortunate events leading to the present deplorable state of the realm, the consensus of the council is that Your Majesty's only course, for the public good, must be to take the next step."

Question-begging advice, following oracular rule number 1: Make pronouncements as empty as possible to minimize the chance of being wrong.

It would be a very good thing if every trick could receive some short and obviously appropriate name, so that when a man used this or that particular trick, he could at once be reproved for it.

—Schopenhauer

Arguments, like men, often are pretenders.

—Plato

Half of being smart is knowing what you're dumb at.

—David Gerrold

Chapter

3

FALLACIOUS REASONING—1

We said in Chapter 1 that we reason fallaciously when we fail to satisfy all three of the requirements of cogent reasoning. Accepting premises that we should doubt makes us guilty of the fallacy *questionable premise;* neglecting relevant evidence guilty of the fallacy *suppressed evidence;* and drawing conclusions not sufficiently supported by evidence guilty of the fallacy *invalid inference.*

Of course, we must remember that the arguments encountered in daily life tend to be vague, or ambiguous, and premises, and even conclusions, sometimes are omitted as understood. As a result, everyday arguments often can be construed in different ways. Consider the following key line in a TV beer commercial:

More people in America drink Budweiser than any other beer.

Taken literally, this isn't an argument, but it clearly implies that the listener also should drink Bud. So its import might be put this way:

    1. More people in America drink Budweiser than any other beer. (premise)
∴ 2. You, too, should drink Budweiser. (implied conclusion)

Construed in this way, the ad does contain an argument, but the argument is defective because it contains an invalid inference. That a beer is the most popular does not imply you should drink it. The most popular beer may not be the best beer, and, anyway, perhaps you should drink a cheaper beer and save money or not drink any beer at all. We could, however, just as well restate the argument this way:

1. More people in America drink Budweiser than any other beer. (premise)
2. The most popular beer is the best beer. (implied premise)
3. You should drink the best beer. (implied premise)
∴4. You should drink Budweiser. (implied conclusion)

Now the argument is valid but contains at least two questionable premises—that the most popular beer is the best beer and that you should drink the best beer.

Like the Budweiser example, most fallacious arguments can be stated in more ways than one. So there often isn't a single "right" label to apply to fallacious reasoning. This doesn't mean that there aren't plenty of wrong labels to apply, and it surely doesn't mean that merely applying a plausible label is sufficient. The point is to understand *why* an argument is fallacious and why a particular label can be shown to be right. In the case of the Budweiser ad, for instance, it's important to see that being the most popular beer is not by itself sufficient reason for most people to conclude that they should go out and buy it. Labeling just helps us to see that an argument is fallacious (*if it is!*) and helps us to understand why it is fallacious.

Notice, by the way, that in calling the argument itself fallacious, rather than reasoners who may have been taken in by it, we have employed the shortcut way of talking mentioned in Chapter 1. To be precise, we should have said, for example, that anyone who was persuaded by it would be guilty of fallacious reasoning.

Although all fallacious reasoning falls into one or more of the three broad categories just mentioned, over the years a number of other, narrower fallacy species have been identified that crosscut the three basic types.[1] These labels have come into common use because experience has shown them to be helpful in spotting fallacious reasoning.

Let's now discuss some of the more important of these common fallacy categories and also add some comments concerning the broad fallacy category *questionable premise*.

1. APPEAL TO AUTHORITY

One of the most serious errors in reasoning is to accept the word of someone, in particular an alleged authority, when we should be suspicious. We all have to appeal to experts for information or advice—only fools don't do so with some regularity. In this technological age we all are nonexperts in most fields. Accepting the word of an authority, alleged or genuine, when we shouldn't makes us guilty of the fallacy called **appeal to authority.**

But which appeals are proper and which fallacious? Clearly, it isn't a good idea to believe that an authority is reliable without having good reason for doing so. Some alleged

---

[1] That is, some instances of a narrower fallacy species may fall into one of the three broad genuses and some into another. Several hundred fallacy categories have been discussed in the literature, but no single source discusses all of them. Only those that occur frequently are discussed in this text, which means that our list is not exhaustive by any means. But the division into the three broad master categories *questionable premise, suppressed evidence,* and *invalid inference* is exhaustive.

authorities don't have the expertise they claim; others can't be relied on to tell it to us straight rather than feed us something more self-serving. Anyway, in some cases we need to do some of our own thinking and research.

So when seeking expert advice, three basic questions need to be addressed if we want to avoid committing the fallacy of appeal to authority:

1. Is the source likely to have the information or good judgment we need?
2. If so, can we trust the authority to tell it to us straight?
3. Do we have the time, desire, and ability to reason the matter out for ourselves (or to understand the expert's reasoning, so that we don't have to rely merely on the authority's word)?

We usually know right away whether we have the needed time and inclination, but the other questions often are rather difficult to answer. However, a few rules of thumb should prove helpful.

Some Authorities Are More Trustworthy than Others

Individuals who are regarded as authorities or experts are not created equal. Some are smart, others stupid; some are well trained in their field, some not; some are more or less honest (a completely honest person being a rarity in any case), others pretty much untrustworthy.

Characters who are less than completely ethical are found in every profession, but some fields attract this type more than others. The fields of law, financial advising, and politics, for instance, notoriously attract sharp operators, but even the ministry is not without its Elmer Gantrys, and doctors who prescribe unneeded surgery are not unknown in the history of medicine.

Anyway, the personal interests of experts are bound now and then to conflict with their duties to clients. Professionals are human, after all, just like the rest of us. Politicians elected to the U.S. Congress are bound to savor the perks, fame, power, and excitement that goes along with their jobs (who wouldn't?), making it rather difficult for them to refuse the fat cat "campaign contributions" (bribes?) needed to gain reelection, and thus more difficult still for them to tell voters the straight truth on important issues. (Remember, though, that politics is the art of compromise and, in particular, that candidates do need to get elected to do good work, so they often need at least to shade the truth for that purpose. See the section in Chapter 10 on political rhetoric for more on this point.)

So when considering expert reasoning or pronouncements, we always need to make a judgment about believability. Does the authority have an axe to grind, a personal interest that might be furthered? Lawyers who speak out against no-fault auto insurance, as they usually do, have to be looked at with a jaundiced eye precisely because the point of no-fault insurance is to reduce legal costs. When members of Congress vote against gun laws, in spite of strong public sentiment favoring gun control in the wake of the tragedies at Virginia Tech and elsewhere, we aren't being overly skeptical if we wonder whether their judgment has been warped by campaign contributions from interested parties or by narrow constituent interests.

The advice of military experts can be equally suspect if their judgment is skewed by conflicts of interest. During the Iraq War, television newscasts were swamped by interviews with high-ranking retired military officers who assured us for years that the war was justified, the insurgents were under control, the suicide bombings weren't so bad, the surge was working, and so on. It turned out that many of these military experts were recruited by the Pentagon to help sell the war in exchange for access to power and the perks that went along with it—including lucrative business affiliations. So much for expert opinion. (See more on this in Chapter 11.)

On the other hand, we should be inclined, other things being equal, to accept the word of dentists who urge their patients to brush and floss regularly and of doctors who exhort us to quit smoking cigarettes, precisely because dentists make money when patients get cavities, and doctors profit when people get cancer, have heart attacks, or come down with emphysema. (Sad but true.) Advice to brush regularly or to quit smoking thus is more likely to be motivated by a professional intent to serve the interests of clients rather than by a desire to further selfish interests.

Authorities in One Field Aren't Necessarily Experts in Another

Famous athletes and movie stars who endorse all sorts of products in television commercials are good examples of professionals speaking outside their fields of expertise. There's no reason to suppose that someone who knows how to act, or to hit home runs, knows any more about washing machines, or shaving cream, than anyone else. The fact that Brad Pitt was paid to endorse Pringles or Tiger Woods to tout Nike products proves nothing about the quality of these products, nor is there any reason to suppose that Panasonic takes better pictures of Shakira than Leicas or Nikons. Yet most of us, irrationally, are suckers when it comes to celebrity TV commercials, unless, maybe, the celebrity is an obvious mismatch with the product. Who would believe that Tiger Woods was dying to drive a Buick, the car he pitched in General Motors' ads for eight years? Since he is half the age of the average Buick owner, GM finally figured out the disconnect and pulled him off the ads. Nonetheless, probably plenty of 60-year-olds bought into the very young, very cool image of the golf star. Age does not preclude gullibility!

Learn How Best to Appeal to Authorities

It generally is easy to know which sorts of experts to appeal to. Sick people need to consult doctors; someone sued for divorce, a lawyer. It's a lot more difficult to find experts in a particular profession who know their stuff and can be relied on. But even after finding them, we need to become adept at picking their brains. Experts often throw up roadblocks to understanding, especially by overwhelming us with professional lingo. They frequently find it tedious to explain complicated matters to laypeople, and, anyway, they may not want to spend the time and effort necessary to do so.

It also is true that laypeople often are unable to follow the complicated reasonings of trained professionals, medical specialists being a case in point. But it usually is possible to get at least a rough idea of what authorities are up to if we are persistent and if we insist that they translate their professional lingo into ordinary discourse. It's hard not to be intimidated by professional jargon or by an authoritarian aura, but it is well worth the effort to resist that sort of intimidation.

Understand What Authorities Can Be Expected to Know

All experts definitely are not created equal. It isn't just that some alleged authorities, as we mentioned before, don't know what they claim to know, or that some aren't completely on the up-and-up. It's also that a good deal more is known about some topics than about others and that some information is much more expensive to obtain than others. True experts in some fields thus are more reliable than those in others.

We all are forced by the nature of modern life to seek advice and expert performance from doctors, lawyers, auto mechanics, and other kinds of trained (and often licensed) professionals. But we can't expect the same sorts of definitive answers to our questions or solutions to our problems when consulting these authorities as we can, say, when consulting physicists or chemists. Medicine, for example, while based on biological theory, still is an art: Doctors cannot always be sure of their diagnoses or of how to treat an ailment; the best of them are bound to be mistaken in their judgments now and then. Lawyers cannot be sure how jurors or judges will respond to evidence. Ministers do not have direct lines to a higher authority.

Become Your Own Expert on Important Controversial Topics

When authorities disagree on a topic of importance, the rest of us need to become our own experts, turning to authorities for evidence, reasons, and arguments, but not conclusions. This is especially true with respect to social and political matters, because experts themselves disagree so much on these issues and because we have to watch out for the intrusion of self-interest into their stated judgments and opinions. Politicians, for example, may be beholden to special interests (as we noted before) or simply be going along with a misguided tide of public opinion. Conservative commentators generally see things differently than do those who are liberal.[2]

But politics is not by any means the only topic where the reasons and reasonings of experts should count for much more than their conclusions. Judges and juries, for example, too often uncritically accept the opinions of psychologists concerning the sanity of those charged with crimes, rather than delving into the reasons behind those opinions. After all, different opinions often can be obtained just by consulting other psychologists.[3] This holds true even in fields like medicine, where we tend to trust the opinions of experts. For instance, a woman who is advised to have a hysterectomy might be wise to seek a second opinion from another physician. (Women with relevant background information know that many unnecessary hysterectomies are performed for conditions that can be treated by less invasive means.)

One way to gauge the judgment of alleged experts is to check their past records. Professional sports has a saying that when in doubt, you should go with a winner. Similarly,

---

[2]Although labels such as "conservative," "libertarian," "liberal," "right wing," and "left wing" tend to be vague and ambiguous, they still have some content: Those labeled by these terms do tend to differ in their viewpoints, and critical reasoners need to take these differences into account.
[3]This observation conforms to B. Duggan's Law of Expert Testimony: "For every Ph.D. there is an equal and opposite Ph.D."

when expert advice is needed, it makes sense to go with a winner—someone whose track record is good. Those who have been right in the past are more likely than others to be right in the future, other things being equal. Remember, however, that other things are not always equal. Auto mechanics may get out of touch with the latest technology, lawyers who have made their pile may become lazy, and textbook writers (with at least two obvious exceptions!) may eventually go over the hill.

Note, by the way, that most fallacious appeals to authority fall under the broader category *questionable premise,* because underlying the acceptance of the word of an authority is the implicit premise that it is wise to do so. In other words, the fallacy appeal to authority is committed by acceptance of expert advice or information when it isn't wise to do so, perhaps because the authority isn't likely to have the information we desire or may have a serious conflict of interest.

Before going on to a discussion of other fallacies, perhaps notice should be taken of the flip side of the fallacy of appeal to authority—namely, failure to take the word of authorities when we should. After all, salespeople frequently do give us the relevant facts straight; TV news programs do provide us with a good deal of useful information, even if they don't provide us with "the whole truth, nothing but the truth"; politicians sometimes do put aside self-interest and speak out against powerful interests. Being careful when evaluating information sources does not mean becoming completely cynical.

2. INCONSISTENCY

We commit the fallacy of **inconsistency** when we are persuaded to accept the conclusion of an argument that contains self-contradictory statements or statements that contradict each other.[4] Obviously, if two statements are contradictory, then one of them must be false.

Consider, for example, the ways in which inconsistencies intrude into campaign rhetoric. (Campaign rhetoric: The pronouncements of most politicians most of the time.) Candidates for public office do not explicitly say *A* and then immediately assert not-*A*. Instead, the contradictory nature of their pronouncements is concealed in one way or another. For instance, in the same speech, a candidate may assure voters that various government services or payments will significantly be increased (to curry the favor of voters who will profit from them), promise large tax reductions (to gain the support of those burdened by high taxes), and favor a huge reduction in the national debt (to appeal to voter beliefs about the virtues of governmental thrift).[5]

That is how the vast majority of candidates for high office, including President Clinton in 1992 and 1996, President Bush in 2000 and 2004, and both major presidential candidates in 2008, have played the game. But government services and benefits cost money, and a majority of government expenses are fixed (most notably interest payments on previously contracted debts), so that a package of increased services and benefits, coupled

---

[4]Recall the discussion in Chapter 2 about tautologies, contradictions, and contingent statements.
[5]Their argument thus can be put this way: If elected, I won't destroy the government services and payments you want, I will significantly reduce taxes, and I will reduce the national debt. Therefore, you should vote for me.

Cartoon by Tom Meyer.

with significant tax and public debt reductions, can be regarded as inconsistent in the absence of a plausible explanation as to how this trick is going to be performed. (In recent times, extremely high military expenditures and huge financial bailouts have made this trick even more difficult than it otherwise would be.) Adding up the figures is one way of determining whether candidates are being consistent, and hence believable, when they promise us the moon.

One reason that politicians get away with inconsistent claims or arguments so often is that voters, being human, tend to see political issues from the point of view of their own self-interest, just as they see personal problems and conflicts with friends and family. Self-interest tends to make us more blind than usual both to fair play and to cogent reasoning. Lots of cigarette smokers, for example, argue against a ban on the sale of cigarettes, on the grounds that we all have a right to ingest harmful substances if we are so inclined, but most of them also, inconsistently, argue against the legalization of heroin because it is harmful to health. Extremist African Americans who get on their high horses about prejudice against blacks have been known at the same time to inconsistently preach hatred of whites.

But when evaluating the various kinds of rhetoric encountered in everyday life, it is important that we don't misjudge deliberately equivocal, ironic, or humorous rhetoric. It won't do, for example, to brand the literally contradictory bumper sticker that says "Good enough isn't good enough" as contradictory, since it isn't intended to be taken literally. It says, in a humorous way, that we should do better than merely minimally well.

Mike Peters, 1986. Reprinted by permission of United Feature Syndicate, Inc.

Note that there are ways to be guilty of the fallacy of inconsistency in addition to the obvious one of being inconsistent within a single argument or statement. The example above about politicians who, in the same speech, promise lots of government services, lower taxes, and a reduction in the national debt is a case in point. So are the cigarette smokers, also just mentioned, who are against making cigarettes illegal while at the same time are against legalizing the use of heroin.

Another way to be inconsistent is to *argue one way at a given time and another way at some other time, or when talking to one person and then to another.* Of course, there is nothing wrong with changing one's mind—of believing *A* at one time and not-*A* at another. That, after all, is the point of learning from experience. It is when we continue to hang on both to *A* and to not-*A*, trotting out one for use when reasoning about one thing and the other when reasoning about something else, that we are guilty of being inconsistent.

In politics, being inconsistent over time or from audience to audience is called "blowing with the wind." What is popular with constituents in one place or at one time may not be in another. Circumstances thus push politicians into being inconsistent in order to

---

We have just gone to some lengths to describe inconsistency as a serious mistake. Yet others have railed against being consistent; witness Ralph Waldo Emerson's famous remark, "A foolish consistency is the hobgoblin of little minds, adored by little statesmen, philosophers and divines."

But there need be no inconsistency in accepting both sides of this coin, provided we notice that consistency is an ambiguous concept. One sense requires us to be consistent in what we believe at any given time. This is roughly the sense meant in this chapter. The other requires us to be consistent now and forever, to stick to our guns no matter what contrary evidence we encounter. This, one must suppose, is the kind of consistency Emerson intended to disparage.

keep up with the latest trends in public opinion or to placate particular audiences. Candidates for office try as much as they can to tell people what they want to hear, and different people want to hear different things. So candidates sometimes switch sides on certain issues to win voter support. John McCain voted twice against President Bush's tax cuts, saying "I cannot in good conscience support a tax cut in which so many of the benefits go to the most fortunate among us . . ."[6] But during the campaign he switched sides and repeatedly said he wanted to make those tax cuts permanent rather than let them expire. He shifted ground on abortion laws as well. Although he has long been against abortion, he has said, "I would not support repeal of *Roe v. Wade,* which would then force x number of women in America [to have] illegal abortions." But he changed his position during the campaign. "I do not support *Roe v. Wade*—it should be overturned," he said during the primaries in South Carolina (a state with a large conservative base).

To some extent, we all engage in this sort of inconsistency—politicians are just better at it than most of the rest of us. Occasionally, we do so deliberately, with conscious intent. But often we are trying to fool not just or even the other guy but rather ourselves. Virtually all of us, for instance, are against cheating others, yet at one time or another we can't resist the temptation to do so to our advantage while providing reasons (excuses) to justify what we have done; for example, the excuse that most other people do it, so it's not wrong for us to do so. (This point is discussed at greater length in Chapter 6, where impediments to cogent reasoning are the subject.)

It also needs to be noticed that large organizations have an interesting way to be inconsistent that tends to be rather hard to notice: They have one representative speak out of one side of the mouth while another speaks from the other side. Let's call this sort of chicanery *organizational inconsistency,* thinking of a large organization as a kind of artificial person. (In regarding this as a fallacy, we are, of course, stretching that concept a bit, but for a good purpose, namely, to call attention to this threat to consistent reasoning.)

Another kind of organizational inconsistency occurs when it seems expedient to ignore company policy. For instance, a few days before the Olympiad's opening ceremonies in the 1998 Nagano games, Nike swooshes were seen everywhere on CBS—not just on athletes in Nike ads, but on the hats, jackets, gloves, and snow boots of CBS network correspondents in their pregame coverage. Yet the CBS ethical handbook clearly prohibits advertiser identification during a broadcast outside of the time devoted to billboards or commercial messages. As an example, ". . . a request for permission to include an advertising logo on the desk of a broadcaster must continue to be, rejected" (*CBS News Standards,* p. 2). When substantial sums of money are at stake, it is clearly more expedient for CBS's practice to be inconsistent with its stated policy. (For more on this and related matters, see *The Nation,* November 30, 1998.)

The CBS chicanery just mentioned also illustrates another way to be inconsistent, namely, by *saying one thing while doing another.* (Calling this a fallacy again stretches that concept to serve everyday purposes. Strictly speaking, saying one thing and doing another does not make one guilty of a fallacy, because it does not involve an inconsistency

---

[6]Quotes from "On His Signature Issues, McCain Has Shown Some Inconsistencies in the Senate," by Elisabeth Bumiller, *New York Times,* March 3, 2008.

Moon Mullins. Reprinted by permission of Tribune Media Services.

between one claim, idea, or argument and another. We include this discussion here to call attention to those who engage in this sort of behavior.

Al Gore was charged with this type of inconsistency when the media revealed that his private consumption of energy was at odds with his praiseworthy public campaign to reduce global warming. The day after he received an Oscar for the best documentary feature, *An Inconvenient Truth*, in which he urged Americans to curb their energy consumption, the Tennessee Center for Policy Research had this to say about Gore's personal energy use: "Gore's mansion . . . consumes more electricity every month than the average household uses in an entire year, according to the Nashville Electric Service . . . more than 20 times the national average. . . . In total Gore paid nearly $30,000 in combined electricity and natural gas bills for his Nashville estate in 2006." Considering how admirable his efforts have been to curb global warming, he might be forgiven a little personal inconsistency. Nonetheless, it would have looked better if he had walked the walk as well as talked the talk.

Of course, mention of the inconsistencies of these politicians should not blind us to the fact that they are not the only ones who are guilty of being inconsistent. The rest of us aren't exactly paragons of virtue where consistency is concerned. Feminists who argue against different "roles" for males and females, yet who don't reciprocate when given expensive engagement rings, or who always leave the driving to their husbands, along with the spanking of errant children, surely are inconsistent.[7]

Inconsistency often is connected in people's minds with hypocrisy—with pretending to believe what one in fact does not, or to be what one is not. The vast majority of candidates for office in the United States during the past 40 years or so have run on platforms opposing legalization of drugs even though lots of them smoked dope or sniffed cocaine (including Al Gore and George W. Bush?). (Forget about the fact that virtually all of them also drank alcohol or smoked cigarettes.) Bill Clinton did own up to smoking marijuana but notoriously claimed that he did not inhale (ho, ho, ho). Should we say that those who were inconsistent in this way were guilty of the sin of *hypocrisy*? (At least Barack Obama admitted past drug use in his teens, but attitudes have changed over the years, and Americans seem more willing to accept youthful lapses than they did before.)

---

[7]See the article by Cynthia Tucker, *Atlanta Constitution* editorial page editor, that ran in many newspapers on March 30, 1996.

Readers may note, when they have completed reading the three fallacy chapters in this text, that a good deal more time is spent on the first two fallacies in this chapter than on any of the others. The reason is that these two are very likely the most important. The importance of the fallacy of appeal to authority is obvious: We all are nonexperts about most of the things that matter in everyday life and therefore regularly have to appeal to authorities for information and advice. The importance of the fallacy of inconsistency also should be obvious: It lies in the crucial importance of consistency to cogent reasoning. *At least one of a set of inconsistent statements must be false!*

That is why trying to be consistent is very likely the best way to improve the quality of one's stock of background beliefs (a point to be discussed again later). Having reasoned to a particular conclusion, consistency requires that we ask ourselves whether we would be willing to carry through that line of reasoning when it applies to other cases. If not, then we must give up that line of reasoning or admit to the intellectual crime of being *inconsistent.*

3. STRAW MAN

While the broad fallacy category *suppressed evidence* seldom is mentioned in traditional logic texts, several species of this genus are given great play. One of these is the fallacy **straw man,** which is committed when we misrepresent an opponent's position, or a competitor's product, or go after a weaker opponent or competitor while ignoring a stronger one.[8]

Straw man has always been the stock-in-trade of advertisers and political smear campaigns. A group called Common Sense Issues made a million automated phone calls to voters in the 2008 South Carolina primaries claiming that John McCain "has voted to use unborn babies in medical research." This was a gross distortion of his position to support research on stem cells gathered from embryos.

Political ads resort to straw man regularly. For example, the McCain campaign ran a 30-second TV spot in battleground states accusing Barack Obama of promoting "comprehensive sex education" for kindergarten children, then asking the provocative question, "Learning about sex before learning to read?" This was a deliberate distortion of a bill Obama voted for in the Illinois state legislature that called for "age and developmentally appropriate" sex education in schools. On a kindergarten level, the objective was simply to teach children how to defend themselves against sexual predators, not to provide comprehensive sex education. Nonetheless, McCain gave this his official consent in the ending line: "I'm John McCain, and I approve this message."

4. FALSE DILEMMA AND THE EITHER-OR FALLACY

In traditional logic, a *dilemma* is an argument that presents two alternatives, both claimed to be bad for someone, or some position. (Dilemmas are discussed further in the appendix.)

---

[8]Note, however, that some cases of this fallacy do not fall into the category of *suppressed evidence*. Should we, by the way, replace the name "straw man" by, say, "straw person" or perhaps "false characterization"?

The general form of a dilemma can be put this way:

> Either P or Q.
> If P then R.
> If Q then S.
> Therefore, either R or S.

Sometimes the undesired outcomes R and S are identical, sometimes quite different. Here is an example in which they are not quite the same: "Either our fellow citizens are good or they're bad. If they're good, laws to deter crime aren't needed. But if they're bad, laws to deter crime won't succeed. So laws to deter crime either are not needed or won't succeed."

A **false dilemma** is a dilemma that can be shown to be false. One way to do this is to demonstrate that the premise having the form "Either P or Q" is false by showing that there is at least one other viable possibility. This is called "going between the horns" of the dilemma. In the case of the dilemma just mentioned, a viable alternative is that our fellow citizens may be both good (in some ways) and bad (in others).

Another way to defeat a dilemma is to challenge one or both of its other two premises. This is called "grasping the horns" of the dilemma. We might challenge the crime law dilemma, for example, by arguing that even if some citizens are bad, they still can be deterred by laws specifying harsh penalties.

False dilemmas usually are a species of the genus *questionable premise* because any set of statements that sets up a false dilemma needs to be questioned. (Note, by the way, that we can have false trilemmas, false quadrilemmas, and so on.)

The **either-or fallacy** (sometimes called the *black-or-white fallacy*) is very similar to that of *false dilemma*. We're guilty of this fallacy when we mistakenly reason from two alternatives, one claimed to be bad (that is, to be avoided) so that we ought to choose the other alternative. The general form of the fallacy is this:

> Either P or Q.
> Not P.
> Therefore, Q.

where there is at least a third viable alternative, or it is questionable that P is bad. For example, "You have to vote either for the Republican or for the Democratic candidate. But you shouldn't vote for the Republican. So you should vote for the Democrat." A third alternative in this case would be to vote, say, for the Green Party candidate (this is like going between the horns of a dilemma), and some people would challenge the claim that you shouldn't vote for the Republican candidate (this would be like grasping a dilemma by its horns).

One notable example of the either-or fallacy was the second President Bush's battle cry after September 11, "You are either with us or against us in the fight against terror." There were, of course, plenty of options in between. This simplification of a complex situation was a rhetorical device rather than an appeal to reason. A more subtle example surfaced much later when he explained the rationale for the troop "surge" into Iraq to stem the increasing violence and incipient civil war. In his address to the nation (January 2007), Bush said, "Their [Congress's] solution is to scale back America's efforts in Baghdad or announce the phased withdrawal of our combat troops." His solution was to send 21,500 additional troops to secure Baghdad and Anbar. Without mentioning other possibilities, he reduced the solution to two alternatives: Either withdraw from Iraq or increase the troops. In fact, there were a number of other policy choices, some outlined by the bipartisan Iraq Study Group, others suggested by members of Congress.

5. BEGGING THE QUESTION

When arguing, either with ourselves or with others, we can't provide reasons for every assertion and then reasons for the reasons, and so on. Some of what we assert must go unjustified, at least for the moment. But when we assume as a premise some form of the very point that is at issue—the very conclusion we intend to prove—we are guilty of the fallacy of **begging the question.**[9] In this sense *to beg* means "to avoid." When the premise simply states another version of the conclusion, the question of proof is avoided, or *begged*. (The fallacy of begging the question usually falls into the broad category *questionable premise* because a statement that is questionable as a conclusion is equally questionable as a premise.)

In real life, of course, this fallacy rarely, if ever, has the form

> *A.*
> Therefore, *A.*

Few would be taken in by anything so obvious. Instead, a premise may state a conclusion in different but equivalent words, so that the conclusion is not so obviously begged. This is the way in which the question is begged in one of the classic textbook cases (from the nineteenth century—human gullibility tends to remain constant): "To allow every man unbounded freedom of speech must always be . . . advantageous to the state; for it is highly conducive to the interests of the community that each individual should enjoy a liberty, perfectly unlimited, of expressing his sentiments."[10]

Although the traditional fallacy of begging the question deals primarily with questions that are at issue, say, as in a debate, over time it has come to have a broader range so as to cover other sorts of questions. Thus, to take a textbook example, we can be said to be guilty of this fallacy when, having asked why chloroform renders people unconscious, we accept the answer that it does so because it is a soporific (a *soporific* being defined as something that induces sleep).

Doctors and other sorts of professionals are frequent perpetrators of this version of begging the question, but they aren't by any means the only ones who set us up for it. Indeed, many times questions are begged quite innocently. Here is an example taken

---

[9]In a sense, all deductively valid arguments beg the question, because what is said by their conclusions already is said in their premises. In the typical case, part of an argument's conclusion is said in one premise, part in another. That is the point of valid deduction; anyone who accepts the premises of a deductively valid argument and yet rejects its conclusion is guilty of being inconsistent. The difference in the case of the fallacy of begging the question is that the premises state the claim of the conclusion in a way that those who reject the conclusion also will reject the premises for being just as questionable as the conclusion.

[10]Cited by Richard Whately in his excellent book *Elements of Logic* (London, 1826). Whately's fallacy classification is more like the one used in this text than are those of any other text in use today.

from an article on exclusive men's clubs in San Francisco. In explaining why these clubs have such long waiting lists, Paul B. "Red" Fay, Jr. (on the roster of three of the clubs) said, "The reason there's such a big demand is because everyone wants to get in them."[11] In other words, there is a big demand because there is a big demand. Fay inadvertently (we hope) gave another version of the conclusion in the premise and thus avoided the question of proof.

Note that the fallacy begging the question also has been broadened over time so as to cover cases in which a premise is different from the conclusion of an argument but is controversial or questionable for the same reasons that typically might lead someone to question the conclusion.

Evading the Issue

One effective way to beg the question at issue is simply to avoid it entirely. Doing this makes one guilty of the fallacy **evading the issue.** This approach succeeds when those taken in fail to notice that the issue has been evaded. Perhaps the best way to hoodwink an opponent or dodge a barbed question is to make it appear that the issue or question is indeed being addressed. Politicians frequently evade an issue concerning a complicated problem (the homeless, the national debt, whatever) by speaking instead about the pressing need to solve it. Savvy citizens are not taken in by this sort of chicanery.

For example, at a White House news conference on July 17, 2003, a reporter asked the second President Bush if he took personal responsibility for including in his State of the Union address earlier that year the disputed claim that Saddam Hussein had tried to buy uranium oxide in Niger, Africa. Bush replied, "I take responsibility for putting our troops in action. And I made that decision because Saddam Hussein was a threat to our security and a threat to the security of other nations. . . . I take responsibility for making the decision, the tough decision to put together a coalition to remove Saddam Hussein." But he didn't take responsibility for including the disputed claim in his address. In fact, he evaded the issue entirely.

Presidential hopeful Mike Huckabee managed a clever evasion in the 2007 YouTube/CNN debate for Republican candidates. When Huckabee, a minister and politician, was asked whether Jesus would support the death penalty, he quipped, "Jesus was too smart to run for public office." And thus he neatly ducked a question suggesting that his Christian scruples were inconsistent with his pro-death penalty stance as governor of Arkansas.

Politicians are masters at evading the issue. When they are asked hard questions in interviews, they skirt the subject with responses like "That's a complex issue . . ." and then shift into the message they want to give. Or they claim the question isn't relevant, which clears the way for topics they do think are relevant. Or they say things like "That's a good question, but before going into that I want to discuss . . ." and then go on to spin their own point of view. Evading the issue is so important to politicians that many of them hire media trainers to help them perfect the art.[12]

---

[11]Quoted in "The Chosen Few," by Adair Lara, *San Francisco Chronicle,* July 18, 2004.
[12]For more on this see a fascinating article on media training, "Answer the &%$#* Question" in *Columbia Review of Journalism,* January/February, 2004.

6. QUESTIONABLE PREMISE—QUESTIONABLE STATEMENT

As we noted earlier, most examples of the fallacies discussed so far fall into the broader category of *questionable premise.* But not all species of questionable premise have received specific names in the literature. So when a premise that is not believable is spotted in an argument and none of these more specific labels apply, we have to fall back on the general term **questionable premise.** That is what we did earlier when we pointed out that a statement in a Budweiser commercial constituted a questionable premise.

Knowing for a fact that a statement is false obviously is a very good reason for questioning it—indeed, for dismissing it. Thus, when a colleague was alleged to be incompetent on grounds that she was an alcoholic, one of the authors of this text rejected the charge on the basis of personal knowledge that the allegation was false. But often we ought to question a statement just because we have no good reason to think it true, even though we also don't have any reason to doubt it. For instance, at one of the debates in the 2007 run-up to the presidential primaries, Rudy Giuliani said, "It's unthinkable that you would leave Saddam Hussein in charge of Iraq and be able to fight the war on terror." Was it? You have to ask the question why it was unthinkable to fight the war on terror if Hussein were still in power. When evidence is lacking, reason requires holding judgment in abeyance.

Remember, though, that hearing something from a trustworthy expert often counts as a reason for believing it to be true. For example, the fact that the overwhelming majority of scientists believe the burning of fossil fuels, such as oil and coal, is polluting the air and causing a rise in worldwide temperatures ought to constitute good reason for believing that there very likely is a greenhouse effect resulting from the use of these fuels.

Finally, it is worth remembering here that in everyday life statements generally do not come labeled as premises or conclusions and also that not all persuasive discourse is put into argumentative form. So there is a good deal of merit in expanding the fallacy of *questionable premise* so that it becomes, say, *questionable statement.*

7. SUPPRESSED (OVERLOOKED) EVIDENCE

The general fallacy category **suppressed evidence,** introduced earlier along with questionable premise and invalid inference, has not received much attention in the fallacy literature, perhaps because theorists tend to see the suppression of evidence as an error in reasoning but not as a fallacy (as they define that concept). Whether thought of as a fallacy or not, however, it is important that we learn how to bring relevant evidence to bear on an argument and learn how to avoid being taken in by others when they suppress evidence.

Of course, people who suppress evidence often do so inadvertently, one reason that a more all-encompassing label for the fallacy might be *overlooked evidence,* or perhaps *slighted evidence.* It's easy, when strongly committed to a particular side of an issue, to pass over arguments and reasons on the other side. In recent years, advocates on both sides of issues such as capital punishment, abortion, the legalization of marijuana, the depiction of violence on TV, and the legalization of prostitution frequently have been guilty of slighting evidence damning to their side of the issue. Those opposed to "three strikes and you're out" legislation, for instance, tend to neglect the ways in which this kind of law might protect society from repeat offenders; those in favor don't like to talk about the high costs associated with keeping people in jail long past the age at which the vast majority of criminals have ceased to commit violent crimes, or about the fact that a great many of those sentenced under these laws have not committed violent or even serious crimes.

We all, of course, sometimes are motivated by more crass considerations than mere overzealousness. Self-interest is a powerful motivator of deliberately shady reasoning. Take, for instance, the way drug companies manipulated data on drug trials that tested the effectiveness of antidepressants like Prozac and Paxil. The published trials showed that these drugs provided significant relief for 60 percent of people on the drugs, compared to only 40 percent for those on placebos. This evidence was convincing enough to persuade doctors and patients that the drugs were effective. But in January 2008, the *Journal of the American Medical Association* ran a report of a new analysis reviewing data from both the published and unpublished trials of the antidepressants. This analysis revealed that 94 percent of the positive trials were published but only 14 percent of the unconvincing ones were. In effect, the drug companies were suppressing the negative data to win over the government and get FDA approval. Once the unpublished trials were taken into account, the antidepressants had only a slim edge over the placebos. No wonder physicians were puzzled that the drugs didn't seem to work as well on their patients as they did in the published trials.

The point of becoming familiar with the fallacy of suppressed evidence is to sharpen one's ability to spot cases in which relevant evidence is being passed over, whether by others or by ourselves. We need, in particular, to learn how to carry through reasoning so as to see whether all likely relevant information has been considered.

Take, for instance, the tax rebates issued in 2008 as part of a stimulus package to invigorate the sinking economy. The theory was that the government would circulate money for consumers to spend in order to stimulate the economy and forestall a recession. The rational was loosely (and erroneously) based on economist John Maynard Keynes theory that spending is the driving force of the economy, no matter who does it—governments, businesses, or consumers. Circulating money through tax rebates, however, was not the answer. Twice in the past 40 years (1975 and 2001) Congress

---

Shall I tell you what it is to know? It is to say you know when you know, and to say that you do not know when you do not know; that is knowledge.

—Attributed to Confucius (which means that we do not know for sure that he said it)

We don't want to be too hasty, or too picky, in leveling a charge of begging the question. Although what Confucius is quoted as saying is literally question begging, it is very likely that what he meant to say (if he actually said it) is that a large part of wisdom is to know what you do and what you don't have good reason to believe and, by implication, not to believe what you do not have good reason to believe. Excellent advice, indeed.

Tokenism: Note that Clint equates his notion of half way with fairness.

agreed to one-time rebates, but they did little to stimulate spending. People either saved the money or used it to pay bills. Yet Congress agreed to issue the same stimulous package again in 2008, ignoring evidence that rebates are not effective responses to economic slowdowns. The rebates did more to placate the public and build goodwill in an election year than to stimulate the economy.[13]

For lots of us, becoming adept at bringing to bear suppressed or overlooked relevant information is perhaps the most difficult knack required by good reasoning. Sometimes the difficulty is compounded by our limited understanding of the issue at hand. Take, for example, the Environmental Protection Agency's decision in 2002 to omit, for the first time in six years, the chapter on global warming from its annual federal budget. The *New York Times* (September 15, 2002) reported that industrial lobbyists were "praising the decision, contending that carbon dioxide, which is believed to cause global warming, is not a pollutant." In one sense the lobbyists were right—carbon dioxide is not a pollutant; it's a natural gas—but scientists would argue that it has the side effect of trapping heat and thus causing temperatures to rise. Understanding the fallacious reasoning in the lobbyists' argument requires most of us to do a bit of research.

Many people have trouble distinguishing between having no evidence or proof for a claim and having evidence or proof that the claim is false. But having no evidence, say, that vitamin C helps us fight the common cold is quite different from having evidence that it does not do so. Similarly, a lack of clinical proof that marijuana has certain medicinal benefits is much different from having clinical proof that it does not. Lack of *clinical proof,* by the way, also is quite different from having no good evidence whatsoever concerning marijuana's medicinal benefits. In fact, there is a good deal of such "anecdotal" evidence.

---

[13]For a more complete analysis, see "Feel-Good Economics," by Bruce Artlett, *Wall Street Journal,* January 19, 2008.

> In the Italian film *Il Postino* (*The Postman*), the big politician promises, again, that pipes will be built so that the people can have indoor running water, and he actually has construction begin before the election. People again vote him into office, and—surprise—construction immediately stops. Voters have again been suckered by a token gesture and only wake up to that fact when it is too late to make a difference.

8. TOKENISM

Tokenism—mistaking a token gesture for the real thing, or accepting a token gesture in lieu of something more concrete—is another common fallacy.

As might be expected, tokenism is one of the politician's best friends. In 2008, as gas prices soared and voters complained, both Hillary Clinton and John McCain endorsed a plan to suspend the federal excise tax on gasoline (18.4 cents a gallon) for the summer travel season. But this was just a token gesture, a short-term fix that would save consumers little in the long run. In the fiercely competitive election campaign, the proposal was a ploy to win over middle-class voters, hard-hit by the recession and the escalating costs of gas and food.

Another example: When, in June 2000, George W. Bush, then governor of Texas, stayed the execution of a convicted felon so as to leave time for DNA tests, his action was taken by some observers to rebut the claim that Bush denied the convicted all of their political rights by failing to use his power of granting 30-day stays of execution. But his action in this case was obviously a token gesture, since, with the one exception of his pardon of a dramatically innocent person, he had failed to act in 131 cases of people on death row, including several in which those convicted were generally held to be clearly innocent or had not been fairly tried.

Actually, his token gesture was a variation on a related ploy—namely, behaving or speaking one way when the heat is on and another when it isn't sufficiently hot to force change. For as long as possible, Bush satisfied those of his Texas constituents and his financial supporters who favored being "tough on criminals," changing when a wider constituency was being wooed during his presidential campaign, much as Texan Lyndon Johnson did on race way back in the 1960s.

SUMMARY OF CHAPTER 3

All fallacious reasoning falls into one or more of the three broad categories of *questionable premise, suppressed evidence,* and *invalid inference.* But other fallacy categories, crosscutting these broad ones, have come into common use.

1. *Appeal to authority:* Accepting the word of alleged authorities when there is not sufficient reason to believe that they have the information we seek or that they can be trusted to provide it to us (for example, when they have a vested interest), or doing so when we ought to figure the matter out for ourselves. *Example:* Taking the word of power industry executives that nuclear plants are safe.

   When appeals must be made to authorities, we should remember that some are more trustworthy than others, and in particular, we should be wary of experts who have an axe to grind. We also should pay attention to the track records of alleged authorities.

2. *Inconsistency:* Accepting the conclusion of an argument that has self-contradictory statements or statements that contradict each other. These contradictory assertions may be made (1) by one person at one time and place, (2) by one person at different times or places (without explaining the contradiction as a change of mind based on reasons), or (3) by different representatives of one institution. While not, strictly speaking, a fallacy, we need to note when there is a contradiction between what someone says and what that person does. *Example:* Al Gore's verbal support of energy conservation compared to his own excessive energy consumption to run his household.

3. *Straw man:* Misrepresenting an opponent's position or a competitor's product to make it easier to attack them or to tout one's own product as superior, or attacking a weaker opponent while ignoring a stronger one. *Example:* Ads accusing John McCain of voting to use unborn babies in medical research.

4. *False dilemma:* A dilemma that can be shown to be false either by "going between the horns" of the dilemma or by "grasping its horns." *Example:* Refuting the dilemma about the futility of laws to deter crime by pointing out that there is a third alternative—namely, that many citizens are both good and bad.

   The *either-or* (*black-or-white*) variation occurs when an argument is based on the assumption that there are just two viable alternatives, one of which is bad (so the other has to be chosen), although there is at least one other viable alternative. *Example:* Refuting the argument that you should vote for Barack Obama because the only alternative is John McCain by pointing to a third possibility, say, voting for Ralph Nader.

5. *Begging the question:* Assuming without proof the question, or a significant part of the question, that is at issue, or answering a question by rephrasing it as a statement. *Example:* In explaining why exclusive men's clubs have such long wait lists, "Red" Fay said, "The reason there is such a demand is because everyone wants to get in them." One way to beg the question is to avoid it entirely and thus evade the issue. *Example:* An elected official who skirts hard questions by shifting into a message he or she wants to give.

6. *Questionable premise—questionable statement:* Accepting a less than believable premise or other statement. *Example:* Accepting the claim that Budweiser is the best beer as a reason for deciding to switch to Bud. (Note that the five fallacies just described are variations of this broader fallacy but that not all species of questionable premise have special names.)

7. *Suppressed (overlooked) evidence:* Failing to bring relevant evidence to bear on an argument. *Example:* Advocates on both sides of the debates about the merits of "three strikes and you're out" laws who slight sensible arguments and objections of their opponents.

8. *Tokenism:* Accepting a token gesture in lieu of the real thing. *Example:* Being satisfied with campaign rhetoric when there is little likelihood of serious intent to carry through.

EXERCISE 3-1

Determine which fallacies (if any) occur in the following passages and state reasons for your answers. Note: Some items may contain more than one fallacy.

Example

Passage: Heard in a debate concerning capital punishment: "Capital punishment is morally wrong. After all, murder is just as wrong when committed by a government as it is when done by an individual person."

Evaluation: The speaker *begged the question at issue.* To say that capital punishment is murder is to say that it is a morally wrong killing (note that only wrongful killings are considered to be murder). But the issue was whether capital punishment—governmental killing—*is* murder, so to assume without argument that it is begs the question.

*1. Overheard in a laundry: "What makes me think abortion is murder? When my pediatrician refused to perform an abortion for me, she said she wouldn't be a party to murder. Babies and childbirth are her business, you know."

*2. When Hillary Clinton was asked in a Bloomberg television interview in 2006 how she thought the Bush administration should try to prevent Iran from building up its nuclear program, she said, "I would certainly take nuclear weapons off the table." A year later, in a discussion about the use of nuclear weapons in the war on terror, she criticized Barack Obama for saying that if he were president, he would rule out using nuclear weapons to get rid of terrorists in Afghanistan or Pakistan. Senator Clinton's response was, "I don't believe any president should make any blanket statements with respect to the use or non-use of nuclear weapons."

3. An item from the *New York Times* Service, March 2000: In 1988 Maureen Dowd, *New York Times* reporter, asked President Bush (the father of George W.) how he could justify claiming that he was a good candidate for blacks when he did nothing to influence the Reagan administration against watering down civil rights laws during his eight years as vice president. Bush replied, "But I helped found the Yale chapter of the United Negro College Fund."

4. Joe Morgan, announcing a Giants–Marlins baseball game and commenting on the Marlins pitcher: "He's been a little erratic, which explains why he hasn't been consistent."

5. Comment by gossip columnist Liz Smith a week after the attack on the World Trade Center, when the stock market was falling fast: "The most important thing for citizens of any age—for themselves and for their Uncle Sam and as a tribute to the thousands who likely died—should be to call a broker and buy stock in American companies this week, and next week and the next."

6. Excerpt from the second President Bush's 2004 State of the Union address: "A strong America must also value the institution of marriage. . . . Congress has already taken a stand on this issue by passing the Defense of Marriage Act signed in 1996 by President Clinton. That statute protects marriage under federal law as the union of a man and a woman, and declares that one state may not

redefine marriage for other states. Activist judges, however, have begun re-defining marriage by court order, without regard for the will of the people and their elected representatives. On an issue of such great consequence, the people's voice must be heard. If judges insist on forcing their arbitrary will upon the people, the only alternative left to the people would be the constitutional process. Our nation must defend the sanctity of marriage."

7. Eric Jubler, in an article in which he argued that America should "open up" its wilderness areas: "The purist [conservationist] is, generally speaking, against everything . . . the purist believes that those who do not agree with him desire to 'rape the land.'"

8. A *New York Times* article on Rudy Giuliani (March 23, 2007) noted that he championed national standards for enforcing gun laws as mayor of New York City, lobbied Congress to outlaw most assault weapons, and complained that gun laws in the South were lax. "He praised President Clinton on gun control, endorsed the Brady Bill . . . and advocated federal laws for semiautomatic weapons." As presidential candidate in 2007, he said, "There can be reasonable restrictions, and they largely should be done by state and by, and then you know, done by legislatures."

9. Calvin Coolidge is alleged to have been the first to say this: "We must keep people working—with jobs—because when many people are out of work, unemployment results."

10. In an interview with Sarah, Duchess of York, Larry King asked whether she was friends with Prince Charles. She replied, "Well, Larry, the important thing is that I have great respect for the royal family."

11. Argument in a student essay: "Prostitution should not be legalized because it encourages the breakdown of the family. Nevada, where prostitution is legal in ten counties, has the highest divorce rate in the nation, almost twice as high as the national average."

12. Notice from the Hyatt Regency Hotel in New Orleans: "We are pleased to confirm your reservation. It will be held on a space-available basis."

13. It is reported that when Socrates was condemned to death his wife cried out, "Those wretched judges have condemned him to death unjustly!" To which Socrates is said to have replied, "Would you really prefer that I were justly condemned?"

14. An article on Nike's Asian factories (*Time,* March 30, 1998) addressed a question asked by an anti–sweat shop activist: "Can't they find more money to pay the workers?" (Labor activist Jeff Ballinger estimated that Vietnamese workers were paid 57 cents per pair of shoes, typically selling for $90—see *Extra! Update,* June 1998). *Time's* response to the question was "The short answer is no. Corporations pay the going rate for labor wherever they are."

15. In a segment of *60 Minutes* on April 21, 2007, Leslie Stahl questioned Lou Dobbs about a report aired on his program by one of his correspondents that there had been about 900 cases of leprosy in this country over a 40-year period,

but 7,000 cases over the past three years. The report was part of a segment on his April 14, 2005, program in which he claimed that "the invasion of illegal aliens is threatening the health of many Americans." When Leslie Stahl said there didn't seem to be much evidence to support these statistics, he replied, "Well, I can tell you this. If we report it, it's a fact."

16. Question to artist's model: "Why did he paint you so often?" Answer: "Because I'm his model."

*17. From a Dr. Joyce Brothers newspaper column: "Question: You should be more fearful of rape at home because rapes occur more frequently in private homes than in back alleys. Answer: TRUE. Studies indicate that more rapes are committed in the victim's home than in any other place. Almost half took place in either the victim's home or the assailant's; one fourth occurred in open spaces; one fifth in automobiles; one twelfth in other indoor locations."

18. From *Slander*, by Ann Coulter, on the attitudes of liberals: "The liberal catechism includes hatred of Christians, guns, the profit motive, and political speech, and an infatuation with abortion, the environment, and race discrimination (or in the favored parlance of liberals, 'affirmative action')."

19. From a *New Republic* review of the James Michener book *Iberia:* "Michener leads off his chapter on bullfights with an argument between your quintessential American and Spaniard about brutal sports—which the Spaniard wins by pointing out that more young men get killed and maimed every year playing American football than in the bullring."

20. After the tsunami struck Southeast Asia in 2004 and devastated some of the world's poorest countries, the secretary of state at the time, Colin Powell, announced that the United States would contribute $15 million to the recovery effort—less than half the amount that the Republicans intended to spend on President Bush's second inaugural celebrations. (Faced with widespread criticism, the administration later upped the financial aid considerably.)

21. A *Washington Monthly* article on celebrity chefs (July/August, 2001) quoted Evan Kleinman, chef of Angeli Café in Los Angeles, as saying, "Basically when it comes to food and food supply, I find it frightening that something so fundamental to life has been left to people whose only concern is profit. . . . I mean as far as I can see, because of that, there are only two kinds of people putting food in their mouths—the ones who have lost the notion that food is something made by human hands and then there are the others . . . for whom there's still some link with food as a culture of nurturance."

22. Paraphrase of part of a letter to the editor (*Washington Post National Weekly Edition*, March 13–19, 1989): "It's true that the Ayatollah Khomeini has gone too far with his death sentence for author Salman Rushdie [because of his "outrageous" book *The Satanic Verses*], but Rushdie also has gone too far by offending all Moslems. I am a strong believer in the freedom of speech. However, books like Rushdie's only create hatred and division and weaken the ties of people to each other. Therefore, his book and others like it should be abolished."

23. When Calvin Klein was asked what the secret of his success was, he answered, "I make clothes women want to wear."

24. *Extra!* (September/October, 2007) quoted a *Washington Post* article (June 10, 2007) arguing that immigrants are "drawn by the great magnet of the American Economy to fill jobs that most Americans won't do."

*25. Sociologist James Q. Wilson: "I am not about to argue [as some sociobiologists do] that there is a 'sympathy gene.' But there must be some heritable disposition that helps us explain why sympathy is so common."

26. The second President Bush in a televised interview with Diane Sawyer (December 16, 2003), explaining why he doesn't read the newspapers: "I get my news from people [in his administration] who don't editorialize. . . . They give me the actual news, and it makes it easier to digest, on a daily basis, the facts."

27. In attacking a proposed equal rights amendment to the state constitution of Iowa, Pat Robertson argued that the proposal was part of a "feminist agenda . . . a socialist, anti-family political movement that encourages women to leave their husbands, kill their children, practice witchcraft, destroy capitalism, and become lesbians."

28. A commercial aired in the 1998 election campaign that uses President Clinton's sex scandal as the theme. The announcer asks, "Should we reward Democratic plans for more big government? More big spending? Should we reward their opposition to more welfare reform? And should we reward not telling the truth?"

    "That is the question of this election. Reward Bill Clinton. Or, vote Republican."

29. The day after the Mitchell report was released detailing the widespread use of anabolic steroids in baseball, a fan made this comment on sfgate.com, the *San Francisco Chronicle*'s website (December 18, 2007): "This will send a shock wave through baseball and steroid usage will stop."

30. In a 2007 debate with other contenders for the Republican presidential nomination, John McCain said, "I am prepared [to be president]. I am prepared. I need no on-the-job training. I wasn't a mayor for a short period of time. I wasn't a governor for a short period of time."

    In August 2008 McCain was asked if his running mate, Sarah Palin, was ready to step in as president if necessary; he answered with a resounding yes, touting her "executive experience" as governor of Alaska (for 21 months), as mayor of Wasilla, Alaska (population 7,000), and as president of the PTA.

31. Jorg Haider, Nazi sympathizer and Austrian Parliament member, in response to an interview with a *Time* magazine reporter (*Time*, February 14, 2000):

    Time: Why did you praise Hitler's employment policies?
    Haider: I think it was only one sentence out of a big debate. My opponents took out one sentence and made a campaign against me, and it was not possible for me to explain myself.

32. Ad for an International Correspondence School journalism course: "Every successful writer started that first story or article with no previous experience. William Shakespeare, Alexander Dumas, Harold Robbins, Danielle Steel, Barbara Cartland—any famous writer you can name started just like you."

33. *Extra! Update* (April 2003) included two quotes on religion by Bill O'Reilly on *The O'Reilly Factor.*

    March 11, 2003: Both sides of the debate [on whether to invade Iraq] are saying God is on their side. . . . I think both sides are wrong. Nobody knows for sure what the absolute right thing to do is. We can only have opinions. Thus, it's intellectually dishonest to be claiming God is on your side when only God knows for sure what the right thing to do is."

    December 4, 2002: "I'm telling you, I'm telling you that President Bush is doing what Jesus would have done."

34. Walter Burns, in an article in which he argues for capital punishment: "When abolitionists speak of the barbarity of capital punishment . . . they ought to be reminded that men whose moral sensitivity they would not question have supported [it]. Lincoln, for example, albeit with a befitting reluctance, authorized the execution of 267 persons during his presidency . . . and it was Shakespeare's sensitivity to the moral issues that required him to have Macbeth killed."

35. Phyllis Schlafley, an outspoken opponent of the women's liberation movement, in her book *The Power of Positive Women:* "The second dogma of the women's liberationists is that, of all the injustices perpetrated upon women through the centuries, the most oppressive is the cruel fact that women have babies and men do not. Within the confines of women's liberationist ideology, the abolition of this overriding inequality becomes the primary goal."

"If the coach and horses and the footmen and the beautiful clothes all turned back into the pumpkin and the mice and the rags, then how come the glass slipper didn't turn back, too?"

Two important factors in critical or creative thinking are the ability to bring relevant background information to bear on a problem and to carry through the relevant implications of an argument or position to determine whether they hang together. The cartoon illustrates the second of these factors: The child carries through the reasoning in the Cinderella story and finds it wanting. The first factor might be illustrated by a child who realizes there are millions of chimneys for Santa Claus to get down in one night and wonders how he could possibly manage to do so in time.

How happy are the astrologers, who are believed if they tell one truth to a hundred lies, while other people lose all credit if they tell one lie to a hundred truths.

—Francesco Guicciardini

It ain't so much the things we don't know that get us into trouble. It's the things we know that ain't so.

—Artemus Ward

Chapter

4

FALLACIOUS REASONING—2

Most instances of the fallacies discussed in the previous chapter fall into the broad fallacy categories *questionable premise* or *suppressed evidence*. Most of the fallacies to be discussed in this and the next chapter belong to the genus *invalid inference*.

1. *AD HOMINEM* ARGUMENT

There is a famous and perhaps apocryphal story lawyers like to tell that nicely captures the flavor of this fallacy. In Great Britain, the practice of law is divided between solicitors, who prepare cases for trial, and barristers, who argue the cases in court. The story concerns a particular barrister who, depending on the solicitor to prepare his case, arrived in court with no prior knowledge of the case he was to plead, where he found an exceedingly thin brief, which when opened contained just one note: "No case; abuse the plaintiff's attorney." If the barrister did as instructed, he was guilty of arguing *ad hominem* — of attacking his opponent rather than his opponent's evidence and arguments. (An *ad hominem* argument, literally, is an argument "to the person.")

Both liberals and conservatives are the butt of this fallacy much too often. Not long after Barack Obama was elected to the Senate, Rush Limbaugh repeatedly referred to him as "Obama Osama" when criticizing the senator and the Democrats in general. While this may have been intended as a humorous play on words, the underlying *ad hominem* is unmistakable. And Limbaugh (as well as other radio hosts) often referred to him as "Barack Hussein Obama," not to clarify his full name but to link him to Saddam Hussein. John McCain suffered similar attacks. In the run-up to the primary elections in 2008, Vietnam War Veterans Against McCain sent out fliers that accused him of selling out his fellow prisoners of war in Vietnam to save his own skin. In fact, McCain refused an early release offered by the North Vietnamese and stayed in prison with his fellow POWs. In both cases the candidates were attacked, not their political positions.

It is important not to confuse *ad hominem* arguments with those in which the fallacy is *straw man*. The difference is that straw man attacks misrepresent an opponent's position, whereas those that are *ad hominem* abuse an opponent directly.

Attacks on Character or Credentials Sometimes Are Relevant

Although attacks on a person usually are irrelevant to that individual's arguments or claims, sometimes they are very relevant indeed. Lawyers who attack the testimony of courtroom witnesses by questioning their expertise or character are not necessarily guilty of arguing *ad hominem*. They may be trying to gauge the integrity of the witness to determine whether his or her testimony is credible.

The judgment of expert witnesses may be particularly difficult to assess because they often express opinions or arguments against which the typical layperson is unable to argue directly. When doctors, lawyers, or other experts testify, often the best we can do is try to evaluate their honesty or judgment. Evidence that a psychologist testifying in court has been convicted of perjury, or spends a great deal of time testifying in court, would be good reason to prefer the conflicting testimony of experts on the other side of the case.

Of course, negative evidence concerning an expert rarely proves that the authority's pronouncements are false. At best, character attacks just provide grounds for disregarding their testimony, not for deciding that it is false. If a doctor who advises operating on a patient turns out to be held in low esteem in the profession, it is rash to conclude that *therefore* no operation is necessary.

What has just been said about attacking the credentials of experts applies to organizations and their pronouncements as well. For example, that a research organization receives most of its funds from the pharmaceutical industry and also regularly issues reports favorable to drug company interests constitutes a very good reason to be suspicious of its output.

Guilt by Association

One of the important variations on *ad hominem* argument is that of **guilt by association.** According to an old saying, people can be judged by the company they keep. But is this true? Is it rational to judge people in this way?

The answer is that it is—up to a point and under certain circumstances. In the absence of contrary evidence, a man frequently seen in the company of several different women known to be prostitutes is rightly *suspected* of being connected with their occupation. Similarly, a person who frequently associates with several known agents of a foreign government is rightly suspected of being an agent of that government.

But suspicion is very different from certitude. Judgments based on a person's associations rarely have a high degree of probability. Suspecting that someone uses the services of prostitutes is much different from knowing that he does. (It is, however, good reason to look further, assuming we care enough about the matter.) Someone frequently in the company of prostitutes may turn out to be a sociologist conducting an investigation. A person often seen in the company of foreign spies may turn out to be a friendly counterspy or even just an associate.

Establishing guilt by association between politicians is particularly tricky. When Jack Abramoff, the Republican lobbyist, was indicted for bribery and corruption, a photograph of him shaking hands with the second President Bush hit the media. The obvious implication was that Bush was involved in Abramoff's nefarious activities, though there was no evidence to suggest that he had ever been with the lobbyist except at a few White House receptions, where it is customary for the president to shake hands with guests. Bush, himself, denied knowing Abramoff at a news conference in January 2006. However, Abramoff claimed that he had seen Bush in almost a dozen settings, and Secret Service records revealed that he had made at least seven visits to the White House—six in 2001 and one in 2004. But so far there is no evidence that Bush was in cahoots with Abramoff and probably there never will be. Unless ongoing investigations prove otherwise, the president cannot be charged with guilt by association.

2. Two Wrongs Make a Right

Those who try to justify a wrong by pointing to a similar wrong perpetrated by others often are guilty of the fallacy sometimes called **two wrongs make a right** (traditional name: *tu quoque*—"you're another"). For example, in the 2000 presidential election, over 1,900 Palm Beach County, Florida, citizens voted for two candidates for the same office, thus invalidating their ballots. Democratic Party representatives claimed that the vast majority of these double votes resulted from confusion brought on by an illegally designed ballot, thwarting voter intent. A Republican Party spokesperson dismissed their complaint by pointing out that in the 1996 presidential election over 15,000 ballots in Palm Beach County were invalidated for that reason, without creating a huge uproar. But surely, the fact that the 1996 election had a problem does not justify having the same problem in the year 2000.

Justifying a vengeful retaliation in sports may fall into this category as well. In recent years the baseball commissioner has clamped down on aggressive acts of retaliation between players by fining and suspending them for violence on the field. But in the rough-and-tumble "good old days," retaliation was the way they settled scores. If a pitcher hit the batter, one of the players on the other team would take him down by sliding into first base, cleats high, when the pitcher was covering the base. The umpires would turn a blind eye, and the players would get revenge and the satisfaction of taking care of the problem themselves.[1] Nonetheless, slamming into a player, like a fullback, because a pitcher on the other team knocked down a batter is using one wrong to justify another.

Fighting Fire with Fire

Like most other fallacies, two wrongs seems plausible because of its resemblance to a more legitimate way of reasoning—in this case to the plausible idea that we sometimes are justified in "fighting fire with fire." Killing in self-defense illustrates this nicely.

---

[1] For more discussion of retaliatory behavior in baseball see, "End of an Age that was Rule by Retaliation," by Murray Chass, *New York Times,* March 18, 2008.

The Handbook of Political Fallacies, by British political philosopher and re-former Jeremy Bentham (1748–1832), is one of the classic works on political rhetoric and fallacies. Here are excerpts from his account of the first of four "causes of the utterance of [political] fallacies" (another excerpt appears in Chapter 6).

First Cause . . . : Self-Conscious Sinister Interest

[I]t is apparent that the mind of every public man is subject at all times to the operation of two distinct interests: a public and a private one. . . .

In the greater number of instances, these two interests . . . are not only distinct, but opposite, and that to such a degree that if either is exclusively pursued, the other must be sacrificed to it. Take for example pecuniary interest: it is to the personal interest of every public man who has at his disposal public money extracted from the whole community by taxes, that as large a share as possible . . . should remain available for his own use. At the same time it is to the interest of the public . . . that as small a share as possible . . . should remain in his hands for his personal or any other private use. . . . Hence it is that any class of men who have an interest in the rise or continuance of any system of abuse no matter how flagrant will, with few or no exceptions, support such a system of abuse with any means they deem necessary, even at the cost of probity and sincerity. . . .

But it is one of the characteristics of abuse, that it can only be defended by fallacy. It is, therefore, to the interest of all the confederates of abuse to give the most extensive currency to fallacies. . . . It is of the utmost importance to such persons to keep the human mind in such a state of imbecility that shall render it incapable of distinguishing truth from error. . . .

Students inclined to complain that too many of the fallacy examples in this text come from politicians should seriously reflect on Bentham's remarks, especially because government today deals with so many matters that determine the quality of all of our lives.

We feel justified in fighting one evil (the unjustified attack on our own life) by doing what otherwise would constitute another evil (taking the life of the attacker). So the two wrongs fallacy is not automatically committed every time one wrong is counteracted by another. The crucial question is whether the second wrong is genuinely needed to fight, or counteract, the first.[2]

---

[2] This passes over questions concerning retributive justice. If retributivists are right, we sometimes are justified in punishing those guilty of unfairly harming others even though in doing so we fail to fight the original harm (or fail to rehabilitate the criminal or deter others from similar offenses).

Two Wrongs and Hypocrisy

The two wrongs fallacy also sometimes seems plausible—not fallacious—for another reason: Those who argue this way may intend to imply that their opponents are being hypocritical, and often this charge is accurate and may even have some merit. The town drunk isn't the one to tell us we've had one too many and are making fools of ourselves, even if we are. (That's the import of the reply, "You're a fine one to talk.") Similarly, the philanderer who finds out about his wife's infidelity is hardly the one to complain that she has deceived him. But when we become outraged at the chutzpah of our accusers, we shouldn't lose sight of the fact that their hypocrisy doesn't justify our own failures.

Common Practice and Traditional Wisdom

As the traditional Latin name *tu quoque* suggests, the fallacy two wrongs make a right originally was intended to cover only those cases in which an individual or group responds to a charge by charging the accuser or accusers with a similar crime. But over time, it has come to take in related, indeed overlapping, sorts of fallacious arguments. One of these is **common practice,** committed when a wrong is justified on the grounds not that one other person or group, but rather lots of, or most, or even all others do the same sort of thing.

For example, when former Senator George Mitchell released an explosive report naming baseball players who took anabolic steroids, many hard-core fans defended superstars like Roger Clemens, Barry Bonds, and Mark McGwire. They argued that these players were taking steroids because lots of other players took them. Since the performance level of everyone on drugs was much better than before, the competition was keener. "How can you blame these guys?" one fan asked. "They did what they had to do to stay competitive." Well, you can blame them, of course, for rationalizing that it was okay to take performance-enhancing drugs because it was common practice to do so.

Another example is the all-too-common rationalization students use for cheating on tests or plagiarizing papers: "Everyone is doing it." That may well be, but common practice is hardy justification for academic dishonesty—particularly from a teacher's point of view.

A related fallacy, sometimes called **traditional wisdom,** is committed when a wrong or an unsuitable practice is justified on grounds that it follows a traditional or accepted way of doing things. We do, of course, want to learn from past experiences, so we shouldn't assume that *just because* things have been done certain ways in the past, that way must be the right, or best, way now. All innovations go against past practices—from the introduction of plows that dig deeper furrows (resisted by North African farmers on the grounds that their fathers and grandfathers had farmed the traditional way) to the elimination of practices based on racial, religious, or gender bias in the United States or to do away with practices based on the caste system in India, which force "untouchables" to do dirty work, such as collecting "night soil." (Interestingly, new methods of planting seeds without plowing at all may make deep furrow plowing obsolete in its turn.)

In some cases, practices that once made perfect sense no longer do because of changing circumstances or increased knowledge. In others, the fallacy in arguing for the retention of common practices is due to the wrongheadedness or unfairness of those old ways of doing things. Those who benefit from these practices find it hard to entertain the idea that there could possibly be anything wrong with them. In England, for instance, women for centuries had no legal rights under the common law. It wasn't just that women were disenfranchised. Fathers could marry a daughter to whomever they pleased,[3] and after marriage a woman's husband became the owner of her property. It took a very long time for these and similar legal injustices to be rectified; they were defended, for one thing, on the grounds that women had no legal rights because they never had had any. (In nineteenth-century England and America, the idea that women should have the vote was met with great hilarity in all-male circles of power, and political cartoons in newspapers and magazines poked fun at "lady suffragettes.")

It's often easier to see the questionable nature of customs in distant times or other cultures than in one's own. Consider the centuries-old tradition in some Middle Eastern countries of "honor" killing, the practice of killing girls or women who have sexual relations out of wedlock. In the Arab world, an unchaste woman brings shame on the family and sometimes the relatives themselves kill her to "cleanse the honor" that has been soiled. Hundreds of women are killed for reasons of honor each year. Yet activists trying to tighten the laws against honor killings are faced with massive opposition that portrays their campaign as an assault on Arab ways. The traditional wisdom is that an unchaste woman deserves to die.

Similar remarks apply to other societies, a very important example being India, where there also is the inhuman practice of murdering a wife whose family fails to come up with a sufficiently large dowry. Note also that in many Middle Eastern and African countries, traditional wisdom requires that young girls, just before puberty, be given a clitorectomy so as to reduce the temptation to engage in sex out of wedlock.

Of course, those who conform to these customs see them as good; it is other people, both inside and outside these cultures, who find fault with them. The point is that traditional beliefs need to be reevaluated and changed when found wanting.

But, again, we don't want to go overboard. Every change brings with it risks that may not have been calculated correctly. The "three strikes and you're out" bills, for example, were generally enacted without careful consideration of the likely consequences of such a serious departure from past practice. The point of such a bill is to assure that those who repeatedly commit serious violent crimes are not released from jail to again commit heinous offenses. But most of these measures enacted so far fail to distinguish correctly between seriously violent repeat felons and others or to consider the cost of incarcerating criminals long past the time when they are likely to commit violent crimes (most of which are committed by young men). They also fail to take account of the motivation these bills provide for two-time losers to shoot to kill rather than allow themselves to be captured and tried a third time.

W. Somerset Maugham summed things up nicely when he said, "Tradition is a guide, not a jailer."

---

[3] Successful resistance to this paternal power forms an important subplot in eighteenth-century novelist Henry Fielding's psychologically insightful novel *Tom Jones,* made into a charming movie in the 1960s, a must-see for all movie buffs.

3. IRRELEVANT REASON (NON SEQUITUR)

Traditional logic textbooks often discuss a fallacy called *non sequitur* (literally, "it does not follow"), usually described as being committed when a conclusion does not follow logically from given premises. In this sense, any fallacy in the broad category *invalid inference* can be thought of as a non sequitur. But other writers describe this fallacy more narrowly.

Let's replace the ambiguous term *non sequitur* with the expression **irrelevant reason,** used to refer to reasons or premises that are irrelevant to a conclusion when the error doesn't fit a narrower fallacy category such as *ad hominem* argument or two wrongs make a right.

Both before and after the outbreak of the 1991 war in the Persian Gulf and the Iraq War in 2003, many Americans railed against antiwar demonstrators on grounds that they were giving the Iraqi leaders the idea that Americans were too soft to go to war, too decadent to take the number of casualties winning might require. (The same charge was leveled against Vietnam War protesters 20 years or so earlier.) This charge may well have been true (Iraq certainly misjudged American resolve), but it was irrelevant to the protesters' arguments against waging war with Iraq (or to those who protested against our fighting in Vietnam).

Sometimes irrelevant arguments defy logic. Shortly after the attack on the World Trade Center, Michael Kelly had this to say in "Pacifist Claptrap."

> Organized terrorist groups have attacked America. These groups wish the Americans to not fight. The American pacifists wish the Americans to not fight. If the Americans do not, the terrorists will attack America again. And now we know such attacks can kill many thousands of Americans. The American pacifists, therefore, are on the side of future mass murders of Americans. They are objectively pro-terrorist.[4]

Ah, those crafty pacifists. Little did we realize their murderous intent.

How about this excerpt from a United Airlines commercial?

> We humans are a social animal. That's why United flies to more places than any other airline.

This commercial says that the reason United flies to more places is that "we humans are a social animal," a fact that is totally irrelevant to [United's] flying to more places than competing airlines. Their use of the phrase "that's why," implying that a reason supports a conclusion, is completely off base. The appeal of United's spiel is to emotion, not to brain power, not to reason. Note, by the way, that a reason is not automatically irrelevant just because it is false. For example, the old superstition about walking under a ladder bringing bad luck is false, but it isn't irrelevant to the question whether a person should or shouldn't engage in this practice; were it true, it would be a very good reason indeed for not walking under ladders.

Note also that a reason may be irrelevant when looking at a matter from one point of view but not from another. Take, for example, the remark by a psychological clinician, quoted in *Science News* magazine, that abandoning the old and standard ways of

---

[4] *Washington Post,* September 26, 2001, quoted in *Extra!,* November/December, 2001.

© Dan Wasserman, *The Boston Globe,* Tribune Media Services

A humorous (we hope) equivocation.

classifying mental disorder in favor of new ones "will result in denial of insurance coverage for treatment of serious psychological disturbances." Looked at from the point of view of psychiatric *theory,* this remark is irrelevant, but from the point of view of psychiatric *practice,* it is very relevant indeed.

4. EQUIVOCATION

A term or expression is used *equivocally* in an argument when used to mean one thing in one place and another thing in another.[5] Accepting an argument that is invalid because we are fooled by an equivocal use of language makes us guilty of the fallacy that you will not be surprised to learn is generally called **equivocation.**

   When a TV evangelist said that we all should stop sinning and "be like Jesus," someone in the audience expressed doubt that he was up to that, pointing out that, after all, "Jesus is the son of God." In reply, the evangelist told the doubter that he could indeed stop sinning because, "You're the son of God, too." But the evangelist was guilty of

---

[5]As used in everyday life, the term *equivocation* often connotes the use of equivocation to deceive. As used here, it does not necessarily carry this connotation. We do, of course, have to remember that equivocation is frequently employed in daily life to make invalid arguments appear to be valid.

equivocation, because the doubter meant that Jesus is the son of God in the special way that (according to Christian doctrine) only Jesus is held to be, while the evangelist had to mean that the doubter was the son of God in the metaphorical sense in which (again according to Christian theology) we all are children of God.

Equivocation is a common fallacy because it often is quite hard to notice that a shift in meaning has taken place. As might be expected, given human nature, less than completely ethical manipulators frequently take advantage of the ease with which people can be fooled in this way. The sugar industry, for instance, once advertised its product with the claim that "Sugar is an essential component of the body . . . a key material in all sorts of metabolic processes," neglecting the fact that it is *glucose* (blood sugar), not ordinary table sugar (sucrose), that is the vital nourishment. It's true, of course, that table sugar does turn into blood sugar in the body, but it provides that necessary ingredient without also providing the other sorts of vital nutrients found in fruits, grains, and other more complete food sources that contain plenty of sucrose.

Advertisements of this kind for food and other health products are successful because a large majority of consumers know very little about how the body functions—what sorts of food are required for good health and what sorts are unhealthy. They tend to get their information about these vital matters from television commercials, other advertisements, and TV talk shows. So they are ready-made suckers for every fad that comes down the pike. For example, many food products have been advertised as especially healthy because they are low in cholesterol, or even cholesterol-free, while containing the usual (high) levels of fats, which the body then uses to make cholesterol. The ambiguity taken advantage of here is, again, the difference between what is in a food and what is in the bloodstream. Low blood cholesterol levels are good; low food cholesterol levels combined with high fat content definitely are not good. (Note that some foods advertised to be cholesterol free, or even fat free, contain partially hydrogenated oils, much less heart healthy than the fats listed on packages by law.)

Sometimes legal action is taken against companies for misleading advertising. When Phillip Morris was sued for deceiving smokers into thinking "light" cigarettes were less harmful than regular ones, a company spokesman said that the word *light* referred to taste, not content, but surely he was equivocating. Most smokers would tend to think that "light" meant that the cigarettes had less tar and nicotine—if only to rationalize their bad habit.

Interestingly, terms that can be used either relatively or absolutely, like *rich* and *poor,* sometimes cause trouble. Poverty, for instance, is exceedingly unpleasant anywhere, at any time. But the poor in the United States today are richer in absolute terms with respect to material wealth than the vast majority of people who lived in days of old or who live today in the so-called Third World countries of Africa, Central and South America, and Asia. This important truth is masked by the fact that the term *poor,* in its relative sense, does apply to those Americans who are poor compared to other Americans, although rich compared to most people who lived in the past or who live in Third World countries today. (Do we make ourselves perfectly clear?)

But Ambiguity Often Serves Useful Purposes

Students sometimes get the idea that *ambiguity,* certainly equivocation, always is bad. But it isn't. Ambiguous uses of language, especially metaphorical ones, and even equivocations, can be employed for all kinds of good purposes. The well-known psychologist,

> It is he that sitteth upon the circle of the earth.
>
> —Isaiah 40:22
>
> ### Ambiguity
>
> *Almost any statement can be interpreted in various ways if we have a mind to do so. The Bible is a happy hunting ground for those intent on taking advantage of the ambiguity of natural languages, because so many people take what it says to be the word of the Ultimate Authority. This passage from Isaiah was once used to prove that the Earth is flat, but when the discoveries of Copernicus, Kepler, and Newton made the idea of a flat Earth untenable, the Isaiah quote was reinterpreted to prove that those who wrote the Bible knew the Earth is a sphere.*

Carl Rogers, for example, used equivocation very effectively in the following passage to emphasize a point:

> As a boy I was rather sickly, and my parents have told me that it was predicted I would die young. This prediction has been proven completely wrong in one sense, but has come profoundly true in another sense. I think it is correct that I will never live to be old. So I now agree with the prediction that I will die young.[6]

Ambiguous uses of language also serve to grease the wheels of social intercourse. Benjamin Disraeli, the nineteenth-century British prime minister, often used ambiguity to soften his replies to letters, while still coming close to being truthful, as in his reply to an unsolicited amateur manuscript: "Many thanks; I shall lose no time in reading it." (In most other contexts, of course, equivocation of this kind is rightly considered to be rather sneaky.)

Ambiguity also serves very useful purposes in literature, particularly in metaphoric passages. It enables writers to introduce multiple meanings quickly into a text in a way that adds significance to what is being said by drawing attention to often rather subtle connections without hitting us over the head with them. For example, the title of Joseph Conrad's great novel *Heart of Darkness* doesn't refer just to the central part of the African jungle but also captures some of the moral horror of the principal character, Kurtz, succumbing to the dark temptations of colonial African life, and by extension it draws attention to the corruption and depravity "civilized" people are capable of when they give in to their base instincts. It also suggests the appalling abuses of power resulting from the exploitation of Africans and their lands by European colonials at the turn of the century. The ambiguity lurking in the title of Conrad's novel thus prepares us for the complex moral issues addressed in his classic work.

---

[6]Carl Rogers, *Journal of Humanistic Psychology* (Fall 1980).

5. Appeal to Ignorance

When good reasons are lacking, the rational conclusion to draw is that we just don't know. But when we greatly desire to believe something, it's tempting to take the absence of evidence, and thus absence of refutation, as justification for believing that it is true. Doing this makes us guilty of the fallacy **appeal to ignorance** (traditionally known as *argumentum ad ignorantiam*). Some people have argued, for example, that we should believe there is no intelligent life on other planets anywhere in our galaxy, since no one has been able to prove that there is; indeed, until recently, when the existence of other planets was confirmed, it was sometimes argued that there were no planets anywhere other than our own tight little island.

The fallacy in this sort of reasoning can be seen by turning it on its head. If appeals to ignorance could prove that no life exists on other planets, then it equally well could prove just the opposite. After all, no one has proved that life does *not* exist on any of these planets. In the absence of good evidence for a claim, the right thing to do is to be *agnostic* on the issue, to neither believe nor disbelieve. Ignorance proves nothing, except, of course, that we are ignorant. During the Iraq War, the Bush administration could have said that the opposition was guilty of appeal to ignorance when it claimed that because no weapons of mass destruction were found, there must not be any hidden weapons. As of this writing, they still haven't been found, but you never know—they may turn up.

There are, however, cases in which the failure of a search does count against a claim. That happens when whatever is searched for would very likely have been found if it existed. Given all the sky watching that has gone on in the past 10,000 years, the claim that there exists a planet-sized object between Earth and Mars is disproved by the failure of anyone to observe it. Similarly, the failure to find evidence of a virus in a blood test justifies a doctor's conclusion that we aren't infected with that virus. These are cases not of reasoning from ignorance but rather of reasoning from the *knowledge* that we would have found the item looked for if it had been there to find.

In 1950, when Senator Joseph R. McCarthy (Republican, Wisconsin), was asked about the fortieth name on a list of 81 names of people he claimed were communists working for the United States Department of State, he responded that "I do not have much information on this except the general statement of the agency that there is nothing in the files to disprove his communist connections."

Many of McCarthy's followers took this absence of evidence as proof that the person in question was indeed a communist, a good example of the fallacy of appeal to ignorance. This example also illustrates the importance of not being taken in by this fallacy. McCarthy never backed up his charges with a single bit of relevant evidence, yet for several years he enjoyed great popularity and power, and his witch hunt ruined many innocent lives before, finally, McCarthy and "McCarthyism" were brought down in congressional hearings that revealed the true character of this miserable person.

Note, however, the importance of *appropriately* searching. That telescopes have searched the sky for several hundred years, and naked eyes for thousands, without spotting a god up there proves absolutely nothing about the existence of a god in the sky, since deities are not conceived of as the kind of entities that can be seen in this way.

6. COMPOSITION AND DIVISION

The fallacy of **composition,** also sometimes called the *salesman's fallacy,* but more accurately the *consumer's fallacy,* is committed when someone assumes that a particular item must have a certain property because all of its parts have that property. Auto dealers, for example, frequently try to get prospective customers to fall for this fallacy by touting low monthly payments while neglecting total costs, hoping their marks will assume that if the monthly payments are low, then the total cost must be low also. Washers and dryers used to be sold by telling customers that it takes "only 50 cents a day" to buy one. Of course, 50 cents a day adds up to $365 in two years (a lot of money until rather recently), something buyers seldom thought to figure out even though the arithmetic involved is on the grade school level.

The fallacy of **division** is committed when we assume that all (or some) of the parts of an item have a particular property because the item as a whole has it. The fallacy of division thus is the mirror image of the fallacy of composition. While infrequently fallen for in everyday life, cases do happen. An example is concluding that all the rooms in a large, fancy, hotel must be large, as guests often do when making reservations at places such as the posh Plaza Hotel in New York (where in fact lots of rooms are rather tiny).

7. SLIPPERY SLOPE

In a typical **slippery slope argument,** an action is objected to on the grounds that once it is taken, another, and then perhaps still another, are bound to be taken, down a "slippery slope," until some undesirable consequence results. According to a slightly different version, whatever would justify taking the first step would also justify all the others, but since the last step isn't justified, the first isn't, either.

Arguing that a slope is slippery without providing good reason for thinking that it is, or when the slope clearly is not, makes us guilty of the **slippery slope fallacy.** For example, a Canadian-style "single-payer" health care system has often been objected

---

Earlier editions of this text at this point had a section on a variation of the fallacy slippery slope called the *domino theory.* Back in the nasty old Cold War days, dominoes were alleged to be in danger of falling all over the globe. Perhaps the chief reason advanced by the Johnson and Nixon administrations for our involvement in the war in Vietnam was that if Vietnam fell to the communists, the rest of Southeast Asia would also, and then countries in Central America (Nicaragua, El Salvador, and so on) and even parts of South America (in particular, Chile). Although we were defeated in Vietnam, it is primarily communist dominoes that have fallen—perhaps the reason that the domino theory has gone out of fashion.

to on grounds that it is a kind of socialized medicine and that its adoption would lead to socialized insurance of all kinds, socialized railroads, airlines, and so on, without sufficient reason being presented for believing this would be the case. (Are there any?) It also sometimes is argued that whatever would justify a single-payer system of health care also would justify all sorts of other socialistic measures, again without justifying this conclusion.

Note, however, that some slopes may well be slippery. The slippery slope fallacy is committed only when we accept without further justification or argument that once the first step is taken, the others are going to follow, or that whatever would justify the first step would in fact justify the rest. Consider this explanation of an economic slide that could have occurred after the housing market crashed in 2007.[7]

> As homeowners see the value of their homes decline, they become more likely to delay purchases of the big items—like automobiles, electronics and home appliances—that are ballasts of the American economy. When those purchases decline, large manufacturing firms, suddenly short on funds, could begin laying off employees. Those workers, uncertain about the future, might in turn stop buying Starbucks lattes and movie tickets, and in a worst-case scenario, that could spur coffee shops and theaters to begin layoffs of their own.

This may seem like a slippery slope fallacy at first glance, but a similar chain reaction did occur during the Great Depression in 1929, resulting in persistent, widespread unemployment. It was, indeed, a slippery slope and one that threatened to repeat itself when the credit markets froze up, and the stock market plunged in 2008.

SUMMARY OF CHAPTER 4

1. *Ad hominem argument:* An irrelevant attack on an opponent rather than on the opponent's evidence or arguments. *Example:* Rush Limbaugh calling Barack Obama "Obama Osama." Note, however, that not all character attacks are fallacious, as they may not be when challenging the integrity of an allegedly expert witness.

    We're guilty of the variation on this fallacy called *guilt by association* when we judge someone guilty solely on the basis of the company that person keeps.

2. *Two wrongs make a right:* Justifying a wrong by pointing to a similar wrong perpetrated by others. *Example:* Baseball players justifying aggressive retaliation against a pitcher on the other team because he hit a batter and knocked him down. Note, however, that when fighting fire with fire, what would otherwise be a wrong often isn't, as when someone kills in self-defense.

    Although there is an air of hypocrisy to a charge coming from an equally guilty party, this doesn't make an accurate charge any less on target.

    Variations: Common practice, in which a wrong is justified because commonly engaged in. *Traditional wisdom,* in which a wrong is justified because that's the way things always have been done.

---

[7]"Depression, You Say? Check Those Safety Nets," by Charles Duhigg, *New York Times,* March 23, 2008.

3. *Irrelevant reason:* Trying to prove something with evidence that is or comes close to being irrelevant. (Some other term, such as *ad hominem argument,* may also apply.) *Example:* Countering the claims of antiwar protesters by arguing that antiwar talk tells the enemy we don't have the resolve to fight.

4. *Equivocation:* Using a term or expression in an argument in one sense in one place and another sense in another. *Example:* The TV evangelist's use of the expression "son of God" to refer to Jesus Christ and to a parishioner. Note, however, that intentional ambiguity, even equivocation, is not always fallacious. It isn't, for example, when used for metaphoric effect.

5. *Appeal to ignorance:* Arguing that the failure to find evidence refuting a claim justifies believing that it is true. *Example:* Arguing that there is no intelligent life on other planets since no one has been able to prove there is. Note, however, that the failure of *appropriate* searches sometimes does support rejection of a claim.

6. *Composition:* Assuming that an item has a certain property because all or most of its parts have that property. *Example:* Assuming a commodity is inexpensive because of low installment payments.

   Division: Assuming that all or most parts of an item have a property because the whole item has it. *Example:* Assuming the rooms in a large hotel are large.

7. *Slippery slope:* Accepting a claim that a slope is slippery when no or insufficient reason has been presented to justify that claim. *Example:* Arguing that adoption of a single-payer health plan will lead to adoption of all sorts of other socialistic measures.

EXERCISE 4-1

Determine which fallacies (if any) occur in the following short passages and justify your answers (as you did when working on Exercise 3-1). (Some of these passages may contain fallacies discussed in the previous chapter.)

1. Letter to the editor, *San Francisco Chronicle:* "What, again? Another jab at the CIA by [columnist and reporter] Jack Anderson? . . . All countries have spy organizations. Most of them sometimes overstep the bounds of propriety. Why single out our own outfit?"

2. In a column about *The Assault on Reason,* by Al Gore, David Brooks roundly criticized the book, but wrote that it was "well worth reading. It reminds us that whatever the effects of our homogenizing mass culture, it is still possible for exceedingly strange individuals [meaning Al Gore] to rise to the top." (*New York Times,* May 29, 2007)

3. Charlton Heston (then president of the NRA), in an interview after the 1999 shootings at Columbine High School, told ABC's *This Week* that he opposed President Clinton's attempt to limit handgun purchases to one a month. "Before you know it, it becomes no guns."

*4. Football player Roger Craig, on George Seifert's promotion to head coach of the San Francisco 49ers: "I think George will do an excellent job, because he's been searching for a head coaching job for some time, and what better place to start his head coaching job." (In fact, Seifert did have an excellent record with the 49ers before being canned.)

5. From a 1972 article in the *Hartford Courant* on the possibility of women priests in the Catholic Church: "Citing the historic exclusion of women from the priesthood, ... the study [of a committee of Roman Catholic bishops] said '... the constant tradition and practice, interpreted as divine law, is of such a nature as to constitute a clear teaching of the Ordinary Magisterium [teaching authority of the church].'"

*6. Bumper sticker seen in California when a handgun bill was before voters of that state:

Gun Registration Equals Mass Extermination
First Register Guns, Then Register the Jews

7. In an article for the *Atlanta Constitution* (March, 1996) Cynthia Tucker pointed out how the rich and powerful often are given special privileges. "These revelations make the case for affirmative action. People of color, who rarely have power or connections, are just seeking the same favors available to those who [already] have them."

8. (In this case, the question is what fallacy, if any, Momma failed to put over on her son.)

Momma by Mell Lazarus. Courtesy of Mell Lazarus and Field Newspaper Syndicate.

9. Jan Berger in the *Baltimore Evening Sun:* "Weeks of patient investigation have revealed that the gas leaked at Bhopal [India—with thousands of casualties] because something went wrong."

10. Rush Limbaugh on opponents to the war in Iraq (quoted in the *Baltimore Sun,* March 9, 2003): "I want to say something about these anti-war demonstrators. No let's not mince words, let's call them what they are: anti-American demonstrators."

11. Claim made by opponents of an initiative to legalize marijuana for medicinal purposes: "It would be foolish to permit the sale of marijuana to seriously ill

people on the recommendation of their physicians. That just opens the floodgates to the complete legalization of that dangerous drug."

12. A letter to the editor of *Connoisseur* magazine defended a previous article favoring bullfighting from "the protesting letters you are sure to receive," by reminding readers that bulls selected for the arena live twice as long as those destined for McDonald's and die in a far more noble fashion.

13. When President Bush attempted to justify sending 20,000 more troops to secure Iraq in 2007, congressional leaders asked him why he thought this strategy would succeed when previous efforts had failed. Bush responded, "Because it has to." (quoted in the *New York Times,* January 11, 2007)

*14. Indian mystic Vivekananda: "There is no past or future even in thought, because to think it you have to make it present."

15. From a conversation with a friend (not verbatim): "Sure, I've told you before that I believe everyone's opinion counts on moral matters like abortion. But not *everyone's* opinion counts—I wouldn't want Hitler's to count. Well, [name deleted] isn't a Hitler, but she sleeps around like sex was going out of style next week or something. She's just a slut, and she's broken up at least one marriage I know about. Why should her opinion count on anything? Why should we listen to her opinion on the abortion business?"

16. President Bush, explaining why he would veto an expansion of the State Children's Health Insurance Program (SCHIP) to cover more children:

> They're going to increase the numbers of folks eligible through SCHIP; some want to lower the age for Medicare. And then all of a sudden, you begin . . . to get more people to be a part of a federalization of health care.

17. Jules Crittenden, an embedded journalist for the *Boston Herald* in the Iraq War, defended himself from criticism for bringing home some illegal "souvenirs" from Iraq (*Boston Herald,* April 23, 2003): "I understand and share the world's concern about the disappearance of legitimate Iraqi national treasures that are in fact treasures of human civilization," Crittenden wrote in an open letter to journalists in this country. "However, those are matters separate from the time-honored tradition among soldiers of bringing home reminders of some of the most intense experiences of their lives. There was no exception to that historical practice in this war . . . [until reporters and soldiers were subject to search by federal agents on returning to the United States]."

18. Argument heard all too frequently in introductory philosophy classes: "We're perfectly entitled to believe there is a God. After all, every effort by atheists to prove otherwise has failed."

19. Lewis Carroll, in *Through the Looking Glass:* " 'You couldn't have it if you did want it,' the Queen said. 'The rule is jam tomorrow and jam yesterday—but never jam *today.*' 'It must sometimes come to jam today,' Alice objected. 'No it can't,' said the Queen. 'It's jam every *other* day: today isn't any *other* day, you know.' "

20. Chris Matthews's comment on *Hardball* about Fred Thompson, 2008 presidential candidate (quoted in *Extra!,* July/August 2007): "Can you smell the English Leather on this guy, the Aqua Velva, the sort of mature man's shaving cream, or whatever, you know, after he shaved? Do you smell the sort of—a little bit of cigar smoke? You know, whatever."

21. Robert Ringer in *The Tortoise Report* touting gold as an investment: "Two thousand years after the human flesh had disappeared, the gold that adorned it [an ancient Egyptian corpse] remained virtually unchanged. That's a real hard act for paper money to follow."

22. Margaret Morissey, an anti-garbage activist, was interviewed on *As It Happens,* a Canadian news program (February 2002) about her arrest for blocking trucks from dumping garbage on a hill overlooking St. Brides, Newfoundland. The arrest occurred despite the fact that it was illegal to use the hill as a dumpsite. When she asked the mayor why the dumping was still allowed, he said, "We've been doing it for 30 years."

23. Overheard on the bus to Atlantic City: "I just play the quarter slots when I go to Atlantic City. That way, I don't lose too much money."

*24. Sigmund Freud: "Our own death is . . . unimaginable, and whenever we make the attempt to imagine it we can perceive that we really survive as spectators."

25. Excerpt from an article in *Extra!* (June 2003) critical of embedding journalists with military units during the Iraq War: "Embedding was the brainchild of Assistant Defense Secretary Victoria Clarke, formerly with Hill and Knowlton, the PR firm infamous for promoting the false baby-incubator story during the first Gulf War."

26. When John Bolton was nominated for the position of ambassador to the United Nations in 2005, repeated testimony was given in Senate hearings about his bad temper and his abrasive manner with subordinates. (One person went so far as to call him a "serial abuser.") But he was defended by Danielle Pletka, a vice president at the American Enterprise Institute, who said, "This is a disgrace, the idea that temperament is suddenly important. There are legions who have gone before John, as well as members of Congress, who have behaved appallingly."

27. St. Augustine, in *De Libero Arbitrio:* "See how absurd and foolish it is to say: I should prefer nonexistence to miserable existence. He who says, I prefer this to that, chooses something. Nonexistence is not something; it is nothing. There can be no real choice when what you choose is nothing."

28. When Ralph Nader announced on *Meet the Press* that he was running for president in the 2004 election, he said, "George Bush is a giant corporation masking as a human being."

29. Item from the *Philadelphia Inquirer* (August 28, 2003) about an atheist, Sherrie Wilkins, suing a school board in Camden, New Jersey, over school uniforms: "Citing the equal protection clause of the U.S. Constitution, Wilkins' lawsuit argues that atheists should have the same rights as religious parents [since the

school district allows parents to opt out of the requirement on religious grounds]. . . . [Furthermore] as an atheist, Wilkins said in court documents, she objects to the uniforms because they 'hinder her children's creativity . . . and freedom of expression.' Uniforms also symbolize militarism, which she opposes, she said."

30. In the run-up to the Senate confirmation of appointments to the Supreme Court, Senate Republicans threatened to strip Democrats (the minority party) of their right to use the filibuster as a way to prevent the confirmation of judges. The Democrats argued that the filibuster had been around for 200 years and scrapping it would be "changing rules in the middle of the game." Further, it would undermine the constitutional principle of "checks and balances" that protected Americans from one-party rule (discussed in "The Framing Wars," by Matt Bai, *New York Times Magazine,* July 17, 2005)

31. A lobbyist, whose job is to get people to call or write to members of Congress, responding to the charge that this sort of activity makes the "political playing field" uneven (because big money can afford these endeavors much better than small): "Everyone knows that the playing field isn't level in this country in the business arena, or in others for that matter. Nobody complains about that. Why fuss about the funding for what I do?"

32. Excerpt from a letter to the editor of the *Pacific Sun* (September 2000): "Nowhere on the official Ralph Nader website is there any mention of concern about how women are treated in the media. I can't help but infer that this kind of human dignity is not high on his agenda."

33. On a *Larry King Live* TV show (November 29, 2000), Republican Senator John McCain defended the acceptance of the Florida presidential election results by saying that the votes in the disputed counties had been counted and recounted and that, although there were ways in which the 2000 election in Florida could have been better conducted, we should remember that many elections in the past have been less than perfect; for instance, in Illinois in 1960 (the year John F. Kennedy was elected president amidst claims of chicanery in Illinois and Texas).

*I*t's dangerous to conclude that A *is the cause of* B *just because* B *follows* A.

Figures don't lie, but liars figure.
                              —Old saying

There are lies, damn lies, and statistics.
                      —Benjamin Disraeli

It's very difficult to make predictions, especially about the future.
                              —Casey Stengel

Chapter

5

FALLACIOUS REASONING—3

Let's now continue our discussion of fallacious reasoning with several fallacies that generally fall into the broad category *invalid inference.*

1. HASTY CONCLUSION

The fallacy of **hasty conclusion** is committed when we draw a conclusion from relevant but insufficient evidence. This fallacy is committed in many different ways and circumstances, ranging from judging political candidates primarily on the basis of 30-second TV commercials to concluding that a neighbor is having an affair on the basis of one or two suspicious clues.

Of course, if we mere human beings were as lucky as Hercule Poirot or Miss Marple, or the other famous fictional detectives, our overly hasty conclusions would frequently turn out to be correct. Here, for example, is the archetype of the great fictional detective, Sherlock Holmes, making one of his amazing "deductions" when first introduced to Dr. Watson in Sir Arthur Conan Doyle's *A Study in Scarlet:*

> Here is a gentleman of the medical type, but with the air of a military man. Clearly an army doctor, then. He has just come from the tropics, for his face is dark, and that is not the natural tint of his skin, for his wrists are fair. He has undergone hardship and sickness, as his haggard face says clearly. His left arm has been injured. He holds it in a still and unnatural manner. Where in the tropics could an English army doctor have seen much hardship and gotten his arm wounded? Clearly in Afghanistan.

What Holmes observed about Watson was consistent with all sorts of other possibilities that in real life might have been actualities. Doctors don't look that much different from other professionals. Some men with a military air (whatever that might be) never have been in the military. Among Englishmen in those days, when Britain ruled the waves, naval military men were just as common as army types. Tanned faces can result from exposure to nontropical sunlight. A still and unnatural arm carriage may be the legacy of a childhood accident, a haggard expression due to anguish at the loss of a close relative. And even supposing the person in question were a military man who had been wounded in battle in Afghanistan, he still might just have come from a funeral in Italy, South Africa, Brighton, or Timbuktu. The conclusion drawn by Holmes may have been a good guess, but stated with the typical Holmes air of infallibility, it surely was hasty.

Fallacies are endemic to political campaigns, and hasty conclusions are no exception. During the 2008 presidential primaries, Hillary Clinton, usually very controlled in public, teared up when asked a personal question about how the rigors of campaigning affected her, and that was enough for one blogger to comment, "If she is breaking down now [before being elected] . . . then how will she act under pressure as president?" The implied conclusion that she would crack under pressure as president is hasty indeed (not to mention a sexist stereotype), particularly in light of the steely emotional control she invariably exhibits in public.

2. SMALL SAMPLE

Statistics frequently are used to project from a sample to the "population" from which it was drawn. This is the basic technique that underlies several kinds of inductive reasoning and is the method employed by most polls—including those conducted by Gallup, Harris, and the Nielsen television ratings. But when we accept a conclusion based on a sample that is too small to be a reliable measure of the population from which it was drawn, we are guilty of the fallacy of the **small sample,** a variety of the fallacy *hasty conclusion.* No sample of 100 to 500 voters, for instance, can possibly be depended on to accurately reflect the entire voting population of the United States.

Scientists, of all people, aren't supposed to commit statistical fallacies (or any fallacies, for that matter), but they're human. In an interesting, one might say comical, example, researchers drew a conclusion about the mating vocal responses of primate species based on a sample of three human couples (each observed engaged in sex exactly once), a pair of gibbons, and one troop of chacma baboons.

The general question as to when a sample is sufficiently large is extremely difficult to answer and is a matter of great interest to statisticians and other scientists. Obviously, though, all other things being equal, the larger the percentage of a population from which a sample is drawn, the more confident we can be that it reflects that population as a whole.

3. UNREPRESENTATIVE SAMPLE

In addition to being large enough, a good sample should be *representative* of the population from which it is drawn. Indeed, the more representative a sample is, the smaller it needs to be to be significant. When we reason from a sample that isn't sufficiently representative, we commit the fallacy of the **unrepresentative sample** (sometimes called

Sample size does not overcome sample bias.

—Saying popular among statisticians

the fallacy of **biased statistics,** although that name also applies to cases where known statistics that are unfavorable to a theory are deliberately suppressed).

The example just mentioned, about primate mating responses, illustrates the fallacy of the unrepresentative sample as well as that of the small sample. For one thing, only three of the dozens of primate species were checked—chimps, gorillas, lemurs, tarsiers, and so forth, may be quite different. (In fact, orangutans turn out to be much different from all other primates in their sex practices.) For another, there is plenty of reason to believe that no sample of three human couples could possibly be representative of all *Homo sapiens,* given the tremendous variety of sex practices engaged in by members of our species.

As usual, relevant background information is crucial when we try to determine whether a sample is likely to be representative of the population from which it was drawn (or is likely to be sufficiently large, for that matter). Good reasoning *always* requires good background information.

4. QUESTIONABLE CAUSE

We commit the fallacy of **questionable cause** when we label something as the cause of something else on the basis of insufficient or unrepresentative evidence, or when doing so contradicts well-established, high-level theories.[1] (Questionable cause is a broader version of the traditional fallacy *post hoc, ergo propter hoc,* literally "after this, therefore because of this." Note that the fallacy questionable cause often overlaps that of hasty conclusion or of small sample.)

As just mentioned, it isn't easy to determine whether a sample is sufficiently large or representative. This is true in particular because judgments on these matters often depend on seeing the relevance of background information and *bringing it to bear.* All too often, people make judgments about causal connections on the basis of observed correlations, often quite small, that contradict very general, very well-confirmed, and quite easily understood higher-level theories about what sorts of causes can result in what kinds of effects. People often do so because they lack the relevant and *accurate* background information; sometimes they are motivated by wishful thinking to ignore contrary evidence or theories (a topic to be discussed at some length in the next chapter).

Many people have little or no understanding of the general way in which things work in this world. As they experience life, they don't try to figure out how things work in general or attempt to gain some of the knowledge that has been gleaned over time by

---

[1] This doesn't mean that these higher-level theories are exempt from refutation. Evidence that persistently runs contrary even to the highest-level, most general scientific theories eventually, and sometimes rather swiftly, overturns them, as, for example, old ideas about the motions of continents, and related matters, were overturned by evidence favoring the currently held theory concerning plate tectonics.

The Small Society. Reprinted by permission of the Washington Star Syndicate, Inc.

It isn't always easy to determine what is the cause of what.

others. Instead, they attend almost exclusively to immediate events and problems. They may see science as some kind of magical box from which gadgets like television sets, computers, and jet planes are extracted by bearded drudges with German accents or by youthful nerds. Having relatively little background information to bring to bear on experience, they are unable to assess either the adequacy of evidence or the possibility that a general idea might be true. Think, for instance, of those who believe in ESP despite the failure of every scientific test to confirm it.

Or consider the apparent rise in autism cases that certain groups have blamed on child immunizations, particularly the measles, mumps, and rubella vaccination (MMR).[2] They reason that since the rise in autism cases has coincided with an increase in recommended childhood vaccinations, certain vaccines must be the cause of autism in some children. The MMR immunization, given to toddlers between 15 and 17 months, comes at about the same time that parents begin to observe signs of autism. But this low-level reasoning fails to take into account the fact that autism typically begins to emerge at the end of the second year, whether the child is immunized or not, as rigorous scientific studies have shown. Yet the coincidental occurrences of autism at the time the vaccine is given, plus the media coverage of the plight of autistic children, have persuaded many people that vaccinations are the cause.

For many people economics is just as baffling as the hard sciences. Critics were inclined to blame the second President Bush for the downturn in the economy during his last year in office. But the fact that the country slid into a recession during his last year doesn't prove that his policies caused the economy to slow down. True, his administration sank billions of dollars into the Iraq War, but wars tend to stimulate the economy in the short run. (The long run is another matter, as future generations will discover when the burden falls on them). The reasons are more complex, and economists are still

---

[2]For more on this see *The Age of American Unreason* (New York: Pantheon Press, 2008), by Susan Jacoby, pp. 219–220, and more specifically, "A Population-Based Study of Measles, Mumps, and Rubella Vaccination and Autism," by Kreesten Madsen, et al., *New England Journal of Medicine, 347,* November 7, 2002.

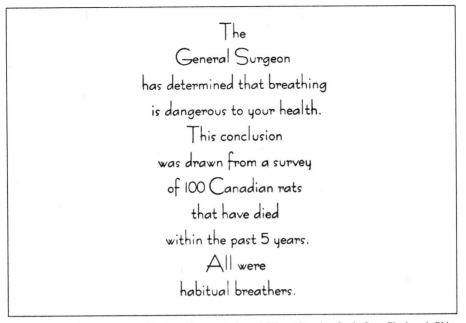

The
General Surgeon
has determined that breathing
is dangerous to your health.
This conclusion
was drawn from a survey
of 100 Canadian rats
that have died
within the past 5 years.
All were
habitual breathers.

Greeting card humor illustrating some fallacy or other, no doubt.

sorting them out, but one cause was certainly the crash of the bloated housing market. When the housing bubble burst in 2007, inflated real estate sank like a stone, home foreclosures skyrocketed, the stock market skittered around, and the nation's largest financial institutions teetered on the brink of bankruptcy as they looked for bailouts from the government. But President Bush did not cause the chain reaction. Although his administration certainly contributed to it by reducing government oversight of the financial industry, the groundwork was laid by previous administrations that deregulated financial markets over a period of thirty years, allowing an unregulated shadow banking system of hedge funds and investment banks to evolve, bypassing the safety regulations imposed on traditional banks, and thus paving the way for the credit crisis in 2008.

In hindsight, the bust after the boom now seems inevitable, but the housing debacle was only one reason for the downturn. The economic well-being of the United States depends on many complex factors, here and around the world, that a president does not and cannot control. This doesn't mean that by promoting unsound economic policies a president cannot be a part of the cause of an economic downturn. The point is that it is simplistic to give him the lion's share of the blame without further argument.

The fallacy questionable cause also sometimes is committed because items are incorrectly classified—poorly sorted into different kinds. Any items, no matter how different from one another, have some things in common, so that there always is some reason for grouping them together in our thoughts. When we classify items to discover cause/effect relationships, we need to make sure we have bunched together just the right sorts of cases. In some areas of the United States, for instance, a larger percentage of nonwhite children do poorly in school compared to students who are white, a fact that has led some people to conclude that being nonwhite is the *cause* of their doing less well in school (that there is a genetic difference involved here), an interesting and very serious example of the fallacy questionable cause.[3]

Issue campaigns often lapse into hasty conclusions based on questionable causes that support their platforms. In 2006 the Brady campaign, the group behind the Brady Law requiring background checks for handgun owners, claimed that "gun laws work." As evidence they cited the decline in violent crimes since the Brady Law passed in 1993 and the ban on assault weapons in 1994. But arguing that gun laws caused the decline fails to take into account other factors, like increased police protection and community watch programs. In fact, the Committee on Law and Justice of the National Research Council could find no "causal relationship between the ownership of firearms and the causes or prevention of criminal violence."[4]

As might be expected, the statistical variety of questionable cause, in which a mere statistical correlation is taken to provide proof of a causal connection, is quite common. It's true that every statistical correlation has some significance and, in the absence of reasons to the contrary, increases the likelihood (probability), however slightly, that there also is a causal connection between the things correlated. But when there are reasons to the contrary, or when the statistical sample in question is too small or unrepresentative, we make a mistake in jumping to the conclusion that we've found a causal connection.

Sometimes alleged causal connections based on statistical surveys are too silly to take seriously, because they are so obviously contrary to well-supported background beliefs. An example is the theory that smoking marijuana causes college students to get better grades, based on one dubious statistical study in which marijuana smokers averaged slightly higher grades than nonsmokers. This theory actually gained modest acceptance in some, ah, . . . "high"-minded circles during the 1970s. (And what are the background beliefs that should make you doubt smoking dope causes an increase in grades?)

It's often very hard, if not impossible, for the layperson to evaluate statistical claims on complicated or technical subjects. Sometimes, the best that nonexperts can do is try to find the best professional advice they can. But sometimes they can evaluate these claims by employing the method described in the following excerpt from a *Psychology Today* article on statistical reasoning:

> *"What do the other three cells look like?"* This slogan should always be invoked to assess covariation [the statistical connection] of events. . . . To determine the effectiveness of chiropractic treatment, for example, one needs numbers from

---

[3]Notice that in the United States, nonwhite is an ethnic, not a racial, category. Most Americans who think of themselves as African American are racially both of white (European) and African American (African) descent; a few are of African and Asian stock; and a very few are descended from European, African, and Asian forebears (Tiger Woods being a well-known example). Similar remarks apply to members of many other groups. Mexican Americans, for example, tend to be descended from European (chiefly Spanish) and Asian forebears. Interestingly, the exact or even approximate place of origin of the Asian peoples who originally populated Mexico is hotly disputed by anthropologists and other scientists.
[4]Example taken from *unSpun, Finding Facts in a World of Disinformation,* an excellent and lively guide to unraveling deception in politics and advertising, by Brooks Jackson and Kathleen Hall Jamieson.

four "cells." How many people were cured after being treated by a chiropractor? How many were not cured after such treatment? How many people got better without treatment? How many didn't get better and went untreated?

Most of us are impressed when we see first cell statistics and fail to realize that we usually need to know about one or more of the others to determine whether we've found a causal connection or just a statistical one. Reading, say, that about two-thirds of those treated by chiropractors get better proves nothing about the effectiveness of chiropractors; it may be that two-thirds of those with similar complaints who were not so treated also got well, or even that three-quarters did (in which case we would have some evidence that chiropractors harm patients more than they help them.)

5. Questionable Analogy

We reason by *analogy* when we conclude from the observed similarity of two or more items in some respects to their similarity in another.[5] Sports fans, for example, reasoned by analogy when they concluded that the 2008 Olympic Games would be fun to watch, given that they were in previous years. Caffeine lovers do so when they reason from the fact that coffee has kept them awake several nights in a row to the conclusion that drinking it again tonight will keep them awake.[6] The general form of such reasoning is that the items mentioned are alike in certain respects, so they will be alike in some other way.

But we aren't always justified in reasoning by analogy. When we do so anyway, we are guilty of the fallacy of **questionable analogy,** sometimes referred to as **faulty comparison.**

Analogical reasoning can be fallacious for several different reasons. The sample on which it is based may be too small or not sufficiently representative, it may conflict with conclusions drawn by higher-level reasoning, or there may be a lack of relevant similarity between the items implied to be alike. Here is an example based on a much too small sample:

> I've won at blackjack twice in a row by drawing a card when holding cards totaling 18, so I conclude by analogy that I'll win next time I draw on 18.

This analogy also is defective because it ignores the higher-level theory of probability, which says that your chances of success when drawing on 18 are quite low.

Some analogies seem to be apt on the surface but collapse under closer scrutiny. For instance, in an op-ed article for the *New York Times* (January 1, 2007), the historian Arthur Schlesinger, Jr., used this analogy to illustrate the folly of ignoring the lessons of the past: "As persons deprived of memory become disoriented and lost, not knowing where they have been and where they are going, so a nation denied a conception of the past will be disabled in dealing with its present and its future." Although both examples deal with a loss of past experience, the first involves forgetting all experience,

---

[5]Analogical reasoning thus is very similar to induction by enumeration. Indeed, the latter can be thought of as a kind of analogical reasoning.

[6]Recall, though, the earlier discussion of the fallacy questionable cause. It isn't easy to be positive that it's the coffee keeping us awake.

as Alzheimer's patients do, but the second involves ignoring past experience—quite a different phenomenon.

In some cases, the analogy is so wide of the mark that its questionable nature should be obvious. For example, after the prisoner abuse scandal at the Abu Ghraib prison, Saudi Arabian Daud al-Shiryan was quoted in the media saying, "This will increase the hatred of America, not just in Iraq but abroad. . . . Abu Ghraib was used for torture in Saddam's time. People will ask now what's the difference between Saddam and Bush. Nothing!" President Bush didn't authorize the prison abuse, to begin with, and the abuse that did occur, though bad enough in its own right, was in no way comparable to the torture and killing that went on under Hussein.

Not uncommonly, questionable analogies surface in a court of law. In 2003 many American tourists were annoyed to discover that credit card companies were charging a currency conversion fee for items purchased abroad. One irate customer filed suit against Visa and MasterCard for intentionally hiding the fee from cardholders. (It only appears—occasionally—in cardholder agreements, buried in legal jargon.) The attorney for MasterCard argued, "That's not hiding, that's not concealing—that's how business is done in this country." The defense went on to explain that "while consumers naturally understand that commercial suppliers of goods and services impose a mark-up over their costs, the proposed decision would condemn as 'embedding' the standard practice that a seller tells its customer its price to them, not which part of the price reflects its cost and which part its mark-up." However, to compare hidden credit card fees to the undisclosed markup of commercial goods is certainly questionable. The consumer knows the cost of an item in a retail store because it is clearly marked on the price tag, but when using a credit card abroad, the consumer has no idea of the total amount because of the hidden conversion fee.

Some analogies are easily seen to be fallacious, others as clearly apt. But the evaluations of still others often require a good deal of thought. Consider this analogy in a letter to the editor arguing against stricter handgun control laws: When a drunk driver runs over a child, we go after the driver, not the car. When someone kills a child with a gun, we go after the gun. But shouldn't we go after the person who murders with a gun, not the gun itself? In this case, there clearly is a relevant resemblance between the two cases—killing with a car or with a gun—so there is something to the analogy. But there also are important differences, as there often are, and the question is whether they are both relevant and sufficient to make the analogy questionable. For example, private autos are an extremely important kind of transportation in our society; banning their use would dramatically change all sorts of things in everyday life. Handguns serve few legitimate purposes in private hands; AK-47s and the like, none at all; restricting their use would make relatively little difference in most of our lives. Furthermore, most auto deaths result from accidents or negligence, rarely from deliberate intent to murder. Guns frequently are used deliberately to murder other people. Note that the letter writer omits the fact that, when people use guns for nefarious purposes, we go after the gun user as well as the gun itself, and also the fact that we outlaw autos believed to be unsafe to drive. The point of all of this is that we don't want to label analogies questionable, or apt, too quickly; in some cases we need to consider all sorts of factors. Good critical reasoners need to become adept at bringing background information to bear when evaluating analogies, just as most other sorts of reasoning.

This example also illustrates the difficulty in bringing one's relevant background beliefs to bear when evaluating an argument. All of the relevant differences just mentioned are common knowledge, yet we all often fail to bring information of this kind to bear when evaluating an argument. (Did you in this case?)

Before turning to a discussion of other fallacies, perhaps it should be noted that we need to distinguish between *explanatory* analogies used to explain and *argumentative* analogies used to prove a point. When we argue or reason analogically, we present evidence for a conclusion; when we use an analogy to explain, we merely liken the thing explained to something already familiar. In Plato's famous analogy of the cave, for example, the people in the cave who merely see the shadows of things are likened to those who restrict themselves to the ever-changing world of everyday experience, while the people who come out into the sunlight and see the objects themselves are likened to the philosophers who reason to the unchanging reality that lies behind everyday experiences. The analogy explains Plato's ideas about a world beyond that of mere everyday experiences, but it doesn't prove that there is such a world or in any way argue that there is. (Plato himself very likely intended his cave myth to be explanatory, not argumentative, but it often is construed otherwise.)

The point here is that we shouldn't accuse those whose analogies are intended to explain of being guilty of the fallacy questionable analogy. (They may, of course, serve very poorly to explain, but that is another matter.) Anyway, as just remarked, explanatory analogies sometimes are mistakenly taken to prove what they merely explain, and in this case we are indeed justified in accusing those who do this of the fallacy questionable analogy.

Finally, we need to notice that in everyday life it often is difficult to determine whether an analogy is intended to explain or to prove; no doubt some are intended to serve both purposes. In any case, as with explanations in general, it is hard to separate the mere explanatory nature of an analogy from its power to persuade. (Recall, for example, the salesperson's explanation about cameras in Chapter 1, where the intent was to persuade a customer to buy a camera, not merely to explain the differences between one set and another.)

6. QUESTIONABLE STATISTICS

Statistics always seem so precise and *authoritative*. It sounds so much more believable, for instance, to claim that the typical child watches an average of 4,286 acts of violence on TV by age 18 rather than just that kids typically watch an awful lot of TV violence. But how could anyone know such an exact fact? There would have to be a lot of guesswork and extrapolation from very small samples to arrive even at an informed rough estimate as to these sorts of matters. This doesn't mean that we ought simply to dismiss these statistics; it just means that we have to understand their limitations.

Statistics on the state of the economy are a case in point. Take the ones published by the federal government on business conditions in the United States. One of the major problems with these statistics is that their *margin of error* (not always provided) often is greater than the "significant" differences they report. This becomes evident when we consider that the government's later revisions of its own figures often reflect a change larger than the alleged margin of error.

In addition, problems arise from the need to use a base year in determining long-run trends. Those who want to show that a given year has had a high rate of growth can choose a low base year; those intent on proving a low rate of growth, a high base year. Meanwhile, the precisely true rate of growth may remain in doubt.

In the case of figures concerning the gross national product, we have several other reasons for being suspicious. One is that a good deal of commerce in the United States today is illegal. Think only of racketeering, gambling, drug traffic, prostitution, and the hiring of illegal aliens to do migrant farm labor or household cleaning and other low-paying, tedious, and often backbreaking jobs. Reliable statistics concerning illegal activities are by their nature hard to come by. Calculating, say, the commerce in illegal drugs has to be done indirectly, by reference to the sale of legal drug equipment, drug busts, and so on. Another reason for suspicion is that a good deal of otherwise legal commerce is done "off the books," so that no taxes need to be paid or so that restrictive laws can be avoided. How are we to assess the value of goods when one kind is bartered for another?

Statistics on corrupt activities are just as hard to come by, particularly in a country like Russia, where corruption is endemic, and bribery is the norm rather than the exception (Russians shell out bribes for all manner of things, from paying off traffic cops to getting better medical treatment.) So when Transparency International, a group monitoring corruption, estimated that corruption in Russia had grown sevenfold from 2001–2006 or that the value of bribes paid to bureaucrats was almost equal to the country's revenue in a given year, we have to assume that these are little more than guess-timates. The same goes for estimates made by INDEM, an independent Russian think tank, that businesses in Russia spend 7 percent of their budget on bribes.[7] How is it possible to come up with these statistics when bribery, by its very nature, usually occurs under the table?

Sometimes statistics are based on soft information and are thus questionable. For years doctors have urged us to reduce our intake of fatty foods, but a 2006 study funded by the Women's Health Initiative (WHI) seemed to contradict this advice. The study— following 48,835 women aged 50–79 for an average of 8.1 years—revealed no significant statistical difference in the rates of colorectal cancer, heart disease, or stroke between the group on the low-fat diet and the comparison group on the normal diet. But the study was problematic because the data were drawn from the participants' memories of what they ate—sometimes up to a year earlier! (Do you remember what you ate last week, let alone a year ago?) Evidence that their memories were unreliable becomes clearer when we consider this finding: Women who weighed 170 pounds on average claimed they consumed 1,700 calories a day at the beginning of the study and 1,500 calories at the end. Yet these women lost only 1 pound over many years in the WHI study.[8] How could that be? Either their memories were faulty or they were shaving off calories. More likely, they consumed 500–700 more calories a day than they reported. Given the apparent unreliability of these reports, it is questionable that low-fat diets fail to protect women from certain illnesses. No matter, this dubious science made headlines and probably allowed many women to rationalize eating the fatty foods they craved.

---

[7]See "Bribery Thrives as Big Business in Putin's Russia," by Michael Mainville, *San Francisco Chronicle,* January 2, 2007.

[8]For more on this see NIH News, "News from the Women's Heath Initiative," March 15 2006, www .nih.gov; and "Down to a Science," by Carol Ness, *San Francisco Chronicle,* March 16, 2006.

The government's figures on unemployment also need to be viewed with a good deal of suspicion. These figures are calculated partly on the basis of information gathered via polls of "representative" individuals. How these people respond depends on the precise wording of the questions they are asked (a point soon to be discussed further), and this in part depends on what the government considers to be full-time, compared to part-time, employment and who is said to be seeking employment, compared to those who have given up the search. (It also depends on how truly representative the government's samples happen to be.) Early in 2008, for instance, the Bush administration was upbeat about the low unemployment rate of 4.9 percent, pretty good considering that the country was sliding into a recession. A closer look, though, revealed that long-term unemployment of six months or more rose to 18.3 percent—a more accurate and ominous indicator of the serious economic downturn. The hundreds of thousands of people out of work for 27 weeks or more were not included in the unemployment rate of 4.9 because they had not applied for work in the four weeks preceding the survey.

All of this certainly does not mean that government statistics on commerce and employment should be tossed into the nearest wastebasket. But it does mean that precise official figures should be taken for what they are: the best *approximations* we have of business activity—valuable primarily in showing very-long-term trends, but often calculated so as to serve short-term political interests.

By way of contrast, consider a correctly cautious claim typical of those frequently made by scientists (*Science News,* January 19, 1991): Scientists using sophisticated techniques to determine the age of ancient cliff drawings in west Texas estimated that the drawings were painted "3,865 years ago, *give or take a century*" (italics added).

Finally, it's important to have some idea as to which sorts of statistics can be known, even in theory. Some statistics simply are unknowable, at least by human beings. How, for instance, could Dr. Dean Edell (whose TV and radio programs usually provide excellent information about health and medical matters) know that the average person tells 13 lies per week, as he stated on one of his programs? How could anyone know? Anyway, here is a letter one of the authors of this text received several years ago that contains examples of unknowable statistics it would be hard to top:

> Dear Friend: In the past 5,000 years men have fought in 14,523 wars. One out of four persons living during this time have been war casualties. A nuclear war would add 1,245,000,000 men, women, and children to this tragic list.

It's ludicrous to present such precise figures as facts. No one knows (or could know) the exact number of wars fought so far, to say nothing of the number of war casualties. (Does anyone even know the true casualty rates just for all of the wars that have occurred in the past ten years?) As for the numbers in a nuclear conflict, the casualty rate would depend on who fought such a war, and, in any event, it is a matter on which even so-called experts can only engage in the wildest sorts of speculations.

7. QUESTIONABLE USES OF GOOD STATISTICS

As we've just seen, statistics that are obviously questionable are a problem. But perfectly good statistics also can cause trouble—for two reasons. The first is the inability of so many people to understand the significance of this statistic or that, made worse by the natural tendency in all of us to pay attention to statistics that support conclusions we already have drawn. The second is the ability of charlatans to bamboozle the rest of us via cleverly employed statistics. (That's the import of the old saying that figures don't lie, but liars figure.)

The ways in which we confuse ourselves seem to be limitless. HMO lobbyists helped us do this, for example, when they tried to dissuade members of Congress from regulating HMOs through patients' rights bills. They cited statistics from polls conducted by the American Association of Health Plans (AAHP)—the main HMO trade association—revealing that most Americans were satisfied with their managed care plans. In one sense, then, the AAHP and their lobbyists were right. A large majority of Americans have historically claimed to be satisfied with the health care they receive from their insurance providers, including HMOs.

But the AAHP suppressed all sorts of relevant facts that point to a different conclusion, including statistics from other polls. To start with, a 1999 CBS poll found that only 69 percent of those insured by HMOs were satisfied with their health care compared to 86 percent of those insured by more traditional fee-for-services plans. In addition, more specific surveys reveal far greater dissatisfaction with HMO care. A 1998 Kaiser Family Foundation/Harvard University poll found that 53 percent of the public said that, in general, HMOs made it harder than traditional plans to get care, as compared to only 29 percent who said it was easier, and that 62 percent claimed HMOs made it more difficult to see medical specialists, with only 23 percent saying it has become easier. Similarly, a 1998 CNN/Time poll found that 43 percent of those interviewed believe health-care coverage had gotten worse during the previous five years (when HMOs made big inroads into the health-care market), with only 18 percent saying it had improved. This poll also found that 64 percent of respondents believe health-care costs have increased, only 11 percent that they have decreased.

We also need to notice that the AAHP lobbyists neglected the obvious thought that it isn't surprising a majority of Americans are satisfied with their health plans, given that at any particular time most of us are not experiencing serious health problems. A more relevant statistic would be one concerning what percentage of those who have had serious health problems are satisfied or dissatisfied with HMO coverage as compared to the more traditional fee-for-service plans still offered, say, by some Blue Cross/Blue Shield organizations. (Of course, as usual, those lacking relevant background information, even of the kind that might lead them to suspect that the AAHP might be concealing relevant facts, are fair game easily taken in by sharp operators.[9])

The misuse of statistics is just as common in economics as it is in medicine. For instance, a libertarian defending the current economy on a radio talk show claimed that less than 10 percent of Americans used to own stocks, but now up to 45 to 50 percent do. Thus, an ordinary wage earner who saves can take part in the increase in wealth the stock market provides. Although his figures are about right, he neglects two important points. First, the 45 to 50 percent includes retirement funds invested by companies, not individuals—the ordinary earner simply draws a pension from the invested fund. Second, a tiny portion of stockholders own most of the stock and get rich, and the gap between the rich and the rest of us has been getting a good deal larger.

---

[9]For more information on this topic, see, for instance, *American Prospect,* December 20, 1999 issue.

Going onto another topic, the Death Penalty Information Center indicated that from 1990 to 2006 the murder rate was higher in states with the death penalty than in those without it. Those opposed to the death penalty on grounds that it does not deter homicides take this to be evidence supporting that conclusion.

But sophisticated critical reasoners wondered whether doing so made them guilty of the fallacy questionable cause (or perhaps hasty conclusion?). For it very well may be that states with death penalties had a higher rate of murder to start with and that perhaps they opted for this harsh penalty to try to reduce the amount of serious crime. To prove their point, those opposed to the death penalty on these grounds would have to present statistics showing that serious crime remained the same, or increased, after a death penalty was imposed in particular states. Otherwise, the comparison is of apples and oranges. (Remember that the number of serious crimes tends to increase in hard economic times and decreases in good.)

8. Polls: An Important Special Case

A well-conceived and well-executed poll can be a fruitful way to find out all sorts of things, from the voter strength of a political candidate to Fido's preferences in dog food. Unfortunately, not all polls are created equal.

One problem is that the way in which a question is asked seriously influences the answers one can expect. It is extremely difficult, if not impossible, to word a question in a way that is completely neutral. At the height of the Watergate scandal, for instance, a Gallup poll asked the question

> Do you think President Nixon should be impeached and compelled to leave the presidency, or not?

Thirty percent said yes. But a Pat Caddell private poll asked the question this way:

> Do you think the President should be tried, and removed from office if found guilty?

Fifty-seven percent answered yes to that one. So 30 percent answered yes to the question worded one way, 57 percent when the same question was put another way.

Information left out of questions can skew poll results enormously. Here, for example, are two different questions on late-term abortion that had radically different responses.[10]

Statistics seem to baffle almost everyone. Several years ago, when 200 educators were asked what percentage of children read at grade level or below, 78 percent failed to provide the correct answer—50 percent. Even teachers have a hard time keeping straight on the difference between comparative and absolute scales.

Another comparative rating that causes confusion is the IQ rating: Half of those who take the test must be rated at 100 or below, given that 100 merely marks the halfway point in results.

---

[10]Quoted in "Framing the Abortion Issue," *Extra!,* July/August 2007.

Cartoon by Tom Meyer © *San Francisco Chronicle*. Reprinted by permission.

An ABC poll asked "Do you think the late-term abortion procedure known as dilation and extraction, or partial birth abortion, should be legal or illegal?" Sixty-two percent said "illegal." But a follow-up question was asked, adding additional information. "What if it would prevent a serious threat to the woman's health?" Only 33 percent responded "illegal" to this question.

The importance of framing the issue has not escaped those intent on skewing poll results one way or the other. Here, for example, are a couple of loaded question in the "2000 Official NRA Gun Owners Survey":

> Do you think gun owner names should be subject to surprise inspection by the Bureau of Alcohol, Tobacco, and Firearms?

> Do you think gun owners like you should be required to pay expensive liability insurance for every gun you own?

What gun owners in their right minds would answer *no* to these questions?

Of course, when it comes to slanted poll questions, the Democratic and Republican Parties take a back seat to no one. Here is an example from the 1999 mailings conducted by the Democratic National Committee of the Democratic Party:

> Should the projected budget surplus be used to support tax cuts that are weighed more heavily toward the rich?

What voters, other than the very rich, would answer yes to this question?

Many surveys ask biased questions to make something seem more popular than in fact it is, because of the "bandwagon" effect of being popular (discussed in the next chapter). An egregious example surfaced during the antitrust trial in 1999 against Microsoft Corporation when the government accused the company of chicanery in Microsoft's attempt to make Bill Gates look good in a Senate hearing in 1998. A Microsoft witness, Richard Schmalansee, cited a survey of independent software vendors who overwhelmingly agreed that Microsoft should hard-wire its web-browsing software directly into its Windows operating system. But the government's lead counsel, David Boies, brought out under cross-examination that the poll was the brainchild of Microsoft's top technologist, Nathan Myhrvold, in response to the following request from Bill Gates: "It would HELP ME IMMENSELY to have a survey showing that 90 percent of developers believe that putting the browser into the (operating system) makes sense" (February 14, 1998).

The next day Myhrvold replied by e-mail: "I think that it is crucial to make [sure] the statement we ask people about in the survey . . . is worded properly. Saying 'put the browser in the [Windows operating system]' is already a statement that is prejudicial to us. The name 'browser' suggests a separate thing." Instead, Myhrvold decided on "a more neutral question about how internet technology needs to merge with local computing." (The issue of integration is central to the charges brought against Microsoft by the Department of Justice and 19 states.) Had the survey questions not been manipulated to elicit the desired response, the software vendors might have answered differently.

And poll results can be twisted to distort the findings. For example, at one point in the run-up to the 2008 presidential primaries, 53 percent of Republican voters rated Rudy Giuliani as the strongest leader in a poll conducted by the *Washington Post*. But political opponents could have undermined Giuliani by claiming that 47 percent of the voters didn't think he was a strong leader. Sometimes polls are only as trustworthy as the people who interpret them.

The biggest problem with polls, though, is the difficulty of tapping a truly representative sample. The 1936 *Literary Digest* poll, based on names lifted from telephone directories and auto registration lists, is perhaps the most famous example of an extremely biased poll. It predicted that Alf Landon would defeat Franklin Roosevelt, while the actual result was a tremendous landslide for Roosevelt. The magazine (which went out of business shortly afterward—questionable cause?) failed to take into account the fact that few people in the bottom half of the American population had telephones or autos in those days, so that their sample was completely unrepresentative of American voters.

Of course, the art of polling has come a long way since 1936, or even 1948, when polls predicted an easy victory for Thomas E. Dewey over Harry Truman. The *Chicago Tribune*—whose motto, incidentally, was and still is "The World's Greatest Newspaper"—was so sure Dewey would win that it grossly misinterpreted early returns and printed one of the most infamous headlines in newspaper history—"Dewey Defeats Truman"—which an exultant Truman held up to the crowd at his victory celebration.

But it still is difficult to get a representative sample of the voting population by polling only 1,500 or so potential voters—the standard practice today. In theory, a very carefully selected sample of roughly this size should be almost as reliable as one of 15,000 (a poll of this size would be much too expensive and is never conducted). But in practice, for all sorts of reasons, things frequently don't work as planned. This doesn't mean that we should not pay attention to polls. They often are the best or even the only way we have of testing the water. It just means we have to pay heed to them in an intelligent manner. A presidential election poll taken in September is of much less value, other things being equal, than one conducted in October; polls paid for by one side or the other are worth less than those conducted by truly independent organizations. But most important, we have to remember that even the best polls have a batting average well below 100 percent.

As recently as 2008, the polls in the New Hampshire primary got it wrong when they had Barack Obama ahead of Hillary Clinton by a comfortable margin of 8 percent right up to the election. But Clinton beat Obama by 12 points. Apparently the polling methodology was sound because John McCain's victory was accurately predicted almost to the exact percentage in the Republican primary. In the Democratic primary, though, it seemed the polls did not sufficiently take into account the fact that poorer, less well-educated white voters are less likely to participate in surveys than whites who are better off financially and better educated. Although samples are usually adjusted to offset this tendency, the polls did not adequately factor in the added variable that the whites who don't take part in surveys tend to have more negative feelings about blacks than those who do. Sometimes polling is such a complicated affair that even pollsters with the most refined methodologies get it wrong. They got it right for the election, though, when they accurately predicted Barack Obama's victory.

Note, by the way, that there is no such thing as a "poll fallacy," even though, as just illustrated, polls do give rise to fallacies such as questionable statistics and hasty conclusions.

9. FALSE CHARGE OF FALLACY

It often is all too easy to charge others with fallacious reasoning. This is particularly true when people change their minds and embrace positions they previously denied. The temptation is to charge them with the fallacy of inconsistency. But making a given statement at one time and one that contradicts it at a later time does not necessarily indicate inconsistency; we may have, and express, good grounds for changing our minds.

Take the person who says, "I used to believe that women are not as creative as men, because most of the intellectually productive people I knew about were men; but I've changed my mind, because I believe now (as I didn't then) that environment (culture, surroundings), not native ability, has been responsible for the preponderance of intellectual men." Surely, that person cannot be accused of the fallacy of inconsistency, since he (or she!) has explained the change of mind.

Anyway, in good textbook style, let's say that those who falsely accuse others of fallacy are themselves guilty of making a **false charge of fallacy.**

Of course, falsely accusing someone of inconsistency is not the only way in which someone might be guilty of false charge of fallacy. Recall, for example, the earlier discussion of the distinction between analogical reasoning and explanatory analogies;

clearly, we are guilty of making a false charge of fallacy if we accuse someone of perpetrating a questionable analogy when his or her intent is not to prove something but merely, via an analogy, to explain it.

We are also guilty of falsely charging someone with a fallacy when we take literally an ironic jab at the opposition. In the following letter to the editor, for example, the writer clearly intends to be ironic:

> Billions of dollars and two decades later, the War on Drugs has successfully eliminated illegal drugs from the face of America. The country is finally free of pot, coke, and heroin. With this as a model, the War on Junk Guns is bound to be successful.

Claiming that the writer is guilty of questionable premise or suppressed evidence because the War on Drugs hasn't eradicated illegal drugs clearly constitutes a false charge of fallacy. The letter writer just employs sarcasm to remind us ironically that the War on Drugs has been a failure.

Note, by the way, that some of the alleged fallacies that have been discussed in logic textbooks since time immemorial are not generally fallacious, at least according to the criteria set up in this text. Take the fallacy called *appeal to force* (traditional name: *argumentum ad baculum*), committed, it is said, when a conclusion is accepted after a threat of force of one kind or another. Lawmakers, for instance, sometimes are charged with commission of this fallacy when they are convinced to vote a certain way by the implied threats of lobbyists to stop the flow of campaign contributions.

But legislators whose arms are twisted in this way generally are not guilty of a fallacy—the arm twisting doesn't convince them of the merits or demerits of particular legislation but rather of the personal (career) benefits to be gained by voting as lobbyists "suggest" they should. We need to know here, though, that self-interest frequently motivates people, lawmakers included, to believe what they otherwise would see to be false. More is said in Chapter 6 about the power of self-interest to influence beliefs.

Exercise item from the second edition of a certain textbook on logic and contemporary rhetoric:

Newspaper story: Thor Heyerdahl has done it again, crossing the Atlantic in a papyrus raft designed according to ancient Egyptian tomb carvings. Landing in the Western Hemisphere on the island of Barbados, he was greeted by the Barbados prime minister, Errol Barrow, who declared, "This has established Barbados was the first landing place for man in the Western World."

This was a very un-PC remark by Barrow, but that is not the point here. The point is that the correct answer to this exercise item was supposed to be hasty conclusion, *but a student from Barbados pointed out that the prime minister was known for his sense of humor. Another false charge of fallacy, this time by the (here nameless) author of the critical reasoning textbook in question.*

Quibbling

When deciding whether someone has or has not committed a fallacy, we don't want to **quibble.** We don't want to take advantage, for instance, of the fact that life is short, and, in everyday life, we don't usually bother to spell out every detail. Some things can, and should, be taken for granted.

Consider the American Medical Association (AMA) ad that stated:

> 100,000 doctors have quit smoking.
> Maybe they know something you don't.

Students have called this ad fallacious because, among other reasons, it suppresses evidence as to what kind of doctors have quit. ("Maybe it was horse doctors." "They don't say if they were doctors of medicine.") But this sort of response amounts to nothing better than quibbling. It resembles the remark of a student who objected to Shakespeare's wonderful line "He jests at scars, that never felt a wound" (*Romeo and Juliet*), on grounds that *he* (the student) had felt a wound—a mere scratch—and still jested at scars. (Other students have objected to the line on the grounds that Shakespeare incorrectly used *that* instead of *who,* but they [the students!] were guilty of another, grammatical sort of quibbling—to say nothing of hubris, in having the temerity to "correct" the grammar of someone who may well be the greatest writer to ever work in the English language.)

This (finally!) concludes our discussion of fallacies, unfortunately restricted to just a few of the more common varieties that have been discussed in one place or another in the literature. While it is useful to become adept at aptly applying specific names to cases of fallacious reasoning, the point of acquiring this skill, after all, is to learn how to improve one's own reasoning and to be better able to spot the fallacious reasoning of others. Remember, though, that what counts is not the ability to apply a label to poor reasoning. Labels certainly are useful in getting adept at spotting bad arguments, but seeing that they are bad and understanding why they are bad is the name of the game.

In any case, we will soon see that spotting fallacies is only part of the larger enterprise of evaluating more complicated passages containing related arguments that are intended to form a coherent whole. *Extended arguments* of this kind—argumentative essays—are discussed in Chapters 8 and 9.

SUMMARY OF CHAPTER 5

1. *Hasty conclusion:* Accepting an argument on the basis of relevant but insufficient information or evidence. *Example:* Sherlock Holmes's conclusion that Dr. Watson was an army man just back from Afghanistan.

2. *Small sample:* Drawing conclusions about a population on the basis of a sample that is too small to be a reliable measure of that population. *Example:* Conclusions drawn about primate mating habits based on a sample of three human couplings, a gibbon mating, and those of one troop of baboons.

3. *Unrepresentative sample:* Reasoning from a sample that is not representative (typical) of the population from which it was drawn. *Example:* The sample of primates just mentioned.

4. *Questionable cause:* Labeling A as the cause of B on evidence that is insufficient, negative, unrepresentative, or in serious conflict with well-established high-level

theories. *Example:* Blaming President Bush for the downturn in the economy when other, more complex factors are at work.

5. *Questionable analogy:* Drawing an analogical conclusion when the cases compared are not relevantly alike. *Example:* Comparing Bush to Hussein in the prisoner abuse scandal at Abu Ghraib.

   Note, by the way, that the quality of statistics sometimes differs a great deal from time to time and place to place.

6. *Questionable statistics:* Employing statistics that are questionable without further support. *Example:* Accepting government statistics on short-term business trends as completely accurate rather than just educated approximations. *Extreme example:* Employing unknowable statistics about how many wars have been fought in the past 5,000 years and how many casualties there have been.

7. *Questionable uses of statistics:* Perfectly good statistics also sometimes are a problem—for two reasons. The first is the inability of so many people to understand the significance of this statistic or that, made worse by the natural tendency in all of us to see statistics as favoring conclusions we already have drawn. The second is the ability of charlatans to bamboozle the rest of us via cleverly employed statistics. *Example:* Accepting evidence that the murder rate in states that have adopted a death penalty for serious crimes is higher than in states that have not done so as proof that the death penalty does not deter crime, without further evidence that this statistical evidence has a causal foundation; it could well be, for example, that states adopting death penalties had even higher murder rates than other states and have adopted a death penalty in an attempt to do something about that unfortunate fact.

8. *Polls:* Although polls are an important source of information, they need to be dealt with cautiously. Polls can be misleading (1) because of the way in which questions are worded—often deliberately, to obtain the desired statistics; (2) because they ask the wrong questions; (3) because respondents don't want to appear ignorant, immoral, odd, or prejudiced; or (4) because they are based on a sample that is too small or unrepresentative. *Example:* The NRA survey asking loaded questions skewed to get negative responses to government control of gun owners.

9. *False charge of fallacy:* Erroneously accusing others of fallacious reasoning. *Example:* Accusing someone of fallacy who has changed his mind about the lack of creativity of women in the light of contrary evidence.

   Note that ironic rhetoric that, if taken literally, would be fallacious, may well not be. Note also that we don't want to be overly critical of the reasoning of others to the point that we are guilty of *quibbling.*

   Some of the alleged fallacies that have been handed down to us in logic textbooks often are not fallacious. For example, legislators who vote so as to satisfy lobbyists are not usually guilty of the fallacy of appeal to force: They become convinced by the implied threats of the lobbyists to vote as "suggested" because of self-interest, not because they change their minds about the merits of the legislation. Sad.

EXERCISE 5-1

1. The National Science Foundation reported that two different polls conducted by telephone two weeks apart came up with much different results on the question of whether Americans support embryonic stem cell research—even through the pollsters used similar methodologies.[11] The Coalition for the Advancement of Medical Research (CAMR) found that nearly 75 percent of Americans supported this type of research, but a poll conducted two weeks later by the United States Conference of Catholic Bishops (USCCB) reported that "48 percent of Americans oppose federal funding of stem cell research that requires destroying human embryos." Only 39 percent approved. Why were the results so different? The answer is in the way the questions were framed.

   CAMR question: I'm going to read you a brief description of embryonic stem cell research, and then get your reaction. Embryonic stem cells are special cells that can develop into every type of cell in the human body. The stem cells are extracted from embryonic cells produced in fertility clinics and then frozen days after fertilization. If a couple decides that the fertilized eggs are no longer needed, they can choose to donate the embryos for research or the clinic will throw the embryos away. Scientists have had success in initial research with embryonic stem cells and believe that they can be developed into cures for diseases such as cancer, Parkinson's, heart disease, juvenile diabetes, and spinal cord injuries. Having heard this description, do you strongly favor, somewhat favor, somewhat oppose, or strongly oppose medical research that uses stem cells from human embryos?

   USCCB question: Stem cells are the basic cells from which all of a person's tissues and organs develop. Congress is considering the question of federal funding for experiments using stem cells from human embryos. The live embryos would be destroyed in their first week of development to obtain these cells. Do you support or oppose using your federal tax dollars for such experiments?

   Evaluate the way the issue is framed in each question and explain how the questions influenced the survey results.

2. Here is a paraphrase of a letter to the editor of the *Nutrition Action Health Letter:*

   I am a diabetic who has found the artificial sweetener NutraSweet to be "a total nightmare." I thought it would be a good substitute for sugar [diabetics have to severely limit their intake of sugar]. But when I started using it, I began to have serious headaches that my doctor could not account for. So under my doctor's supervision, I stopped using NutraSweet and my headaches stopped. Going back onto NutraSweet was followed by a renewal of my headaches. I did this back and forth three times and the scenario was the same each time: "no NutraSweet, no headache; NutraSweet, headache."

   Do you agree with the unstated implication of this letter—that taking the NutraSweet was the cause of the headaches? Defend your answer against likely objections.

---

[11]For further discussion see "Public Attitudes about S & T [Science and Technology] in General," nsf.gov/statistics, (2006).

3. Comment on this quote (attributed to Rush Limbaugh) from an ad urging people to join the National Organization for Women. "What if a man claimed the right to rape using the same principle found in the theory that it is his body and he has the right to choose?"

4. Earlier in this chapter, we questioned the use of Death Penalty Information Center (DPIC) statistics concerning the death penalty to show that that extreme form of punishment does not deter crime more than lesser penalties. What about a *Harper's Index* item indicating that the chances of a white teenager arrested on a drug charge being tried in adult court, rather than a juvenile court, are about 1 in 70, while for blacks the chances are 1 in 18? Is the implied conclusion that black teenage offenders are discriminated against compared to whites justified on the basis of this evidence?

*5. Comment on the following statistic listed in the November 2000 *Harper's Index:* Points by which the average SAT score of a home-schooled student exceeds that of other United States students—81.

EXERCISE 5-2

Determine which fallacies (if any) occur in the following short passages and justify your answers (as you did when working on Exercises 3-1 and 4-1). (Note again that some of these passages may also contain fallacies discussed in previous chapters and some *may* not contain fallacious reasoning.)

1. *Bangkok Post* (June 7, 1990): "In sweltering California, a Red Indian brave performed a water ceremony in Claremont in the middle of last month. Now everyone is raving about the fact that just nine days after he returned to his teepee, 'the skies opened up and a 2.54 cm deluge soaked the region.' Three Valleys Municipal Water District supremo Paul Stiglich insists there is a connection. 'The Indians came, they danced, it rained,' he said."

2. The *New York Times* (January 20, 2005) reported that Germaine Greer, a well-known Australian feminist and literary scholar, quit the cast of *Celebrity Big Brothers,* a British reality show, after only five days. On this program celebrities are confined in a house where they interact with one another while viewers vote on who should go or stay. Greer complained that contestants were encouraged to bully, living conditions were poor, food was stale, and towels were filthy. Even worse, she claimed that they were subjected to "lockdowns" in their bedrooms, where they were prohibited from eating, using the bathroom, or sleeping. When other contestants refused to join her revolt against *Big Brothers* thought police, she quit in disgust and denounced the show as a "fascist prison camp."

3. From a Bob Schwabach "On Computers" newspaper column: "There aren't just a couple of brands [of IBM-compatible computers] for those [very low] prices; there are dozens. Do they work? Someone I know has been running one continuously for five months, and it's never missed a beat."

4. During the wars in Afghanistan and Iraq, the U.S. government placed a value on human lives that suffered wrongful deaths caused by the U.S. military and made "condolence payments" to family members. They did the same for Americans

killed in al Qaeda attacks on September 11, 2001. Here are some statistics on the worth of human life taken from "A Scale for the Price of Life," by Tom Engelhardt (*San Francisco Chronicle,* May 20, 2007).

A civilian killed in Haditha, Iraq, by U.S. Marines: $2,500.

A civilian killed near Jalalabad, Afghanistan, by U.S. Marines: $2,000.

A civilian killed by al Qaeda terrorists on September 11: $1.8 million.

5. Smoking pot definitely leads to heroin use. A report by the U.S. Commissioner of Narcotics on a study of 2,213 hard-core narcotics addicts in the Lexington (Kentucky) Federal Hospital shows that 70.4 percent smoked marijuana before taking heroin.

6. Susan Brownmiller, arguing against the legalization of pornography: "Pornography, like rape, is a male invention designed to dehumanize women, to reduce the female to an object of sexual access, not to free sensuality from moralistic or paternal inhibition."

7. From a student essay: "It is wrong to criticize advertisers for manipulating people through psychological ploys because that's what makes ads effective."

8. Overheard in a local bar: "You women are wrong to be for censoring pornography, even if it's true, and I'm pretty sure it isn't, that porno stuff makes a few men more likely to rape. Would you want to ban miniskirts, bikini outfits, low-cut dresses, and such—require women to wear Muslim-style outfits—if it's true that scanty clothes make some men more likely to rape?"

9. A *Wall Street Journal* headline (July 29, 2002):

Man's Lawsuit Claims Fast-Food Restaurants Caused His Obesity

The article went on to explain that Caesar Barber ". . . a 5-foot-10 maintenance worker who weighs 272 pounds had heart attacks in 1996 and 1999 and has diabetes, high blood pressure and high cholesterol. He said he ate fast food for decades, believing it was good for him until his doctor cautioned him otherwise. . . . His lawyer, Samuel Hirsch, said the restaurants should list ingredients on their menus. 'There's direct deception when someone omits telling people food digested is detrimental to their health.'"

10. A disgusted baseball fan on hearing about Barry Bonds alleged use of performance-enhancing drugs: "They ought to let him play ball. The next thing you know, they'll be taking away records from people because they had an extra bowl of Cheerios." (*San Francisco Chronicle,* September 2, 2006)

11. The president of a college who shall go unnamed here justifying the reduction of salaries for adjunct (part-time) teachers who are paid only 75 percent of the rate paid to full-time staff per course: "I don't see the problem here. No other college in the state pays more than we do."

12. Comment in *Time* article (May 14, 2001) by Tom Green, a self-proclaimed fundamentalist Mormon, who was indicted in Utah on four counts of bigamy: "Mormons say polygamy is immoral and wrong, but the church was founded by polygamists. That is hypocrisy."

*13. In February 1999, Larry King said on his program *Larry King Live* that since the Lewinsky story broke in January 1998, we'd had an excellent year: crime down, business up, unemployment lower. So he asked his guests, Wasn't Monicagate good for the country?

14. In a speech at the Naval Postgraduate School in Monterey, California, Albert Gonzales, the president's White House counsel, justified the second President Bush invading Iraq without a congressional declaration of war. When one officer asked how Bush could legally do this, Gonzales said that we had conducted 100 military actions in the past without a congressional declaration of war; furthermore, past presidents often declared war without a congressional declaration.

15. When Joseph Lieberman was the Democratic senator from Connecticut, he supported the war in Iraq, despite the fact that Connecticut was an antiwar state. But in an uphill battle to win the 2006 Democratic primary against antiwar challenger Ned Lamont, he said "The sooner we are out [of Iraq] the better" and predicted we would "begin to draw down significant troops" by the end of 2006. After he was re-elected to the Senate as an Independent, he sent a letter to President Bush saying "[I] strongly urge you to send additional American troops to Iraq."

16. Bill Gates, commenting on the government's antitrust suit against Microsoft: "Forcing Microsoft to include Netscape's competing software in our operating system is like requiring Coca-Cola to include three cans of Pepsi in every six-pack it sells." In response, the chief of the Justice Department antitrust division, Joel Klein, said Microsoft's actions are similar to one company owning all the supermarkets and refusing to carry any soda brand other than its own. In your opinion, who won this little to-and-fro, and why?

17. From a student essay: "The U.S. Department of Health states that only 3–5 percent of sexually transmitted diseases in this country are related to prostitution."

18. Paraphrase of part of a letter in a December 1990 "Ann Landers" advice column: "My parents didn't give me much guidance about social behavior, morals, or sex. But I read your column—you were one person I learned from. You said not to go for looks and popularity, but to pay attention to 'the quiet one in the corner.' So about nine years ago, I married an average-looking guy who is a 'great father and a good provider,' and have been very happy. Thanks very much for your excellent advice."

19. Paraphrase of part of a letter to the editor, *Marin* (California) *Independent Journal:* "When the first heart transplant was done by Dr. Christian Barnard, he was praised, not his scalpel. It was Cain, according to the Bible, not a rock, that killed Abel. Why, then, listen to the pseudoliberals and other nitwits when they blame crimes on guns rather than on people who use guns?"

*20. Wayne LaPierre, executive vice president, National Rifle Association: "I think that [the ban on assault weapons] has as much to do with crime control as making a wish while you blow the candles out on a birthday cake." He then provided reasons that he believed showed that such a ban would not reduce the crime rate.

21. In September 2005, a Danish Newspaper, *Jyllands-Pasten,* published cartoons of the prophet Muhammad that were reprinted in several other countries over the next few months, causing a storm of protest throughout the Islamic world. Current Islamic interpretation decrees that the Koran prohibits depicting the image of Muhammad (though it has not always been interpreted this way in the past), but one cartoon went so far as to caricature the prophet as a terrorist. The outcry was even greater when a report later emerged that two years earlier the paper had refused to print cartoons of Christ because they might be offensive and were not funny. The editor claimed that the case was "ridiculous to bring forward now. It has nothing to do with the Muhammad cartoons. In the Muhammad drawings case, we asked the illustrators to do it. I did not ask for these cartoons [of Christ]. That's the difference."

*22. Comment on the following *Associated Press* item, November 10, 1997: "Americans spent $57.3 billion on illegal drugs in 1995, a catastrophic amount but down from previous years, a report by the White House Office of National Control Policy says. The report . . . said [that] estimated spending on . . . illicit drugs compared with 57.5 billion in 1994 and continued a downward trend from 1988 . . . [when] drug sales were estimated at 91.4 billion."

23. Comment by Dr. James M. Orient, Executive Director of the Association of American Physicians and Surgeons, on President Clinton's February 2000 proposed $3,000 fine on tobacco manufacturers for each underage smoker:

What's next? Fining auto makers for each speeding driver, nailing Hershey for every diabetic who eats a candy bar, or gouging MacDonald's for all obese people who order a Big Mac?

EXERCISE 5-3

Here are a few more short passages to be evaluated.

*1. A response to the criticism of the danger of the *Cassini* space mission because it contained 72.3 pounds of plutonium: "Would you decide not to drive a car because you might have an accident and harm others?"

*2. Although traditional Jewish practices forbid eating the meat of the pig, a large minority of Jews in Israel have developed a taste for bacon, pork, and the rest. This offended Orthodox Jews, who wanted to pass a law prohibiting the sale of these products. Explained Rabbi Avraham Shapira, a leader of Orthodox Jews (in the fall of 1985—a law concerning meat from the pig was passed in 1990): "Our law is not to forbid people to eat pork. We are very democratic here. What we want is people not to be able to sell pork. It hurts every religious man when he passes through a city in Israel and he sees a shop with pork in the window."

3. When Arnold Schwarzenegger announced his decision on the *Tonight Show* to run for governor in the 2003 California recall election, he vowed he would rid the government of special interest politics, implying that he was the ideal candidate to do so because he didn't "need to take money from anybody." In the weeks

that followed, he received millions of dollars in campaign contributions from some of the largest corporations in the state.

4. In discussing Jet Blue's decision to sponsor the Yearly Kos Convention, Bill O'Reilly made this comment on his program (July 1, 2003) about the Daily Kos, a liberal blog: "There's no difference between the KKK and the Nazis who have websites, than the Daily Kos because the Daily Kos is basically saying 'We're allowing this thing [hate commentary] to come on'" (quoted on mediamatters.org). O'Reilly was referring to a few offensive viewer comments (not blog posts) about Tony Snow and Dick Cheney.

5. Taken from a student's paper (paraphrased): "The prohibition amendment, which made drinking alcohol illegal early in this century, reduced consumption by 50 percent. When the amendment was repealed, the consumption of alcohol almost tripled. This shows that Americans take the law seriously; when something is illegal, they tend to stay away from it."

   Instructor's comment on the student's paper: "This must be why we have no drug problems today."

6. Item from Molly Ivins's column during the Democratic challenge to the Florida vote, November 2000: "George [W.] Bush claime[ed] throughout the campaign 'We trust the people,' then complain[ed] after the election: 'No way can you trust the people. What idiots are counting these votes?'"

7. Newspaper Association of America's spokesperson Paul Luthringer (quoted in *Extra!*, September/October 1995), responding to a survey that found only 19 percent of sources quoted or referred to on newspaper front pages were women: "The fact that women are quoted less than men has nothing to do with the state of journalism, but has more to do with who—male or female—is the first to return a reporter's call."

*8. From a *Science News* article:

   [Scientists] produced their map of the vegetation existing 18,000 years ago by sifting through published reports on ancient pollen and other plant remains in sediments from around the world. They then estimated how much carbon dioxide was locked within the plants, soil and peat in specific regions. Continental vegetation and soils contained far less carbon dioxide during the Ice Age than they do today, researchers report. . . . Carbon storage on the continents totaled 968.1 billion tons 18,000 years ago, compared with 2,319.4 billion tons now, an increase of 140 percent.

9. *New York Times* article: "When several women's groups protested the Pakistani law that accords the legal testimony of women half the weight of the testimony of men, Qazi Hussain Ahmed, leader of the Islamic party, said, 'These laws do not affect women adversely. Our system wants to protect women from unnecessary worry and save them the trouble of appearing in court.'"

10. Craig Stoll, a San Francisco restaurant owner, defended his decision to prohibit diners from bringing their own wine into his pizzeria. "I don't know why people feel so entitled to bring their own [bottle]. What if you collected fine table cloths

from all over the world and you don't ever cook at home so you want to bring one in to eat off of? It's ridiculous." (taken from "The Taming of the Screw," *San Francisco Chronicle,* April 6, 2006)

*11. Item in *Science 80* (November/December 1979): "The chief trouble with the word 'superstition' is that it always applies to the beliefs of someone else, not your own. The entire history of science shows that, in varying degrees, much that even the greatest scientists believed to be fact is today either false or else somewhat less than factual, perhaps even superstitious. It follows that what the best scientists today believe to be fact will suffer the same fate."

12. On a segment of "Your World" (Fox News, January 4, 2008), host Neil Cavuto asked author Marc Rudov why he said that Hillary Clinton's nagging voice was the reason men overwhelmingly picked Barack Obama rather than Clinton in Iowa (at the Democratic caucuses). Rudov replied, "When Barack Obama speaks, men hear, 'Take off for the future.' And when Hillary Clinton speaks, man hear, 'Take out the garbage.'"

13. An item from the *New York Times* (June 13, 2001) reported that the Justice Department announced in June 2001 that violent crime had fallen 15 percent the previous year, the largest drop on record. The report, based on a survey of 160,000 crime victims nationwide indicated that "[s]imple assaults accounted for 61.5 percent of all violent crime . . . and because they declined by 14.4 percent in 2000 compared with 1999, they accounted for most of the drop in violent crime. . . ." Two weeks earlier, "the FBI reported that serious crime had remained stable in 2000, ending an eight year period of significant declines. . . . [It] measures only the most serious crimes . . . but does not include simple assaults like pushing and shoving."

14. A letter to the *San Francisco Examiner* from a physician argued that if juries award sums like $10.5 million to plaintiffs who have contracted toxic shock syndrome—even though that disease wasn't known to medical science when the damage took place—perhaps we can now expect lawsuits against pharmaceutical companies and physicians by the relatives of people who died of pneumonia before 1943, on the grounds that as-yet-undiscovered penicillin hadn't been prescribed.

*15. When it was pointed out to Stephen Schneider, a climatologist at Stanford's Institute for International Studies, that he was recommending action now even though he was only 90 percent sure that global warming was occurring because of atmospheric emissions, he replied, "Why do we need 99 percent certainty when nothing else is that certain? If there were only a 5 percent chance the chef slipped some poison in your dessert, would you eat it?"

16. Peter Singer in his book *Animal Liberation:* "The racist violates the principle of equality by giving greater weight to the interests of members of his own race when there is a clash between their interests and the interests of those of another race. The sexist violates the principle of equality by favoring the interests of his own sex. Similarly, the speciesist allows the interests of his own species to override the greater interests of members of another species. The pattern is identical in each case."

17. When Charles Gibson, ABC anchor, asked vice-presidential candidate Sarah Palin about her foreign policy experience, Palin made an off-the-cuff remark that she could see Russia from her house. Katie Couric, CBS anchor, followed this up in another interview, asking her to explain how proximity to Russia "enhances your foreign policy credentials."

Palin: "Well it certainly does because our, our next-door neighbors are foreign countries, there in the state that I'm executive of. And there . . ."

Couric [interrupting]: "Have you ever been involved in any negotiations, for example, with the Russians?"

Palin: "We have trade missions back and forth. It's very important when you consider even national security issues with Russia. As Putin rears his head and comes into the airspace of the United States of America, where do they go? It's Alaska. It's right over the border. It is from Alaska that we send those out to make sure that an eye is being kept on this very powerful nation because they are right there. They are right next to our state."

18. Hitler's version of Darwin's theory of evolution by natural selection (from *Mein Kampf*): "No more than Nature desires the mating of weaker and stronger individuals, even less does she desire the blending of a higher with a lower race, since if she did her whole work of higher breeding over perhaps hundreds of thousands of years, might be ruined with one blow."

19. In defending one of the Menendez brothers charged with murdering their parents, the lawyer, Leslie Abramson, argued, "What they did is not the issue. It's why they did it. These boys were not responsible for who they turned out to be. They were just little children being molded."

20. Part of a political column by George Weigel (November 29, 1992), in which he argued against the *Roe v. Wade* Supreme Court decision: "The hard sociological fact is that abortion on demand (the regime established by *Roe*) has been the greatest deal for irresponsible or predatory men in American history. Why? Because whatever else is said, *Roe* frees men from responsibility for the sexual conduct they consensually enter. *Roe* is alleged to have empowered women; in fact, *Roe* legally disempowered women from holding men accountable for their sexual behavior where that behavior had unplanned results."

*21. From an article in the January/February 1994 issue of *Quill* magazine about the claim by Dr. John Pierce (University of California, San Diego) that the Joe Camel cigarette ads were responsible for "a sharp increase in teen smoking": "His study shows that first-time smokers among Californians from the ages of 16 to 18 had steadily declined from 12.5 percent in 1975 to 6.2 percent in 1988, but then began sharply increasing again. Joe Camel, a cool-looking, cartoonish character, was introduced as the Camel symbol in 1988. Teenage smoking immediately began increasing by 0.7 percent a year, through 1990. In 1992, Pierce conducted another study that showed Joe Camel was as familiar a character as Mickey Mouse to children as young as six."

The *Quill* article also indicated that because of his research, Dr. Pierce stated that he believes we should ban all tobacco advertising. When asked whether this wasn't censorship contrary to the Constitution's First Amendment, he replied, "There is no free speech [issue] here. The issue is to protect our children from being influenced into an addiction that will cause cancer."

*22. Since the 55-mile-per-hour speed limit was introduced by President Carter, traffic fatalities in the United States have dropped almost in half. So now that the Republican Congress (in 1995) has repealed the 55-mph limit we can expect traffic fatalities to go back to where they were—almost double what they are now. (Note: We now have the advantage of hindsight, since we can find out whether the repeal did or did not go back to where they were or significantly increased. But do this exercise item without resort to later information of this kind. By the way, did traffic fatalities significantly increase?)

23. Paraphrase of part of a letter to the editor in the *Honolulu Advertiser,* July 17, 1999, disagreeing with the Supreme Court ruling that flag burning was protected as free speech: "Rights entail responsibilities. Since you can't yell fire in a crowded theater and can't utter racial slurs in a schoolroom, you shouldn't be allowed to burn the flag. There should be limits to speech that is hateful or that harms people."

*24. Taken from an item in *Extra!* (December 2003): "Fox News anchor Brit Hume . . . argued (August 26, 2003) that U.S. soldiers were better off than Californians. 'Two hundred seventy-seven U.S. soldiers have now died in Iraq, which means that statistically speaking U.S. soldiers have less of a chance of dying from all causes in Iraq than citizens have of being murdered in California, which is roughly the same geographical size. The most recent statistics indicate California has more than 2,300 homicides each year, which means about 6.6 murders each day. Meanwhile, U.S. troops have been in Iraq for 160 days, which means they're incurring about 1.7 deaths including illness and accidents each day.'"

25. The *Los Angeles Times* ran an article in November 2005 about the covert U.S. military practice of paying Iraqi newspapers and television stations to run articles with reassuring news about the war in Iraq. Although propagandistic in nature, the articles were presented as unbiased news accounts. In defending the policy on National Public Radio, Charles Krohn, a former Army spokesman, said, "I don't think there's any need for secrecy, but I think it's pretty well understood that it's the custom in that country to pay journalists and to pay newspapers. And certainly I think the record that Saddam [Hussein] has done this and others do it is pretty well established."

EXERCISE 5-4

*A letter to the editor of *Free Inquiry* (Winter 1999/00) argues against hanging copies of the Ten Commandments in public schools on the grounds that it may promote church attendance, which may well be harmful. As evidence, the writer cites statistics from two different issues of *Scientific American.* The first (July 1999) notes the percentage of adults in the United States and in European countries who attended church at least once a month in the 1990s. The second (August 1999) lists the criminal population per hundred thousand behind bars during that period. Evaluate these statistics and explain why you think they do or don't support the claim that churchgoing may be harmful.

40 Percent or More Attending Church

Country	Percentage Attending Church	Number in Jail per 100,000
Ireland	88	55
Poland	74	170
U.S.	55	668
Italy	47	85
Canada	40	115
Mean	61	219

Under 20 Percent Attending Church

France	17	95
Norway	13	55
Sweden	11	65
Finland	11	60
Iceland	9	40
Mean	12	63

EXERCISE 5-5

The ACLU has been severely criticized by many for opposing a ban on commercial advertising of cigarette companies while taking large contributions from those companies (for example, from Phillip Morris since 1987 to the tune of $500,000 and similar large quantities from R. J. Reynolds). But the ACLU claims that it has opposed bans on commercial ads on First Amendment grounds for more than 50 years. If true, are the opponents guilty of questionable cause? Do some research. (See, for example, *Public Citizen's Health Letter,* April 1999, or *The Progressive,* February 1999.)

EXERCISE 5-6

Find several fallacy examples of your own, perhaps gleaned from newspapers, magazines, television programs, textbooks (hopefully not this one, but anything is fair game), or what have you, provide a name in each case if you can, and carefully explain why the passage is fallacious.

*Memory says, "I did that." Pride
replies, "I could not have done that."
Eventually, memory yields.*

        —Nietzsche

Every dogma has its day.

        —Abraham Rotstein

Think with your head, not your guts.

        —Old saying

Populus vult decipi. *(The people want to
be deceived.)*

        —Ancient Roman saying

*Nothing is so firmly believed as what we
least know.*

        —Montaigne

*How strange it is to see with how much
   passion
People see things only in their own
   fashion.*

        —Molière

*I wouldn't have seen it if I hadn't
believed it.*

        —Insightful takeoff on an old saying

Chapter

6

PSYCHOLOGICAL IMPEDIMENTS TO COGENT REASONING: SHOOTING OURSELVES IN THE FOOT

Good reasoning is a matter of character as well as brain power. If human beings were completely rational animals, learning how to reason well would be a relatively easy task. We would simply learn which patterns of reasoning are good and which bad, and then make all of our reasoning conform to good patterns while avoiding the bad. Even if we started out with poor background beliefs, repeated use of valid deductive and inductive inferences, based on all of what we have experienced so far, would soon set things straight.

Unfortunately, human beings are not completely rational, although rationality is an important part of our makeup. This chapter is concerned with that other part of human nature—the nonrational, emotional component that prevents us from being perfect reasoners. While no one can completely eliminate these nonrational impediments to cogent reasoning, any more than a leopard can change its spots, understanding how they work can help us to reduce the harm they do to our attempts at completely rational thought.

1. Loyalty, Provincialism, and the Herd Instinct

Throughout history, individual chances for success at most things—getting enough food, attracting and holding a mate, successfully raising children—have depended on two fundamental factors. The first is the success of the groups we belong to in their competitions with other groups. Members of primary in-groups (nations, tribes, cultures) defeated by competing out-groups generally suffer serious harm to their chances of having a good life or any life at all. That is why we all feel a tug of **loyalty** to our own in-group; a society that has too many disloyal people has little chance against other, more cohesive groups. (Note, however, that the strength of this tug differs greatly from person to person.)

But being a member of a successful in-group is of little value if others in the group do not allow us reasonable chances for success in whatever it is we want to do. That is an important reason why we all are so anxious to get along with the other members of the groups to which we owe loyalty. The person who is completely out of step with everyone else is not likely to be successful, even if the group as a whole thrives and multiplies.[1] Enter the **herd instinct** that tends to keep our beliefs, and thus our actions, within the bounds of what society as a whole will accept. Finding ourselves in a culture in which everyone covers certain parts of the body, we feel uncomfortable leaving those parts naked. Those belonging to Muslim or Orthodox Jewish groups find eating parts of the pig abhorrent. In Western societies, virtually everyone avoids eating the meat of horses and dogs; in China, dog meat is a delicacy.

Of course, there is no harm in feeling embarrassed if caught in public with the wrong attire or in finding shellfish repugnant. But the herd instinct sometimes leads people to do horrendous things, as they do when mobs carry out vigilante justice or when whole nations acquiesce to unfair practices. Refraining from eating the flesh of the cow is one thing; branding some of one's compatriots as "untouchables" is another.

The point is that it is part of human nature to find it easy and natural to believe what everyone else in our society believes and foolish to believe what others find foolish. This is no doubt one reason for what sociologists call **culture lag**, the tendency of practices and beliefs to persist long after whatever conditions made them useful or sensible have disappeared.

We all desire to have at least a minimal status in the groups that we belong to, for the reasons just mentioned. But the higher our status, the better our chances. That's why most of us have such a strong desire to make a better than minimally good appearance when in public. We want to look intelligent, informed, and decisive—to shine compared

---

[1]For more on this way of looking at the human repertoire, see Howard Kahane, *Contract Ethics: Evolutionary Biology and the Moral Sentiments* (Lanham, Md.: Rowman & Littlefield, 1995), and James Q. Wilson, *The Moral Sense* (New York: Free Press, 1993).

> Man is a social animal; only in the herd is he happy. It is all one to him whether it is the profoundest nonsense or the greatest villainy—he feels completely at ease with it—so long as it is the view of the herd, and he is able to join the herd.
>
> —Søren Kierkegaard

to others. And that is why, for instance, millions of Americans who had never heard of Osama bin Laden before the devastating terrorist attack on the World Trade Center, who had no idea what the Taliban was until it gave refuge to bin Laden, and who knew next to nothing about Islam and the Muslim religion, let alone the meaning of *jihad,* formed almost instant opinions on the invasion of Afghanistan and later Iraq. After the two-pronged war began, newspapers across the country were filled with letters to editors expressing demands for this action or that. The need to be in the swim, to talk "intelligently" about topics of the day, leads us to form and broadcast these quick opinions based on superficial evidence. And once we have pronounced them, the need to avoid appearing to have been wrong in public leads us to hang onto those beliefs, often in the face of conflicting evidence. The underlying psychological mechanism is the desire to gain, and retain, the status in the eyes of others in our group that is vital to success in everyday life.[2]

It also should be noted that hardly any of the large societies common in today's world are completely cohesive. Nations such as the United States, Canada, India, and Russia are composed of all sorts of diverse subgroups, the United States being one of the two most diverse cultures in history. (The other was the Soviet Union before its disintegration.) Most people are completely loyal to their own nation but also have a special interest in the fates of subgroups. They therefore tend to see things not just from the point of view of the mainstream culture but also from that of smaller groups within the primary culture. We see the results of this in current political rhetoric designed to appeal to "special interest" groups such as religious fundamentalists, African Americans, Latinos, Jews, and so on. (Note, by the way, that we all have a very special interest in the welfare of members of our own families.)

Provincialism stems in large part from this natural tendency to identify with the ideas, interests, and kinds of behavior favored by those in groups with which we identify. That is why blacks tend to sympathize with blacks, Jews with Jews, women with women. (Think of the polls in the 2008 presidential primaries that showed blacks and men in general favoring Barack Obama and women favoring Hillary Clinton—until well into the primaries.)

Of particular importance is the fact that we tend to see things from the point of view and interests of our primary culture—our primary in-group—especially when there is conflict with other groups. The result is a kind of belief provincialism operating at various levels—leading Americans, for example, to pay relatively little attention to what happens to the peoples of the rest of the world and to misconstrue what is happening there. That is why, although the United States was founded on the principles of democracy and fair play, a great many Americans have failed to notice that since World War II

---

[2]Erving Goffman's fascinating book *The Presentation of Self in Everyday Life* (New York: Doubleday, 1959; Penguin, 1969) still is an excellent source of information on these matters.

the United States government has helped to overturn several democratically elected governments around the world (for instance, in Chile) and attempted to murder Cuba's Fidel Castro. It is difficult to swallow unpleasant truths when loyalty and the herd instinct reinforce what others in our group vehemently assert, and when provincialism narrows our range of interests and tends to make us see everything in terms of the interests of our own primary group.[3]

2. PREJUDICE, STEREOTYPES, SCAPEGOATS, AND PARTISAN MIND-SETS

Loyalty and provincialism often lead to **prejudice,** including prejudice against all or almost all members of other groups, and to thinking in terms of unverified **stereotypes** that support prejudicial beliefs. But being prejudiced against others is quite different from simply having a bad opinion of them. We are prejudiced only when our nasty beliefs about others are not justified by sufficient evidence. So prejudice can be defined as thinking ill of others without sufficient warrant.

African Americans in particular have been the butt of prejudice in this country, flagrantly before the civil rights movement, but after that in more devious ways. Racial slurs were masked in code phrases like "welfare mothers" or "crime in the streets" or "states rights." Over time, these covert references were driven underground by politically correct attitudes that put the lid on anyone who "played the race card," but political correctness also tended to dampen healthy discussions about race. It wasn't until Barack Obama ran in the 2008 presidential primaries that discussions of prejudice and race returned to the public forum—and, sadly, so did racial slurs.

Prejudicial attitudes often lead to stereotypical thinking that involves attributing certain oversimplified characteristics, often negative, to a specific group of people. Of course, no group of any size is composed of people who resemble one another as do peas in a pod, so it is foolish to be prejudiced against every member of such a group. It's just silly to think that the French all are great lovers, that all Jews and Scots are unusually frugal, or that all women are more emotional than men. It *is* true, though, that people in a given large social group generally are different in many ways from those in other groups. The French as a group are modestly different from Germans, as are Iranians from Pakistanis, something anyone can notice simply by going from one of these countries to the other. The trouble with stereotypical thinking is rather that, even when accurate with respect to groups as a whole (and they often are not), it fails to take account of the differences among individual members.

During the 2008 presidential primaries, Hillary Clinton was a lightning rod for stereotypical and sexist comments about women. Her positions on the issues were often drowned out by media hype on her appearance and her emotional control (or lack thereof). At various times she was criticized for having thick ankles, wearing pants suits, styling her hair like a helmet, and—showing cleavage. If tears came to her eyes

---

[3]Another reason for this difficulty is that public school textbooks and the mass media generally play down or try to justify these kinds of breaches of professed ethical ideals. See Chapters 11 and 12 for more on this topic.

(which happened once), she was a weak sister; if she remained controlled, she was an ice princess. Her past as well as present behavior were called into question. Some people criticized her for putting up with an adulterous husband, behaving like a stereotypical maternal enabler; others praised her for standing by her man as a good woman should. (There was no winning that one.) In an ironic twist, the public seems to have forgiven the adulterer. If as much attention had been paid to her policies as to her gender and personality, maybe voters would have had a better yardstick to measure her by.

Then along came Sarah Palin, John McCain's pick for vice president on the Republican ticket. When the news broke that she had recently given birth to a Down syndrome baby and that her 17-year-old daughter was pregnant out of wedlock, she was criticized for putting her own political ambitions above the needs of her family. And questions were raised about whether she could balance her duties as vice president with her stereotypical responsibilities as a mother of five children. These questions were never asked about John McCain, by the way, who was an absentee father on weekdays (when he stayed in Washington) and flew home to Arizona on weekends to be with his family.

One of the most widely stereotyped groups, particularly in this country, is teenagers. Consider this quote: "Our youth now love luxury. They have bad manners, contempt for authority; they show disrespect for their elders, and love to chatter in places of exercise. They no longer rise when elders enter the room. They contradict their parents, chatter before company, gobble food, and tyrannize their teacher." And who is responsible for that rant against teens? None other than Socrates, that wise old philosopher, though whether he actually said it is debatable. Nonetheless, it reminds us that teenagers have had a bad rep throughout the ages and are stereotyped today much as they were in the fifth century BCE. Yet most people, even parents of teens, know that the great majority of young people are reasonably well behaved, polite, and respectful of their elders.

The flip side of prejudice and intolerance directed against members of other groups is overtolerance of, even blindness to, the defects and foibles of our own group and its members. Loyalty tends to make us see our own leaders as a good deal more intelligent, informed, and honest than in fact they are (or than it would be reasonable to expect the leaders of any society to be) and to regard the general run of our compatriots as better on average than the people in other societies. People are particularly prone to loyalty to the government in times of war, as was evident during the early months of the war in Iraq, when the media were so uniformly patriotic that it was considered taboo for journalists to break rank and criticize the government—this, despite the fact that unprecedented protests were occurring throughout the world. (More discussion on this is in Chapter 11.) Clear thinkers need to overcome this reverse prejudice in favor of people in their own in-groups, especially of in-group leaders (an important reason for the inclusion in this text of so many examples illustrating the clay feet of quite a few elected officials).

Prejudice against members of other groups, particularly of minorities within a larger culture, often is reinforced by the need to find **scapegoats**—others we can blame for the ills of the world—when in fact we ourselves may bear a large measure of responsibility. That a group being trashed cannot possibly have produced the troubles it is charged with rarely makes a difference.

This tendency to put the blame elsewhere is captured with chilling effect by Shirley Jackson in "The Lottery," her classic story of scapegoating. The residents of a small village gather in the town square for the annual lottery, an archaic ritual performed for so many years that the people have forgotten its original purpose. They know that one of them must draw the fateful lot, but beyond that they only remember how to use the pile of stones that figures prominently in the story. Until the lot is drawn, the villagers behave in a decent, kindly manner to one another, but once the "winner" is known, they grab stones from the pile and pelt her viciously, driven by the herd instinct to satisfy a barbaric practice of scapegoating whose purpose they no longer understand. The story is an allegory for practices that have unfortunately prevailed for centuries.

The classic scapegoat in the Christian world has always been the Jews. In days of old, when Christian theology was interpreted to say that lending money at interest constituted usury (a sin), Jews therefore became important moneylenders. Blaming them for calamities then sometimes at least had the practical motive of serving as an excuse for the repudiation of outstanding loans. But at most times, the primary point of anti-Semitism has been simply to place the blame for ills elsewhere.

Everyone nowadays is familiar with the way in which the Nazis used the Jews as scapegoats and with their attempt to exterminate all European Jews. So it might be supposed that picking on the Jews would have little appeal these days. Yet anti-Semitism is still very common in many places. In Russia, to take one example, Jews are commonly held responsible for the ills produced by 70 years of Soviet communism. (The thin thread of truth behind this ridiculous idea—note that Stalin was not Jewish—is that a very few of the high officials in the Communist Party and in the Soviet government were Jews.) In other Eastern European countries, Jews were similarly often held responsible for the problems generated by Soviet domination. This was true even in Poland, where only about 10,000 out of more than 3 million Jews survived the German attempt at genocide and still resided in Poland.

One might suppose that the murder of millions of Jews in Europe during World War II, and the still existing anti-Semitism just described, would make Jews, of all people, the least likely to relegate others to second-class citizenship. And yet, in Israel, the first primarily Jewish state in about 2,000 years, Israeli Arabs do not have the same status as Israeli Jews, and Arab lands in the West Bank have been taken from them and given to Jewish "settlers." Not that the Arabs have been paragons of virtue—think only of the stated objective of several surrounding Arab countries to destroy Israel.

And then there are the genocidal tribal battles going on in Africa, the mass destruction and murder in the former Yugoslavia, hostilities between Hindus and Muslims, the savage revenge killings between Shiites and Sunnis, and so on. In every case, those on both sides in these ethnic battles feel justified in their vindictive hatred and prejudice against the "enemy."

Prejudice and scapegoating, of course, also occur in the United States. As usual, small or less powerful groups tend to be the ones picked on, including people of African or Asian descent, Latinos, Native Americans (American Indians), and, naturally, Jews. Since the attack on the World Trade Center, an irrational prejudice against Middle Easterners has sprung up in this country. Yet almost all Middle Easterners in the United States are peaceful, productive members of society who are just as horrified at the terrorist attacks as everyone else. Only a handful are involved in terrorist activities.

More recently, we have been scapegoating immigrants, particularly Latinos. They are blamed for taking jobs from Americans, draining our education and medical resources, and posing the threat of terrorism. Anti-immigration sentiment is highest in areas where unemployment is at its worst, and people look for someone else to blame when faced with job losses and higher costs of living. Scapegoating immigrants has a long history in this country, as it has in most countries for that matter. When a wave of Irish immigrated to the United States during the potato famine in the 1840s, they were stereotyped as dirty, ignorant, alcoholic, and violent and were blamed for society's ills. The same thing happened to the Poles when a million and half swamped Ellis Island in the early twentieth century. That's when Polish jokes started making them out to be stupid, lazy, and inferior. It is a sad tendency of human nature that people tend to move blame and responsibility away from themselves and project it onto others by vilifying and blaming them for things they didn't do.

Thinking in terms of unverified stereotypes and scapegoats often results from a **partisan mind-set** that leads people to perceive evidence and to judge arguments via an "us against them" or a "my right view against your wrong view" attitude. We all are tempted to arrange facts to fit our side of an issue and tend to be blind to the import of evidence supporting any other side. Good reasoners fight this tendency in all of us to favor ideas already held and automatically to see our side as right and the other guy's as wrong. Those with a partisan mind-set give in to this all too human tendency, generally without being aware that they have done so. This is true, for example, of some individuals who are vigorously engaged in the social or political arenas. That is why it can be so maddening to discuss touchy issues with some very committed people — they tend to be deaf to counterevidence and counterarguments. (Another reason, of course, is that we ourselves may be "hearing impaired" when it comes to their reasons and arguments.)

A really good critical reasoner has a mind-set that is completely different from those who see everything from a partisan point of view. This does not mean that good reasoners lack a sense of loyalty! It means simply that they have an open mind rather than a mind that sees everything from the point of view that "our side always is right and the other side always wrong" — a mind open to the truth, wherever it may lie.

3. SUPERSTITIOUS BELIEFS

Prejudice against members of other groups at least has group loyalty going for it. That can't be said about **superstitions.** It is true, though, that superstitions often are based on some small scrap of evidence or other. Bad things obviously do occasionally happen after a mirror is broken. Coincidences do happen. And even newspaper astrology columns are moderately accurate once every blue moon.

The difference between superstitious and sensible beliefs is that sensible beliefs are based on sufficient evidence that justifies those beliefs, not on carefully chosen scraps of support. Superstitious beliefs are generally based on biased evidence or on small or unrepresentative samples (discussed in Chapter 5) — evidence from which all negative cases have been removed. Bad things do happen on Friday the 13th, but so do lots of good things. And bad things happen on other days also, so that there is nothing remarkable about the fact that they happen on Friday the 13th. Superstitious people ignore facts of this sort and pay attention just to the evidence supporting their superstitious convictions.

The odd thing about superstitious beliefs is that their complete irrationality doesn't seem to stop even the most brilliant people from having them. Chess grand masters, for example, display amazing intelligence and insight when playing that great intellectual game, not to mention incredible memories. (The "grand old man of chess," George Koltanowsky, several times played more than 40 games simultaneously—blindfolded.) Yet a former world chess champion, Garry Kasparov, thinks the number 13 is his lucky number (he was born on April 13—well, he's Aries, so that explains his great ability— and he was the 13th world chess champion). The previous champion, Anatoly Karpov, changes his suit every time he loses a game.

4. WISHFUL THINKING AND SELF-DECEPTION

As we have just seen, loyalty, prejudice, stereotypical thinking, the herd instinct, and superstition tend to give us beliefs that do not square with reality. Beliefs acquired in these nonrational ways often result from **wishful thinking**—believing what we would like to be true, no matter what the evidence—or from **self-deception**— consciously believing what at a deeper level we know to be dubious. It is a very human trait indeed to believe that which we would like to be true and to deny those things we find unpalatable (or, as in the case of our own eventual death, extremely hard to accept).

An extreme example in literature is Jay Gatsby's idealization of Daisy Buchanan in *The Great Gatsby,* by F. Scott Fitzgerald. Gatsby persists in deceiving himself about her character despite mounting evidence that she not only is self-centered, irresponsible, and fickle but also has let him take the blame for a crime she has committed. His self-deception is so great it could be called a **delusion**—one that leads tragically to his own death. Gatsby's adoration of Daisy is an exaggerated example of what many people feel in the early stages of love. We commonly indulge in wishful thinking about our lovers and deceive ourselves about their imperfections despite evidence to the contrary (hopefully imperfections of much less magnitude than Daisy's).

When the stakes are high, we have a natural tendency to deceive ourselves rather than face reality. This tendency is just as prevalent in world leaders as it is in the average person. A classic case is British Prime Minister Neville Chamberlain's decision to sign an agreement with Hitler in 1938 to achieve, in his words, "peace in our time." Chamberlain was so conscious of the horror another world war would bring, and so desperately anxious to spare his nation and the civilized world from such a disaster, that his judgment was destroyed, and he failed to see Hitler's intent in spite of all sorts of evidence that many others, including Winston Churchill, perceived for what it was.[4]

The difficulty is in catching ourselves in the act of believing what we want to believe rather than accepting what the evidence indicates to be the reality. Of course,

---

[4] In fairness to Chamberlain, note that a very few historians claim, on rather sparse evidence, that Chamberlain knew chances for peace were not great and wanted to gain time for Britain to rearm.

In Chapter 4, we presented the first of four "causes of the utterance of fallacies" that Jeremy Bentham described in his famous book The Handbook of Political Fallacies. Here is an excerpt from the second of the four, which happens to be relevant to the topics discussed in this chapter:

Second Cause: Interest-Begotten Prejudice

If every act of the will and hence every act of the hand is produced by interest, that is, by a motive of one sort or another, the same must be true, directly or indirectly, of every act of the intellectual faculty, although the influence of interest upon the latter is neither as direct or as perceptible as that upon the will.

But how, it may be asked, is it possible that the motive by which a man is actuated can be secret to himself? Nothing, actually, is easier; nothing is more frequent. Indeed, the rare case is not that of a man's not knowing, but that of his knowing. . . .

When two persons have lived together in a state of intimacy, it happens not infrequently that either or each of them may possess a more correct and complete view of the motives by which the mind of the other is governed, than of those which control his own behavior. Many a woman has had in this way a more correct and complete acquaintance with the internal causes by which the conduct of her husband has been determined, than he has had himself. The reason for this is easily pointed out. By interest, a man is continually prompted to make himself as correctly and completely acquainted as possible with the springs of action which determine the conduct of those upon whom he is more or less dependent for the comfort of his life. But by interest he is at the same time diverted from any close examination into the springs by which his own conduct is determined. From such knowledge he would be more likely to find mortification than satisfaction.

When he looks at other men, he finds mentioned as a matter of praise the prevalence of . . . social motives. . . . It is by the supposed prevalence of these amiable motives that he finds reputation raised, and that respect and goodwill enhanced to which every man is obliged to look for so large a proportion of the comforts of his life. . . .

But the more closely he looks into the mechanism of his own mind, the less able he is to refer any of the mass of effects produced there to any of these amiable and delightful causes. He finds nothing, therefore, to attract him towards this self-study; he finds much to repel him from it. . . .

Perhaps he is a man in whom a large proportion of the self-regarding motives may be mixed with a slight tincture of the social motives operating upon the private scale. In that case, what will he do? In investigating the source of a given action, he will in the first instance set down the whole of it to the account of the amiable and conciliatory motives, in a word, the social ones. This, in any study of his own mental physiology, will always be his first step; and it will commonly be his last also. Why should he look any further? Why take in hand the painful probe? Why undeceive himself, and substitute the whole truth, which would mortify him, for a half-truth which flatters him?

most of us, luckily, have no opportunity to make mistakes of the kind that Chamberlain committed. Our self-deceptions tend to result in less global evils, although they still may have catastrophic consequences for ourselves or friends. Think of the large number of people who drink and then drive. Or consider the significant percentage of adults in every industrial country who still smoke cigarettes or chew tobacco in the face of overwhelming evidence linking tobacco to all sorts of fatal illnesses, including heart disease, various kinds of cancer, and emphysema. Millions of people everywhere continue to puff or chew away, undeterred even by warning labels on tobacco products like this one:

> SURGEON GENERAL'S WARNING: Smoking Causes Lung Cancer, Heart Disease, Emphysema, And May Complicate Pregnancy.

5. RATIONALIZATION AND PROCRASTINATION

Perhaps the most common form of self-deception is **rationalization.** We engage in this kind of psychological ploy when we ignore or deny unpleasant evidence so as to feel justified in doing what we want to do or in believing what we find comfortable to believe. Rationalization is nicely illustrated by the old joke about the psychiatrist and a delusional patient who believes he is dead. To prove to the patient that he is alive, the psychiatrist first gets him to agree that dead men don't bleed and then makes a cut in the man's arm, which, of course, bleeds. Smiling, the psychiatrist tilts his chair back and waits. "Well," says the dismayed patient, "I guess I was wrong. Dead men do bleed." He thus manages to sustain his delusion by rationalizing away undeniable proof to the contrary.

Another example, from the play *Cabaret:* A credulous German is reading the latest Nazi propaganda. Scowling he says, "The Jews own all the banks. And they're behind an international communist conspiracy too." Whereupon his clearer-thinking companion observes, "But bankers are capitalists and communists are opposed to capitalism. How can Jews be both?" The first man pauses, then nods knowingly and rationalizes: "They're very crafty."

Rationalization is often used to justify an act that violates one's personal code. In a revealing study of prison staff who worked on execution teams, a group of Stanford psychologists found that team members were more likely to disengage themselves morally from executing criminals than prison guards not on the team.[5] The "executioners" were more inclined to dehumanize inmates on death row, to claim that they were a threat to society ("they can escape and kill again"), and to cite the financial burden on society of life imprisonments. Such rationalizations (buttressed by suppression and denial) let them slide out of taking moral responsibility.

---

[5]See more on this study in "When Death Is on the Docket, the Moral Compass Waivers," by Benedict Carey, *New York Times,* February 7, 2006.

And then there are media rationalizations, like the ones Nancy Grace and a CNN spokeswoman came up with after they aired a grueling interview with a mother who committed suicide not long after appearing on Grace's talk show. In it, Grace badgered the woman about the disappearance of her 2-year-old son, demanding that she disclose her whereabouts at the time her son went missing. The woman, a suspect in the case, stumbled over her words, groping for answers, as Grace pressed her for a confession. At the bottom of the screen, a text box appeared noting "Since show taping, body [of the mother was] found at grandparent's home." When a viewer called to ask if Grace thought she had pushed the woman over the edge, she replied that her show wasn't to blame for what happened. "The truth is not always nice or polite or easy to go down. Sometimes it's harsh and it hurts." Well, that's one way of rationalizing the effect of a brutal attack. A CNN spokeswoman justified the broadcast, saying that they decided to air the interview just hours after the suicide with the idea that it would continue to draw attention to the case in the hope of helping to find the missing 2-year-old. Right. So CNN was actually helping the police investigation—not rationalizing a sleazy attempt to sensationalize a tragic event.[6]

Rationalization often leads to **procrastination**—to putting off for tomorrow what common sense tells us needs to be done today. Young smokers often tell themselves that they'll quit a few years down the pike before any serious harm is done; students are famous for delaying work on term papers until the day before they're due. (Recall the old song about how "Mañana is good enough for me" and the Spanish saying "Mañana será otro día," "Tomorrow will be another day.") It is an all-too-human tendency to favor immediate gratification at the risk of possible long-term harm. In general, the more likely or more serious the long-term harm, the less likely that an intelligent person will choose immediate gratification. The trouble is that most of us tend to weigh long-term harms or losses too lightly when compared with short-run gains.

Sometimes these types of self-deception affect an entire nation. When Thomas Jefferson wrote the line "all men are created equal" in the Declaration of Independence, he didn't mean all men: He meant all property-owning men, and that certainly didn't include African Americans. Nonetheless, he did not think slaves should be considered property and believed that slavery was morally at odds with the principles of the American Revolution. Yet he rationalized owning slaves himself (200, more or less, at any given time), selling them off when he needed the money and freeing only a handful at his death. Jefferson was a complicated man, who seemed able to hold two opposing ideas in his mind yet remain enough in denial of the moral contradictions not to worry too much. And so he procrastinated raising the issue of freeing the slaves, partly out of ambivalence and partly out of the very real opposition from the South, where slavery was endemic and fiercely defended. Eventually he said it was up to the next generation to free the slaves.[7]

The unwillingness of human beings to face unpleasant reality often is revealed strikingly in important works of fiction. In his novel *Heart of Darkness,* for example,

---

[6]From "CNN Talk Show Reaches a New Depth of Sleaze," by C. W. Nevius, *San Francisco Chronicle,* September 15, 2006.

[7]For more on Jefferson's attitudes on slavery, see *American Sphinx,* an excellent, engaging biography of this complex man, by Joseph Ellis.

> *Here is a short excerpt from Jane Austen's celebrated novel Sense and Sensibility that nicely reveals a kind of rationalization all too common in real life. The excerpt (from Chapter 2) starts with John Dashwood explaining to his wife Fanny why he intends to give his stepmother and half-sisters 3,000 pounds from his very comfortable inheritance:*
>
> "It was my father's last request to me, . . . that I should assist his widow and daughters."
>
> "He did not know what he was talking of, I dare say; ten to one but he was light-headed at the time. Had he been in his right senses, he could not have thought of such a thing as begging you to give away half your fortune from your child." [In fact, it was very much less.]
>
> "He did not stipulate any particular sum, my dear Fanny; he only requested me, in general terms, to assist them, and make their situation more comfortable than it was in his power to do. . . ."
>
> "Well, then, *let* something be done for them; but *that* something need not be three thousand pounds. . . . [W]hen the money is once parted with, it never can return. Your sisters will marry, and it will be gone forever. If, indeed, it could ever be restored to our poor little boy—"
>
> "Perhaps then, it would be better for all parties if the sum were diminished by one half—five hundred pounds [each] would be a prodigious increase in their fortunes!"
>
> "Oh! beyond anything great! What brother on earth would do half so much for his sisters, even if *really* his sisters! And as it is—only half blood! . . ."
>
> ". . . As it is, without any addition of mine, they will each have above three thousand pounds on their mother's death—a very comfortable fortune for any young woman."

Joseph Conrad describes the way in which Europeans who invade Africa in the nineteenth century rationalize their exploitation and degradation of native populations. He thus chronicles a case of self-deception and rationalization engaged in by a whole group of people over an extended period of time. In his novel, set in the Belgian Congo at the turn of the century, European invaders claim that their aim is to enlighten and civilize the African natives—to "wean those ignorant millions from their horrid ways." But it becomes evident as the story develops that the colonial traders have only one mission—to plunder the land for ivory.

Although a work of fiction, *Heart of Darkness* was based on the true conditions that existed in the Belgian Congo at the turn of the century. In 1876, when the Belgians began their colonization of the Congo, their monarch, King Leopold, who literally took personal ownership of the Congo, described his intent as "to open to civilization the only part of our globe where Christianity has not yet penetrated and to pierce the darkness which envelops the entire population." But in fact the king was a tyrant; the colonials, profiteers; and the Congolese, virtual slaves. When news of the atrocities committed

"To be sure it is: and, indeed, strikes me that they can want no addition at all. . . ."

"That is very true, and, therefore, I do not know whether, upon the whole, it would not be more advisable to do something for their mother while she lives rather than for them. . . . A hundred a year would make them all perfectly comfortable." . . .

"[I]t is better than parting with fifteen hundred pounds at once. But then if Mrs. Dashwood should live fifteen years, we shall be completely taken in. . . . [P]eople always live forever when there is an annuity to be paid them. . . ."

"I believe you are right, my love; it will be better that there should be no annuity in the case. . . . A present of fifty pounds now and then will prevent their ever being distressed for money, and will, I think, be amply discharging my promise to my father."

"To be sure it will. . . . I am convinced within myself that your father had no idea of your giving them any money at all. . . . Altogether they will have five hundred a-year amongst them, and what on earth can four women want for more than that?—They will live so cheap! Their housekeeping will be nothing at all. They will have no carriage, no horses, and hardly any servants; they will keep no company and can have no expenses of any kind! Only conceive how comfortable they will be! . . . They will be much more able to give *you* something!"

And so, the wealthy Dashwoods not only manage to rationalize their way out of helping John's stepmother and half-sisters but convince themselves that their much poorer relatives are better able to give something to them!

against African natives reached Europe, a vague uneasiness rippled across the continent, but Europeans managed to deal with these reports by rationalization. If the natives rebelled, the sentries had to defend themselves, didn't they? Weren't some natives bound to die in the civilizing process in any case? Et cetera.

In *Heart of Darkness,* Conrad punctured European rationalizations about what they were doing in Africa in a graphic way by concentrating on a few characters whose development revealed the underlying truth that the European claim to be bringing civilization to the Africans was a smokescreen whose consequence (and unconscious intent?) was not to deceive the natives but rather to deceive the Europeans themselves.

Anyone who dismisses the *Heart of Darkness* portrayal of mass self-deception as just fiction—a story—or thinks that this sort of thing only happened a long time ago might reflect on the present-day confiscation of native lands in Brazil, Indonesia, and elsewhere, where the destruction of indigenous ways of life and peoples is justified in the name of "the integration of native populations into modern life" or "maximal uses of resources."

Reprinted by permission of Paul Miller.

6. OTHER DEFENSE MECHANISMS

When we rationalize or procrastinate, we usually are consciously aware of our actions. But there are a number of psychological strategies (defense mechanisms) that we generally are not consciously aware of using to avoid negative emotional feelings. Because they involve distortion of reality, these defense mechanisms can seriously undermine our ability to think critically.

In **suppression,** we avoid thoughts that are stressful by either not thinking about them or, more commonly, by thinking nonstressful thoughts. In this way we manage to avoid the anxiety associated with the stress-provoking situation. Although suppression may reduce stress in the short run, it often has negative consequences later on. For instance, a student failing a statistics course may block his anxiety by thinking about happier events—his new girlfriend, an upcoming dance, a sports event—or anything else that will suppress his deep-seated fear of failure. Yet in the long run he'd be better off to face the problem, get help, and work to improve his grade.

Denial involves some suppression, but instead of replacing the stressful thoughts with more benign ones, we change our interpretation of the situation to perceive it as less threatening. When a love relationship goes bad, we may remain in denial until our partner walks out on us—even though the signs of discontent are apparent to other people. Instead of paying attention to these signs, we may reinterpret our partner's negative behavior by making excuses for it, or blaming ourselves, or ignoring it. Our need to protect ourselves against separation and loss may prevent us from facing the problems in our relationships and, perhaps, finding solutions.

Albert Camus created an extreme case of denial and suppression in his existentialist novel *The Stranger.* The protagonist, Meursault, kills an Arab on an Algerian beach for no apparent reason and remains in denial about his own motivation, blaming it on the scorching heat of the sun instead. Thus, he reinterprets the situation to diminish his own responsibility and the psychological threat it entails. Later, in jail, he suppresses the

Cartoon by Beattie. Reprinted by permission of Copley News Service.

Instant denial.

anxiety one would expect him to feel about the upcoming trial and thinks instead about his bedroom at home. He spends literally hours recalling every crack in the wall, every chip in the paint, every item in the room—and successfully manages to avoid stress-provoking thoughts. Suppression and denial prevent him from devising his own best defense—that he shot the man in self-defense—a claim for which there is some evidence in the novel, but that, of course, would undermine the existential theme.

People who remain in denial about life-threatening physical ailments run the risk of losing their lives or forfeiting the lives of others. A particularly troubling example is the AIDS "denialists," who claim that HIV is harmless, a belief that contradicts the scientifically proven fact—not theory—that HIV causes AIDS.[8] These people advocate against taking antiretroviral drugs because they think such drugs cause AIDS rather than curb it. If only a few people were affected, this wouldn't be an issue, but when the head of a country advocates this claptrap, thousands suffer. In the last decade, the president of South Africa, Thabo Mbeki, so firmly persisted in denying the cause and treatment of AIDS that his administration curbed access to antiviral drugs. As a result, only about a quarter of those needing treatment received it, despite generous assistance from foreign donors. To make matters worse, the South African health minister, who believed antiviral drugs were poison, promoted nutritional alternatives like lemons, garlic, and olives to treat HIV, thus

---

[8]For more on this, see "AIDS and South Africa: Deadly Quackery," by John Moore and Nicoli Nattrass, in *International Herald Tribune,* June 4, 2006.

using pseudoscience to provide worthless "cures," which ultimately resulted in the deaths of many South Africans. Why people persist in this form of denial despite widely publicized evidence to the contrary is both puzzling and troubling.

7. The Benefits of Self-Deception, Wishful Thinking, and Denial

Our account of human beings as self-deceivers, as well as rational agents, has been objected to on several grounds, perhaps the most important being that such a harmful device could not have evolved and, if it did, would long since have been weeded out by natural selection.[9] There are at least two important responses to this objection. First, whatever any theory may say, it seems clear that human beings do in fact deceive themselves and do engage in wishful thinking that sometimes results in harmful behavior. Those who accept a theory of evolution and natural selection have to make their theory conform to this fact—they cannot deny the fact because of their theory. (One of the great virtues of science is that scientists are not permitted to engage in this kind of monkey business.)

The second response is that self-deception and wishful thinking do in fact provide important survival benefits as well as harms; it thus makes sense to conclude that they evolved because of these beneficial effects. Although these benefits are not yet clearly understood, we now are beginning to grasp how this side of human nature works.

One important function of self-deception is to reduce anxiety or stress, giving us greater ability to make decisions and to act when delay might bring on disaster. One of the authors of this text, for example, was in a serious auto accident a few years ago during which he felt no fear whatsoever. He thus was able to control his car during the crucial moments in a way that would have been impossible had he been paralyzed by conscious fear. (After the accident was over, of course, he pretty much fell apart.) Psychologists would say that his fear was repressed during the crucial moments.

Anxiety reduction also is crucial with respect to long-term dangers and potential failures. Scientists are beginning to understand the biological effects of long-term anxiety on the body, and they are not good, to say the least. Stress is related to reduced effectiveness of the immune system and perhaps also to problems with other important body systems.[10] The relationship between anxiety or stress and belief systems is still not very well understood by psychologists, but this much seems to be true: Doubt, particularly doubt about important matters, produces anxiety in most people. Settling doubt and coming to some belief or other thus reduces anxiety and makes us feel better. So it isn't only the need to act, to do something, that sometimes leads us to premature or unwarranted beliefs. Even when there is nothing to be done right now, doubt may produce

---

[9]That the rational, intelligent side of our nature should have evolved seems quite natural, given its immense value in solving life's problems, and this idea was held even in the 19th century, for instance, by Charles Darwin and Charles Peirce, among many others.
[10]For an excellent and very readable account of the relationship of self-deception to anxiety reduction and of how the unconscious mind selects what comes into consciousness, see Daniel Goleman's *Vital Lies, Simple Truths* (New York: Simon & Schuster, 1985). For a short account of one theory concerning the relationship between stress and the immune and endocrine systems, see the May 1987 *Scientific American*, pp. 68B–68D.

Andy Capp by Reggie Smith. © 1976 Daily Mirror Newspapers Ltd.
Dist. Field Newspaper Syndicate. Reprinted with permission.

Self-deception at work.

ongoing anxiety (sometimes referred to as *generalized anxiety*), and wishful thinking that eliminates this doubt may reduce the anxiety.

Perhaps the classic case in which self-deception helps people to feel better and to act more effectively occurs when, in spite of medical evidence, the terminally ill deny the proximity of death, thus reducing the numbing effect of terrible fear. We all need defenses against the knowledge of the certainty of death; those close to it much more than the rest of us. Similarly, it may be useful to be able to deny the seriousness of ailments that are not life-threatening, as it was for Franklin D. Roosevelt, whose denial for some time of the permanence and debilitating nature of his paralysis may well have been an important reason that he was able to persevere and become president of the United States.

Self-deception also plays a positive role in life for those who tend to relive in memory the good experiences life has afforded them while tending to forget the bad ones. Why, years later, dwell on the bad? Why drag ourselves down in this way? (It's important, of course, to remember the mistakes one has made in order to make sure not to repeat them. The point is that nothing useful is accomplished by dwelling on them needlessly, as so many depressed people do.)

A widespread example of beneficial self-deception called the *placebo effect* occurs when people take dummy pills that they think are a form of medication but, in fact, are not. Because they expect the pills to make them well, they often do feel better even though the substance contains no medication whatsoever. Medical researchers have long understood the effect of placebos and regularly use them as a control in experiments to test the effectiveness of drugs. But a study published in the *Journal of the American Medical Association* (March 2008) showed that the cost of the pill as well as the placebo effect raised patients' expectations. Investigators gave dummy pain pills to half of the 82 participants, who read that they cost $2.50 a dose. The other half read that the pills had been discounted to 10 cents each. Participants were asked to rate the pain caused by electric shocks to their wrists before and after taking the pills. Although all the pills had a strong placebo effect on both groups, 85 percent of those taking the expensive ones said that they experienced significant pain relief compared to 61 percent taking the cheaper ones—yet the pills taken by both groups were identical. Studies like this illustrate the extent to which the mind will trick the body into responding, and in this sense the self-deception is beneficial. People who take untested alternative medicines often experience similar placebo effects even though the drugs may be worthless. The danger is that they may be trying to cure serious ailments with bogus pills, and no amount of self-deception will do that.

In some cases, however, there may be a serious difference of opinion concerning the benefits of the denial that death lurks nearby. It is notorious, for example, that most young men who find themselves in the lethal killing zones typical of modern wars are able to function even though terrified in a way that most of the rest of us can hardly imagine. They can fight (those who can—many cannot) in large part because they tend to see the flying bullets and exploding shells hitting the other guy, not themselves. Soldiers tell stories of the extreme surprise some individuals show when they realize that they have been hit and are dying. The people who send young men into battle rely on this ability of the young to deny consciously what in some sense they know all too well—that they may be the next one to get it. The obviously good function of this kind of self-deception is that it enables soldiers to fight for their country when outside forces threaten its existence. The not entirely good consequence is that tyrants and other megalomaniacal leaders find it easier to get the young to risk their lives in immoral or foolish endeavors.

8. The Pull of Pseudoscience and the Paranormal

That scientists, particularly those in the "hard sciences," generally know what they're talking about is vouchsafed by the everyday miracles that science makes possible, from computers to automobiles, TV sets, electric lightbulbs, nylon, toilet paper, eyeglasses, insulin, and clean water, hot or cold, flowing out of kitchen faucets. **Pseudoscientific theories** continue to be accepted by a significant number of people in spite of the fact that they produce no positive results whatsoever. Why is that?

A 2007 Harris interactive poll showed that a large number of Americans believe in ghosts (41%), UFO's (35%), witches (31%), and astrology (29%). Why are they all so gullible? The answer lies in the strength of the various psychological mechanisms that we have been discussing in this chapter. Although science produces results, it doesn't always provide easy or satisfying answers to our problems. Instead, it often confirms what we would like very much to deny, including, unfortunately, the fact that we are not entirely rational animals; that the virtuous are not always rewarded, nor the guilty punished; that hard work is the fate of most of us; and that in the end we all die. (It also says nothing one way or the other about the possibility of life after death.)

Pseudoscience, on the other hand, while it often titillates with predictions of disasters others will experience, generally has rosy things to tell us about our own futures. It sometimes allays fears that it itself has generated—for instance, by transforming the fear that extraterrestrials lurk about by making them into benign cuddly creatures. It tends to be comforting, uplifting, optimistic. It often provides relatively easy solutions to our problems. Astrologers tell us that we, too, can be successful in business, provided, of course, that we schedule economic transactions on the "right" days. Fortune-tellers predict success in romance and marriage. Mediums claim to put us into contact with departed loved ones (implying the happy thought, by the way, that we too will survive death).

Nevertheless, it is bound to seem odd that pseudosciences are so widely believed, given that they are regularly proved worthless. Astrology, for example, has been disproved countless times over the centuries. Pliny the Elder (Roman scholar and naturalist, 23–79 CE), for instance, stated a simple yet devastating objection to astrology way back then when he said, "If a man's destiny is caused by the star under which he is born, then all men born under that star should have the same fortune. But masters and slaves and kings and beggars all are born under the same star." Can wishful thinking alone generate the considerable acceptance so many pseudosciences enjoy in the face of constant refutation? Whatever the answer to that question, it is clear that a pseudoscience like astrology retains much of its appeal in spite of crushing objections in part because charlatans have devised ways to make it seem plausible to the very suggestive (most of us in weak moments).

One weapon in the con artist's arsenal is what some psychologists call the "Barnum effect," after 19th-century circus magnate P. T. Barnum. Barnum is deservedly famous for remarking that "There's a sucker born every minute," but he also maintained that the secret of his immense success was in providing a little something for everyone. Con artists disguised as astrologers follow this advice very carefully. They word their horoscopes ambiguously, so that virtually everybody who wants to can see themselves in the descriptions under their sign. Here is part of a "typical Barnum profile":

> You have a great need for other people to like you and admire you. You have a tendency to be critical of yourself. You have a great deal of unused capacity which you have not used to your advantage. While you have some personality weaknesses, you are generally able to compensate for them. . . . You pride yourself on being an independent thinker and do not accept others' statements without satisfactory proof.

In fact, this description fits relatively few people, but it does fit how most of us think of ourselves—or want to think of ourselves.

However, not all statements in horoscope columns are of the Barnum type. The typical "Aries" is generally said to be "bold, energetic, assertive, selfish, insensitive, and aggressive." Only some of these characteristics are highly thought of. Typical horoscopes mix statements listing these kinds of character traits with statements of a general Barnum nature. "People tend to be impressed by the specific details that appear to fit (and pay less attention to those that do not), while the general Barnum-type statements provide readily acceptable 'padding'."[11]

Extrasensory perception (telepathy, clairvoyance, precognition, and so forth) is another form of pseudoscience widely believed by the public. But, in fact, over a century of research fails to confirm the existence of ESP in any of its alleged forms. After reviewing a large body of research in this area for the National Research Council, a scientific committee concluded that "despite a 130-year record of scientific research on such matters our committee could find no scientific justification for the existence of phenomena such as extrasensory perception, mental telepathy, or 'mind over matter' exercises. . . . Evaluation of the large body of the best available evidence simply does not support the contention that these phenomena exist."[12]

---

[11]Taken from a fascinating article by Christopher C. French, Mandy Fowler, Katy McCarthy, and Debbie Peers entitled "Belief in Astrology: A Test of the Barnum Effect," *Skeptical Inquirer* (Winter 1991).

[12]*American Psychological Association Monitor,* January 1988—more recent evaluations come to the same conclusion.

Con artists are pikers in the great sweep of things. They titillate, comfort, and do a small amount of harm, and that's about it. But the great mesmerizers, the Benito Mussolinis and Ruholla Khomeinis, who sell whole nations a bill of goods, are another matter. Here are a few pronouncements about mass propaganda by Adolf Hitler, an intuitive master at the game (culled from his writings by the Secular Humanist Bulletin, March 1988):

All propaganda must be popular and its intellectual level must be adjusted to the most limited intelligence among those it is addressed to.

All effective propaganda must be limited to a very few points and must harp on these slogans until the last member of the public understands what you want him to understand by your slogan. . . . [T]he masses are slow-moving, and they require a certain time before they are ready even to notice a thing, and only after the simplest ideas are repeated thousands of times will the masses finally remember them.

Propaganda's effect . . . must be aimed at the emotions and only to a very limited degree at the so-called intellect. [Italics added.]

The very first axiom of all propagandist activity: to wit, the basically subjective and one-sided attitude it must take toward every question it deals with. The function of propaganda is . . . not to weigh and ponder the rights of different people, but exclusively to emphasize the one right that it has set out to argue for. Its task is not to make an objective study of the truth, . . . its task is to serve our own right, always and unflinchingly.

Does this sound like the formula to which most political rhetoric in the United States today is tailored?

In the face of such findings, why do people continue to believe in ESP? We mentioned a few reasons a few pages back, but Thomas Gilovich, a cognitive psychologist at Cornell University, concludes (from surveys asking people to explain the origin of their beliefs) that personal experience also plays an important role. When by chance or coincidence people experience a run of good or bad luck they often attribute it to some special power. Gamblers who have streaks of luck at blackjack or roulette have trouble accepting the fact that the theory of probability predicts that streaks of luck are likely to occur every once in a while. They often become convinced that some special power is at work—that unseen forces are on their side—rather than accept the fact that coincidences are bound to happen now and then.

Premonitions fall into the same category. A premonition is really a coincidence that occurs between someone's thoughts and actual events in the real world. A young man dreams about his ex-girlfriend, and lo and behold, she calls him the next day. If he thinks his dream is a premonition, he has forgotten for the moment the many times he has dreamed about her when she didn't call. After all, people frequently dream about ex-lovers, but rarely do they telephone the next day. When they do, it's coincidental. This element of chance applies as well to extraordinary premonitions that foretell an important event that really does occur. A woman has a dream that a TWA DC 6 will crash in the Florida Everglades—and it does! Of what significance is this? The question to ask is whether such events occur more often than we would expect them to by chance. People have an unfortunate tendency to believe premonitions that come true and to forget those that don't. This, by the way, nicely illustrates the difference between pseudoscience and science. Pseudoscience pays attention to successes and ignores failures; science never ignores failures. It puts its hypotheses to severe tests, requiring independent repetition of observations and experiments rather than relying simply on coincidence and anecdote.

9. Lack of a Good Sense of Proportion

The kinds of irrationality catalogued in this chapter so far—provincialism, self-deception, and so on—seem to have evolved primarily because they are advantageous in certain kinds of circumstances. Self-deception, as mentioned before, may reduce stress, and provincialism tends to increase group cohesiveness. But explanations as to why so many of us lack a good *sense of proportion* are much harder to come by.[13] In any case, there can be no doubt that on occasion we all lack a good sense of proportion when we make decisions and come to conclusions in everyday life. The trick is to learn how to minimize this natural impediment to cogent reasoning.

Prudence is one of the chief components of a good sense of proportion. In the sense intended here, prudence consists in being provident—of tempering what we do today to maximize our overall, long-run interests. Of course, being prudent does not mean becoming a drudge, or a workaholic. It doesn't mean always putting off until tomorrow pleasures that could have been had today. But it does mean carefully weighing today's pleasures against long-term interests.

Note, though, that imprudence frequently is not a factor when people lack a sense of proportion. The impediments to cogent reasoning already discussed certainly play an important role here. A sense of loyalty, for example, sometimes clouds the perspective of even the most level-headed among us, leading us to exaggerate the wonders of our own society while neglecting its defects. And wishful thinking certainly plays an important role. People play state lotteries not just because they have little understanding of what it means to say the odds are a million or a hundred thousand to one against winning

---

[13]Part of the explanation lies, no doubt, in the benefits of the psychological mechanisms already discussed. But perhaps another part lies in two important facts about human evolution. The first is that behavior guided by intelligence is a later arrival on the scene than responses motivated purely by desires and emotions (something that is confirmed by what is known about the development of the brains of vertebrate animals—in particular, mammals). Strong emotions that appropriately guided behavior at much earlier times now sometimes skew rational thought and motivate responses that are less than optimal. The second relevant fact is that until quite recently, very little was known about what philosophers used to call the "secret powers" that move things, and a great deal that was "known" has turned out to be false. (Think only of medicine until about 150 years ago, when practices such as bloodletting were common.) If we go back, say, just 10,000 or 20,000 years in human history—an eye blink on the evolutionary time scale—we are back to a time when exceedingly few accurate general beliefs about cause-and-effect relationships can have been known. So it is only recently in the great sweep of things that it has slowly become increasingly beneficial to moderate the urges of immediate desire and strong emotions in terms of what intelligence can learn from experience. Perhaps, then, the lack of a better sense of proportion is partly explained as being due to a kind of "evolutionary lag."

It often is difficult to know whether someone is irrationally self-deceived, or perhaps imprudent, rather than being completely rational. Take the case of professional boxers and football players. Do they deceive themselves about the likelihood of permanent and serious damage to their bodies? Are they being extremely imprudent? Or do they so value their professional life (and its financial rewards) that to them it is worth the pain and suffering likely at a later date? Some retired professional football players, for instance, say that they were foolish to take the pounding week after week that has left them walking wounded; others say it was worth it. Are the latter still deceiving themselves?

the big prize but also because of wishful thinking. ("This is my lucky day," or "I was born on 1/23/45, so 12345 is my lucky number.")

But there are plenty of cases, some of a much more serious nature, in which wishful thinking or self-deception plays little or no role. After the attack on the World Trade Center, for instance, Americans stopped flying just about everywhere. While this reaction was understandable, given the terrifying nature of the event, the odds against being killed in this way were millions to one. (Again, driving to work every day is much more life-threatening.) Many Americans refuse to fly commercial airplanes from one city to another even though driving is many times more dangerous. In fact, flying commercial airlines is just about the safest way to travel ever invented, yet lots of people, including one of the authors of this chapter on pseudoreasoning, have serious bouts with fear every time they fly.[14]

In fact, failure to see things in proper perspective is one of the most serious errors in reasoning that most of us are guilty of. As might be expected, politicians frequently (one might say continually) take advantage this tendency in our nature. They know that people can be diverted from important issues and problems by being given "bread and circuses" and that, for instance, the best time to announce unpopular measures is when the minds of masses of people are riveted on the private lives of celebrities like Lindsay Lohan or Britney Spears. Sometimes these measures slide under the radar when other, more riveting news hits the media. For instance, in 2007 when the subprime mortgage debacle surfaced and the stock market skittered around, President Bush vetoed a bill to expand health-care coverage to include more children under the State Children's Health Insurance Program (SCHIP). The cost of this program—$60 billion over a five-year period—was a drop in the bucket compared to the staggering cost of the Iraq War, at $607 billion in direct funding, plus uncalculated billions in hidden costs. This, in itself, shows a skewed sense of proportion, but apparently members of Congress didn't get things in perspective either, because they failed to muster enough votes to override the president's veto, and the American people, sidetracked by other issues, paid the matter little attention.

---

[14]In some of these cases, psychologists understand the mechanisms leading to the poor sense of proportion—for example, a fear of unfamiliar threats as compared to the familiar and, in the case of airline flying, a lack of personal control of the plane (similar to fear felt when sitting in the back seat of a car). But they don't understand why people are prone to these kinds of irrationality.

SUMMARY OF CHAPTER 6

Human beings are not completely rational animals. There also is a nonrational component to our makeup that often interferes with our ability to argue or reason cogently.

1. Our reasoning sometimes is skewed from the truth because of *loyalty,* which inclines us to see our own society and its beliefs in a more favorable light than the evidence may warrant; because of *provincialism,* which tends to narrow our interests and knowledge of what goes on in the world; and because of the *herd instinct,* which makes it easy and natural for us to believe what most others in our society believe. *Example:* Failing to notice the undemocratic and nasty things our own government does on the international scene.

2. Loyalty and provincialism are related to *prejudice*—in particular, to prejudice against members of other groups, and to thinking in terms of unverified stereotypes. *Example:* The stereotype that was common in the United States until about the late 1950s, which pictured African Americans as foot-shuffling, obsequious children. But believing bad things about others constitutes prejudice only when not justified by sufficient evidence.

   Prejudice against others often is conjoined with an overtolerance of the defects and foibles of one's own group and its members, and it may be reinforced by the need to find *scapegoats*—others who can be blamed for our own troubles and mistakes. *Example:* Blaming the Jews for the transgressions of others.

   Thinking in terms of stereotypes and scapegoats often stems from a *partisan mind-set*—viewing everything in terms of "us against them" or "my right opinions against your wrong ones." Good reasoners, by way of contrast, have minds open to the truth, wherever it may lead.

3. *Superstitions* often are supported by a small amount of evidence. What makes them superstitions is that we believe them on the basis of insufficient and, frequently, biased samples from which all negative evidence has been eliminated. *Example:* Overlooking the fact that good things sometimes happen on Friday the 13th and bad things on other days.

4. Beliefs acquired in the irrational ways just described generally result from *wishful thinking*—believing what we want to believe, no matter what the evidence— or from its variant, called *self-deception*—consciously believing what, at some deeper level, we know to be dubious. *Example:* British Prime Minister Neville Chamberlain wishfully believing that the Munich agreement with Hitler had assured "peace in our time."

5. Two other important ways to cut the wishful thinking pie are *rationalization, suppression,* and *denial. Example:* Smoking cigarettes after being exposed to all sorts of evidence that they're bad for one's health. Rationalization often supports *procrastination*—putting off until tomorrow what ought to be done today. *Example:* Starting to write a term paper the day before it's due.

6. While we can't yet be sure why nonrational mechanisms have evolved, scientists are beginning to understand some of their beneficial effects. Loyalty and provincialism increase group cohesiveness when there is competition or strife with other groups. The herd instinct helps individuals to work well with others in their

group. And self-deception frequently aids in the reduction of anxiety and stress, both of which can be harmful to health. Prolonged doubt about serious matters tends to produce stress and anxiety; coming to firm beliefs about these matters tends to combat depression and thus be good for one's physical well-being. *Example:* Denying the seriousness of a terminal illness, thereby reducing grief at the end of one's life.

7. *Pseudoscientific beliefs* are adopted, and endure, in spite of their failure to help us deal successfully with everyday problems, because of wishful thinking, self-deception, and similar psychological mechanisms. *Pseudoscience* is comforting and upbeat concerning our own welfare and the satisfaction of our deepest desires. *Example:* Seances that practitioners claim can put us into contact with deceased friends and relatives.

   But pseudosciences also gain widespread acceptance because charlatans have learned how to manipulate us in our unguarded or weak moments. *Example:* Alleged astrologers papering over the phoniness of their forecasts by larding them with "Barnum" profiles that tend to fit everybody. Note that the con artists who play on our weaknesses in this way are two-bit operators compared to such great political mesmerizers as Adolf Hitler, who expertly manipulate masses of their compatriots by clever and sophisticated appeals to the irrational side of the human psyche.

8. On occasion, most of us lack a good *sense of proportion,* a defect in reasoning that critical reasoners try to minimize. *Example:* Being persuaded by political rhetoric to pay more attention to relatively unimportant matters than to those that are more serious. Being *prudent,* in the sense of provident—acting so as to maximize long-run interests—is an important component of a good sense of proportion that we often lack. *Example:* Weighing today's small pleasure more highly than the long-run benefits of doing well on a final exam, thus not preparing until the last minute. But people often fail to see things in proper perspective for other reasons; for example, because of group loyalty or wishful thinking or because of other emotional interferences with cogent reasoning. *Example:* Being more afraid of small risks than of much bigger ones.

EXERCISE 6-1

1. How about this *Luann* cartoon?

Luann reprinted by permission of United Features Syndicate, Inc.

2. When France defied the United States and came out against the Iraq War in 2003, the same sort of stereotypes surfaced among some Americans as did at the end of World War II when the GIs liberated Paris: The French don't bathe, they're cowardly collaborators, their women are loose, and the like. Explain the psychological impediments involved and compare the political climates that gave rise to these attitudes.

3. Explain how this conversation between a student and a teacher (not quite verbatim) relates to topics discussed in this chapter:

   Student: I've come to your office to see about getting a B in this course.
   Teacher: But you're doing C work, the semester ends next week, and you missed two assignments. What makes you think you can get a B?
   Student: Well, I need to get a B, to get into Berkeley [University of California at Berkeley] next fall.
   Teacher: But why didn't you come in sooner and talk to me about this and perhaps get help to do better work?
   Student: Yes. But I really need to get that B, or I can't get into Berkeley.

4. Explain how this conversation between two students (again not quite verbatim, with names changed to protect the guilty) relates to topics discussed in this chapter:

   Smith: Loan me 20 bucks. I'm strapped and have a heavy date with you-know-who.
   Jones: You're always asking me for favors, but you never do any for me. I always do the favors you ask of me; you regularly turn me down. Sorry, Charlie.
   Smith: Hey! What about last year when I got you a date with Charlene? You never got me a date with anyone. So how about it?

5. Do you believe that loyalty really does skew people's beliefs away from what the evidence will support? If so, support your belief with at least one example not mentioned in the text. If not, show that the examples given in the text are somehow mistaken.

6. Do human beings really have a herd instinct, or is that just true of cows and such? Defend your answer.

7. How does the text use the expression "belief provincialism"? Give some examples, other than those mentioned in the text, and explain why they are examples.

8. According to the text, what is wrong with categorizing, say, the French as great lovers, Germans as obedient automatons, and so on? After all, doesn't experience show that the members of a given group tend to be different from the members of other groups, as Greeks are different from Pakistanis and Mexicans from Nigerians?

9. Give at least two examples of other people engaging in self-deception or wishful thinking, and explain why you think their actions fit the relevant descriptions provided in the text. Do you ever engage in this sort of funny business? Explain and defend your answer. (Hint: You do.)

10. What are some of the good consequences of wishful thinking and self-deception that are mentioned in the text? Explain. Can you think of others?

11. Critically evaluate the following argument. (Does it contain a correct use of induction?) "Several of my friends have been very lucky in life so far, and I've read of quite a few other lucky souls. So when I say that my lucky friends will continue to have good luck, I'm basing my conclusion on experience, not wishful thinking."

12. If you had been interviewed for the Harris poll discussed on page 140, would you have been among those expressing belief in at least one of the claims asked about by that poll? If so, explain. If not, you get a free ride on this question. (Note the temptation for those who would have been among the ones with the appropriate beliefs to engage in a tiny sort of "lie of silent assertion" by simply passing over this question!)

13. Carefully explain the so-called Barnum effect. How did the typical Barnum profile reprinted in this chapter fit you?

14. The box on page 142 lists some of the principles underlying Adolf Hitler's propaganda technique. Find at least two examples from the speeches of American presidents, members of the U.S. Congress, or Supreme Court justices that seem to be in accordance with these principles. Explain and defend your choices. (It's cheating to use examples that appear in this text.)

15. We all suffer to some extent from the impediments to rational thinking described in this chapter, the authors of this text not being exceptions. (Actually, one of us is an exception, but the other isn't.) Doesn't this textbook, for example, reflect the provincialism of its authors in some ways? If so, how? If not, why might some readers think otherwise? What about any other ways in which you think the text could be construed so as to indicate rational failures—of the kind discussed in this chapter—on the part of its authors? (Be brief!)

*A*n important art of politicians is to find new names for institutions which under old names have become odious to the public.

— Talleyrand

If concepts are not clear, words do not fit. If words do not fit, the day's work cannot be accomplished, morals and art do not flourish. If morals and art do not flourish, punishments are not just. If punishments are not just, the people do not know where to put hand or foot.

—Confucius, *Analects,* XIII: 3

When an idea is wanting, a word can always be found to take its place.

—Goethe

He who defines the terms wins the argument.

—Chinese proverb

Beware of and eschew pompous prolixity.

—Charles A. Beardsley

Chapter

7

LANGUAGE

Language is the indispensable tool used in formulating arguments. We all are familiar (or should be!) with the power of language when it is employed by fine writers of fiction—Shakespeare, Fielding, Austen, Conrad (to name just a few who wrote in the English language)—the list is very long. The principal point of literature classes is precisely to make this apparent. But good writing can be equally effective when used in the construction of argumentative essays and other argumentative passages. The trouble is that language also can be used effectively in the service of fallacious as well as cogent arguments, deceiving the unwary or unknowing into accepting arguments they should reject.

1. COGNITIVE AND EMOTIVE MEANINGS

If the purpose of a sentence is to inform or to state a fact, some of its words must refer to things, events, or properties of one kind or another. These words must thus have what is commonly called **cognitive meaning.** (The sentences they compose also are said to have cognitive meaning.)

But most words also have **emotive meaning,** which means that they have positive or negative overtones. The emotive charges of some words are obvious. Think of the terms *wop, kike, nigger,* and *fag,* or the so-called four-letter words that rarely appear in textbooks, even in this permissive age.

The words just mentioned have negative emotive charges. But lots of words have positive overtones. Examples are *freedom, love, democracy, springtime,* and *peace.* And plenty of others have either neutral or mixed emotive force. *Pencil, run,* and *river* tend to be neutral words. *Socialism, politician,* and *whiskey* get mixed reviews.

In fact, almost any word that is emotively positive for some people or in some contexts may be just the opposite for others. One person's meat often is indeed another's poison. Perhaps the paradigm case is the word *God,* which has one kind of overtone for true believers, another for agnostics, and still another for strident atheists. To the average person, the word *student* has positive connotations, but not to a landlord or landlady.

Terms that on first glance may appear to be emotively neutral often turn out to have at least modest emotive overtones. The terms *bureaucrat, government official,* and *public servant,* for instance, all refer to the same group of people and thus have approximately the same cognitive import, but their emotive meanings are quite different. Of the three, only *government official* comes close to being neutral in tone.

2. EMOTIVE MEANINGS AND PERSUASIVE USES OF LANGUAGE

The fact that expressions have emotive as well as cognitive meanings has not escaped the notice of con artists, advertisers, politicians, and others whose stock in trade is the manipulation of attitudes, desires, and beliefs. Over the years, they have learned how to use the emotive side of language to further their own ends, whether benevolent or self-serving.

One common way in which the emotive force of language can be used to con, as Talleyrand observed some time ago, is to mask the odious nature of an institution or practice by giving it a nice name rather than a more accurate, nasty one. Why call the Chinese dictatorship by an accurate name when it can be called the *People's Republic of China?* When Saddam Hussein took control of Iraq, why should he have fiddled with the increasingly inaccurate name *Republic of Iraq?* The ruling clique in Myanmar (formerly Burma) surely has no reason to call its thugs who engage in mass murder and other kinds of nasty business anything other than the *State Peace and Development Council.* In a slightly different vein, why call diluted beer *watered-down beer* when you can call it *lite?* Why should a minority political group call itself *The Moral Minority,* when it can puff itself up into *The Moral Majority?* (Note, by the way, the implication that the individuals in this group are more moral than other people.) And doesn't *Department of Defense* have a much sweeter ring to it than the original and more accurate name *War Department?* And how about the *Clear Skies Initiative,* Bushspeak for the set of pollution laws that dumb down the *Clean Air Act?*

I am firm, you are obstinate, he is pigheaded.

—Bertrand Russell's example of words having similar
cognitive meanings but much different emotive senses

The language of diplomacy is particularly prone to tricky manipulation, especially when it refers to provocative international issues. A good case in point was cited by William Safire in his column on language.[1] In 2006, when things were heating up between Israel and the new Hamas government in Palestine, the prime minister, Ehud Olmert, wanted to move 90,000 Israelis from West Bank villages into secure areas behind the antiterrorist fence under construction, but instead of using the word *retreat,* he wanted a synonym that would not suggest weakness for withdrawing, or imply that the new border was permanent. The Hebrew word chosen was *hitkansut,* or coming together (in a safe place), which seemed an appropriate choice for the Israelis, but the problem came with translating the term for the international community. After several false starts, Olmert and his aides decided on *realignment,* which suggests shifting of the lines to describe their withdrawal plan. Safire notes, "By adjusting the line of separation without seeking to establish a formal border, Israel's purpose is to minimize friction while retaining its historic claim on the land in dispute." Thus, the carefully chosen translation was an attempt to gain international support for establishing a firm line of separation from Palestine for the present, while leaving open the possibility of reclaiming the disputed land in the future. This type of language manipulation goes on all the time in diplomatic circles, where word choice is often critical in policy explanations.

In recent years, manipulative uses of language have been given a spate of emotively negative names, each with a slightly different connotation, including *doublespeak* (deliberately ambiguous or evasive language), *bureaucratese* (governmental doublespeak), *newspeak* (media doublespeak), *academese* (the academic variety), *legalese* (lawyer talk), *gobbledygook, bafflegab,* and *jargon.*

Take *militaryese.* The military at all times and places has devised expressions intended as much as possible to hide the fact that war is, to put it mildly, unvarnished hell. For example, the term *waterboarding* sounds more like a harmless water sport than what it really is, a brutal method of torture. Here are some more examples:

Comfort women	Women of conquered countries forced to work as prostitutes "servicing" soldiers (term used by the Japanese during World War II)
Preemptive action	Our side attacking first
Battle fatigue	Insanity suffered as a result of the unbearable horrors and strains of battle
Incursion	Invasion
Collateral damage	People who are inadvertently killed or property that is inadvertently destroyed in warfare
Ethnic cleansing	Driving out unwanted citizens of a country, burning their houses, and killing some along the way (as in Kosovo, 1999)
Enhanced interrogation technique	Torture

---

[1]William Safire, "When Diplolingo Does the Job," *International Herald Tribune,* June 11, 2006.

Friendly fire	Shelling friendly villages or troops by mistake
Servicing a target or visiting a site	Bombing a place flat (used during the Gulf War)
Information extraction	Torturing people into giving confessions
Pacification center	Concentration camp (itself originally doublespeak)
Termination	Killing (also used by the CIA, where *termination with prejudice* means *assassination*)
Selective ordinance	Napalm (used to kill by incineration)
The Final Solution	Plan of the Nazis to murder all European Jews

During World War II—one of the most awful of all wars—the expression *dehousing industrial workers* was used by the British and Americans to mean killing civilians, including women and children via *saturation* air raids. The indescribably horrible massive air raids on Germany and Japan that created incredible firestorms were said to result in *self-energized dislocation,* not widespread death by either incineration or asphyxiation. The term *war* itself has been euphemized into *conflict* or *operation.* Bush the elder waged "Operation Desert Shield"; Bush the younger, "Operation Iraqi Freedom." In the latter conflict the term *war* was used to describe the War on Terrorism or the War for Peace (!), but not the Iraq War, until we were several years into the conflict. During that war, both sides manipulated terminology to suit their own bias. In the United States the networks used the term *coalition forces* for what the Arab media called *occupation forces.* And when CNN reported that 16 "insurgents" were killed in an Iraqi uprising (May 7, 2004), the Arab media described them as "resistance fighters." George Orwell got it right when he said "If thought corrupts language, language can also corrupt thought." Few people would realize that the harmless terms cited above were devised to sugarcoat the truth, or create a bias, or mask sinister, even hideous practices—unless it were pointed out to them.

The military isn't the only master of doublespeak. The law has its own version— legalese, a hybrid of French, English, and Latin that baffles the average person. In plain English a *writ* is a claim form, and a *plaintiff* is someone who makes a complaint against another party. Meetings with the judge *in camera* are just private meetings behind closed doors. Why all this turgid terminology? The principal reason is to ensure certainty, to protect clients by using phrases defined by statutes or case law. Using different expressions may raise doubts as to precisely what is meant. But why can't plain English accomplish the same thing? Another justification is that it's cheaper and less trouble to use archaic language than to rewrite everything. Maybe, but then again, lawyers might have to charge lower fees if legal documents were clear.

Of course, bureaucratese, governmentese, and politicalese (we all can play at this game) don't exactly suffer from a paucity of examples. Political attack groups seem particularly prone to giving themselves euphemistic names. In the run-up to the 2008 presidential primaries, a group called Common Sense Issues launched a smear campaign against John McCain. It made millions of phone calls to South Carolina voters claiming he "has voted to use unborn babies in medical research," and to Iowa voters accusing him of creating "The most restrictive assault on free speech [the McCain-Feingold bill] ever passed in America" because his bill tightened the rules on campaign contributions![2] Given the irrational distortion of these attacks, the term *common sense* in the group's name can only be a euphemism for *nonsense*. John Kerry suffered similar attacks in the 2004 presidential campaign by a group called Swift Boat Veterans for Truth (a euphemism if there ever was one) that launched a barrage of slanderous ads smearing his military record.

These examples illustrate the use of *euphemistic language*—locutions from which as much negative emotive content as possible has been removed—and the replacement of accurate names with more high-flown locutions. The point generally is to conceal or to mislead, which could be one reason that this kind of talk has become so popular with government officials, lawyers, military officers, doctors, and (alas!) a large number of academics. (Is this one reason why so many other[!] textbooks are so dull?)

In recent years, however, it's possible that doublespeak in the business world has managed to surpass even that of militaryese in its deviousness. Well, maybe not. But consider these examples of euphemisms used when someone is fired:

> *bumped, decruited, dehired, deselected, destaffed, discontinued, disemployed, dislocated, downsized, excessed, involuntarily separated, nonretained, nonrenewed, severed, surplussed, transitioned, vocationally relocated*[3]

Firing large numbers of workers is *corporate rightsizing,* by the way, and the place where you get *downsized* is sometimes called the *outplacement office.*

This euphemistic trend in the business world is often satirized in the media. For instance, in a *Doonesbury* cartoon (November 20, 1999) satirizing the owners of startup companies that earn no money but make millions from IPOs (initial public offerings of

---

Everyone knows that politics is fertile ground for doublespeak. All political parties use it when it suits their purposes. Here are a few examples noted in John Leo's article "Double Trouble Speak" (*U.S. News & World Report,* July 4, 2005).

Republican	Democrat
climate change	global warming
trial lawyer	personal injury lawyer
faith-based	religious
school choice	school vouchers
tax relief	tax cuts
illegal	undocumented
fetus	uterine contents
military difficulties	quagmire

---

[2]Quotes from "McCain Parries a Reprise of '00 Smear Tactics," by Elisabeth Bumiller, *New York Times,* January 17, 2008.
[3]New York Times Service (March 8, 1996); mentioned in the July 1996 issue of the *Quarterly Review of Doublespeak.*

*A play on words that distorts paying off the national debt to mean paying down the debt
that the G. W. Bush character owes to his campaign contributors.*

stock), one character says, "We'll probably walk away with a fortune. It's only the small
investors who get burned. It's called socializing the risk while privatizing the profit."

Interestingly, class differences have always been mirrored euphemistically. Average
people *rent* apartments; the rich *lease* them. The nonrich talk of *social climbers;* social
climbers like to think of themselves as *upwardly mobile* or (more recently) *changing
course,* and not as *pushy* but rather as *emphatic.* The wealthy don't earn a *salary,* they
receive *compensation* or have an *income.*

In the field of education euphemisms abound (and why should we be different?). One
college gives placement tests in *Student Success Workshops,* presumably to soften the
blow to the many students who place in remedial (uh, developmental) classes. Teachers
no longer *teach* but *facilitate* in *comfort zones* where *collaborative learning* occurs.

The deliberate use of euphemistic language has been going on at least since the beginning of recorded history, but it seems to have increased dramatically in recent years,
perhaps because of the professionalization of most trades. Titled professionals want to
sound objective and authoritative, not opinionated or biased. Also, controversial topics
can be toned down when dressed in euphemistic language. For instance, to lessen its
negative connotation, the term *abortion* comes in many guises nowadays: *effecting fetal
demise, planned cessation of gestation, interrupted pregnancy, termination,* and *selective reduction.*

It's true that euphemisms can and often do serve useful, nonmanipulative functions. Circumlocutions used to replace offensive four-letter words are good examples. Using expressions like *put to sleep, passed gas,* and *for the mature figure* often is just a matter of politeness. Why shock or offend when we don't have to? Nevertheless, all too often euphemisms are used to further Machiavellian purposes. Indeed, the nastier something is, the greater the need to clothe it in neutral garb.

Doublespeak has become so common that we hardly notice it. Euphemisms slide past us without registering and soften our grasp of reality. When politicians "misspeak" rather than lie, we are less likely to hold them accountable. When the military "deploys troops" rather than invades a country, we are less alarmed. When mayors refer to neighborhoods with "substandard housing" rather than slums or ghettos, we are less likely to think of people living in poverty.[4] Doublespeak hoodwinks us into thinking wrong is right, dangerous situations are benign, poverty is nonexistent, and we are lulled into a deceptive calm. A misleading phrase here and there may not seem like much, but the cumulative effect is to erode our understanding of what is actually going on in the world. When doublespeak is a buffer between us and reality, we are more likely to be manipulated into mindless acceptance of half truths, distortions, and lies.

Of course, sometimes attempts to whitewash bad news are so obvious that the American public simply rolls its collective eyes. When a recession loomed in 2008, President Bush avoided the R word and talked, instead, about "economic challenges" and "uncertainties," as in ". . . we have a dynamic economy, but there are some uncertainties." It didn't take an economist to recognize the code language for recession. Given the sinking economy and the drain on their pocketbooks, most people fully understood what was going on, and no amount of hedging could convince them otherwise. Unfortunately, many people have trouble seeing through doublespeak until they are personally affected, and sometimes that is too late.

Doublespeak is especially deadly when it comes in whole sentences or runs on for whole paragraphs. Academese illustrates this nicely. Here, for example, is a tiny snippet from Zellig Harris's well-known text *Structural Linguistics* that makes a simple idea seem more profound:

> Another consideration is the availability of simultaneity, in addition to successivity as a relation among linguistic elements.

This seems to mean (there is a certain amount of vagueness here) that we can do two things at once, like gesture while we talk. (You didn't know that, did you?)

Now that appetites have been whetted, how about a sampling of truly impenetrable prose?

> Indeed dialectical critical realism may be seen under the aspect of Foucauldian strategic reversal—of the unholy trinity of Parmenidean /Platonic/Aristotelian provenance; of the Cartesian-Lockean-Humean-Kantian paradigm, of foundationalism . . . new and old alike; of the primordial failing of western philosophy, ontological monovalence, and its close ally, the epistemic fallacy with its ontic dual. (*New York Times,* February 27, 1999, report of a Modern Language Association [MLA] speech)

---

[4]Examples are taken from *Doublespeak Defined,* by William Lutz, a perceptive compilation and commentary of misleading language.

> *The popularity of the writings of George Orwell is an important reason that dou-blespeak has received more than a usual amount of attention in recent years. In this excerpt from his 1948 classic "Politics and the English Language," he explains one reason why politicians favor this less-than-straightforward kind of rhetoric:*
>
> In our time, political speech and writing are largely the defence of the indefensible. . . . Thus political language has to consist largely of euphemism, question begging, and sheer cloudy vagueness. Defenceless villages are bombarded from the air, the inhabitants driven out into the countryside, the cattle machine-gunned, the huts set on fire with incendiary bullets: This is called *pacification*. Millions of peasants are robbed of their farms and sent trudging along the roads with no more than they can carry: This is called *transfer of population* or *rectification of frontiers*. . . .
>
> The inflated style is itself a kind of euphemism. A mass of Latin words falls upon the facts like soft snow, blurring the outlines and covering up all the details. *The great enemy of clear language is insincerity. When there is a gap between one's real and one's declared aims, one turns as it were instinctively to long words and exhausted idioms, like a cuttlefish squirting out ink.* [These italics added.]

This little gem earned the author, Roy Bhaskar, first prize for bad writing by "serious" scholars, awarded by the New Zealand–based *Journal of Philosophy and Literature.*

Both these examples of academese are badly written in one way or another (actually several). They use inflated or obscure language and, of special note, are full of *jargon.* There are several senses of this term, one being nonsensical, incoherent, or meaningless talk; another the specialized language used by professionals when talking (or writing) to each other. The trouble is that jargon intended in the professional sense can and often does turn out to be jargon in the meaningless or incoherent sense, making vacuous or otherwise simple and easily understood remarks appear to be profound. The MLA item quoted here may well illustrate the incoherent variety (who can be sure?); the Harris remark exemplifies the obvious made to seem important.

Note the connection here, by the way, with what we said in Chapter 3 in the discussion of appeals to authorities about not being intimidated by professional lingo. Telling patients that they have a *malignant melanoma,* for example, may leave them ignorant of the fact that they have a form of skin cancer, which, if untreated, quickly leads to death.

We need to remember, though, that technical terms used by professional people generally do have an important function—namely, to ensure precision when it counts. Lawyers want contracts to be airtight. Doctors need to be sure they understand each other when they talk about patient illnesses. It may be adequate for a layperson to talk, say, about rapid or irregular heartbeats, but cardiologists need a more precise way of distinguishing the various kinds—distinguishing, for example, *supra ventricular tachycardia* from *atrial fibrillation* or from the immediately life-threatening *ventricular fibrillation.* Use of these technical expressions quickly conveys rather precise and absolutely vital information from one doctor to another. Technical jargon used by people in the same field is an essential form of communication, but when it deteriorates into incoherent or meaningless verbiage, it is puzzling at best and incomprehensible at worst.

As the world changes, language inevitably changes with it. New words come into common use for things and procedures that didn't exist just a few years ago; old words take on new meanings. The computer age illustrates this nicely. We now talk glibly of an inanimate variety of mouse, clipless clipboards, nonedible menus, floppy and hard discs, RAM, ROM, bytes and even megabytes, and glass-less windows. We cut and paste without scissors or glue, and not only delete but also unerase. We surf the (dry) Net and zero in on spiderless websites, navigating with a cursor.

Initially, these new locutions were used and understood primarily by computer nerds and functioned, as professionalese generally does, to exclude the uninitiated. But they quickly worked their way into the vocabularies of everyone who uses computers, even though much of what we do with them is word processing or game playing, not mathematical computation. So it goes.

Another common feature of jargon, by the way, is *padding*—adding significant-sounding sentences here and there that in fact say little or nothing. Here is an example typical of a common variety in psychological writings: "Although the effects of mental attitudes on bodily disease should not be exaggerated, neither should they be minimized." True. And here is an example of another type: "As soon as there are behaviors you can't generate, then there are responses you can't elicit." Yes. And another: "In order to achieve products, outputs, and outcomes through processes, inputs are required." Absolutely.

3. OTHER COMMON RHETORICAL DEVICES

Let's now look at a few of the many other rhetorical devices that are frequently used to manipulate the unwary or less knowledgeable. (This does not mean that these devices cannot be used in the services of truth and justice!)

Tone

Good writers or speakers try to choose the **tone** best suited to their audience, as students are taught to do in writing classes. Tone expresses attitudes or feelings—of compassion, anger, levity, humility, congeniality, and so on—and can be quite powerful when

Reprinted by permission of Stuart Hample.

employed properly in argumentative passages. Using the proper tone, even though doing so clearly plays to emotions, isn't like arguing fallaciously or from premises known to be false, but rather is just a matter of common sense; arguments aren't won by unnecessarily ruffling the other guy's feathers.

But tone can be employed for nefarious purposes, not just virtuous ones. Lawyers addressing juries are masters of the art, as are politicians addressing constituents. Success in politics requires knowing how to use the tone of "Mom and apple pie" rhetoric when addressing, say, families of soldiers returning from overseas duty and humor when dealing with matters of a lighter nature. Here, for instance, is an excerpt from the veto by Adlai Stevenson, then governor of Illinois, of a bill to protect birds by restraining the roaming of cats:

> It is in the nature of cats to do a certain amount of unescorted roaming. . . . That cats destroy some birds, I well know, but I believe this legislation would further but little the worthy cause to which its proponents give such unselfish effort. The problem of the cat versus the bird is as old as time. If we attempt to resolve it by legislation who knows but what we may be called upon to take sides as well in the age-old problem of dog versus cat, bird versus bird, or even bird versus worm. In my opinion, the state of Illinois . . . already has enough to do without trying to control feline delinquency.

Just the right touch to put the quash on a bill that members of the legislature cared little about anyway. By using elevated language to explain his decision on a rather minor matter, and by carrying the consequences of the vetoed bill's logic to ridiculous lengths, Stevenson managed to undermine the opposition with gentle humor and without offending anyone. (Stevenson, by the way, was rightly famous for his ironic humor; witness his remark when accused of being an "egghead": "Eggheads of the world unite; all we have to lose are our yolks.")

Contrast the tone of the Stevenson veto with the following excerpt from the best-known speech by Winston Churchill, a master at the trade. It is taken from the end of an address to the British Parliament in the summer of 1940, during the darkest days of World War II, when the British expected to be invaded by German armies flush with

Farley by Phil Frank; *San Francisco Chronicle,* April 22, 1998. © Phil Frank. Used by permission.

The double meaning of the expression Piggy Bank nicely makes the suggestion that a big dose of good old greed might be the motive for lots of today's megamergers.

recent and spectacular victories in France—a time when most observers believed Britain was about to be crushed by German military power:

> We shall not flag nor fail. We shall go on to the end. We shall fight . . . on the seas and oceans; we shall fight with growing confidence and growing strength in the air. We shall defend our island whatever the cost may be; we shall fight on beaches, landing grounds, in fields, in streets and on the hills. We shall never surrender and even if, which I do not for the moment believe, this island or a large part of it were subjugated and starving, then our empire beyond the seas, armed and guarded by the British fleet, will carry on the struggle until in God's good time the New World, with all its power and might, sets forth to the liberation and rescue of the Old.

The point of Churchill's rhetoric was to buck up the courage of the British people—to stiffen their resolve to fight in the face of terrible odds—and the tone of his speech, not to mention its content, accomplished exactly that. (Incidentally, Churchill's address was not recorded; the recording frequently heard of this momentous speech is by someone else, later.)

Slanting

Slanting is a form of misrepresentation. In one version, a true statement is made so as to imply or suggest something else (usually either false or not known to be true). For example, a defense lawyer may try to blunt damaging testimony by stating, "All this

---

Monroe C. Beardsley was one of the first to write a textbook dealing strictly with critical reasoning (as opposed to formal logic). In this excerpt from his book Thinking Straight, *he explains an example of* suggestion:

On November 30, 1968, the *New York Times* reported on the construction site for a new jetport in the Everglades, 40 miles from Miami:

> Populated now by deer, alligators, wild turkeys, and a tribe of Indians who annually perform a rite known as the Green Corn Dance, the tract could someday accommodate a super jetport twice the size of Kennedy International in New York and still have a one-mile buffer on every side to minimize intrusion in the lives of any eventual residents.

A more horrible example of suggestion could hardly be found. First, note that by putting the Indians in a list with deer, alligators, and wild turkeys, the writer suggests that they belong in the same category as these subhuman species. This impression is reinforced by the allusion to the "Green Corn Dance," which (since it is irrelevant to the rest of the story) can only suggest that this kind of silly superstitious activity sums up their lives. And the impression is driven home sharply at the end when we get to the need to "minimize intrusions on the lives of any eventual residents"—the Indians, of course, can hardly be counted as real residents.
— *Thinking Straight,* 4th edition (Englewood Cliffs, N.J.: Prentice Hall, 1975)

proves is that . . . " or "Since we willingly admit that . . . ," implying that the testimony is of little importance when in fact it is quite damaging. Or an advertisement may say, "Try our best-quality knife, *only* $9.95," implying that the price is very low when in fact it may be just the ordinary price. Punctuation also can be used to make a point. In this headline from the *New York Times* (June 22, 1999)—"In Principle, A Case For More 'Sweatshops'"—the quotation marks around the term *sweatshops* create doubt that such things as sweatshops exist in the United States. (Alas! They do.)

Slanting creeps into objective news reports, as in this example from a *Washington Post* article (October 4, 2007) describing comments by Dennis Kucinich to a mainly Latino audience in the run-up to the Democratic primary. "Kucinich (Ohio), the opening act, went with the naked, Latino pander" when he greeted the crowd with "Buenos dias" and concluded with "Si se puede." Since the word *pander* means to appeal to the baser instincts, pandering to Latinos implies that Kucinich was disparaging them by thinking he could win them over with base appeals to their emotions, though how "good day" and "if we can" qualify as pandering is a mystery. It is worth noting that the media tend to describe politicians as "pandering" to ethnic groups but rarely to corporations. Another example: In a *San Francisco Chronicle* article (October 29, 2003) about a White House press conference on the rebuilding of Iraq, the comment "Much of Bush's black-and-white view of the war persists" implies that the president habitually ignored not only the complexity of postwar problems in Iraq but of all other issues he faced as well.

Slanting also can be accomplished by a careful selection of facts. (So slanting often invites the fallacy of suppressed evidence, discussed in Chapter 3.) For example, the authors of most U.S. history texts used in public schools select facts so as to sanitize American history as much as they can (given the general stricture against wandering too far from the straight and narrow). The point of public school history texts, after all, is not to produce disaffected citizens. Slanting, also, subtly promotes textbook biases. Now that multiculturalism has nudged out Eurocentrism, history books tend to romanticize Native Americans, for instance, and criticize the actions of white settlers. The word *massacre* is invariably used to describe whites attacking Native Americans but not when the situation is reversed and settlers are the victims of atrocities committed by Native Americans. (More said on these topics in Chapter 12.)

It's no secret that political parties slant information to favor their political bias. Under the second President Bush, for example, health information on government websites was subtly changed to reflect the administration's ideology. On the National Cancer Institute website, the statement that there was "no association between abortion and breast cancer" was changed to "the evidence is inconclusive." And the website for the Center for Disease Control and Prevention used to explain that condoms could protect people effectively from HIV infection, but the revision claimed that "more research is needed."

Slanting sometimes goes under the name *suggestion* or, in some cases, the more pejorative name *innuendo.* The latter term might well be applied to the politician who responded to a statement by Dan Quayle, Vice President under the first President Bush: "Well, I admit he wasn't lying *this time.*" The nice thing about slanting, so far as practitioners of the art are concerned, is that you can always deny that you implied or suggested what you in fact have implied or suggested.

Weasel Words

Weasel words (or phrases) are locutions that appear to make little or no change in the content of a statement while in fact sucking out all or most of its content.[5] Typical is the use of the terms *may* or *may be,* as in this example from a student paper: "Economic success *may be* the explanation of male dominance over females" (italics added). Using the expression *may be* instead of the straightforward verb *is* protected the student from error by reducing the content of her statement close to zero. What she said is consistent with the economic success of males *not* being the reason for male dominance. By the way, note the assumption that males do dominate females in the last analysis, a contention some males (and females!) would deny. The term *arguably* is another weasel word frequently employed to spruce up weak arguments. The student quoted here might just as well have protected herself by stating that "Economic success *arguably* is the explanation for male dominance over females."

Weasel words are the stock and trade of most politicians when discussing controversial issues—and they can be subtle. For example, when the second President Bush justified his plan for a troop "surge" in Iraq in 2007, he claimed that military commanders who reviewed the strategy reported that this plan *can* work. However, some critical thinkers agreed that maybe the plan *can* work, but that doesn't mean it *will* work.

Fine-Print Disclaimers

Another common trick is to take back unobtrusively in the (usually) unread fine print what is claimed in the most easily read part of a document. Schlock insurance policies are notorious for their use of this device. They tout wonderful coverage in large type while taking it away in the fine print. When private property is damaged by earthquakes, tornadoes, or hurricanes, for instance, people usually think they are sufficiently insured against damage from natural disasters, but they often discover to their chagrin that upfront promises of replacement cash are severely limited in the fine print of their insurance policies.

Advertisers regularly use very small asterisks to direct readers to the bottom of ads, where they find out, say, that to get the "low-low" airline fare, tickets must be purchased 21 days in advance and cover a stay over at least one Saturday and also learn that "other restrictions may apply" (note the weasel word *may,* hiding the fact that they do).

Fine-print disclaimers have become so odious that advertisers have begun to play on the fact with a bit of humor, announcing (as some Lexus auto commercials did) that their lawyers have gone into paroxysms of joy while writing the fine print that is then scrolled across the TV screen (very quickly, so it can't be read—but that's part of the humor).

A variation of the fine-print disclaimer is the sneaky stipulation buried in contracts. A blatant example of this fine-print finagling occurred in the case of a fellow named Jim Turner, who rented a car in Connecticut, but discovered when he returned it to the car rental company that he had been charged $450 because of a stipulation in the contract that "fined" the driver $150 every time the speed exceeded 79 miles per hour.

---

[5]Weasels often suck out the content of eggs without breaking their shells. The expression, by the way, was first used by Theodore Roosevelt.

His car had been tracked by satellite over seven states! Alas, poor Mr. Turner didn't read the fine print in the contract when the agent asked him to sign his initials by the X.

Another variation on the fine-print disclaimer gambit is the *reinterpretation ploy.* Having said what turns out to be unpopular, or perhaps offensive, the best strategy for a politician often is just to reinterpret the ill-advised remark. On one of the tapes released by Gennifer Flowers, Bill Clinton is heard making a remark that clearly implies he thought Mario Cuomo (then governor of New York) acted like a mafioso. When the tapes became public, an embarrassed Clinton apologized, which is the right thing to do when caught with . . . uh . . . one's pants down, but also stated that "I meant simply to imply that Governor Cuomo is a tough, worthy competitor," which was a clever, but somewhat shady, reinterpretation of his remarks.

Obfuscation

Dictionaries tell us that to *obfuscate* is "to be so confused or opaque as to be difficult to perceive or understand" or "to render indistinct or dim." George W. Bush wins a prize for opacity in his response to the question "Do you support affirmative action?"

> What I am against is quotas. I am against hard quotas, quotas they basically de-lineate based upon whatever. However they delineate, quotas, I think, vulcanize society. So I don't know how that fits into what everybody else is saying, their relative positions, but that's my position.

Since *vulcanization* is the process of treating rubbery material with chemicals, one won-ders what mischief those quirky quotas will do to society—not to mention what Bush's position is on the issue.

Let's stretch the definition of *obfuscation* a bit here to cover cases in which an issue or question has been *evaded* by *wandering from the point* or by snowing one's audience with an immense amount of detail in the hope that they either won't notice or at least won't press the point. For example, in the run-up to the 2008 election, ABC news anchor Charlie Gibson questioned Governor Sarah Palin about whether she had the national security credentials to serve as vice president, perhaps president of the country. He noted that she did command the Alaskan National Guard and that Alaska was close to Russia and then asked, "Are these sufficient credentials?" Palin replied:

> . . . it [running the country] is about reform of government and about putting government back on the side of the people, and that has much to do with foreign policy and national security issues. Let me speak specifically about a credential that I do bring to the table, Charlie, and that's with the energy independence that I've been working on for these years as the governor of this state . . .

And off she went on her energy policy. Well, government reform is important, and so is putting government back on the side of the people, but Palin's response told us nothing about her national security credentials. And so she evaded the issue, then wandered from the point when she slid into her energy policy. One can hardly single her out, though, for what has become standard political obfuscation. Nowadays that's just common practice (as in *two wrongs*).

By the way, it needs to be said that not all wandering from the point constitutes obfuscation. We have to say this here because the many asides in this textbook

("Interestingly, . . ." and "By the way, . . . ," for example) definitely are not intended as obfuscations but merely as remarks about related or secondary matters that it is hoped the reader will find either interesting or informative.

4. LANGUAGE MANIPULATORS

People manipulate language for all sorts of reasons: to flatter, to impress, to persuade, to obfuscate, and to distort the truth—to name a few. Sometimes language manipulation is benign, but when it is done to benefit those in power, it can undermine the rights of others. Often the point of redefining language is to circumvent legal stipulations or to justify inequities—as noted below.

When the torture scandal at Abu Ghraib hit the news, officials in the Bush administration claimed it was the work of a few bad apples, but skeptics dug deeper and came up with the Justice Department's interpretation of existing laws banning torture abroad (posted on the *Washington Post* website, June 14, 2004). In Section 2340 of the U.S. Criminal Code, torture is defined as any act "specifically intended to inflict severe physical or mental pain or suffering . . . upon another person within his custody or physical control." The Justice Department's legalistic explanation (written in June 2002) was that "mere" pain wasn't enough. "Physical pain amounting to torture must be equivalent in intensity to the pain accompanying serious physical injury, such as organ failure, impairment of bodily function, or even death."[6] This interpretation seems to make torture legal, unless it is extreme.

As for the fate of interrogators "who might arguably cross the line drawn in Section 2340" and be charged with torture—not to worry: They could claim they acted out of "necessity" or "self-defense," pleas that "would potentially alleviate criminal liability." In other words, they could get off the hook.

Those Who Control the Definitions . . .

Calling something by just the right name is crucial when you want to bend the law in your favor, influence public opinion, or justify funny business of one kind or another. For example, employers who want to pay employees less than the legal minimum wage or escape contractual obligations to provide health and other benefits to employees need only categorize them as *subcontractors* and arrange paperwork accordingly. Minimum wage laws in the United States apply to employees but not to subcontractors; union-brokered agreements concerning employee health insurance don't cover subcontractors.[7] Attempts at this kind of chicanery via definition occasionally have been overturned by the courts, but often they are successful. However, since the number of independent contractors has mushroomed over the past decade, lawsuits and union protests demanding job reclassification are expected to increase.

---

[6]Taken from "Small Comfort," in the *Washington Post,* June 15, 2004.
[7]While billionaire Bill Gates was becoming the richest person in the world, his Microsoft Corporation was using the subcontractor ploy to stiff over a thousand of his employees out of several perks other employees were entitled to. At one time or another, Microsoft has been embroiled in court battles over classification since 1990.

The food industry is plagued with misleading labels initiated by special interest groups who change the meaning of words used to describe food. For example, in 2003 the House and Senate passed a huge federal spending bill with the last-minute provision that meat, poultry, and dairy products could be labeled "organic" even if the animals were fed partly or entirely nonorganic feed. This rider was added to the bill on behalf of Fieldale farms, which complained about the supply of organic feed (though organic farmers say that what is really at issue is the price, not the supply—which is sufficient). So when does organic mean organic?

Closer to home, college administrators manage to cope with shrinking budgets by hiring lots of cheap labor, often referred to as *adjunct faculty* to distinguish them from "tenure-line" professors. Teachers hired as adjunct faculty earn a good deal less per course than do their tenured colleagues, receive many fewer, if any, fringe benefits, and don't enjoy similar job security. This division of labor can be thought of as an academic analogue to the "downsizing" that goes on in the business world.

On a worldwide level, rich nations manage to undercut the labor force of poor ones by manipulating the language of international agreements to their advantage. Farm subsidies unfairly undercut the agricultural industry of developing countries, particularly in Africa, where most farmers are desperately poor, partly because they cannot compete with the subsidized products from the United States and European Union (EU). A world trade agreement was drawn up to prevent this situation from occurring, but the United States and the European Union managed to slide out of it by simply using different language for export subsidies. For instance, instead of violating the agreement with "trade-distorting" subsidies by paying farmers according to the amount they produce,

---

How much can you squeeze out of a single word, like folks, *for example? A lot, according to Susan Anthony. In a trenchant analysis of the dumbing down of America, she explains how the ubiquitous use of* folks *is symptomatic of the erosion of cultural standards in this country.*

The word is everywhere, a plague spread by the President of the United States, television anchors, radio talk show hosts, preachers in megachurches, self-help gurus, and anyone else attempting to demonstrate his or her identification with ordinary, presumably wholesome American values. Only a few decades ago, Americans were addressed as people or, in the more distant past, ladies and gentlemen. Now we are all folks. . . . [as in "our prayers go out to those folks" or "I've been in contact with our homeland security folks"]

The specific political use of folks . . . designed to make the speaker sound like one of the boys or girls, is symptomatic of a debasement in public speech inseparable from a more general erosion of American cultural standards. . . . Look up any important presidential speech in the history of the United States before 1980 and you will not find one patronizing appeal to folks. Imagine: "We here highly resolve that these folks shall not have died in vain . . . and that government of the folks, by the folks, for the folks, shall not perish from the earth."

—*The Age of American Unreason* (New York: Pantheon, 2008), pp. 3–4 the European Union gives them direct grants that have almost the same effect on the price of these crops as before but are now called "non-distorting" because grants are determined by the amount of land a farmer owns and how much the land produced in the past.[8] Thus the EU is able to undercut the labor force of developing countries without breaking the trade agreement.

Although the United States Constitution grants Congress the sole right to declare war, this has rarely deterred American presidents from waging war without obtaining any such declaration. As we noted earlier in the chapter, they have simply renamed their escapades or declared them not to be wars. Assuming the December 1990 congressional measure allowing President Bush (the elder) to carry out United Nations resolutions did indeed constitute a declaration of war, even though it didn't actually say we were declaring war, then the Gulf conflict is very likely the only legal war out of at least five fought by the United States since World War II.

In 2002 Congress gave President Bush (the younger) authorization to use the Armed Forces as he considered necessary to defend our country's national security against the threat of Iraq and to enforce the United Nations Security Council resolutions with regard to Iraq. Thus Congress gave Bush the authority to wage war on Iraq but managed to avoid a congressional declaration of war. This equivocation enabled Congress to pass the buck and avoid criticism if the war went badly.[9]

In the war in Afghanistan, the Bush administration classified as "enemy combatants" hundreds of suspected al Qaeda and Taliban fighters detained by the United States at Guantanamo Bay Naval Base. Had they been called "prisoners of war," they would have been entitled to release when the war was over, but as "enemy combatants," not only could they be detained indefinitely for questioning without charge, they couldn't challenge their imprisonment in court, nor were they entitled to any other constitutional rights. The case to reverse this decision was appealed for years until it finally worked its way up to the Supreme Court in 2008. In *Boumediene v. Bush*, the Court ruled that aliens detained as enemy combatants in Guantanamo have a constitutional right to challenge their detention in American courts. Will this ruling stand or will the term *enemy combatants* morph into another category that manages to slide past the law?

Not all attempts at victory via definition are successful. In the Microsoft antitrust case, the Justice Department wasn't persuaded by Microsoft's claim that its Internet Explorer was an integral part of its Windows operating system, "not an add-on, like a flash on a camera or a car radio," but an integral part of Windows, like "a shutter on a camera or a car's transmission." The point was crucial to whether bundling Internet Explorer into Windows was a violation of antitrust laws and thus unfair to competition, chiefly Netscape and its Internet browser. But the analogies didn't convince the Justice Department. (By the way, why shouldn't it have?)

Sometimes common sense prevails, and redefinition backfires outside the courtroom. In 2008 when the biggest financial institutions were sliding into bankruptcy and the economy was in free fall, John McCain reassured the American people that the fundamentals of the economy were still good. That didn't play well with the liberals or the conservatives or anyone else, for that matter. So McCain quickly revised his message and

---

[8]For more on this see the (London) *Guardian,* June 3, 2003.
[9]See "Is the War on Iraq Lawful?" by Michael C. Dorf, March 19, 2003. writ.findlaw.com/dorf.

© 1996 Don Wright, Inc.

redefined *fundamentals* to mean the *workers,* not unemployment rates nor trade statistics nor any of the usual economic guideposts. Those hardworking Americans, the backbone of our country, were the fundamentals that were good. Well, no one would argue that the workers weren't good, but whether they were economic fundamentals was another matter. That redefinition unleashed a raft of satiric responses that eventually laughed it into oblivion.

When language is manipulated, it isn't always easy to determine whether there is some sort of sleight of hand going on. For years, the psychologist Thomas Szasz has been campaigning against the use of the expression *mental illness,* on grounds that there is no such thing as *mental* illness. Declaring John Hinckley "not guilty by reason of insanity" after his attempt to assassinate President Reagan was for Szasz just an extreme example of what happens when we take the analogy between physical illness and alleged mental illness seriously. (He does believe, however, that sometimes what is thought of as mental illness really is physical dysfunction.)

But Szasz is in the minority on this point, with the result, he claims, that various kinds of serious abuses of civil rights occur. One is that close relatives of the "mentally ill" often are able to have them "hospitalized for treatment" against their will. Forcing people into institutions in this way is a practice some see as not unlike the one that used to be common in the Soviet Union of confining political opponents in "mental institutions." In a similar vein, Szasz argues, "we call self-starvation either *anorexia nervosa,* a *hunger strike,* a *suicide attempt,* or some other name, depending on how we want to respond."

Well, then, is Szasz right about this? A number of psychologists find his position modestly persuasive, while the majority do not. The reason for this split of opinion is

> *Conservative, n.* A statesman who is enamored of existing evils, as distinguished from the Liberal, who wishes to replace them with others.
>
> —Ambrose Bierce (*The Devil's Dictionary*)

that good arguments can be made on both sides of the issue, making it difficult to choose one over the other. Which choice we should make may well depend, as Szasz notes, on how we wish to deal with whatever circumstances our decisions affect. (Philosophy students might note the connection of this sort of case to the age-old conundrum about whether, when every part of an old ship has been replaced over the years by a new part, it is still the same ship; the answer, at least half of this writing team believes, is that it depends on who we wish to have title to ships repaired in this way, not on any truth written in the sky.)

Those Who Frame Public Policy

Redefining words is one way to influence public opinion; another is to use loaded language to evoke a worldview that persuades people to adopt policies—even if these policies go against their own interests. Over the past decade, George Lakoff, a professor of linguistics at the University of California, Berkeley, has become well known (and controversial) for developing a theory about the science and art of framing the debate that has attracted attention across the political spectrum.

Lakoff defines frames as "mental structures that shape the way we see the world. As a result they shape the goals we seek, the plans we make, the way we act, what counts as a good or bad outcome of our actions. In politics our frames shape our social policies and the institutions we form to carry out policies."[10]

We recognize frames through language, and since people usually make decisions about politics based on their values, the language creates the frame that evokes those values. Lakoff uses as an example the loaded phrase "tax relief," conjured up by Republicans to hype their campaign for tax cuts (a neutral, but accurate term). The notion of relief suggests that there is an affliction that must be removed. Those who remove the affliction are the good guys; those who oppose it, the bad guys. The "frame" taps into the voters' value systems, and they, in turn, buy into the idea. Meanwhile the media repeats the phrase over and over until it enters the political lexicon. Other examples include the ominous sounding "death tax" and the emotionally charged "partial birth abortion," loaded phrases that nudge voters into supporting tax cuts and banning third-term abortions.

Democrats invented their own political frames. When Republicans threatened to eliminate the filibuster procedure that Democrats were using to prevent a quick confirmation of Bush-appointed judges, the Democrats framed their attack as an "abuse of power." Day after day they hammered away at the message that they were fighting for

---

[10]George Lakoff, *Don't Think of an Elephant* (White River Junction, V.: Chelsea Green Publishing, 2004), p. xv.

democracy against a Republican abuse of power that was not what our founders intended. This frame evoked the world view that we value democracy and want to preserve it. Republicans were attempting to undermine democracy by eliminating the filibuster, an American birthright that is central to our republic. In fact, the filibuster is a parliamentary procedure (not a birthright) that is typically used to prevent the Senate majority from ending a debate. The Democrats were actually breaking tradition in using it to block the confirmation of an entire slate of judges. Nonetheless the public was persuaded, and Republicans backed down under pressure.[11]

Whether or not we agree with Lakoff's theory, there is enough truth in it to make us wary of the way politicians use language to manipulate us to side with them on critical issues.

Psychologists use the term *framing effects* to describe similar phenomena that influence our decisions. For instance, weight-conscious people are more likely to eat hamburgers described as 90 percent lean rather than 10 percent fat, even though the amount of fat is the same in either case. Charities rake in more money when they urge donors to give pennies a day rather than dollars per year. People are more likely to spend money described as a bonus (because it is extra income and thus dispensable) and more likely to save money described as a rebate (because it implies a return on money spent within their income that should not be squandered). Politicians could have used this ploy to good effect in 2008 if they had coined the term *tax bonus* instead of *tax rebate* to describe money returned to people so that they will spend it and thus stimulate the lagging economy.[12] And, of course, advertisers regularly rely on framing effects to manipulate consumers into buying their products.

5. LANGUAGE REVISION

Languages aren't artificial products constructed by "linguistic experts" in some laboratory or think tank. They are living, changing products of human intelligence designed to perform various functions, including not just communicating ideas from one person to another but also issuing commands, asking questions, and certifying relationships and bargains (as in wedding ceremonies). This being the case, languages tend to mirror the foibles, aspirations, loyalties, and (alas!) prejudices of those who speak them. English is no exception. Like all languages, English undergoes revision on a regular basis.

The Reform of Sexist Language

In the past 20 or 30 years, a minor revolution has taken place in the United States, as well as many other countries, in the attitudes of most people toward members of minority groups and women. Inevitably, this revolution has been mirrored in the linguistic practices of those caught up in it. The pejorative terms mentioned at the beginning of this chapter are not often heard in polite circles these days, and expressions like "free, white, and 21," common until about 50 years ago, are now as outdated as "23 skidoo."

---

[11]For more on this see "The Framing Wars," by Matt Bai, *New York Times Magazine,* July 17, 2005, an in-depth discussion of Lakoff's theory.
[12]See "Rebate Psychology," by Nicholas Epley, *New York Times,* January 31, 2008.

But the most extensive linguistic changes of this kind have been those reflecting the changing attitudes of most people concerning relationships between men and women and the roles played by women in society. A large majority of previously common sexist locutions have disappeared from everyday speech. This linguistic change has occurred very quickly, as these things go, no doubt in part because of the persistent demands of women's rights advocates. But it also has happened quickly because of the swiftness with which attitudes toward women and their roles in society have changed and because of the speed with which women have entered fields previously reserved primarily for men.

Not so long ago, when the overwhelming majority of those in high offices were men, it may have made some sense to refer to these people as business*men* and congress*men*. But in this day and age, with increasing numbers of women taking on these roles, it makes much less sense. In addition, there is a general realization that these sexist terms imply not just that those holding these offices always are male but also, and wrongly, that only males are supposed to, or are competent to, fill them. The old sexist language implies in subtle but persuasive ways that positions of power should be *manned*, not *personed* or *womaned*, and this in turn implies that only men are capable of holding these important positions. Thus, substituting nonsexist words for the old sexist terms puts women on an equal linguistic footing with men that not only reflects their growing equality but also helps make it possible. Our thoughts about the world—how it works and how it should work—always are framed in language; sexist locutions tend to introduce sexist thoughts into our minds.

So today, people who head committees or departments are generally called *chairs,* not *chairmen* ("I would like to address the chair about . . . " or "The chair has ruled that . . . "). Similarly, people who deliver the mail tend to get called *letter carriers,* not *mailmen.* We say *firefighter* instead of *fireman* and *police officer* rather than *policeman.* The term *man* and its many derivatives now often are replaced by *people, person,* and the like. Publishers don't cotton to manuscripts that contain locutions like "Of course, a *man* might be described as taking a . . . " when it would be more accurate to say "*Someone* might be described as taking a . . . " or to phrases like "even if *he* is willing to allow . . . ," when what is meant is *he or she.*[13]

One of the more interesting language changes accompanying the feminist revolution has been the widespread use of the term *Ms.,* intended to serve when the marriage status of a woman is not considered relevant. The point of this change was to foster equal treatment of the sexes. Men, whether married or single, have always been referred to by the same term, *Mr.,* whereas women have had to be called either *Miss* or *Mrs.,* depending on their marital status. In magazine and newspaper articles the trend is to drop the title entirely and simply refer to women by their last names—the way men always have been. A similar, and perhaps much more significant change, is the fact that women nowadays don't always take on the last name of their mates, although, interestingly, they still usually do (while men rarely do). But even when women do adopt their husbands' last names, they often also hang onto their own, so that, for example, we refer to Hillary *Rodham* Clinton, not just Hillary Clinton.

But an even more important language change may be the elimination of locutions like this one, once typical of the language encountered in all sorts of places, including public school history textbooks: "Pioneers moved west, taking their wives and children with them." That made all of the pioneers into men, while women and children were just accessories. A text written today would get it right and say something like "Pioneer families moved west."

On the other hand, things can get carried too far. It would be unnecessary, wouldn't it, for Germans to stop referring to their homeland as the *Fatherland,* or Englishmen— that is, citizens of England—to their *mother tongue?* What purpose would be served by replacing *Uncle Sam* with *Aunt Sarah?* And why worry about using the term *manhole* when talking about those round excisions in streets and avenues, as did the Public Works Departments of several American cities? (Would it be wrong to change biblical references to God from the *He* employed in the original versions to some more neutral term?) The term *humankind* seems an apt substitute for *mankind,* but somehow the "era of ordinary people" doesn't have the same ring as the "century of the common man."

In any case, the changes in linguistic style brought on by the feminist revolution have also raised questions of aesthetic taste—of what sounds right or wrong rolling off the tongue or when reading a book. The expression *her or his,* to take one example, rings false, perhaps because it calls attention to the avoidance of *his* (used to mean *his* or *her*) or of *his or her,* and thus detracts from what is being said. Good taste sometimes dictates other sorts of moves, for instance, employing plural rather than singular pronouns, thus saying things like, "when students read their textbooks . . ." rather than "when a student reads his textbook . . . ." (That's one reason for the plethora of plural expressions that occur in this textbook. Note, by the way, that the term *congressperson* nowhere appears on these pages, although *member of Congress* is used quite often.)

Interestingly, no one seems overwrought by the fact that Liberty always is portrayed as a woman. (Think, for instance, of the Statue of Liberty in New York harbor.) Note also that, although there are lots of complaints about sexist terms like *waitress* and *actress,* no one seems bothered by the equally sexist term *widower.* Women still receive an award each year for best *actress.* And freshmen still are called *freshmen.* Ah, well.

---

[13]Both of these examples are taken, alas, from a journal article coauthored back in the bad old days by the male coauthor of this text.

The Los Angeles Times, *one of America's best newspapers, now has a guideline concerning "Ethnic, Racial, Sexual and Other Identification" that prohibits the use, among others, of the following words when describing individuals:*

Co-ed, deaf, deaf-mute, biddy, bra-burner, crazy, divorcee, gal, ghetto, gypped, handicapped person, hillbilly, Hispanic, holy rollers, Indians, inner city, lame, male nurse, normal, pow-wow, queer, WASP, welsher.

Commenting on the Times' *guidelines, syndicated columnist Robert Novak had this to say:*

The *Times* forbids reporters to write about a "Dutch treat" because this phrase is allegedly insulting to the Dutch. Nor can one report that a person "welshed on a bet" because that would be insulting to the Welsh. . . . I asked one of the *Los Angeles Times* editors, "How do you refer to Indian summer? Is it now Native American summer?" He replied that he would substitute "unseasonably warm weather late in the year." This is what political correctness can do to language; it destroys meaning. It also demeans the ethnic groups it supposedly protects. Do we really think that these groups are so unintelligent as to be unable to distinguish between conventional idioms and genuine prejudice? Is their identity so fragile that it must depend on censorship?

Well, then, is Novak right about his thoughts concerning what he sees as overzealous PC?

PC (Politically Correct) Terminology

The revolution concerning gender rhetoric is part of a larger movement that also has dramatically changed the ways in which we speak of minorities. As attitudes have changed, language, inevitably, has followed suit.

The result is that certain locutions have become "in," while others are "out." Some are politically correct, some politically incorrect. Careers have been wrecked by publicly using expressions like "fat Jap" and "Nigra." It would be political suicide today to say publicly, as someone did in the 1970s, when then Governor Tribbitt (Delaware) hired a woman as his press secretary at $20,000 a year, "If he wants to pay $10,000 a mammary, that's his business." We aren't supposed to use phrases like *admitted homosexual* (because it implies that being a homosexual is bad) or *tidal wave of immigrants* (because of its negative implication concerning immigrants).

On the whole, of course, changes of this nature are all to the good and are applauded by just about everybody. But problems do arise, and it is quite possible that an excess of zeal causes some of them. One of the authors of this textbook, for example, received letters from students and teachers accusing him of race prejudice, or at least insensitivity, for having used the term *black* in the sixth edition of this textbook, on the grounds that the politically correct, nondenigrating, term for the minority in question is *African*

> *Robert Hughes, an Australian who lived in Europe before settling in the United States, is an iconoclastic commentator of the American scene. He has this to say about what he perceives to be an excess of PC in this country:*
>
> . . . There are certainly worse things in American society than the ongoing vogue for politically correct language, whether of the left or the right. But there are few things more absurd and, in the end, self-defeating.
>
> We want to create a sort of linguistic Lourdes, where evil and misfortune are dispelled by a dip in the waters of euphemism. Does the cripple rise from his wheelchair, or feel better about being stuck in it, because someone in the days of the Carter administration decided that, for official purposes, he was "physically challenged"?
>
> . . . The notion that you change a situation by finding a newer and nicer word for it emerges from the old American habit of euphemism, circumlocution, and desperate confusion about etiquette, produced by fear that the concrete will give offense. And it is a particularly American habit. The call for politically correct language . . . has virtually no resonance in Europe. In France, nobody has thought of renaming the Frankish King Pepin le Bref, Pepin le Verticalement Defie. . . .
>
> . . . When the waters of PC recede—as they presently will, leaving the predictable scum of dead words on the social beach—it will be, in part, because young people get turned off by all the carping of verbal proprieties on campus. The radical impulses of youth are generous, romantic, and instinctive, and are easily chilled by the atmosphere of prim, obsessive correction.
>
> —Robert Hughes, *Culture of Complaint* (New York: Oxford University Press, 1993), pp. 18–24.

American.[14] But when the sixth edition was published, the politically correct term happened to be *black,* which earlier had replaced the term *Negro* (which, of course, happens to mean "black" in several romance languages).

Anyway, the academic world is particularly fertile ground for PC talk. For example, the University of Cincinnati Student Senate has declared their higher institution of learning "a Columbus-myth-free campus." (The allusion, in case you missed it, is to the fact that Columbus could not possibly have "discovered" America—Native Americans having been here for at least 10,000 years before Columbus was born.) At Stanford University students can be punished for violating speech codes designed to suppress racist, sexist, and homophobic speech that carries no legal penalty in the "real" world. An administrator at the University of California, Santa Cruz, was even wary of phrases like a "nip in the air" and "a chink in one's armor" because certain of these words could be construed as racial slurs in other contexts.

---

[14]Whether this is or isn't the PC term, many members of the group—for example, African American politicians on television and students in many college classes—often refer to themselves as *black.* (Interestingly, both of these terms conceal the fact that most of the people so labeled also are genetically part Caucasian—indeed, often primarily Caucasian—or part Asian. The point is that both of these labels are social/political, not scientific, referring to class, not race.)

Sometimes the attempt to be PC defies all logic. The reading passages of the New York State Regents English exam were edited to delete anything that might make "any student feel ill at ease when taking the test." For example, all references to Judaism were cut from an excerpt from a work by Isaac Bashevis Singer about Jewish life in Europe! In one revision, for instance, "most Jewish women" was changed to "most women." For this PC passage, the New York State Regents were given the NCTE Doublespeak award for 2002.

Are we getting a bit overzealous in our, shall we say, *linguistic cleansing*? It no doubt is a good idea, now that the children of unwed parents are not looked down upon, to refer to them as *nonmarital children* rather than *bastards,* thus getting rid of the unfair opprobrium of that nasty term. And why not change the name of the Italian Welfare Agency to the *Italian-American Community Service Agency*?

But is there anything wrong with calling "mixed-breed" dogs *mongrels,* "visually impaired" people *blind,* or the "psychologically impacted" *insane*? Don't those who call the *Sports Illustrated* swimsuit issue *pornographic* rob that word of its legitimate meaning? (Is there a risk here that the door will be opened to wrongheaded legislation?) Was Newt Gingrich just being polite when he said President Clinton was "factually challenged" instead of calling him a liar? (Was he just trying to be cute, snide, or clever?) Anyway, was the First Amendment bruised when the University of Michigan punished students for having uttered "hate speech" when they aired their belief that homosexuality is a disease in classroom discussions? And didn't certain Native Americans make some kind of mistake when they demonstrated during the 1995 World Series against the "demeaning symbols" used by the beloved Cleveland Indians and the Atlanta Braves?

SUMMARY OF CHAPTER 7

1. Most words have emotive meanings (in addition to cognitive meanings). Words like *oppression, kike,* and *bitch* have more or less negative (con) emotive overtones; words like *spring, free,* and *satisfaction* have positive (pro) emotive overtones; and words like *socialism, marijuana,* and *God* have mixed overtones.

2. Con artists use the emotive side of language (1) to mask cognitive meaning by whipping up emotions so that reason is overlooked and (2) to dull the force of language so as to make acceptable what otherwise might not be. The latter purpose often is accomplished by means of *euphemisms* (less offensive or duller expressions used in place of more offensive or emotively charged locutions).

3. Common rhetorical devices often are used in a slippery manner. *Examples: Slanting* words and expressions ("All this proves is that . . ."); *weasel words* that suck out all or part of the meaning of a sentence ("Economic success may be . . ."); *fine-print disclaimers* that take back part of what was originally asserted ("Tickets must be purchased 30 days in advance, subject to availability . . ."); *obfuscation* that, for example, may mask failure to respond to questions (Sarah Palin wandering from the point of the question about whether she had the national security credentials to serve as vice president). Note that employing the right tone can be used to mask lack of cogent reasoning or content or to sway audiences via emotional appeals.

4. The meanings of words and expressions sometimes are changed so as either to get around or to take advantage of laws, rules, or customs. *Example:* Calling an employee a *subcontractor* to avoid paying a minimum wage or Social Security taxes. But it isn't always easy to determine whether terms have been used rightly or wrongly. *Example:* Psychologists disagree about whether it makes good sense to use the expression *mental illness,* because they disagree about whether the implied analogy to physical illness is useful or accurate. Loaded language can "frame" issues and thus influence the way we think about public policy. *Example:* Calling tax cuts "tax relief" or estate tax "death tax."

5. The recent social revolution that changed the roles played by women in society, as well as the attitudes of most Americans concerning male-female relationships, has resulted in matching linguistic changes. *Examples:* Replacing expressions in which the term *man* is used to refer to people in general by more neutral words such as *person;* using *Ms.* in some cases instead of *Miss* or *Mrs.;* not repeatedly using *his* to mean *his* or *her;* or switching to the plural form to avoid this use of *his.* (Note that when use of dechauvinized language may ring a bit false—*her or his* can sound somewhat forced—there always are aesthetically acceptable ways to avoid sexist locutions.) But do we go a bit too far when we start talking, say, about *personhole* covers?

6. The linguistic revolution that has replaced sexist language with locutions that are more congenial with today's attitudes and beliefs also has changed many of the ways in which we refer to members of minorities and other groups, as well as to activities in several important areas of life. Using current lingo, we can say that some ways of speaking are *politically correct* (PC), others not. *Examples:* The terms *Native American, physically challenged,* and *Latino* are "in"; *Indian, crippled* (or *handicapped*), and *Hispanic* (used to refer, say, to Mexican Americans) are "out." In some cases, the PC revolution may have gone a bit too far. *Example:* Objecting to the use of Indian symbols by baseball teams.

EXERCISE 7-1

In the run-up to the 2008 presidential elections, Barack Obama gave a speech, "A More Perfect Union," hailed by many people as one of the most important speeches on race and the American experience since those given by Martin Luther King. Evaluate this excerpt and explain why it might be effective, persuasive rhetoric. Consider the language (positive and negative), tone, examples, repetitions of words and phrases, choice of pronouns, and anything else you can think of. Conclude with a discussion of the world-view it reflects.

> . . . we have a choice in this country. We can accept a politics that breeds division, and conflict, and cynicism. We can tackle race only as spectacle—as we did in the O.J. trial—or in the wake of tragedy, as we did in the aftermath of Katrina—or as fodder for the nightly news. . . . We can pounce on some gaffe by Hillary Clinton as evidence that she's playing the race card, or we can speculate on whether white men will all flock to John McCain in the general election regardless of his policies.
>
> We can do that.
>
> But if we do, I can tell you that in the next election, we'll be talking about some other distraction. And then another one. . . . And nothing will change.
>
> That is one option. Or, at this moment in the election, we can come together and say, "Not this time." This time we want to talk about the crumbling schools that are stealing the future of black children and white children and Asian children and Hispanic children and Native American children. This time we want to reject the cynicism that tells us that these kids can't learn: that these kids who don't look like us are somebody else's problem. The children of America are not those kids, they are our kids, and we will not let them fall behind in a 21st century economy. Not this time.
>
> This time we want to talk about how the lines in the emergency room are filled with whites and blacks and Hispanics who do not have health care, who don't have the power on their own to overcome the special interests in Washington, but who can take them on if we do it together.
>
> This time we want to talk about the shuttered mills that once provided a decent life for men and women of every race. . . . This time we want to talk about the fact that the real problem is not that someone who doesn't look like you might take your job; it's that the corporation you work for will ship it overseas for nothing more than a profit. . . .
>
> I would not be running for president if I didn't believe with all my heart that this is what the vast majority of Americans want for the country. This union may never be perfect, but generation after generation has shown that it can always be perfected. And today, whenever I find myself feeling doubtful or cynical about this possibility, what gives me the most hope is the next generation—the young people whose attitudes and beliefs and openness to change have already made history in this election.

EXERCISE 7-2

1. Louisiana license plates feature the motto "Sportsman's Paradise." Is this sexist? Defend your answer.

2. Over the past decade, the term *illegal alien* has been euphemized as "undocu-mented worker" or even "guest without status." What is the point of these euphemisms and who would be most likely to use them?

*3. Translate the following statement, found on the back of a Hallmark greeting card, into everyday lingo:

Printed on recycled paper. Contains a minimum of 10% post-consumer and 40% pre-consumer material.

Aside from the euphemistic use of language in this statement, is there something a bit sneaky going on here?

4. Here is a passage from a thankfully out-of-print edition of the United States history textbook *America: Its People and Values:*

A friendly Indian named Squanto helped the colonists. He showed them how to plant corn and how to live in the wilderness. A soldier, Captain Miles Standish, taught the Pilgrims how to defend themselves against unfriendly Indians.

How is language used to slant this account? In what other ways is it slanted? Rewrite the passage from the point of view of the "unfriendly Indians" (that is, Native Americans) in question.

5. Explain in plain English Annette Koloday's "reconceptualization" of the term *family* in this quote from her book *Failing the Future: A Dean Looks at Higher Education in the Twenty-First Century.* (This passage was nominated for the Doublespeak Award, *Quarterly Review of Doublespeak,* January 2002.)

To conceptualize what I am calling the "family-friendly campus" means reconceptualizing what we include in the term family. The family in the twenty-first century will no longer be identified by blood ties, by legalized affiliations, by cohabitation, or by heterosexual arrangements.

How, then, would you define *family*?

*6. Translate into plain English the following remark by Admiral Isaac C. Kidd when he was chief of navy matériel:

We have gone with teams of competent contract people from Washington to outlying field activities to look over their books with them . . . to see in what areas there is susceptibility to improved capability to commit funds.

7. During the 2000 presidential campaign and thereafter, Republicans high up in government started referring to the federal tax hitherto known as the *inheritance tax* as the *death tax.*
    a. Does *death tax* more accurately describe the tax in question than *inheritance tax*?
    b. Why do you suppose Republican bigwigs continually use the locution *death tax* intead of the older, traditional name of this tax?

8. An animal rights organization wants to replace the term *pet owner* in San Francisco laws with the expression *pet guardian* because the term *owner* implies that animals are property. Defend or challenge their view on this.

9. Several groups opposed to legal abortions, as well as a few state legislatures in recently enacted laws, refer to a fetus as an *intact child,* a *partially born infant,* or an *unborn child* (see, for example, the March–April 2000 edition of *Extra!*).
    a. What is the point of their use of these locutions instead of the medical term *fetus*?
    b. To which sections or topics of this chapter is this example relevant?

EXERCISE 7-3

1. Find at least one good example of an inappropriate name (for example, *subcontractor*) that is applied so that the law, a custom, or whatever deals with them differently, and explain the chicanery. (No, you aren't supposed to "find" the example in this textbook.)

2. Check your local newspaper, magazines, television programs, the Internet, or some such; find at least two examples of doublespeak or jargon, and translate them back into plain English.

3. Do the same with a particularly obtuse use (as opposed to a "mention") of academese from one of your textbooks (*definitely* not from this one!).

4. Do the same with respect to sexist locutions, but this time translate into PC language.

EXERCISE 7-4

1. Reread Robert Hughes's criticism of politically correct language. Do you agree or disagree with him that Americans have gone overboard in their use of PC? Defend you answer and give examples.

*2. Each chapter in this text starts out with a few (hopefully) apt quotes. But doesn't one of the quotes that starts this language chapter use one of the devices railed against in this chapter? Which one might this be? If it doesn't, why doesn't it? If it does, wasn't it a mistake to use this quotation? Explain. (By the way, does a different one of these quotes commit the fallacy slippery slope?)

3. Previous editions of this text have been criticized by some for implying that in some cases the recent linguistic revolution has gone a bit overboard. This edition contains the question "Why worry about using the term *manhole* when talking about those round excisions in streets and avenues, as did the Public Works Departments of several American cities?" Should we worry? Why, or why not?

4. Do you think universities should develop speech codes designed to suppress racist, sexist, and homophobic speech on campus? Write an argument for or against this policy.

The prejudice against careful analytic procedure is part of the human impatience with technique which arises from the fact that men are interested in results and would like to attain them without the painful toil which is the essence of our moral finitude.

— Morris R. Cohen

There is no expedient to which a man will not resort to avoid the real labor of thinking.

— Sir Joshua Reynolds

Chapter

8

EVALUATING EXTENDED ARGUMENTS

Our principal topic in this chapter is the evaluation of extended passages, or **essays,** that argue to a conclusion. Up to this point, we've considered mainly short arguments, and these primarily to illustrate fallacious reasoning or manipulative uses of language. But in daily life, we frequently encounter longer passages, generally containing several related arguments, offered in support of a thesis — the overall conclusion of the passage.

We should recall, however, that there are other kinds of persuasive essays in addition to the argumentative variety. Even simple description or narration often is used for this purpose. For example, in his essay "A Hanging," George Orwell argues with some force against capital punishment simply by graphically describing a hanging and one person's gut-wrenching response to it. (The ongoing abortion debate is studded with detailed descriptions of aborted fetuses.) And just explaining something may effectively persuade others to our point of view. An article on chlorofluorocarbons, for instance, may simply describe how these chemicals deplete the ozone layer, thus increasing our chances of getting skin cancer, and yet convince readers of the implied conclusion that the use of Freon in refrigerators and other modern equipment should be stopped.

But our main concern in this chapter will be rhetoric in which there is an attempt to present reasons for conclusions. We need to remember, however, that a conclusion can be argued for in various ways. We may, for example, weigh the merits and demerits of a possible course of action, instead of just presenting favorable reasons. A **pro and con argument** of this kind can be very effective because it tends to answer questions or objections the reader or listener may have about the thesis being argued for. This also is why essays often provide a **refutation to counterarguments,** as in the case of politicians who, after arguing for their position, may then go on to say, "Now my opponent will no doubt respond _____; but I say _____," and then attempt to refute their opponent's objections. An essay may also argue for a course of action by showing that likely alternatives are less desirable, which means arguing by a **comparison of alternatives.**

Note, by the way, that a legitimate appeal to experts in a field may count as a reason for accepting their conclusions, even in the absence of an account of their reasoning processes. During World War II, for example, President Roosevelt accepted the conclusion of physicists Leo Szilard and Albert Einstein (conveyed to the president in a famous letter) that it was possible to build an atomic bomb, even though Roosevelt, like every other lay person, would have been unable to comprehend the reasoning behind their conclusion (which, no doubt, is why the two scientists didn't bother to provide it).

Finally, note that essay writers frequently employ more than one of the methods just mentioned. They first may argue, for instance, by a general comparison of alternatives and then, finding the alternative that seems to be the most attractive, zero in on it for a more careful analysis. Or they may provide reasons that support the essay's thesis and are in turn supported by expert opinion.

1. THE BASIC TASKS OF ESSAY EVALUATION

There are almost as many ways to evaluate extended passages as there are evaluators. What works best for one person may not work so well for others. And time and interest always need to be taken into account. Even so, there are guidelines that most people find of value, in particular, those who initially have a bit of trouble handling lengthy or complicated passages. (Most of the discussion that follows will deal with written passages, but applies also to those that are verbal.)

The next few sections of this chapter describe a method for evaluating essays when the topic being dealt with is of great importance and we have the time necessary to do a thorough job. In daily life, of course, these two conditions are not often met. But getting good at a method like the one described here is a good way to become adept at the quicker kinds of evaluations that we do frequently have to make in everyday life.

Find the Thesis and Keep It in Mind

The most important thing, obviously, is to *locate the thesis*—the main conclusion of the argument. The thesis isn't always obvious because the passage may be poorly written, or because the thesis may be implied but not explicitly stated, or simply because the author may build up to it and reveal it only near the end of the work. The thesis is the point of an essay, so you have to keep it in mind to determine whether sufficient *reasons* are provided for accepting it. In many sports, the trick is to keep your eye on the ball; in evaluating extended passages, the trick is to keep your mind's eye on the thesis, so that you can better judge whether the reasons do, or don't, adequately support it.

Find the Reasons that Support the Thesis

Obviously, then, the next task after locating the thesis is to *find the reasons*—the *premises*—that are provided in support of the thesis. Again, this will be hard or easy depending on the author's style and competence. But it may also be hard because the reasons themselves are supported by reasons, so that the sheer complexity of an extended passage makes analysis difficult.

Typically, however, it isn't all that hard to see what the thesis of an essay is and to discover the principal reasons offered in its support. For example, a newspaper columnist arguing for the thesis that cigarettes should be made illegal supported his conclusion by pointing out that cigarette smoking kills millions of people; then supported that claim by presenting statistics concerning smoking and heart disease, cancer, and emphysema; and then claimed that anything so bad for us should be illegal. The logical structure of his essay thus was something like this:

> *Thesis:* Cigarettes should be made illegal.
> *Reasons:* 1. Cigarette smoking is deadly.
>   2. Anything so deadly should be illegal.
> *Support for 1:* Statistical proof linking smoking cigarettes with heart disease, cancer, and emphysema.

The columnist assumed (wrongly) that most people would accept his second reason without further justification.

Identify the Evidence

Effective extended arguments usually provide evidence, or support, for the reasons they present. That is, they provide reasons for believing their reasons. In the cigarette example, statistical evidence was cited in support of the claim that cigarette smoking is deadly. But many other sorts of evidence may be appealed to, including authoritative pronouncements, examples, personal experiences, generally accepted facts or common knowledge, and so on. In the Szilard/Einstein letter mentioned before, the evidence for the conclusion that an atomic bomb could be built was just the authority of the letter's authors. Someone might defend the claim that cigarette smoking is deadly simply by appealing to what by now is common knowledge—that it causes lung cancer, heart disease, and so on. A powerful argument against war might well contain specific examples of wars—for example, World War I—that produced incredible misery with little else to show for them.

In a sense, of course, all reasons or premises offered in support of a thesis constitute evidence in its favor. The important point here is that reasons themselves often need, and receive, supporting evidence. Indeed, good essay writers always support reasons in this way except when confident that readers will accept them without further argument.

Identify Responses to Likely Objections or Counterarguments

The sample essay concerning cigarette smoking did not discuss likely objections or counterarguments, but essays often do. The cigarette essay, for instance, might have raised and argued against the objection that we have a right to risk shortening our lives by smoking, or taking other sorts of risks, if we want to. If this objection had been included in the essay, then it would have been important to note and take account of it.

Skip Whatever Doesn't Argue for (or Against) the Thesis

People write essays to persuade other people. So they sometimes include irrelevant material if they think it will help them to persuade others. This kind of "flavoring" material makes reading more fun, but it shouldn't influence the assessment of an argument.

Add Relevant Information or Reasons

Everything needed to prove a thesis is *never* included in an essay, no matter how long it may be. There is no point in trying to prove things that are obvious or generally accepted. Good writers try to provide just the information their audiences will need in order to see the merit of the writer's point of view. For instance, someone writing about education for an audience of teachers doesn't need to prove that plenty of students graduate from high school today without having developed sufficient ability in reading, writing, and basic arithmetic. Every teacher knows that.

Of course, writers, being human, often fail to do the best job of supporting their theses. They often overlook important evidence, or they reason incorrectly to a conclusion that can be supported by better logic. Good critical thinkers try to evaluate the best version of an argument, adding material that its author may have neglected. By the same token, of course, good reasoners also bring to bear whatever negative evidence or reasons they may know about.

Consider Tone and Emotive Language

Although tone and emotive language are not part of the formal elements of argument, they are subtle manipulators that deserve attention, particularly when considering a strongly emotive topic or one that uses irony or humor to persuade. When Adlai Stevenson argued against a state Senate bill to restrain cats (quoted in Chapter 7), his droll exaggeration of the consequences was part of the persuasive power. The idea that the Senate might be "called upon to take sides in the age-old problem of dog versus cat, cat versus bird, or even bird versus worm" made the bill seem just plain silly and thus not worth passing.

One way to identify these hidden persuaders is to underline or circle the emotive words or humorous phrases and then see how they nudge the reader into agreeing with the writer's thesis. Becoming aware of these expressions helps us guard against their undue influence.

Come to an Evaluation

While evaluation is logically the last thing we need to do when dealing with an argumentative passage, good critical thinkers start evaluating from the word go. They keep in mind questions such as, Do I already accept this thesis? Does it fit well with what I already know and believe? If not, in what way is the argument fallacious and why? What sort of reasons or evidence might change my mind? And they continue to evaluate as they go along, bearing in mind questions such as, Is this reason acceptable without further justification? Does that reason really defend the thesis at hand? Do the facts alleged seem plausible, given my background beliefs? Has the writer forgotten a serious counterargument or omitted important counterevidence? Is the use of tone and emotive language unduly persuasive? It's true that a completely confident judgment about a work can't be reached until an essay has been thoroughly examined, but it still is useful to make provisional evaluations right from the start.

Successfully bringing relevant background information to bear clearly is the key to good evaluations, but other relevant thoughts often play an important role. We often simply don't know enough to come to a confident evaluation but still may be able to speculate intelligently by thinking about the right questions that need to be raised either for or against a particular thesis. For example, one of the important reasons often given in favor of laws requiring capital punishment for heinous crimes is that these laws will act as a deterrent—criminals may think more carefully before committing murder if they know conviction means death. This sounds like a very plausible reason given the strength of the urge most of us have to stay alive. But does it in fact work this way? Not knowing the answer may be a good reason for withholding judgment, or for seeking further information, or for at least only *provisionally* assuming that the threat of death deters criminals more than do lesser penalties. The point here is that coming to a justified evaluation requires us to think of what it would be useful to know that we don't as yet know—it requires us to raise the right sorts of questions. (Raising questions of this kind, of course, also serves as a guide to research that might have to be undertaken.)

When the entire structure of an extended argument has been figured out, its relevant passages will divide into those that are argued for within the essay and those that are not. The latter are the writer's basic *assumptions*—*starting points*—assumed without being justified. When evaluating an extended passage, you need to ask and answer three vital questions, corresponding to the three basic requirements of cogent reasoning (discussed in Chapter 1):

1. Are the writer's assumptions and stated reasons justified by what you already believe?
2. Do you know other relevant reasons or arguments? (If so, then you need to add them before coming to a final conclusion as to the essay's cogency.)
3. Do the reasons (plus any relevant material you may have added) justify acceptance of the thesis—that is, is the reasoning valid?

If an assumption or reason is not supported by your background beliefs, if you know of relevant information that refutes or casts doubt on the thesis, or if the reasoning is not completely valid (taking into account material you may have added), then clearly you should not be convinced by that particular extended argument. It may be, of course, that your background beliefs neither support nor conflict with an argument's assumptions or reasons, in which case you can't either accept or reject the argument's thesis; you need to withhold judgment or delve further into the matter.

A note of caution: It is common for some of the subsidiary arguments in a long essay to be cogent, while others are fallacious. When this is the case, reason dictates accepting only the untainted portions of the overall argument. But it would be wrong to automatically toss out the whole extended argument—wrong to reject the thesis of the essay—if that thesis can stand on the basis of the legitimate portions of the essay (along with relevant material you may have added from your background beliefs). This point often is characterized as one of *charity*—of being fair to the other side on an issue—but it also is an important requirement of good critical reasoning.

EXERCISE 8-1

Here are several short passages (taken from longer works). Reveal the structure of each passage, including reasons that support the thesis, reasons for the reasons, counterarguments, extraneous material, and so on, as in this simple example. (Remember, sometimes a reason or thesis may be implied.)

Example
Original passage (from an essay by Baruch Brody on the abortion issue): "There is a continuity of development from the moment of conception on. There are constant changes in the foetal condition; the foetus is constantly acquiring new structure and characteristics, but there is no one state which is radically different from any other. Since this is so, there is no one stage in the process of foetal development after the moment of conception which could plausibly be picked out as the moment at which the foetus becomes a living human being. The moment of conception is, however, different in this respect. It marks the beginning of this continuous process of development and introduces something new which is radically discontinuous with what has come before it. Therefore, the moment of conception, and only it, is a plausible candidate for being that moment at which the foetus becomes a living human being."

Rewritten Passage
Reason (premise): After the moment of conception, there is a continuous development of the human fetus, with no one state being much different from the next.
Conclusion: No moment after conception can be selected as the moment the fetus becomes a human being. (This conclusion then becomes a reason [premise] in the larger argument.)
Reason (premise): But the moment of conception introduces something radically different from what came before.
Conclusion (thesis): The moment of conception is the only plausible moment when the fetus becomes a human being.

1. Payday loan stores prey on low-income people and drive them into debt. There are now so many of them that they outnumber most fast-food franchises. Companies with names like EZ Money and Check Into Cash give two-week loans with no credit checks, but they charge huge fees. It's not uncommon for a company to charge a fee of $22 per two weeks for every $100 borrowed; at this rate a $500 loan would rack up an annual interest rate of 572 percent. Loan companies like this take advantage of poor people who are desperate to make ends meet from one paycheck to the next. Borrowers begin by taking out one loan to tide them over, and then another if they still run short, and then another. For example, one woman had to take out loans from four different companies and wound up

paying $600 in finance fees alone for a debt of $1,300. Borrowers like this, who live on the margin as is, are driven deeper and deeper into debt by the loan shark practices of payday stores. This is little better than thievery and should be stopped. State governments should prohibit payday lending. It's bad enough that these borrowers are living on the edge. Loan companies that take advantage of them are unconscionable. (Data taken from "Payday Loans, Nonprofit Style, Emerge to Mixed Response," by John Leland, *New York Times,* August 28, 2007)

2. Excerpt from "The Case for Censorship," by Roger Kimball, the *Wall Street Journal* (October 8, 2000):

> ... What's wrong with a little censorship? Until quite recently all sorts of things were censored in American society. There were very strict rules about what you could show on television and in movies, what you could describe in books and what you could reproduce in magazines. Were we worse off then?
> ... There are plenty of reasons to support government censorship when it comes to depictions of sex and violence. For one thing, it would encourage the entertainment industry to turn out material that is richer erotically. ... Another reason ... is that it would help temper the extraordinary brutality of popular culture.
> ... [Society] has an interest in protecting the moral sensibility of its citizens, especially the young. Freedom without morality degenerates into the servitude of libertinage. Which is why judicious government censorship is not the enemy of freedom but its guarantor.

*3. Thomas Paine, in his classic *The Age of Reason:* "Revelation is a communication of something which the person to whom that thing is revealed did not know before. For if I have done a thing, or seen it done, it needs no revelation to tell me I have done it or seen it, nor to enable me to tell it or to write it. Revelation, therefore, cannot be applied to anything done upon earth, of which man himself is the actor or the witness; and consequently, all the historical and anecdotal parts of the Bible, which is almost the whole of it, is not within the meaning and compass of the word 'revelation,' and therefore, is not the word of God."

4. Argument implied in this excerpt from the *International Herald Tribune* (July 3, 2003): "The federal appeals court in Atlanta has ordered the chief justice of the Alabama Supreme Court to remove a monument engraved with the Ten Commandments from the rotunda of his courthouse. The 11th U.S. Circuit Court of Appeals concluded the monument violates the First Amendment's prohibition on government establishment of religion. In its ruling Tuesday, the court was unusually blunt in responding to the assertion by Chief Justice Roy Moore in court papers in the case that he did not recognize the authority of the federal court in this matter. The appeals court compared Moore to those Southern governors [George Wallace and Ross Barnett] who attempted to defy court orders during an earlier era."

5. Philosopher John Locke, in his classic *The Second Treatise on Government:* "Though the earth and all inferior creatures be common to all men, yet every man has a property in his own person; this nobody has any right to but himself. The labor of his body and the work of his hands, we may say, are properly his.

Whatsoever then he removes out of the state that nature has provided and left it in, he has mixed his labor with, and joined to it something that is his own, and thereby makes it his property. It being by him removed from the common state nature has placed it in, it has by this labor something annexed to it that excluded the common right of other men. For this labor being the unquestionable property of the laborer, no man but he can have a right to what that is once joined to, at least where there is enough and as good left in common for others."

6. Abstract of an article by Joyce Neu, "The United States Should Seek Alternatives to Military Action":

Americans are justifiably angry at the terrorists behind the September 11 attacks. Many call for military reprisals. However, war has failed to deter terrorism and inevitably kills innocent bystanders and civilians. The United States should reject calls for war and revenge and instead seek out alternative ways of bringing the terrorists to justice and work to remove the underlying causes of terrorism. By responding with restraint and magnanimity, America can help prevent terrorism in the future.

7. From an article on genetically engineered foods, by John B. Fagan: [1]

Giant transnational companies are carrying out a dangerous global experiment by attempting to introduce large numbers of genetically engineered foods widely into our food supply. Because genetic manipulations can generate unanticipated harmful side-effects, and because genetically engineered foods are not tested sufficiently to eliminate those that are dangerous, this experiment not only jeopardizes the health of individuals, but could also lead to national health threats. . . . Tampering with the genetic code of food is reckless and poses a serious threat to life. It could easily upset the delicate balance between our physiology and the foods that we eat. There is already ample scientific justification for an immediate ban on genetically modified foods in order to safeguard our health.

8. Philosopher Sidney Hook, on recovering from a near-fatal stroke:

A few years ago, I lay at the point of death [following the stroke]. . . . At one point my heart stopped beating; just as I lost consciousness, it was thumped back into action again. In one of my lucid intervals during those days of agony, I asked my physician to discontinue all life-supporting services or show me how to do it. He refused. . . .

   A month later I was discharged from the hospital. In six months I regained the use of my limbs [and voice]. . . . My experience . . . has been cited as an argument against honoring requests of stricken patients to be gently eased out of their pain and life. I cannot agree. . . . As an octogenarian, there is a reasonable likelihood that I may suffer another "cardiovascular accident" or worse. . . . It seems to me that I have already paid my dues to death—indeed . . . I suffered enough to warrant dying several times over. Why run the risk of more?

---

[1] From "Genetically Engineered Food: A Serious Health Risk," posted online February 26, 1997, www.natural-law.org/issues/genetic/gehazards.html.

Secondly, I dread imposing on my family and friends another grim round of misery similar to the one my first attack occasioned. My wife and children endured enough for one lifetime. . . .

EXERCISE 8-2

In general, we do not read poetry with the intent of constructing a summary and then evaluating for cogency. We read out of love for effective poetic expression. Nevertheless, it is a fact that poems often argue for a conclusion. Andrew Marvell's wonderful (one might say "Marvell-ous") poem "To His Coy Mistress" is a case in point. Clearly, there would be no point in constructing a detailed summary of this, or perhaps any, poem, citing every bit of support given for the reasons provided for its thesis. So in this case, after first reading the poem for the enjoyment of the experience, simply state in a general way and in your own words the poem's thesis; the reason, or reasons, provided in its support; and a rough idea of the support provided for the reason or reasons.

To His Coy Mistress

Had we but world enough, and time,
This coyness, Lady, were no crime.
We would sit down and think which way
To walk and pass our long love's day.
Thou by the Indian Ganges' side
Shouldst rubies find: I by the tide
Of Humber would complain. I would
Love you ten years before the Flood,
And you should, if you please, refuse
Till the conversion of the Jews.
My vegetable love would grow
Vaster than empires and more slow;
An hundred years would go to praise
Thine eyes and on thy forehead gaze;
Two hundred to adore each breast,
But thirty thousand to the rest;
An age at least to every part,
And the last age should show your heart.
For, Lady, you deserve this state,
Nor would I love at lower rate.

But at my back I always hear
Time's winged chariot hurrying near;
And yonder all before us lie
Deserts of vast eternity,
Thy beauty shall no more be found,
Nor, in thy marble vault, shall sound
My echoing song; then worms shall try
That long preserved virginity,
And your quaint honor turn to dust,
And into ashes all my lust;
The grave's a fine and private place,
But none, I think, do there embrace.

Now therefore, while the youthful hue
Sits on thy skin like morning dew,
And while thy willing soul transpires
At every pore with instant fires,
Now let us sport us while we may,
And now, like amorous birds of prey,
Rather at once our time devour
Than languish in his slow-chapped power.
Let us roll all our strength and all
Our sweetness up into one ball,
And tear our pleasures with rough strife
Through the iron gate of life,
Thus, though we cannot make our sun
Stand still, yet we will make him run.

EXERCISE 8-3

The Declaration of Independence contains a thesis and reasons supporting that thesis. Get a copy of that important document, and (1) determine what its thesis is and (2) list the reasons provided in defense of that thesis. Is the argument inductive or deductive? What is the worldview?

2. The Margin Note and Summary Method

The **margin note and summary method** is a good method to use when an evaluation has to be right. The idea behind this method is that a summary can be more easily worked with than the longer work from which it is drawn, provided the summary is *accurate*. (Making a summary helps us to remember things better and thus is a good study technique—one, in fact, that instructors often use when preparing class material.)

The margin note and summary method has four basic steps:

1. Read the material to be summarized.
2. Read it through again, this time marking the important passages with an indication of their content written in the margin. (The point of the first reading is to enable you to spot the important passages more accurately when you read through the material a second time. First readings often don't catch the drift.) Margin notes need not be full sentences or grammatically correct. They may contain abbreviations or whatever shorthand notes you care to employ.
3. Use the margin notes to construct a summary of the passage, indicating which statements are premises (reasons) and which conclusions, so that the structure of the passage's argument is laid bare.
4. Evaluate the essay by evaluating your summary, checking back and forth to be sure there are no significant differences between the essay and your summary.

Two things need to be remembered about the margin note and summary method. First, when we skip portions of a passage, we make a judgment that the passed-over material is relatively unimportant. It takes practice and skill to know what to include and what to omit, and even those with a good deal of experience may differ on such matters. (This does not mean, however, that anything goes!) Second, margin notes and summaries are shorthand devices; they should be briefer than the passages they summarize—if possible, a good deal briefer. The risk in this process, obviously, is falsification. We don't want to commit the straw man fallacy by making judgments about the shortened version that would not be valid for the original.

3. Extended Evaluation of an Argument

An exended evaluation examines an argument in some detail, using the critical thinking tools covered throughout this text. The first step is to summarize the article using the margin note method explained in the previous section. Then identify the thesis, the reasons and the main points of the argument. The next task is to determine whether the argument is convincing. Do the reasons really defend the thesis or are they fallacious? Is the evidence plausible? Has the writer included important counterarguments? Is the use of emotive language persuasive or manipulative? Is the worldview convincing? These are some of the questions to consider when evaluating arguments.

It is important to keep in mind that there is no such thing as a perfectly reasoned, totally convincing argument (though there are plenty of really bad ones out there). Even brilliant thinkers slip up once in a while or get carried away with their own rhetoric. A good analysis determines what is convincing and what is not, then comes to an overall evaluation of the argument.

Here is a condensed version of an argument on capital punishment by probably the most famous trial lawyer of the 20th century, Clarence Darrow, followed by an evaluation. One of Darrow's most celebrated cases was his defense of Richard Loeb and Nathan Leopold, two teenagers who pled guilty to kidnapping and murdering a 14-year-old boy. The prosecution was determined to hang the killers, but Darrow's brilliant 12-hour summation, an eloquent attack on the death penalty, was so effective that the presiding judge wept at its conclusion and gave Leopold and Loeb a life sentence instead of the death penalty. (An interesting footnote on Darrow is that no client of his was ever executed.) The following essay was published a few years after the trial. Although written in the first half of the 20th century, the arguments Darrow made are still used by abolitionists today. Given his legendary prowess in a court of law, one might think his arguments were airtight, but even the great Darrow lapsed into fallacious reasoning and used rhetorical tricks to persuade.

The Futility of the Death Penalty[2]

. . . It is my purpose in this article to prove, first, that capital punishment is no deterrent to crime; and second, that the state continues to kill its victims, not so much to defend society against them—for it could do that equally well by imprisonment—but to appease the mob's emotions of hatred and revenge. . . .

Behind the idea of capital punishment lie false training and crude views of human conduct. People do evil things, say the judges, lawyers, and preachers, because of depraved hearts. . . .

If crime were really the result of willful depravity, we should be ready to concede that capital punishment may serve as a deterrent to the criminally inclined. But it is hardly probable that the great majority of people refrain from killing their neighbors because they are afraid; they refrain because they never had the inclination. Human beings are creatures of habit; and, as a rule, they are not in the habit of killing. The circumstances that lead to killings are manifold, but in a particular individual the inducing cause is not easily found. In one case, homicide may have been induced by indigestion in the killer; in another, it may be traceable to some weakness inherited from a remote ancestor; but that it results from *something* tangible and understandable, if all the facts were known, must be plain to everyone who believes in cause and effect.

Of course, no one will be converted to this point of view by statistics of crime. In the first place, it is impossible to obtain reliable ones, and in the second place, the conditions to which they apply are never the same. But if one cares to analyze the figures, such as we have, it is easy to trace the more frequent causes of homicide. The greatest number of killings occur during attempted burglaries and robberies. The robber knows that penalties for burglary do not average more than five years in prison. He also knows that the penalty for murder is death or imprisonment. Faced with this alternative, what does the burglar do when he is detected and threatened with arrest? He shoots to

---

[2]From Clarence Darrow, "The Futility of the Death Penalty," in *Verdicts Out of Control*, edited by Arthur and Lila Weinberg (Chicago: Quadrangle Books, 1963), pp. 225–234. This essay first appeared in *The Forum*, September 1928.

kill. He deliberately takes the chance of death to save himself from a five-year term in prison. It is therefore as obvious as anything can be that fear of death has no effect in diminishing homicides of this kind, which are more numerous than any other type.

The next largest number of homicides may be classed as "sex murders." Quarrels between husbands and wives, disappointed love, or love too much requited cause many killings. They are the result of primal emotions so deep that the fear of death has not the slightest effect in preventing them. Spontaneous feelings overflow in criminal acts, and consequences do not count.

Then there are cases of sudden anger, uncontrollable rage. The fear of death never enters into such cases; if the anger is strong enough, consequences are not considered until too late. The old-fashioned stories of men deliberately plotting and committing murder in cold blood have little foundation in real life. Such killings are so rare that they need not concern us here. The point to be emphasized is that practically all homicides are manifestations of well-recognized human emotions, and it is perfectly plain that the fear of excessive punishment does not enter into them.

In addition to these personal forces which overwhelm weak men and lead them to commit murder, there are also many social and economic forces which must be listed among the causes of homicides, and human beings have even less control over these than over their own emotions. . . . the United States has gathered together people of every color from every nation in the world. Racial differences intensify social, religious, and industrial problems, and the confusion which attends this indiscriminate mixing of races and nationalities is one of the most fertile sources or crime.

Will capital punishment remedy these conditions? Of course it won't; but its advocates argue that the fear of this extreme penalty will hold the victims of adverse conditions in check. To this piece of sophistry, the continuance and increase of crime in our large cities is a sufficient answer. No, the plea that capital punishment acts as a deterrent to crime will not stand. The real reason why this barbarous practice persists in a so-called civilized world is that people still hold the primitive belief that the taking of one human life can be atoned for by taking another. It is the age-old obsession with punishment that keeps the official headsman busy plying his trade.

And it is precisely upon this point that I would build my case against capital punishment. Even if one grants that the idea of punishment is sound, crime calls for something more—for careful study, for an understanding of causes, for proper remedies. To attempt to abolish crime by killing the criminal is the easy and foolish way out of a serious situation. Unless a remedy deals with the conditions which foster crime, criminals will breed faster than the hangman can spring his trap. Capital punishment ignores the causes of crime and, like the methods of the witch doctor, it is not only ineffective as a remedy, but is positively vicious in at least two ways. In the first place, the spectacle of state executions feeds the basest passions of the mob. And in the second place, so long as the state rests content to deal with crime in this barbaric and futile manner, society will be lulled by a false sense of security, and effective methods of dealing with crime will be discouraged. . . .

. . . while capital punishment panders to the passions of the mob, no one takes the pains to understand the meaning of crime. People speak of crime or criminals as if the world were divided into the good and the bad. This is not true. . . .

Human conduct is by no means so simple as our moralists have led us to believe. There is no sharp line separating good actions from bad. The greed for money, the display of wealth, the despair of those who witness the display, the poverty, oppression, and hopelessness of the unfortunate—all these are factors which enter into human conduct and of which the world takes no account. Many people have learned no other profession but robbery and burglary. The processions moving steadily through our prisons to the gallows are in the main made up of these unfortunates. And how do we dare to consider ourselves civilized creatures when, ignoring the causes of crime, we rest content to mete out harsh punishments to the victims of conditions over which they have no control? . . .

Even now, are not all imaginative and humane people shocked at the spectacle of a killing by the state? . . . How can the state censure the cruelty of the man who—moved by strong passions, or acting to save his freedom, or influenced by weakness or fear—takes human life, when everyone knows that the state itself, after long premeditation and settled hatred, not only kills, but first tortures and bedevils its victims for weeks with the impending doom?

For the last hundred years the world has shown a gradual tendency to mitigate punishment. We are slowly learning that this way of controlling human beings is both cruel and ineffective. . . . There is no doubt whatever that the world is growing more humane and more sensitive and more understanding. The time will come when all people will view with horror the light way in which society and its courts of law now take human life; and when that time comes, the way will be clear to devise some better method of dealing with poverty and ignorance and their frequent byproducts, which we call crime.

Analysis

In "The Futility of the Death Penalty," Clarence Darrow argues against capital punishment because it is "no deterrent to crime" and it is the state's attempt "to appease the mob's emotions of hatred and revenge." His overall argument is valid and often persuasive, but he sometimes reasons fallaciously, and though he uses language effectively, he also uses it cleverly, to manipulate the reader. He is at his best, however, when he urges us to consider the humane world view at the heart of his argument.

Darrow's first premise, that capital punishment is no deterrent to crime, is hypothetical, based on common sense and his own background experience as a defense lawyer. Darrow himself concedes that "no one will be converted to this point of view by statistics of crime" partly because "it is impossible to obtain reliable ones." Although recent studies seem to provide some statistical corroboration that the death penalty is a deterrent, Darrow's reservations about crime statistics are just as relevant today as they were then. The *New York Times* published a survey in September 2000 revealing that the homicide rate in states with the death penalty has been 48 percent to 111 percent higher over the past 20 years than in states without the death penalty. However, these findings suggest the fallacy of questionable cause, since the states cited may have had a higher rate of murder to start with and may have instituted the death penalty to reduce the number of homicides.

Instead of using questionable statistics to make his point, Darrow reasons that most killers are not deterred by the death penalty when they kill in the heat of the moment—during attempted burglaries, in sex-related quarrels, or in cases of uncontrollable rage. Our own background beliefs would probably confirm his assumption that people aren't likely to think of the consequences under these circumstances. But he is guilty of suppressing evidence when he dismisses the idea of premeditation in his claim that "men deliberately plotting and committing murder in cold blood have little foundation in real life." Countless examples of premeditated murder could be used to refute this claim, but the most obvious in Darrow's case is the gruesome crime committed by his own clients, Leopold and Loeb, who systematically planned to commit the perfect crime to kidnap and murder their 14-year-old victim. His argument that a "great majority of people refrain from killing their neighbors . . . because they never had the inclination" probably applies to most people but doesn't take into account those who *do* have the inclination to kill and who *are* deterred by the fear of punishment.

There is some truth to his second premise that the state continues to kill its victims to appease the mob's emotions of hatred and revenge. Politicians do, indeed, pay attention to the attitudes their constituents have about capital punishment. In Texas, for instance, candidates who take a stand against the death penalty would have a hard time getting elected. But Darrow relies more on provocative rhetoric than reasoning to make his point. He argues that those who favor the death penalty are a " mob," incited by "hatred and revenge," and the state is a murderer in the questionable premise that "the state itself, after long premeditation and settled hatred, not only kills but first tortures and bedevils its victims for weeks with the impending doom." By presenting the criminal as the "victim," he transforms the entire legal process—from the interrogation, to the trial, sentencing, and appeals—into torturous treatment of the murderer, all of which evade the issue that a real victim is dead at the hands of a killer.

Darrow's argument is driven by highly emotive, often persuasive language, used to engage the reader in his crusade. His tone is characterized by compassion for the hapless killer and moral outrage at the harsh retribution exacted by the state. Capital punishment is condemned as a "barbarous practice," the "easy and foolish way out of a serious situation." Those who favor it are "moralists" with "crude" notions of human conduct, people with the "primitive belief" that executing the killer will atone for the murder. To counter these uncivilized tendencies in human nature, Darrow describes right-thinking people as "imaginative and humane," "shocked at the spectacle of killing by the state." This is an effective ploy to jar the reader into seeing the state in a different light—as a killer not far removed from the murderer it condemns. Less persuasive is the linguistic sleight-of-hand he reserves for the criminals, whom he repeatedly refers to as "victims"—of social forces, emotional drives, or biological quirks—implying that they commit crime through no fault of their own because of the questionable premise that their behavior is the result of "conditions over which they have no control."

Perhaps more than anything else, his argument stands or falls on his worldview, which encompasses his attitude toward the criminal class and the responsibility of society in dealing with it. Darrow's philosophy of determinism is evident throughout when he claims that homicides may be "traceable to some weakness inherited from a remote ancestor" or "the result of primal emotions" or "uncontrollable rage," or that criminals are "victims of conditions over which they have no control." Although it is true that we have no control over the environment we are born into or the genes we inherit, most of us believe that we not only can but should control our actions, despite the problems inherent in our background. A more compelling reason for abolishing capital punishment is rooted in his humane worldview that a civilized society should not sink to the level of the criminal, that it should resist the primitive urge to exact retribution, and that it should deal with criminals in a humane manner, by mitigating punishment and trying to remedy the conditions that foster crime. In this way he appeals to our better natures and presents his most convincing argument.

EXERCISE 8-4

1. The above analysis of Darrow's argument is one person's evaluation and may not agree with your own. In what ways would you agree or disagree with it? Analyze the premises, reasoning, language, and worldview of Darrow's argument and come up with your own evaluation.

2. Find a 2- to 3-page argument in a magazine or on the Internet and evaluate it, using the critical thinking tools covered in the text.

4. DEALING WITH VALUE CLAIMS

By now, it should have become clear how often the reasons presented in favor of a thesis are at least in part about values, not facts. It is a *fact,* for example, that sugar sweetens coffee; it is a *value judgment* that sweetened coffee tastes better than unsweetened. It is a fact that the Earth goes around the sun once every 365 days or so; it is a value judgment that, other things being equal, those who give to the poor are better people than the Scrooges who don't. (Note the slanting word used in the previous sentence.)

When someone argues, say, that vacations are better taken in the spring, because spring is the best time of the year, that person uses a value judgment as a reason (premise) supporting the conclusion that vacations are best taken in the spring. (Note, by the way, that this conclusion is itself in part a value judgment, as are all conclusions that depend on at least one reason that is a value judgment.)

Value judgments typically are justified, or defended, in ways that are different from judgments about facts. Someone who claims, for example, that gold does not rust can support that claim by citing the fact that nothing made of gold has ever been observed to rust and that all attempts to rust gold have failed. But the person who says that gold makes beautiful jewelry has to cite a different sort of evidence—for example, that people generally like the look of gold jewelry. That is why many philosophers say that value judgments concern matters that are *subjective,* while judgments about alleged facts deal with matters that are *objective.*

The idea that values are subjective is captured nicely by the saying that beauty is in the eyes of the beholder and by the old precept that there is no disputing about taste. According to these maxims, the fact that some people like string beans, or Bach fugues, while others don't doesn't make those who do or those who don't wrong. By way of contrast, those who make a nonvalue, factual claim—for instance, that the Earth is flat (so-called "flat earthers")—are wrong; the rest of us who believe that it is spherical (well, extremely close to being spherical) are right. (Yes, there are people who still, in this day and age, believe that the Earth is flat. Recall the discussion of self-deception in Chapter 6.) Merely believing that something is a fact doesn't make it a fact; nor is such a belief justified in the absence of evidence (experience about something relevant) to support that belief.

It's true, of course, that lots of philosophers would argue against the idea that value judgments are by their nature subjective. Some would say, for example, that beauty is in the object, not just in the eyes of the beholder, so that the person who doesn't see the beauty in beautiful objects is like someone who is color-blind. (One of the points of a philosophy course in which value judgments are discussed is precisely to deal with disagreements of this kind.)

Fortunately, when the value judgments relevant to an argument are about beauty, or taste, or other aesthetic matters, we generally can come to an evaluation without having to deal with underlying philosophical issues like the one about objectivity versus subjectivity. Suppose, for example, that some people in a community want to make uncovered auto junkyards illegal, on the grounds that they constitute an "eyesore." Voters don't need to decide whether being an eyesore is an objective or a subjective property to figure out how to vote. They can just find out whether most people find them to be ugly, or at least whether they themselves see junkyards as a good deal less than attractive. (There may, of course, be good reasons against banning open auto graveyards, but that is another matter.) The point is that, in these cases, we can appeal to something subjective—namely, whether we see junkyards as ugly or not—without answering the underlying questions about whether the ugliness of something is in the thing itself or merely in the eyes of the beholder.

But other sorts of value cases are more problematic, the prime case being *moral values*. If it is true that moral values are subjective, then claims about them can be justified simply by appealing to evidence that most people hold these values. Enslaving people and working them to death then become morally wrong just because virtually everyone finds this sort of behavior wrong or unfair. But if moral values are objective, judgments about them cannot be defended in this way. Subjective feelings become irrelevant if moral principles are objective—if there is something outside us, be it biblical commandments, natural rights, the greatest good for the greatest number, or whatever, that determines which actions are right and which wrong.[3] Thus, those who hold that moral standards are objective need to think carefully as to what sorts of justifications—appeal to cultural norms, natural rights, religious principles, or something else—they believe should count in assessing moral claims and whether these allegedly objective standards in turn can be justified without appeal to subjective values or standards.

The point here, however, is that when someone makes a moral value claim in an argument, it may be crucially important to find out what makes that person hold the value in question. Those who argue against legal abortions, for example, often present as their principal reason the claim that taking a human life is morally wrong; but if their justification is the biblical commandment "Thou shalt not kill," then those who do not accept

---

[3] All of these, and many other allegedly objective factors, have been argued for, and against, by philosophers and theologians.

the Bible as the ultimate authority on moral matters have not been given a persuasive reason for accepting this claim about the immorality of taking a human life.[4] Similarly, those who argue in favor of legalizing prostitution often claim that a woman has a right to use her body in any way that she sees fit; but if their justification is a theory of objective natural rights, then those who reject the idea of objective rights have not been given a satisfactory reason for being in favor of legal prostitution.

In any case, good critical reasoners accept premises that contain moral value judgments only if those judgments conform to their own moral standards. Socialists, for instance, sometimes argue that it is not just impractical but also immoral to allow some workers in a community to earn thousands of times more than others (as is currently the case in the United States and some other industrial countries), and they use this claim as a reason for overturning, or at least modifying, the free enterprise system now in place in most industrial countries. Good critical reasoners accept or reject moral claims of this sort by seeing how they fit with the moral principles they already accept.

This does not mean, of course, that moral standards and values are exempt from challenge. Those who believe, say, that it always is morally wrong to violate legally enacted legislation may see the matter differently if laws are enacted forbidding the practice of their own religion or forcing acceptance of another faith.

It also needs to be noted that there often are no simple principles—say, those like the Ten Commandments—to apply in determining moral right and wrong. It seems morally right to many people that income should be proportionate to what one produces, a standard encapsulated in the idea that one should reap what one sows. According to this *principle of just desserts,* the fruits of a cooperative effort ought to be distributed according to the relative contributions of the various parties, whether in labor, capital, or whatever. But even supposing this idea is accepted, how are just desserts to be determined in actual cases? How do we compare, for instance, the efforts of a corporate chief executive officer who oversees the successful introduction of a new product with the engineers who designed and perfected that product, or with workers on the line who actually produce the goods? How do we compare the contributions of those who put up the money (stockholders) with those of company executive or production line employees?[5]

Finally, it is important to remember that those who go through life without carefully examining and questioning their moral principles run the same risk of mistake as do those who fail to acquire accurate factual beliefs about how things work in this complicated world of ours. This is true even if the subjectivist view of moral right and wrong is correct, for it still could well be that a person's unexamined feelings about this or that moral issue will fail to agree with how that individual might see the matter after giving

---

[4]Note that appeals to documents such as the Bible can be tricky. With respect to the abortion case, for instance, it has been argued that the original Hebrew has been mistranslated and that what the commandment says is better translated as "Thou shalt not *murder,*" so that the question remains as to whether abortion is murder—immoral killing. There also is the problem that most who deny the legitimacy of abortion believe certain kinds of killing are justified—for instance, in wartime or in self-defense; those who believe this would have to show why killing fetuses is not also sometimes justified.

[5]For more on this topic, see Howard Kahane, *Contract Ethics: Evolutionary Biology and the Moral Sentiments* (Lanham, Md.: Rowman & Littlefield, 1995).

it careful thought or after bringing to bear relevant background information. The first thought that virtually all of us have about infanticide, to take an interesting case, is that it always and everywhere is the worst sort of murder; but thinking carefully about the hard choices life presents to some parents has changed the minds of more than a few thinking and even compassionate individuals.[6]

EXERCISE 8-5

In a *New York Times* op-ed piece (April 16, 2008), James Alan Fox argues that colleges and universities are creating an "unwarranted and unhealthy level of fear" by beefing up campus security with measures that might well be ineffective. Fox, a professor of criminal justice and law at Northeastern University, believes that colleges are overreacting to shootings at Virginia Tech and other institutions by developing security measures like lockdowns and mass notification "that not long ago would have been considered unnecessary, if not absurd." Lockdowns, or plans to seal off buildings to prevent a gunman from moving from one place to another, "may do little to prevent casualties . . . [since] almost all college shootings have taken place in one location." They have the added disadvantage of preventing a potential victim from fleeing the building that has been sealed off. Mass notification may be equally ineffective. Emergency sirens could be set off by other causes other than gunfire, and text message alerts on cell phones wouldn't reach a lecture hall full of students required to turn off cell phones. Professor Fox argues that security measures like these raise the level of student fear without providing reliable protection. He does believe in taking sensible precautions, like having an adequate security forces and well trained staff members, but he thinks colleges have overreacted to violence on campus, creating fear and apprehension that undermine the "carefree atmosphere of campus life." Would you agree or disagree? Do some research on security measures at your campus and evaluate them for effectiveness.

EXERCISE 8-6

A while back (Exercise 8-1, number 5), you were asked to summarize excerpts from the writings of philosopher John Locke.

1. Indicate which of his assertions, if any, in his essay concern values, moral or nonmoral.

2. Use the summary of the article that you constructed before, along with your beliefs about any value statements the essay in question may contain, to come to an evaluation of Locke's view on the matter, indicating where you think his argument is weak, where strong, and what your overall evaluation is, making sure, of course, to explain why you think so.

---

[6]It sometimes happens that the only alternatives open to parents in poor societies, or societies in the throes of famine, are to do away with a newborn child so as to be able to keep their other children alive or else to see all of their offspring slowly starve to death.

EXERCISE 8-7

Follow the instructions for Exercise 8-6 for the following excerpt from "On Date Rape," by Camille Paglia:

> Dating is a very recent phenomenon in world history. Throughout history women have been chaperoned. As late as 1964, when I arrived in college, we had strict rules. We had to be in the dorm under lock and key by 11 o'clock. My generation was the one that broke these rules. We said, "We want freedom—no more double standard!" When I went to stay at a male friend's apartment in New York, my aunts flew into a frenzy: "You can't do that, it's dangerous!" Still, we understood in the '60s that we were taking a risk.
>
> Today these young women want the freedoms that we won, but they don't want to acknowledge the risk. That's the problem. The minute you go out with a man, the minute you go to a bar to have a drink, there is a risk. You have to accept the fact that part of the sizzle of sex comes from the danger of sex. You can be overpowered.
>
> So it is women's personal responsibility to be aware of the dangers of the world. But these young feminists today are deluded. They come from a protected, white, middle-class world, and they expect everything to be safe. Notice it's not black or Hispanic women who are making a fuss about this—they come from cultures that are fully sexual and they are fully realistic about sex. But these other women are sexually repressed girls, coming out of pampered homes, and when they arrive at these colleges and suddenly hit male lust, they go, "Oh, no!"
>
> These girls say, "Well, I should be able to get drunk at a fraternity party and go upstairs to a guy's room without anything happening." And I say, "Oh, really? And when you drive your car to New York City, do you leave your keys on the hood?" My point is that if your car is stolen after you do something like that, yes, the police should pursue the thief and he should be punished. But at the same time, the police—and I—have the right to say to you, "You stupid idiot, what the hell were you thinking?"
>
> I mean, wake up to reality. This is male sex. Guess what, it's hot. Male sex is hot. There's an attraction between the sexes that we're not totally in control of. The idea that we can regulate it by passing campus grievance committee rules is madness. My kind of feminism stresses personal responsibility. I've never been raped, but I've been very vigilant—I'm constantly reading the signals. If I ever got into a dating situation where I was overpowered and raped, I would say, "Oh well, I misread the signals." But I don't think I would ever press charges. . . .[7]

EXERCISE 8-8

In the fall of 2003, Californians were asked to vote on Proposition 54, a measure that prohibits state and local governments from classifying any person by race, ethnicity, color, or national origin. Your task is too evaluate the argument for Proposition 54 and decide whether you would vote for or against it.

---

[7]From Camille Paglia, "On Date Rape," *San Francisco Examiner,* July 7, 1991. Copyright © 1991. Reprinted by permission of the *San Francisco Examiner.*

Argument in Favor of Proposition 54

"'What is your race?'"

African-American? Mexican-American? Asian-American? White? Native American? Or, the mysterious 'other?'

If you're like most Californians, you're getting tired of that question.

Californians are the most racially and ethnically diverse people in the world—and we are proud of it. We are also among the most independent; and we resent being classified, categorized, divided and subdivided based on our skin color and the origin of our ancestors.

When you're asked to check a government form with row after row of these rigid and silly little 'race' boxes, have you ever just wanted to say, "None of your business; now leave me alone?' Proposition 54 seeks to eliminate racial categorization, by the government, in all areas except medicine, health care and law enforcement.

The advocates of racial categorization maintain that you have no right to privacy concerning your ancestry and racial background. They see no problem if your employer or school officials label you AGAINST YOUR WILL often without telling you—or charge you with 'racial fraud' if their 'racial' definitions are different from yours.

Dare we forget the lessons of history?

Classification systems were invented to keep certain groups 'in their place' and to deny them full rights. These schemes were not invented by the Civil Rights movement! They were anathema to it. In fact, former Supreme Court Justice Thurgood Marshall once said, "Distinctions by race are so evil, so arbitrary and invidious that a state bound to defend the equal protection of the laws must not involve them in any public sphere."

Throughout history, government-imposed racial classifications have been used to divide people. They have been used to set people against each other. The slave owners and segregationists of the American past knew it when they labeled European Jews a separate and inferior 'race'; American judges knew it when they had to determine if Asians or part-Asians were white or non-white for the purposes of naturalization. Now, the advocates of racial categorization tell us that government-imposed racial categories will somehow yield the very opposite of what they were originally intended to do! They insult our intelligence!

The unrelenting daily racial categorization of people by the government is one of the most divisive forces in American society. It is constantly emphasizing our minor differences, in opposition to our better instincts that tell us to seek our common interests and common values.

It's time for a change!

The government should stop categorizing its citizens by color and ancestry, and create a society in which our children and grandchildren can just think of themselves as Americans and individuals.

The colorblind ideal—judging others by the content of their character rather than the color of their skin—is more than a dream in California; it is central to the definition of who we are as a people, because, in California, we don't just dream; we do what others dream of doing.

Vote 'YES' on Proposition 54 (*www.racialprivacy.org*)!

Ward Connerly, *University of California Regent*
Martha Montelongo Myers, *Columnist*
Joe Hicks, *Human Relations Consultant*

1. Using the margin note and summary method, or whatever method works best for you, construct a summary of the excerpt, and then identify the thesis and the main premises.

2. Critically evaluate the article, using your summary as your guide, making sure that your evaluation accurately reflects the excerpt itself, as well as your summary.

3. Drawing on your background knowledge and beliefs, decide how you would vote on this issue and defend your decision.

5. EVALUATING IRONIC WORKS

Jonathan Swift, author of *Gulliver's Travels,* wrote a famous satire called "A Modest Proposal" in which he suggested that the Irish should raise babies to be eaten in order to solve the myriad problems confronting that famine-stricken land back in the 18th century.

But the point of his essay, of course, was completely other than that people should literally carry out the plan he proposed. He was, to be plain, writing in an **ironic** vein, saying one thing but meaning something entirely different. So when evaluating ironic works it is a mistake to take them literally; you need to evaluate them in terms of their underlying message. Swift's point was to force his British audience to face the mass starvation and misery in Ireland that British policies had produced; his ironic suggestions were intended to shock his audience into a recognition of what they were doing in Ireland.

Irony often is combined with humor or exaggeration to form a potent weapon in the hands of a master at the trade. Telling us what is true in a funny or exaggerated way makes it harder to deny than if it is put to us in a straightforward, serious manner. Ironic writing is particularly effective in penetrating the kinds of self-serving psychological defenses—denial, rationalization, and so on—that were discussed in Chapter 6.

EXERCISE 8-9

Today, political columnists such as Gail Collins and Maureen Dowd use a combination of irony and humor to make points about the current social/political scene. Here is an example, written in 1999 by the late and sadly missed Arthur (Art) Hoppe. It is just as relevant today as it was when written.

Our Deserving Rich

Let us pray that not a hand is laid on the $792 billion tax cut passed by the House when the Senate takes it up today. Never has a piece of legislation been so pure in its concept, so efficient in its means, so right on the mark.

As you may have read, the Republican measure passed by the House proposes giving 79 percent of the income-tax reductions to the richest one-fifth of our citizens and .03 percent to the poorest. The richest's take would average $4,592, while the poorest would haul in $15.

Before I pronounce you man and wife, a brief word from Archer Daniels Midland.

Irony and exaggeration work well not only in written works but also in drawings and cartoons.

It is high time we recognized the tremendous contributions the rich have made to this great land of ours. Hitherto, we have punished them for their well-earned money. The harder they labor and the more they make, the more we penalize them financially. What sort of a message does this send to every little tad in the land?

At the same time, we have rewarded the poor for their inability to find well-paying jobs. The less money they make, the more we subsidize them with our taxpayer dollars. There can be no doubt that they take far more from us than they give.

Let's ask ourselves: What has poverty ever done for America? The answer is absolutely nothing. Do the poor endow the symphonies and operas that flood our souls with musical grandeur? Of course not. Do they build the museums that increase our knowledge of the world or the galleries where hang the masterpieces of human creativity? Do they donate vast acreages of untouched land as a heritage for generations yet unborn? Don't be silly.

How many poor people have adopted a highway or saved a baby harp seal? Their commitment to the environment is infinitesimal at best. Indeed, rather than devoting themselves to improving our surroundings, they go out of their way to make our cities and towns far less inviting.

Their ghetto tenements, their sleazy housing projects and their skid row hotels are a blight on the landscape. Generally speaking, their wardrobes are tasteless, if not downright appalling. And those who live in the country have a penchant for littering their yards with unsightly collectibles such as broken-down washing machines and rusted-out cars.

Contrast this utter disregard for our sensibilities with the care the rich lavish on their surroundings. How pleasant it is to stroll through a wealthy neighborhood, graced with high flower-bedecked walls, verdant hedges and stately cast-iron fences.

How pleasing to the eye is the sight of an immaculately tuxedoed man and his bejeweled wife in her haute couture gown stepping from a limousine to attend a culture-improving function. Never could a poor person hope to equal their gratifying splendor.

Yes, as we would say in the rosy Ronald Reagan days, "It's morning in Palm Beach."

So hail the Republicans! Let us take comfort in the adage that the rich will always be with us—at least as long as the Republicans are in power. As for the Democrats, they would foolishly squander our hard-won budget surplus on Social Security, Medicare and other give-aways to the less successful members of our society.

Let's admit that the Democrats were not totally defeated. In what was obviously a last minute compromise, the Republicans agreed to give the poor families that $15. I can't for the life of me think why. It will only encourage them.[8]

1. What is Hoppe's point—his unstated thesis?

2. Why does Hoppe bash the poor and praise the rich? What is the point of such questions as "What has poverty ever done for America?" or "Do the poor endow symphonies and operas that flood our souls with musical grandeur?"

3. In your opinion, is he on target or not? Explain.

4. Does he make you take account of something that you already knew or that you hadn't paid sufficient attention to or appreciated the significance of? If so, explain. If not, why not?

---

[8]From Art Hoppe, "Our Deserving Rich," *San Francisco Chronicle,* July 28, 1999. © *San Francisco Chronicle.* Reprinted by permission.

Summary of Chapter 8

Chapter 8 concerns the evaluation of extended arguments—essays.

1. Most types of essays are straightforwardly argumentative, but some—for instance, descriptive or explanatory essays—may mask their theses in one way or another. *Example:* Orwell's essay, "A Hanging."

   Essays may argue by considering reasons *pro and con* a thesis, by providing a *refutation to counterarguments,* or by making a *comparison of alternatives,* as well as simply by presenting *reasons (premises)* in support of a *thesis.*

   There are several guidelines to use in evaluating argumentative passages: (1) Find the thesis and keep it in mind as you read; (2) find the reasons (premises) that support the thesis, and (when there are any) the reasons for the reasons, and so on, taking into account the evidence presented; (3) identify responses to likely objections or counterarguments; (4) skip whatever doesn't support (or argue against) the thesis; (5) add relevant information, pro or con, that you may know of; (6) consider the tone and emotive language; and (7) come to an evaluation.

   Coming to an evaluation consists primarily in asking and answering three questions, corresponding to the three basic requirements of cogent reasoning introduced in Chapter 1: (1) Are the writer's (or speaker's) assumptions and stated reasons justified by what you already believe? (2) Do you know other relevant reasons or arguments? (If so, they need to be added to the mix.) (3) Do the reasons (plus any added material) justify acceptance of the thesis—that is, is the argument then valid?

2. The *margin note and summary method* is a useful way to clarify the main ideas of an essay before analyzing it. This method has four steps: (1) Read the material carefully, (2) read it again and add margin notes at the relevant spots in the essay, (3) construct a summary from the margin notes, and (4) evaluate the summary, making sure to bring relevant information to bear.

3. Reasons offered in support of a thesis may be about *facts* or about *values.* Claims about values typically are justified differently than those about facts.

   It often is said that facts are *objective,* values *subjective.* On this view, the shape of a gold ring, for example, is an objective fact about the ring itself; the beauty of the ring is "in the eye of the beholder." A contrary view is that values inhere in the valuable objects themselves, so that they too are objective.

   Among value claims, those about *moral* matters tend to be both controversial and important. If moral values are subjective, then moral claims can be justified by evidence that the writer or speaker, or most or even all people hold that value. But if moral right and wrong are objective facts, then how people feel about them is irrelevant, and something outside our feelings—for example, biblical commandments—need to be appealed to in order to justify a particular moral claim. So when one is evaluating arguments containing moral claims, it often is important to try to find out what makes the writer or speaker make such a claim and to then assess the claims in view of one's own moral standards, however one has arrived at them. Of course, one's own moral standards should not be exempt from challenge and improvement (for example, in subtlety). Those who accept, say, the Ten Commandments need to see that they do not automatically answer all questions—they don't answer all economic ones, for example—and thus are in need at the very least of interpretation and perhaps also augmentation. Careful consideration of a standard may lead to a change of mind, say, about abortion or infanticide in view of the dire situations some people find themselves in.

4. Ironic essays argue for a point indirectly and thus are not to be taken literally. (For example, Swift did not espouse the eating of Irish babies.) The point in irony is not to present reasons for a conclusion so much as to get readers to see something clearly that they may have overlooked, or not paid sufficient attention to, or defended against by some sort of self-serving self-deception. An honest evaluation of ironic writing requires us to determine whether, as implicitly claimed, we have overlooked or denied something important.

There are no dull subjects. There are only dull writers.

—H. L. Mencken

Learn as much by writing as by reading.

—Lord Acton

He can compress the most words into the smallest idea of any man I ever met.

—Abraham Lincoln

A deluge of words and a drop of sense.

—John Ray

Chapter

9

WRITING COGENT (AND PERSUASIVE) ESSAYS

The discussion in Chapter 8 should make clear the essential contents of an argumentative essay: a thesis (grand conclusion) and reasons (premises) supporting the thesis. It also should be clear that in most cases the reasons themselves need to be supported by evidence or secondary reasons and that it often is useful to consider and refute likely objections.

But it should quickly become evident that writing a cogent and effective essay is much more difficult than summarizing and evaluating someone else's effort. Writing is character forming; it does indeed make evident the truth that writing is nature's way of letting us know how sloppy our initial thoughts on a topic often are. There are three reasons for writing essays, and one is without doubt that it is the very best way to sharpen sloppy thoughts into ideas that are clear, sensible, and well supported by good reasons and evidence. (The other two are to convince others and—obviously—to satisfy course or other requirements.)

1. THE WRITING PROCESS

Experienced writers tend to keep their basic goals firmly in mind as they write and, indeed, as they prepare to write. They usually develop a plan of attack designed to meet their goals, but they don't generally move relentlessly from one idea to the next. Rather, they frequently revise their original plans in the light of new evidence or ideas or in the face of unexpected difficulties. One task often interrupts another. (Interestingly, editing seems to have a higher priority with most experienced writers than any other writing task and tends to interrupt others at any time. Having used an inaccurate word, for example, writers tend to put aside whatever they are doing and search for one that is more precise.) The point is that for most people essay writing is a convoluted process, not a straightforward, linear one.[1] Skilled writers constantly rework their ideas as they plan and then write. The process itself leads to discovery, including, alas, the discovery of the inadequacy of our previous thoughts.

2. PREPARING TO WRITE

Students generally are asked to write short argumentative essays on specific topics—for instance, literacy in the United States or legalizing marijuana. Suppose your assignment is to write an essay on the topic of regulating the possession of firearms.

The first task is to determine what the precise thesis of your essay will be. Gun regulation might involve restricting the carrying of handguns to specific places or perhaps only to specified individuals. Your thesis might be for, or against, the legal possession of automatic, quick-firing weapons, or it might focus just on handguns such as pistols.

Once you have provisionally decided on a thesis, your research and greater thought on the matter may well urge a change of mind, perhaps even a switch from pro to con, or vice versa. Unless a precise thesis is forced on you, say, by your instructor, the very process of thinking about the topic and investigating the evidence and the reasonings of others is likely to motivate you to revise your thesis in one way or another. Poor thinkers often decide on a thesis and hang on to it no matter what the evidence seems to indicate, as though changing one's mind indicates failure. Good thinkers realize that changing one's mind *for good reason* is the hallmark of intelligent thought. In the case of laws concerning firearms, for instance, evidence about the incredible destructive firepower of handheld automatic weapons such as Uzis might convince you to argue for the banning of these weapons.

After you have provisionally selected a thesis and have developed reasons and evidence in its favor, it often is useful to construct an outline of the essay that is to be the finished product. It's true, of course, that we all are different. Some people do better just starting out writing, doing research, and even altering their thesis as they go along rather than following the order suggested here. (Recall the earlier remark about writing being a convoluted process.) But most writers, in particular those with little experience, find it useful to do a good deal of preparation, including the construction of an outline, before starting to write the essay itself. (That is an important reason why essays written the night before they're due seldom get good grades—the fact that they are "off the top of the head" is obvious to instructors.) At the very least, an outline should include a provisional thesis and the principal reasons and supporting evidence expected to be presented

---

[1] There have been a very few exceptions to this rule, the philosopher Bertrand Russell, interestingly, being a case in point. His handwritten first drafts, with extremely few changes here and there, often were used by publishers to set final type. We ordinary writers can only examine these drafts with a sense of awe, not with the intent to acquire the knack ourselves.

in its favor. Outlines need not be written in grammatically correct or even whole sentences. Phrases and key words often are sufficient. But it is a good idea for inexperienced writers to state the thesis and principal reasons in complete sentences.

Calvin (of the Calvin and Hobbes duo) found it overly tedious having both to write an essay about bats and to do research on the topic, but research—diligent research— usually is essential. When doing research, take notes (including citations!) of pertinent evidence—statistics, examples, the opinions of experts, and so on. Regularly review what you have discovered in the light of your thoughts on the topic to see how the evidence supports, or undermines, your thesis or important reasons. If research undermines your thesis, it obviously needs revision (making the thesis narrower, perhaps) or a significant change in the reasons you intend to offer in its support. *Never simply ignore counterarguments or reasons!*

Some reasons involve legal matters that require us to review the law and interpretations of it. For instance, many arguments address issues that involve constitutional law (such as abortion, gun control, pornography, and so on). Because the Constitution often is used to support either side of an argument, it needs careful interpretation to be persuasive. For this reason, it's a good idea to research judicial opinion (the majority and dissenting opinions of high-court judges) in court cases addressing the issue you are writing about. Consulting expert opinion will help you understand the kind of careful deliberation needed in arguing complex legal matters.

Of course, you don't want to snow readers with a mountain of reasons or evidence. Plan to stick to your best reasons—those that reflect your most convincing evidence. Remember, though, that not all reasons are based on factual research or evidence. When relevant, moral convictions and standards, or beliefs about aesthetic or other values, constitute very good reasons indeed. For instance, the belief that taking the life of animals solely for our own purposes—for food or for furs—is morally wrong certainly is relevant to issues concerning the treatment of animals.

Finally, before starting to write an essay, make sure that its thesis follows logically from the reasons (premises) you intend to offer in its support. After all, validity— deductive or inductive—is an absolutely necessary condition of cogent argument. And reasons that do not genuinely support a thesis are useless.

3. WRITING THE ESSAY

Argumentative essays typically divide into three parts: an introduction (usually including the essay's thesis), the body of the essay, and a conclusion. Each part helps to develop, organize, and support the argument.

The Introduction

A good introduction engages the reader's attention and lays the groundwork for an essay's thesis, which usually is stated toward the end of the introduction but may be placed right at the beginning. The point of the introduction is to start persuading readers to accept your thesis, perhaps before it is even stated. (Remember, you have two goals in mind. One is to write an essay that is cogent. The other is to persuade readers to accept your thesis. A perfectly cogent essay that is not well written may very well not convince many readers.)

Reprinted by permission of the *Detroit Free Press*.

An essay can be started in all sorts of ways, a good one being to quote from an authoritative source. For instance, an essay on the need for greater adult literacy might begin with the following statistics:

> According to the National Adult Literacy Survey, 40 to 44 million adults[1] have either very basic or below basic reading skills, and that number has not improved since 1992.

The essay might then tie this quote into the rest of the introduction:

> These alarming statistics suggest that there is something drastically wrong with a system of education that turns out so many poorly prepared adults. . . .

After a few more introductory remarks, provide readers with a clear statement of the essay's thesis, followed by an enunciation of the three major reasons that are offered in its support:

> We, as a country, must do what is necessary to ensure that our people are literate [thesis], not only to improve the lot of those who suffer from illiteracy [reason 1], though that is reason enough, but to reduce the economic burden on society [reason 2] and to strength our democracy with an informed citizenry [reason 3].

Starting the essay in this way prepares the audience to read the body of the essay intelligently. Although it isn't necessary to include the main reasons after the thesis, doing so helps to keep both the writer and the reader on track.

The Body of an Essay

The body of an essay develops the reasons and evidence offered in support of the essay's thesis. How much support is needed depends on how resistant the intended audience is likely to be (or on how much space is available to make your case). You don't want to hit people over the head with what they already believe or know. The body of the essay on illiteracy might contain two subsidiary reasons offered in defense of the first major reason that illiterate individuals suffer personally. The first might be this one:

> The humane argument for a completely literate population is quite simply that illiterate people suffer a great deal from their affliction—both on a psychological and a practical level. Consider the man who is so embarrassed at being unable to read that he *pretends* to read so as to conceal his ignorance. . . .

Note the use of an example to illustrate the first subsidiary reason.

After providing several examples that make the point about the psychological problems facing the illiterate, the essay might then describe other problems that the functionally illiterate face in everyday life:

> Personal humiliation, however, is only one consequence of illiteracy. Perhaps even more important are the ways in which the lives of functional illiterates are severely restricted. Imagine, for instance, how difficult perfectly ordinary, everyday tasks become for those unable to read product labels, telephone books, ...

The stage has now been nicely set for the essay's second major reason—that society as a whole suffers when many of its citizens are illiterate, stated perhaps in a way that at the same time counters a likely objection to the essay's thesis that America should act to greatly reduce its rate of illiteracy:

> It may be argued that the expense of tracking down and stamping out illiteracy is more than our pocketbooks can bear. But that argument fails to take into account how much we, as a society, have to pay for the illiteracy of a third of our people. . . .

At this point, after providing examples of how illiteracy is an economic drain on society as a whole, the essay might continue in this way:

> Even more important, though, literate citizens are more likely to strengthen our democracy because they have the ability to be well informed. For example, ...

The Conclusion

The conclusion of an argumentative essay often restates the thesis—perhaps with emphasis. If the essay is rather long or complicated, the main points may need to be summarized. Here, for instance, is part of what would make a good conclusion to the illiteracy essay:

> In sum, everyone will benefit from the eradication of functional illiteracy. Certainly the illiterate one-third of our adult population has a great deal to gain by learning to read. They will be better able to cope with such simple practical tasks as . . . . Those of us who enjoy the advantages of literacy will also benefit because . . . .

Here, now, is what the entire essay on illiteracy might look like. It is rather short as essays go, intended primarily to serve as an example, but it nevertheless does a satisfactory job of clearly presenting and defending an important thesis:

> According to the National Adult Literacy Survey,[1] 40 to 44 million adults have either very basic or below basic reading skills, and that number has not improved since 1992. These alarming statistics suggest that there is something drastically wrong with a system of education that turns out so many poorly prepared adults. Those with rudimentary skills have trouble functioning effectively in society, finding employment or training for new jobs. Yet fewer than 10 percent of those needing help are being reached.[2]
>
> The National Committee on Education was right in claiming that we are "a nation at risk." We, as a country, must do what is necessary to ensure that our adult population is literate, not only to improve the lot of those who suffer from

illiteracy, though that is reason enough, but to reduce the economic burden on society, and to strengthen our democracy with an informed citizenry. The humane argument for a literate population is quite simply that people who cannot read suffer a great deal from their affliction—both on a psychological and practical level. Consider the man so embarrassed by his illiteracy that he *pretends* to read books on buses and in restaurants, just to save face, or the woman who can't read street signs and is ashamed to ask someone to read them for her. The functionally illiterate regularly suffer embarrassment because of their affliction. I once knew a young man who, to avoid ridicule, went to great lengths to hide the fact that he could not read. Although in constant fear of discovery—by friends, his boss, even his relatives—he sometimes was forced to accept help, for instance, when filling out simple forms—much to his mortification.

Personal humiliation, however, is only one consequence of illiteracy. Perhaps even more important are the ways in which the lives of functional illiterates are severely restricted. Imagine, for instance, how difficult perfectly ordinary, everyday tasks become for those unable to read product labels, telephone books, prescriptions, or even bills or letters from friends. Think of how illiteracy prevents them from getting any but the most menial jobs. At the turn of the century, when the economy was more dependent on factory and farm workers, nonreaders might have been able to support themselves reasonably well, but in this age of technology, where computers dominate the workplace, employees *must* be literate. These days it is a rare job that doesn't require reading ability.

It may be argued that the expense of tracking down and stamping out illiteracy is more than our pocketbooks can bear. But that argument fails to take into account how much we, as a society, have to pay for the illiteracy of a third of our people. The functionally illiterate are disproportionately on welfare rolls, or in jail.[3] Unable to earn good incomes and often ignorant of simple preventive health or birth control measures, they increase the cost of programs such as Medicaid. Taxpayers, already heavily burdened by high taxes, can ill afford the additional expense of an illiterate population.

The business sector of the economy suffers as well. The U.S. Department of Labor estimates that illiteracy costs businesses up to $225 billion a year in lost productivity. "The costs stem from employee mistakes . . . absenteeism, tardiness, missed opportunities, and other problems associated with illiteracy."[4] The illiterate are much more likely to be injured on the job, costing employers several billion dollars every year in workmen's compensation and other insurance premiums and in the expense of replacing damaged equipment. These losses are ultimately passed on to us, the consumers.

Even more important, though, literate citizens are more likely to strengthen our democracy because they have the ability to be well informed, unlike the illiterate one-third of the nation. They need not rely on television, as most illiterates do, for watered-down versions of the news, but can read about issues in greater depth and make informed decisions at the polls. (Note that the illiterate even have trouble following voting instructions when they go to the polls, let alone make informed decisions.) They are less likely to be manipulated by demagogues and charlatans and more likely to reason critically about matters of national importance. Democracy guarantees freedom to discuss issues and allows for the uncensored distribution of news and critical commentary—rights that can be practiced effectively only by a literate citizenry.

In sum, everyone will benefit from the eradication of illiteracy. Certainly those who are illiterate have a great deal to gain by learning to read. They will be better equipped to find decent employment, to function well in everyday life and thus to feel better about themselves. Those of us who enjoy the advantages of literacy will also benefit because the expense of supporting illiterates will be considerably reduced and we will have a more reliable, more efficient workforce. Above all, a literate, informed citizenry is more likely to benefit our democracy as a whole. We thus have everything to gain and nothing to lose by helping everyone to become literate.

NOTES

1. Compiled by the National Assessment of Adult Literacy, 2003.
2. "The Scope of Illiteracy in This Country," Adult Literacy Service, accessed August 10, 2000, <http://www.indian-river.fl.us/livingservices/als/facts.html>
3. Jonathan Kozol, *Illiterate America* (New York: Anchor Books/Doubleday, 1985).
4. Shelly Reese, "Illiteracy at Work." *American Demographics* (April 1996), accessed August 12, 2000, <http://www.demographics.com/publications/ad/9604AB02htm>

4. SUPPORTING REASONS EFFECTIVELY

Perhaps the most difficult part of writing an argument is to provide convincing evidence. It's not enough to have sensible reasons to begin with. You need to convince the reader that those reasons are worth believing. Here are a few guidelines.

Provide Concrete Evidence

When possible, provide evidence that is specific. Use examples, cite statistics, compare or contrast relevant material, and draw on factual information. Reasons are more likely to be convincing when they can be verified by specific information than when they are explained in terms of generalities. Statistics reported in the National Adult Literacy Survey are a case in point. The fact that 40 to 44 million adults are functionally illiterate and 50 million more read on a fourth- or fifth-grade level is persuasive evidence for the need to reduce illiteracy in our country.

Specific information of this kind is usually drawn from these three sources:

1. *Personal experiences:* Suppose your thesis is that the food served at school should be improved. In this instance you, yourself, have had personal experiences that can be used to support your position. Every time you have eaten lunch in the cafeteria, the food has been terrible: the bread is hard as a rock, and the spaghetti tastes like rubber. Citing these personal experiences provides good support for your reasons, though usually other kinds of evidence are needed as well.

2. *The experiences of others:* When using this type of evidence, you need to make sure that their information is accurate. You know what your own experiences are, but judgment is required in evaluating what others claim has happened to them. (Sad, but true.)

3. *Authoritative sources:* These include such sources as reference books, journals, and people who have extensive knowledge about a subject—experts. But here, too, judgment must be used. Reputable encyclopedias, dictionaries, and handbooks on specific subjects can usually be relied on with respect to bare facts or matters that are not politically controversial. You have to be more careful with magazines, newspapers, television programs, and particularly the Internet because people can put anything on-line they want to and claim to be authorities when they aren't.

Note this important point: *Authoritative sources must always be credited,* either in a footnote or in the text itself. And direct quotations must always be indicated by the use of quotation marks. Using someone else's material without acknowledging the source constitutes **plagiarism,** an extremely serious offense.

Provide Transitions

A good essay obviously has to have a logical structure, but you also want to write so that one thought flows into another—so that the logical structure of your essays is easy to follow. Transition terms and expressions highlight the flow of an essay, helping readers to know what to expect next—to know which expressions serve as reasons and which as conclusions and, in general, how things hang together. Note the use in the illiteracy essay of the words *but, thus, however, consider, although, yet* and the expressions *think how, for instance, above all, it may be argued that,* and *in sum.*

Think Your Position through Carefully

Having to write so as to convince others—much more than speaking extemporaneously—is an excellent way to get clear in your own mind as to where the truth lies. Writing a good argumentative essay requires mental discipline—the ability to see through the natural tendency to hang on to opinions once formed, even in the light of their inadequacy—to root out inconsistencies and fuzzy beliefs, and to arrange thoughts into a coherent whole.

Consider Your Audience

Writers who seriously intend to influence others have to keep their audience firmly in mind. It's all too easy to forget the audience as we sit alone at a desk scribbling away (well, these days also tapping away). But experienced writers learn that they must always

---

The plural of anecdote is not evidence.

—Bill Lockyer, attorney general of California

Block Those Metaphors!

Metaphor is a time-honored linguistic device. In the hands of careful writers, it often can express ideas swiftly and more effectively than more literal language. The trouble is that writers often go overboard in their enthusiasm for this linguistic tool. Here is an example from the writings of Guy Gugliotta in the Washington Post *(carried as one of the* New Yorker's *occasional metaphoric overkill items):*

There was no time, Acting Chairman Matthew F. McHugh (D-N.Y.) said last week, and the committee was tired of stoking public outrage with fortnightly gobbets of scandal. It decided to publish everything it had left, warts and all.

Now everyone is tarred with the same ugly brush, and the myth that forever simmers in the public consciousness—that the House shelters 435 parasitic, fat-cat deadbeats—has received another shot of adrenalin.

This little snippet also illustrates another writing no-no: the use of obscure words few readers can be expected to understand. Or did you know what gobbet *means without having to look it up?*

---

write with the intended readers in mind. Past failures—having had manuscripts rejected, severely criticized, or simply passed over by others—motivate them to figure out who they are writing for and how best to engage the interest of that particular audience.

One way to develop a sense of audience is to have one immediately at hand. Much has been written about the importance of writing with an audience in mind, but this advice needs to be augmented by actually having others respond to your work. In college, papers are usually directed to an audience of one—the teacher who evaluates your work and provides valuable advice intended to improve your writing ability.

However, what do you do in the hazy prewriting stage when you have the glimmer of an idea but aren't sure whether it will work, or when you have thought of a thesis and reasons but don't know whether they are convincing? In this stage of the writing process, it is helpful to try your ideas out on other people. Their feedback will give you a sense of audience response. Some teachers divide their classes into response groups so that students can discuss their ideas and read drafts aloud to each other. Some schools have tutors who can act as an audience. The point is to use whatever resources happen to be available so as to become accustomed to addressing a real audience.

Here are some questions to ask about the audience:

1. What is your intended audience?

2. What are their worldviews and background beliefs?

3. What tone is appropriate?

Think of how different your approach would be if you were arguing for gun control either to a group of mothers or to a local gun owners' organization. Most likely their

Reprinted by permission of Paul Miller.

worldviews and background beliefs would differ considerably, and undoubtedly the gun owners would be harder to convince than the mothers. Once you have the audience firmly in mind, you can begin to see what reasoning and evidence would be most likely to persuade and what tone would be appropriate.

Rewrite! Rewrite! Rewrite!

The difficulty of arranging thoughts coherently is an important reason why rewriting almost always is necessary. When writing a critical essay, we often realize that our thoughts aren't as focused or penetrating as we supposed. The writing process itself constitutes an important part of the reasoning process.

That's why most writers, definitely including the authors of this text, construct the first draft of an essay as a learning, or thinking, device. They do the best job they can on the first draft and then critically evaluate it as they would an opponent's essay. The next draft then can take account of what has been learned, perhaps by introducing new reasons and arguments that aren't open to the criticisms made of the first draft.

But one thing is clear. Only a few of the very best writers can construct a really good critical essay in one draft. Writers like philosopher Bertrand Russell (recall that his manuscripts often showed only a word or two changed here and there to mark the transition from first to final draft) are extremely rare in this world. The rest of us have to write at least two drafts, usually more, to get our thoughts into good order and to express them so they can be easily understood by others. And you shouldn't be surprised to find out that learning to do this well takes . . . practice, practice, practice. (The good news here is that computers, those marvelous "word processors," make the task of seemingly endless revision a good deal easier for many—but not all!—writers.)

If the need to practice, practice, practice has been mentioned, can lots of exercise chores be far behind? Here are a whole bunch of exercises—just how many you will need to sweat over is up to your instructor.

Good Writers Respect Their Audience

F. L. Lucas, once fellow and lecturer at King's College, Cambridge University, stressed the writer's obligation to readers in his essay "What Is Style?" from which this excerpt is drawn:*

The writer should respect his readers; therefore [he should behave with] courtesy. . . . From this follow several other basic principles of style. Clarity is one. For it is boorish to make your reader rack his brains to understand. One should aim at being impossible to misunderstand—though men's capacity for misunderstanding approaches infinity. Hence Molière and Po Chu-i tried their work on their cooks; and Swift on his men-servants—"which, if they did not comprehend, he would alter and amend, until they understood it perfectly." Our bureaucrats and pundits, unfortunately, are less considerate.

Brevity is another basic principle. For it is boorish, also, to waste your reader's time. People who would not dream of stealing a penny of one's money turn not a hair at stealing hours of one's life. But that does not make them less exasperating. Therefore, there is no excuse for the sort of writer who takes as long as a marching army corps to pass a certain point. Besides, brevity is often more effective; . . . And because one is particularly apt to waste words on preambles before coming to the substance, there was sense in the Scots professor who always asked his pupils—"Did ye remember to tear up that fir-r-st page?"

*Holiday magazine, March 1960

EXERCISE 9-1

One good way to get practice in writing well is to critique poor writing. Here is a tiny (142 words) tongue-in-cheek essay from the delightful book *Ordinary Money* by Louis B. Jones (New York: Viking, 1990). For many years, Jones was a reader for freshmen English and other college writing courses. As a warm-up exercise, explain the various writing bloopers, of the kind that might move your instructor to make negative margin comments—blunders that Jones constructed into his little "student-written" essay (described by one of the book's characters as "complete bull___, but Ohrbach [the instructor] never notices"):

> The comparison/contrast of the Greeks and Romans is a very important comparison/contrast. Since the beginning of time, people have pondered this question. In the hustle-bustle world of today, the comparison/contrast of the Greeks and Romans is very important and relevant. For example, the Romans were after the Greeks and therefore they had a more technology-oriented advancement. For example, they had plumbing and flush toilets and they had lead in the pipes which made everybody gradually insane. For example, Caligula, which caused the Decline and Fall of the Roman Empire. Another comparison/contrast

Student Essay Bon Mots

Here are a few extreme examples from student essays to serve as a reminder that good writing requires care and—yes—extensive revision. (Our thanks to English students at Knowname College.)

The elementary school I first attended was racial towards minorities.
  (Poorly expressed thought.)
Women have sat on the back burner long enough.
  (Unfortunate figure of speech.)
She was a rabid typist.
  (Malapropism.)
Secondly, the American school system is more loose, thus encouraging students to be creative rather than Japanese.
  (Faulty comparison.)
Every day at 4:00 thousands of people evacuate on their jobs.
  (Poor choice of words and construction.)
The octopus of communism spread its testacles over the continent.
  (Really!)
Do punctual errors count?
  (Yes, they do.)
He resorts to name calling and puts himself on a peddle stool.
  (What a motor-mouth.)
A broader view also prevents the student from charging blindly into a brick wall of unconceptuality.
  (Block that metaphor!)
I have a fool-time job.
  (Freudian slip?)
The vowels we made at the alter.
  (Double display of ignorance.)
I am in favor of capital punishment particularly in cases of murder and rape and aggravated napping, child or otherwise.
  (Unintended humor.)
And here are a few gems culled from Jaime O'Neill's article "The Goal Is Garbage In, Writers Out" (*San Francisco Chronicle*, September 4, 2005)

  "I believe in my second amendment that is the right to bare arms."
  "I have this udder glow of happiness."
  "I placed a reef on my grandmothers' grave."
  "My ex-best friend is so stuck on herself. She's like a pre-Madonna."
  "I was in the mist of studying when my cell phone rang."

Ah, well, everyone can't go to the head of the class in this doggy dog world. But at least we all can have self-of-steam.

of the Greeks and Romans is, the Greeks were very sane. For example, Plato and other world-famous philosophers pondered the greatest question of all time. Plato believed that everything was ideal. This is still true today. . . .

EXERCISE 9-2

Here are many issues that should be of some interest to college students. Select one and, bearing in mind the writing suggestions just discussed, write an essay (about 1,000 to 1,500 words), taking one side or the other of the issue. Then write a critical analysis in reply to your own essay (as though you were a competent—and fair!— opponent attacking your position). And then rewrite your original essay to try to take account of your own criticisms. Think of your fellow students, not your instructor, as your audience. Pick a topic that will let you show how well you can reason about a complicated issue. Do not pick an issue that you think has an obviously right solution to it. For example, do not select number 12 if all you are going to say is that of course we should not offer absinence-only sex education, because we all have the right to learn about contraception. Every issue is more complicated than that, and there always are serious pros and cons to consider. This is a difficult and very important assignment; it absolutely cannot be done satisfactorily the night before it is due—if for no other reason than that a certain amount of research very likely is in order. (Your instructor definitely and without doubt will quickly tell when reading your essay if it's a last-minute concoction.)

1. Should all college students be required to take at least basic introductory courses in math and science? In a foreign language?

2. Should illegal aliens be allowed to get driver's licenses?

3. Should people be allowed to download music from the Internet for free?

4. Should affirmative action with respect to the education or employment of women and minorities be the law of the land? (If you write on this topic, you must carefully explain what you mean by "affirmative action," and you should restrict your topic either to education or to employment.)

5. Should colleges and universities support big-time football and basketball teams?

6. Should speech codes be instituted in colleges and universities to fight racism on campus?

7. Should Congress raise fuel-economy standards for SUVs and other light trucks?

8. Are the salaries paid to movie stars and sports stars too high? If so, what should be done about this? If not, rebut those who would argue otherwise. In either case, support the side of the issue that you chose.

9. Should stem cells from embryos be used in medical research?

10. Should we have a military draft?

11. Is banning indecent material on the Internet unconstitutional?

12. Should high school courses in Human sexuality offer abstinence-only sex education and eliminate discussion of contraception?

13. Should homosexuals enjoy the same legal benefits as other married couples?

14. Should we legalize marijuana for medical use?

15. Should voters be required to show government-issued photo IDs in order to vote at the polls?

16. In recent years some pharmacists have refused to fill prescriptions for birth control pills or devices, arguing that their religious or moral beliefs prevented them from doing so. Should pharmacists have the legal right to refuse this service?

17. As of spring 2001, discoverers of human genes are allowed to patent their discoveries, so that, for instance, certain tests for a propensity to breast cancer cannot be conducted on your genes without paying a royalty to the patent holder. The principal argument in favor of gene patenting is that allowing it dramatically increases the incentive to discover such genes. Should we allow human genes to be patented?

18. Most scientists believe that increased use of fossil fuels (coal, oil, and so on) is leading to increases in global warming that will have adverse effects such as raised sea levels and the inundation of low-lying coastal areas. But some scientists deny this is true, and a very few argue that the good effects of global warming will outweigh the bad ones. Take sides in this debate.

EXERCISE 9-3

1. Online college courses have become so popular that one in five students took at least one course online in fall 2007, and the number is growing. These courses work well for students who live far from a campus or have jobs and cannot attend regularly scheduled classes. They offer everything a conventional classroom provides except live participation. But some educators worry that the virtual classroom is no substitute for the real thing. They argue that electronic conversations can't match classroom discussions where students are stimulated by the spontaneous exchange of ideas and by professors who are better able to clarify and channel discussions in person than online.

   Interview students who have studied online and professors who have taught these courses. Use the evidence you gather, along with current research on the subject, to support an argument for or against taking courses online.

2. Hip-hop has been controversial for decades. It has a reputation for using bad language, for glorifying sexism, racism and crime, and for popularizing an anti-snitch attitude that discourages cooperation with the police. Critics of the genre argue for censoring hip-hop, but advocates of free speech believe that rappers have the right to say whatever they want. Although the media usually bleep out offensive remarks, the recording industry does not.

   Write an essay arguing for or against the recording industry censoring bad language and offensive attitudes expressed in hip-hop.

3. A Florida technology company has developed a computer ID chip that could be implanted inside the body. The implant, about the size of a grain of rice, can be encoded with a wide range of information—everything from secret codes to sensitive medical data. Such a device would be invaluable to the medical community for giving emergency workers access to an unconscious patient's medical history, but it raises questions about privacy rights. Lee Tren, a senior attorney for a privacy advocacy group, cautioned that ". . . you always have to think about what the device will be used for tomorrow. . . . At first a device is used for applications we all agree are good, but then it slowly is used for more than it was intended."

   Write an argument either defending or rejecting the use of embedded ID chips.

4. Here are brief arguments for and against public colleges and universities soliciting private funding from corporations and wealthy benefactors. Take a stand on this issue and write an argument defending your position. Good sources of information might be professors, department chairs, and deans in your own school.

   An argument for soliciting private dollars is that state and federal budget cuts have been so severe in the past decade that public schools have had to look to the private sector for funding in order to ensure a high-quality education, to do cutting edge research, to replace outdated equipment, and to upgrade deteriorating buildings.

   The opposition argues that private funding transforms public schools into appendages of private industry, preoccupies the faculty with fund-raising instead of teaching, pits one department against another, and undermines the curriculum through corporate influence.

5. DDT, once used to control malaria-bearing mosquitoes, has been banned for decades because of its harmful effect on animals and humans. Fish-eating birds, in particular, were threatened with extinction from eating fish that had concentrated DDT in their tissues. But humans eating contaminated fish were afflicted as well, accumulating DDT in their systems and passing it onto their babies through breast milk. Since the chemical has been banned, however, malaria rates in developing countries have soared, and a movement is underway to start spraying houses in these countries to protect people from mosquitoes carrying the disease.

   Do some research on this subject and write an argument for or against using DDT in developing countries to prevent the spread of malaria.

EXERCISE 9-4

Here are excerpts from Adolf Hitler's *Mein Kampf,* a book in which he explained his philosophy and his goals for a "Thousand Year Reich."

1. Construct a summary of Hitler's arguments.

*2. Write an essay in which you critically evaluate these arguments. (In this case, the friendly authors of this text provide a summary in the answer section at the back of the book but not a critical evaluation. You should, of course, construct your own summary first and then compare it with the authors' summary at the back of the book.)

Nation and Race

There are some truths which are so obvious that for this very reason they are
not seen or at least not recognized by ordinary people. They sometimes pass by
such truisms as though blind and are most astonished when someone suddenly
discovers what everyone really ought to know. Columbus's eggs lie around by
the hundreds of thousands, but Columbuses are met with less frequently.

Thus men without exception wander about in the garden of Nature; they
imagine that they know practically everything and with few exceptions pass
blindly by one of the most patent principles of Nature's rule: the inner segrega-
tion of the species of all living beings on this earth.

Even the most superficial observation shows that Nature's restricted form
of propagation and increase is an almost rigid basic law of all the innumerable
forms of expression of her vital urge. Every animal mates only with a member
of the same species. The titmouse seeks the titmouse, the finch the finch, the
stork the stork, the field mouse the field mouse, the dormouse the dormouse,
the wolf the she-wolf, etc. . . .

Any crossing of two beings not at exactly the same level produces a medium between the level of the two parents. This means: the offspring will probably stand higher than the racially lower parent, but not as high as the higher
one. Consequently, it will later succumb in the struggle against the higher
level. Such mating is contrary to the will of Nature for a higher breeding of
all life. The precondition for this does not lie in associating superior and inferior, but in the total victory of the former. The stronger must dominate and
not blend with the weaker, thus sacrificing his own greatness. Only the born
weakling can view this as cruel, but he after all is only a weak and limited man;
for if this law did not prevail, any conceivable higher development of organic
living beings would be unthinkable. The consequence of this urge toward racial
purity, universally valid in Nature, is not only the sharp outward delimitation of
the various races, but their uniform character in themselves. The fox is always
a fox, the goose a goose, the tiger a tiger, etc., and the difference can lie at
most in the varying measure of force, strength, intelligence, dexterity, en-
durance, etc., of the individual specimens. But you will never find a fox who in
his inner attitude might, for example, show humanitarian tendencies toward
geese, as similarly there is no cat with a friendly inclination toward mice.

Therefore, here, too, the struggle among themselves arises less from inner
aversion than from hunger and love. In both cases, Nature looks on calmly,
with satisfaction, in fact. In the struggle for daily bread all those who are weak
and sickly or less determined succumb, while the struggle of the males for the
female grants the right or opportunity to propagate only to the healthiest. And
the struggle is always a means for improving a species' health and power of
resistance and, therefore, a cause of its higher development. . . .

No more than Nature desires the mating of weaker with stronger individuals, even less does she desire the blending of a higher with a lower race, since,
if she did, her whole work of higher breeding, over perhaps hundreds of thousands of years, might be ruined with one blow.

Historical experience offers countless proofs of this. It shows with terrifying
clarity that in every mingling of Aryan blood with that of lower peoples the

result was the end of the cultured people. North America, whose population consists in by far the largest part of Germanic elements [Hitler classified the English as Germanic] who mixed but little with the lower colored peoples, shows a different humanity and culture from Central and South America, where the predominantly Latin immigrants often mixed with the aborigines on a large scale. By this one example, we can clearly and distinctly recognize the effect of racial mixture. The Germanic inhabitant of the American conti-nent, who has remained racially pure and unmixed, rose to be master of the continent; he will remain the master as long as he does not fall a victim to defilement of the blood.[2]

EXERCISE 9-5

Here are two essays arguing opposing points of view on the value of computers in the classroom. Identify the thesis and reasons of each article; then write an essay taking one side or the other or arguing for a modified use of computers in education. As supporting evidence use your own experiences as well as research on the topic.

Computerized Lessons Help Motivate Kids

Need a stock tip? Ask one of Mark Neal's fourth-graders.

Students researched, "bought," and tracked stocks in their portfolios via Yahoo. Then, they developed final profit/loss reports for their shareholders that included spreadsheet-generated graphs of stock values during the project.

Look out Wall Street—here they come! Students in Rick Needham's and Joanne Zachariades' seventh-grade science classes simulated forming their own engineering companies to build bridges. Student companies designed the bridges and purchased materials with class "money." Company accountants kept check-ing account balances on spreadsheets, and workers built the bridges as the group's architect scanned plans into digital form for multimedia presentations. . . .

What was life like for a runaway slave in the South? If you could just talk to one. Well, you can—through Colonial Williamsburg interactive electronic field trips. Students in Patsy Lockhart's eighth-grade language arts/social studies class took a virtual trip back in time to Colonial Williamsburg. Via satellite broadcast, they watched three live re-enactments in the life of a runaway slave. After each segment, students' call-in questions were answered by the actors and on-site historians in real time. Students interacting with history—what an experience! . . .

These are just a few examples of the technology-integrated instruction that is taking place in classrooms in the New Haven Unified School District in Union City.

Computers, video, video conferencing, virtual field trips, multimedia and—motivation. Technology motivates students to do the everyday basics they often

---

[2]From Ralph Manheim's translation of *Mein Kampf* (Boston: Houghton Mifflin, 1971), pp. 284–287. Copyright 1943 and renewed 1971 by Houghton Mifflin Company. Reprinted by permission of Houghton Mifflin Company and The Random Century Group Ltd.

dread. The key is integration, not stand-alone technology for its own sake. As shown in the examples above, when technology is integrated into instruction, students still do the basics—reading, writing and math. The technology provides access to information, simulations, publishing tools, creative extensions and real-world connections.

Technology also helps provide students with instruction based on their needs—not a one-size-fits-all model that loses the struggling students and bores the others.

When teachers divide classes into groups based on the needs of their students, they can work with smaller rotating groups and focus on instruction. But what are the other students doing during these groups? They learn through a variety of independent activities. From skills practice to research to creative extensions, technology can provide activities that allow teachers to focus directly on instruction.

So what do we give up to put technology in schools? If the technology is integrated into instruction, very little. What's to be gained? Motivation, access to the basics, focused instruction, creative extensions and real-world connections. Technology is already thoroughly integrated into everyday life—from cell phones and checkout scanners at stores to dot-coms and Internet purchasing. We owe it to our students to join the real world and integrate technology in our classrooms.[3]

Computers Dumb Down Education

Thinking about buying a computer for your kids? Everyone else is. Indeed, our children are being sold down the river of technology. Throngs of educators, lemminglike, line up to wire schools. Parents grin as they plunk down credit cards to buy electronic machines for their children, anticipating an educational jump-start or quick fix. Meanwhile, English teachers cope with semiliterate students who are itching to play with computers but can't read a book.

Computer literacy doesn't demand the same level of instruction as English, American history or physics. It doesn't require the same amount of effort, either. Today, practically all office workers know word processing. Most learned it late in life.

But some subjects, while easy for a child to learn, are impossible for adults, like languages, for instance. The earlier you start, the easier it is to become fluent. The same with playing a musical instrument. Or drawing. Or public speaking.

Which gives you more advantages in business: having a long history of - computer experiences going back to programming Logo or fluency in Japanese, German, French or Chinese? Which is more likely to lead to a rich, happy life: a childhood of Nintendo and PlayStations or a childhood of hikes and bikes?

---

[3] From Stephen W. Politzer, "Computerized Lessons Help Motivate Kids," *San Francisco Chronicle,* August 14, 2000, Copyright 2000. Reprinted by permission of the author.

Probably because computers are so easy for students to learn, educators love to teach computer techniques. But what are their students prepared for? A lifetime of poking at a keyboard for eight hours a day. It's one more way to dumb down the school, giving the appearance of teaching futuristic subjects while dodging truly challenging topics. . . .

Plenty of job skills get bypassed in our rush to get online. Today in the [San Francisco] Bay Area, Web programmers get $40 or $50 an hour—pretty good wages. Yet plumbers charge twice as much. How come? One reason plumbers charge so much is that almost every Bay Area school teaches computing. Almost none teach the trades: auto mechanics, carpentry or plumbing. When every student—good and bad—is pressed to become a computer maven, and only the incompetents are allowed to become plumbers, neither our programs nor our pipes will hold water.

Computers aren't compatible with the clay, dirt and cookie crumbs of a 5-year-old's life. Kids mustn't pour sand into the keyboard or smear peanut butter on the monitor. . . .

In Columbus, Ohio, Dana Elementary School installed three Compaq Presario computers in its kindergarten class, despite the kindergarten teacher telling the principal that computers were superfluous. Nevertheless, the technicians lugged in the equipment, only to haul out the sandbox and block table. There wasn't enough room for both. . . .

There's plenty wrong with our schools—lack of discipline, low interest in scholarship, leaky roofs, big classes, politically inspired curricula. But more computers and video monitors won't improve this. Do the politicians who promote wiring our schools really believe that Internet access will develop a love for mathematics, physics, history, reading or playing the violin?

So what computer should you buy your kids? Save your money and go hiking with them on Friday afternoons. Rather than checking into some science Web site, go to the kitchen and experiment with ice cubes sprinkled with salt, sugar and baking soda. Rather than a virtual online trip to the Louvre, bicycle over to the deYoung Museum and see real Asian art. Instead of a copy of *Reader Rabbit,* spend a half-hour every night reading stories.[4]

EXERCISE 9-6

The tragic shootings at Virginia Tech in 2007 by a psychotic student raised questions about the way colleges and universities deal with mentally ill students. Warning signs of Cho Seung Hui's troubled mental state surfaced well over a year before the killings. Mental health officials knew of his suicidal tendencies, two women students complained to the police about annoying contacts initiated by Cho, and several English teachers informed university officials about his deeply disturbing writing, full of violent images, persecution, and anger. Yet the university was limited in taking action by federal privacy and antidiscrimination laws. Colleges and universities are restricted by the disabilities

---

[4]From *San Francisco Chronicle,* August 14, 2000. Reprinted by permission of Cliff Stoll.

act from screening prospective students for mental health problems. They cannot put a student on involuntary medical leave on the grounds of mental illness, nor can they notify parents of their child's mental condition or release medical records without the student's consent. Although these laws are designed to curtail discrimination and the invasion of privacy, they make it harder to detect seriously disturbed students like Cho and to take the steps necessary to prevent violent behavior.

Consider the complex issues involved and write an argument for or against amending laws that restrict colleges and universities from dealing with students who have serious mental illness.

EXERCISE 9-7

The Patriot Act, passed by Congress after the September 11, 2001, terrorist attack on the World Trade Center and the Pentagon, gave federal authorities the power, in cases involving national security, to get an order from a secret court giving them permission to obtain various records relevant to an investigation—including medical files, library records, and business documents. Groups like the American Library Association and civil rights advocates have opposed the legislation because of the far-reaching, invasive powers it gives the government. Advocates of the Patriot Act have countered that the Justice Department must have the authority to examine the records in question in order to identify terrorists dangerous to our country. The provisions of the act were due to sunset in 2006, but Congress reauthorized the bill with minor modifications in 2006.

Do some research and examine both sides of the issue. Then write an argument defending your position.

EXERCISE 9-8

The opinions written by high court judges constitute a good source for essay topics because they often are written on matters of general concern and tend to be logical, or at least somewhat intelligent. Here are four short excerpts from opinions of judges of the U.S. Court of Appeals concerning suits challenging state laws against assisted suicides. Write an essay in which you evaluate the statements made in these excerpts, being sure to consider whether at least two remarks in them that might be thought to commit fallacies discussed earlier in this text in fact do so.

Judge Stephen Reinhardt, Ninth Circuit: Those who believe strongly that death must come without physician assistance are free to follow that creed, be they doctors or patients. They are not free, however, to force their views, their religious convictions or their philosophies on all the other members of a democratic society, and to compel those whose values differ with theirs to die painful, protracted, and agonizing deaths.

Judge Roger Miner, Second Circuit: Physicians do not fulfill the role of "killers" by prescribing drugs to hasten death any more than they do by disconnecting life-support systems.

Judge Andrew Kleinfeld, Ninth Circuit: It is very difficult to judge what ought to be allowed in the care of terminally ill patients. The Constitution does not speak to the issue. People of varying views, including people with terrible illnesses and their relatives, physicians and clergy, can, through democratic institutions, obtain enlightened compromises of the complex and conflicting considerations. They can do so at least as well as we judges can.

Judge Robert Beezer, Ninth Circuit: If physician-assisted suicide for mentally competent, terminally ill adults is made a constitutional right, voluntary euthanasia for weaker patients, unable to self-terminate, will soon follow. After voluntary euthanasia, it is but a short step to a "substituted judgment" or "best interest" analysis for terminally ill patients who have not yet expressed their constitutionally sanctioned desire to be dispatched from this world.

EXERCISE 9-9

Here is an excerpt from an essay that is interesting because it argues for a more or less anti-PC thesis—that is, it defends a currently frowned-on side of an issue. Although written in the 1990s, it is still relevant today and involves issues that currently come before the Supreme Court.

1. Construct a short summary.

2. Write an essay either attacking or defending the thesis, being sure to take account of what is said in the work in question, as well as in other writings that occur in this text. (Again, note that there is no law against doing outside research.)

Demystifying Multiculturalism

If you believe the multiculturalists' propaganda, whites are on the verge of becoming a minority in the United States. The multiculturalists predict that this demographic shift will fundamentally change American culture—indeed destroy the very idea that America has a single, unified culture. . . . But has America truly become a multicultural nation? And if not, will those who capitulate to these demands create a self-fulfilling prophecy?

At the heart of the argument is the assumption that the white population is rapidly declining in relation to the non-white population. . . .

In fact, white males will still constitute about 45 per cent—a plurality—of the workforce in the year 2000. The proportion of white men in the workforce is declining—it was nearly 51 per cent in 1980—but primarily because the proportion of white women is growing. They will make up 39 per cent of the workforce within ten years, according to government projections, up from 36 per cent in 1980. Together, white men and women will account for 84 per cent of all workers by 2000—hardly a minority share.

But the business world is behaving as if a demographic tidal wave is about to hit. A whole new industry of "diversity professionals" has emerged to help managers cope with the expected deluge of non-white workers. These consultants . . . train managers to "value diversity." [But what] precisely does valuing diversity mean? The underlying assumptions seem to be that non-whites are so different from whites that employers must make major changes to accommodate them, and that white workers will be naturally resistant to including non-whites in their ranks. Public-opinion polls don't bear out the latter. They show that support among whites for equal job opportunity for blacks is extraordinarily high, exceeding 90 per cent as early as 1975. As for accommodating different cultures, the problem is not culture—or race, or ethnicity—but education. Many young people, in particular, are poorly prepared for work, and the problem is most severe among those who attended inner-city schools, most of them blacks and Hispanics.

Nevertheless, multiculturalists insist on treating race and ethnicity as if they were synonymous with culture. They presume that skin color and national origin, which are immutable traits, determine values, mores, language, and other cultural attributes, which, of course, are learned. In the multiculturalists' world view, African-Americans, Puerto Ricans, or Chinese-Americans living in New York City have more in common with persons of their ancestral group living in Lagos or San Juan or Hong Kong than they do with other New Yorkers who are white. Culture becomes a fixed entity, transmitted . . . in the genes, rather than through experience. Thus, "Afrocentricity," a variant of multiculturalism, is "a way of being," its exponents claim. According to a leader of the Afrocentric education movement, Molefi Kete Asante, there is "one African Cultural System manifested in diversities," whether one speaks of Afro-Brazilians, Cubans, or Nigerians (or, presumably, African-Americans). Exactly how this differs from the traditional racist notion that all blacks (Jews, Mexicans, Chinese, etc.) think alike is unclear. What is clear is that the multiculturalists have abandoned the ideal that all persons should be judged by the content of their character, not the color of their skin. Indeed, the multiculturalists seem to believe that a person's character is determined by the color of his skin and by his ancestry.

Such convictions lead multiculturalists to conclude that, again in the words of Asante, "[T]here is no common American culture." The logic is simple, but wrong-headed: Since Americans (or more often, their forebears) hail from many different places, each of which has its own specific culture, the argument goes, America must be multicultural. And it is becoming more so every day as new immigrants bring their cultures with them. . . .

The urge to assimilate has traditionally been overpowering in the United States, especially among the children of immigrants. Only groups that maintain strict rules against intermarriage with persons outside the group, such as Orthodox Jews and the Amish, have ever succeeded in preserving distinct, full-blown cultures within American society. (It is interesting to note that religion seems to be a more effective deterrent to full assimilation than the secular elements of culture, including language.) Although many Americans worry that Hispanic immigrants, for example, are not learning English and will therefore fail to assimilate into the American mainstream, little evidence supports the case. By the third generation in the United States, a majority of Hispanics, like other ethnic groups, speak only English and are closer to other Americans on most measures of social and economic status than they are to Hispanic immigrants. On one of the most rigorous gauges of assimilation—intermarriage—Hispanics rank high. About one-third of young third-generation Hispanics marry non-Hispanic whites, a pattern similar to that of young Asians. Even for blacks, exogamy rates, which have been quite low historically, are going up; about 3 per cent of blacks now marry outside their group. . . .

Affirmative-action programs make less and less sense as discrimination diminishes in this society—which it indisputably has—and as minorities improve their economic status. Racial and ethnic identity, too, might wane if there weren't such aggressive efforts to ensure that this not happen. . . .

Multiculturalism is not a grassroots movement. It was created, nurtured, and expanded through government policy. Without the expenditure of vast sums of public money, it would wither away and die. That is not to say that ethnic communities would disappear from the American scene or that groups would not retain some attachment to their ancestral roots. American assimilation has always entailed some give and take, and American culture has been enriched by what individual groups brought to it. The distinguishing characteristic of American culture is its ability to incorporate so many disparate groups, creating a new whole from the many parts. What could be more American, for example, than jazz and film, two distinctive art forms created, respectively, by blacks and immigrant Jews but which all Americans think of as their own? But in the past, government—especially public schools—saw it as a duty to try to bring newcomers into the fold by teaching them English, by introducing them to the great American heroes as their own, by instilling respect for American institutions. Lately, we have nearly reversed course, treating each group, new and old, as if what is most important is to preserve its separate identity and space.

It is easy to blame the ideologues and radicals who are pushing the disuniting of America, to use Arthur Schlesinger's phrase, but the real culprits are those who provide multiculturalists the money and the access to press their cause. Without the acquiescence of policy-makers and ordinary citizens, multiculturalism would be no threat. Unfortunately, most major institutions have little stomach for resisting the multicultural impulse—and many seem eager to comply with whatever demands the multiculturalists make. Americans should have learned by now that policy matters. We have only to look at the failure of our welfare and crime policies to know that providing perverse incentives can change the way individuals behave—for the worse. Who is to say that if we pour enough money into dividing Americans we won't succeed?[5]

EXERCISE 9-10

In a very well-known, often reprinted lecture, "The Idea of a University," Cardinal John Henry Newman (1801–1890) argued that the principal work of the university is to provide a liberal education, not merely, or even primarily, professional training. He said that a liberal education

> gives a man a clear conscious view of his own opinions and judgments, a truth in developing them, an eloquence in expressing them, and a force in urging them. . . . it prepares him to fill any post with credit and to master any subject with civility.

---

[5]By Linda Chavez. © 1994 by National Review, Inc., 150 E. 35th Street, New York, NY 10016. Reprinted by permission.

Do you agree with Cardinal Newman's assessment of a liberal education and agree that the primary job of a university (or college) is to provide such an education? Write an essay defending your opinion.

EXERCISE 9-11

High-tech cheating has increased dramatically now that almost all students have access to the Internet. Some examples: 78 students at Dartmouth College were caught copying online answers to homework assignments; 150 students from two classes at the University of California, Berkeley, were caught plagiarizing papers from the Internet; and 30 engineering students at Northeastern University were caught gaining access to each other's online homework assignments.

It has been suggested that this new wave of cheating is due in part to there being a relatively low risk of detection and even more to the lenient nature of punishments when caught. In view of this and the fact that cheaters do harm to those who do not cheat, would you approve expulsion from college for first-time proven cheaters? Or flunking the course? Or suspension for one semester? Defend your answer.[6]

EXERCISE 9-12

In May 2008 the California Supreme Court ruled in a 4–3 decision that same-sex couples have a constitutional right to marry, making it the second state after Massachusetts to allow same-sex marriage. In a majority opinion, Chief Justice Ronald George wrote that "[i]n view of the substance and significance of the fundamental constitutional right to form a family relationship, the California constitution properly must be interpreted to guarantee this basic right to all Californians, whether gay or heterosexual, and to same-sex couples as well as opposite-sex couples."

In a dissenting opinion, Justice Marvin Baxter said that the majority should have deferred to the state legislature, which banned same-sex marriage in a law enacted in 1977, a decision reaffirmed by voters as a ballot initiative in 2008. Further, he wrote that "the majority does not have the right to erase, then recast, the age old definition of marriage as virtually all societies have understood it, in order to satisfy its own contemporary notions of equality and justice."

When lawyers for the opposition argued that tradition and the will of the majority were justification for reserving the term *marriage* for heterosexual unions, Chief Justice George said neither was sufficient. He conceded that "as an historical matter in this state marriage has always been restricted to a union between a man and a woman. But tradition alone does not justify the denial of a fundamental constitutional right." He noted that bans on interracial marriage had also been sanctioned by the state for many years, but California was the first state to overturn them.

Conservative religious groups have submitted petitions with more than a million signatures for an initiative to amend the state constitution to ban same-sex marriage and thus overturn the court's decision. (Voters have approved similar amendments in at least 20 states.) How would you cast your vote on this issue? Write an argument defending your position.

---

[6] See the article by Ted Wallach, *San Francisco Chronicle,* August 14, 2000.

Summary of Chapter 9

The essential contents of an argumentative essay are a *thesis* and *reasons (premises)* supporting the thesis. Usually, reasons need to be supported in turn by evidence or secondary reasons.

1. Experienced writers tend to keep their basic goals in mind as they prepare to write, developing a plan of attack to meet those goals, revising their original plans in the light of new evidence or unexpected difficulties. But they don't generally write in a linear fashion; writing tends to be a convoluted process.

2. The first task when preparing to write is to determine precisely what your thesis will be. Later, of course, you may change your mind, perhaps by narrowing the topic or zeroing in on it more carefully. While preparing to write and during the writing process itself, changing one's mind for good reasons is the hallmark of intelligent thought.

   After selecting a thesis and developing your principal reasons in its support, you may find it useful to construct an outline of the proposed finished product. When doing the generally inevitable research, be sure to take notes, including reference citations. If research undermines your thesis, or reasons in its support, you must revise. Never simply ignore counterarguments or reasons. Before starting to write, make sure your thesis follows logically from the reasons you intend to offer in its support.

3. Argumentative essays typically divide into three parts. The *introduction* generally states and lays the groundwork for the thesis, either before or after stating it explicitly. The *body* of the essay should contain the reasons and evidence, perhaps also reasons in support of the reasons. It is likely to be more convincing if it contains examples. If counterarguments are to be discussed, the right time to do so is in the body of an essay; and similarly for comparing or contrasting with other ideas. The *conclusion* of your essay may restate the thesis or perhaps provide a short summary of the essay's most important points.

4. The point of writing an argumentative essay is to persuade readers to accept your thesis. To do so, effective writers provide convincing reasons and supporting evidence. They also keep the reader firmly in mind by considering the background beliefs of their audience and the appropriate tone to take given that audience.

5. Good writers also try to achieve a natural flow by providing readers with transition words and expressions such as *but, although, for instance,* and *nevertheless.*
   But (note the transition word), however well planned an essay may be, rewriting almost certainly will be necessary. A first draft may thus serve as a learning device, so that later drafts can take account of what has been learned.

The ads of our times are the richest and most faithful daily reflection that any society ever made of its entire range of activities.

—Marshall McLuhan

Advertising is legalized lying.

—H. G. Wells

Doing business without advertising is like winking at a girl in the dark. You know what you are doing, but nobody else does.

—Stuart Henderson Britt

Would you persuade, speak of interest, not reason.

—Ben Franklin

Advertising persuades people to buy things that they don't need with money they ain't got.

—Will Rogers

Advertising is what you do when you can't go see somebody. That's all it is.

—Fairfax Cone (ad executive)

Chapter

10

ADVERTISING: SELLING THE PRODUCT

Advertising is so obviously useful that it's surprising it has such a bad name. Ads tell us what is new and what is available, where, when, and for how much. They tell us about a product's (alleged) quality and specifications. All for free, except for the effort of reading or paying attention.

Yet there are legitimate gripes about advertising. Ads don't tell us about product defects. They often mislead, either via exaggeration or, occasionally, downright lies. And because some products are advertised more heavily or more effectively than others, ads tend to skew our choices in unreasonable ways.

It also has been argued that advertising increases the costs of goods to consumers. It isn't uncommon for a quarter, or even a third, of the price of an item to be due to advertising costs, and critics have argued that this constitutes a tremendous waste.

But this charge is misleading. Advertising does cost a great deal of money, and this expense has to be factored into the costs of finished goods. Nevertheless, advertising greatly reduces the prices of those goods in the marketplace compared to what they would cost were advertising abolished or greatly restricted. It does so because it lowers production costs by making mass production profitable, thus enabling producers to obtain a mass market. In short, advertisers advertise because it reduces the costs of *selling goods*. It is not an accident that virtually all businesses advertise; they do so because they don't know of a better or cheaper way to sell their products. Those who argue otherwise generally forget that if a company doesn't advertise, it will have to increase other selling costs, especially sales commissions. (Advertising also has been objected to on the grounds that it gives an unfair advantage to large organizations when they compete against smaller ones, but objections of this kind raise large issues best left unexplored here—for example, about the desirability of large versus small businesses.)

It is worth noting, though, that advertising techniques and markets have changed dramatically over the past 40 years. In 1965 companies poured most of their advertising dollars into the three major TV networks: ABC, NBC, and CBS, the market that reached 80 percent of the prime target audience—the 18- to 49-year-olds. Today, most Americans have more than a hundred channels to choose from and the hi-tech tools to mute or bypass ads altogether. Since fewer people read newspapers and magazines (once major marketing outlets) and more turn to the Internet for information and entertainment, the advertising industry has had to reach far broader and much more complex markets than ever before. But advertisers are nothing if not inventive. So over the years, ad agencies have metamorphosed into marketing companies that hawk their products through public relations promotions, in-store displays, and direct mail gimmicks. They use product placement, show ads in movie theaters, and inundate the Internet with pop-up ads and TV commercials that stream on (and on and on) to websites like YouTube.com, giving them an eternal shelf life. But no matter how glitzy or numerous the innovations are, the bottom line is that they still manipulate consumer attitudes about beauty, status, relationships, and sex, using age-old gimmicks to sell us the goods.[1]

1. PROMISE AND IDENTIFICATION ADVERTISEMENTS

Virtually all ads are one or another (or both) of two basic kinds. **Promise advertisements** promise to satisfy desires or allay fears. All you have to do is buy the product advertised (remove bad body odor by using Old Spice deodorant; enjoy life more by driving a Ford Explorer). Most promise ads provide "reasons why" the product will do the job or do it better than competitors (Kleenex tissues are softer; a bowl of Total cereal has more vitamins and minerals). Then there are ads that promise to satisfy our bodily needs,

> Promise, large promise, is the soul of advertising.
>
> —Samuel Johnson

---

[1]For a summary of the changing world of advertising, see "The New Pitch," by Ken Auletta, *The New Yorker,* March 28, 2005.

Many advertising executives subscribe to the idea, mentioned before, that there are just two ways to influence people: via promises and identification. This Marine Corps advertisement invites young men to identify with the Marines pictured handsomely decked out in fancy dress uniforms. It was so successful that it spawned several even more successful TV commercials, one showing a piece of steel being made into a sword that was then nicely placed into its scabbard by a handsome Marine in dress uniform, while the voiceover intoned, "We're looking for a few good men—with the mettle to be Marines!" An absolutely brilliant ad series.

like the taglines for Snickers candy bars, "When you're hungry, reach for a Snickers" or "Hungry, why wait?" The implication is that Snickers is a food that will satisfy hunger when, in fact, the only food value is in a few peanuts—the rest is sugar, chocolate, nougat, and caramel—none of which will ward off hunger for long. But this immensely successful campaign boosted sales 3½ percent, no small amount for the best-selling candy bar in the world.

Identification advertisements sell the product by getting us to identify with the product. They are a kind of promise ad, since they promise that somehow or other you will be better off using the product. But the promise is made indirectly through identification with respected institutions or individuals (or occasionally simply by fostering identification with the product directly, as in the case of some Pepsi commercials). We all tend to identify with our own group and with those whom we respect—people who are famous, rich, accomplished, unusually brave, or powerful. Identification ads take advantage of this very human trait. Celebrity ads work precisely because we identify with the famous people they feature and thus with the products they tout; we become like them in some small way by using Chanel No. 5 (Nicole Kidman), by playing golf with Nike golf balls (Tiger Woods), or by reading a good book (Oprah Winfrey).

Identification ads—indeed, all ads—work for another interesting reason. When people shop, say, in a supermarket, they tend to purchase products whose brand names are familiar to them. Few of us, for example, will buy a brand of toothpaste we have never heard of or never seen advertised; we buy a brand we recognize even though we know no other "reason why" we should buy that brand and not a competing one. (When was the last time you chose an unadvertised product rather than an advertised competing product?)

Among identification ad campaigns, celebrity ads have the strongest consumer appeal. Now that the lives of celebrities are chronicled around the clock on websites, in tabloids, and on television, people are eager to wear the same clothes, drink the same beer, and drive the same cars as their idols. When Nicole Kidman pumped new life into the aging Chanel No. 5, women ran out and bought it. (Sales went up 30 percent after she signed on.) Reeboks seemed trendier when Jay-Z hawked them; American Express cards, more accessible when Ellen DeGeneres pitched them; and chic, expensive handbags, more desirable when Gwyneth Paltrow fronted for Todd's, a luxury goods company. Nothing sells like celebrity. Consumers live vicariously through big stars and identify with the products they endorse.

2. THINGS TO WATCH OUT FOR IN ADVERTISEMENTS

The good news about advertising, you will recall, is that it often provides true and useful information about products and entertains us with humor, storytelling, or just nice scenes or sentiments. Time enjoyably spent is time not completely wasted. *Examples:* The Budweiser Christmas TV commercials featuring their magnificent Clydesdales in winter scenes; Black & Decker's: "You don't have to be crazy to buy a Black & Decker cordless screwdriver. You just have to have a screw loose." Or the Billy Graham billboard ad:

> You're born.
> You suffer.
> You die.
> Fortunately, there's a loophole.

How Visuals Distort Reality

This excerpt from "The Archenemy of Flavor," by David Harris, appeared in Harper's *magazine (May 1999).*

The equation of beauty and taste is a false one, for nothing ever tastes as good as it looks in advertisements or food magazines. It is widely known that the fantastical foods in glossies such as *Gourmet* and *Bon Appétit* are actually inedible, that the voluptuous centerfolds of these gastronomical *Playboys* and *Penthouses* have communicable diseases, that those "willowy wonton strips gracing the salad" are the equivalent of prosthetic food, toxic concoctions of varnish, hair spray, and shoe polish. Wedges of cheese have been swabbed with rubbing alcohol to bring out their color, piping hot sauces are actually ice-cold so that they won't congeal, the grill marks on chicken have been drawn in with Magic Marker, and desserts made of gelatin have been so fortified with artificial thickeners that they are as indestructible as hockey pucks and are often tossed around among the staff, who exhibit the macabre sense of humor of medical students in the morgue.

The bad news about advertising stems from the increasing ability of advertising geniuses—and some of them, alas, *are* geniuses—to manipulate audiences via sophisticated psychological ploys. Everyone realizes how others are conned by advertising, but most of us think that we somehow are exceptions. Young people, including college students, often deny that they are influenced by advertising. They typically say that they don't wear designer jeans or Adidas shoes because of advertising but rather that they just "like" these products, self-deceptively ignoring the effect of advertising on their preferences. In fact, *no one* is immune to the influence of advertisements. (A Madison Avenue bigwig owned up to this when he said, "Even I fall for the stuff.") So we all are faced with the problem of how best to use advertising without being used. One way is to become familiar with the advertising devices and gimmicks used to appeal to our weaknesses, prejudices, and emotions unguided by intelligence. No doubt we'll still get taken now and then, but perhaps less often and with less seriously harmful consequences.

Ads Invite Us to Reason Fallaciously

We've already noted that ads often feature celebrity endorsements to manipulate us into buying the product. They thus invite us to commit the fallacy appeal to authority. We don't stop to think whether Justin Timberlake really does prefer Pepsi to Coca-Cola or whether he just gets paid to say he does. Anyway, what difference would it make to you if he didn't drink soft drinks at all? (*Consumer Reports* taste tests, by the way, show hardly anyone can distinguish between Pepsi and Coke. Can Justin Timberlake? Can you? Hint: In several actual classroom tests conducted by one of the authors of this text over a period of years, students consistently failed to distinguish their favorite brands of beer from competing brands.)

In the case of Justin Timberlake advertising Pepsi, it seems obvious that he is no authority on the taste of soft drinks, which, anyway, certainly are a matter of individual preference. But some celebrity ads are different, sports endorsements being a case in point. In recent years, Tiger Woods has dominated the golf scene, many professional golfers stand in awe of his accomplishments at that game, and he is often said to be the greatest golfer in the history of that sport. So his endorsement of Nike's Tour Accuracy golf balls carries great weight with golf duffers intent on improving their scores. But in fact Woods doesn't use these ordinary golf balls in tournaments. Instead, he hits custom-made balls not available to the general public (as do, by the way, some other pro golfers who endorse other brands). (Why millionaire actors and professional athletes feel that they need to make extra money by touting products they don't use is one of those mysteries of human nature that, perhaps fortunately, is not our topic here.)

Anyway, moving on to a related topic, it should be clear by now that ads generally are designed to invite us to overlook their *suppression of evidence*. They tell us the good features of products but always hide their product's warts. (Why should they do otherwise?) Cigarette ads contain probably the most obvious examples of this fallacy, given what we know about the lethal effects of smoking. When R.J. Reynolds Tobacco launched a feminine version of Camels called Camel No. 9, you can be sure the ads made no mention of the fact that far more women die of lung cancer today than breast cancer. Instead, they played up the feminine appeal of the cigarette, giving it a name that evokes images of perfumes like Chanel No. 19 and packaging it in pink and green floral boxes labeled "light and luscious." Getting women to identify with a brand that has long played to male

> There is an art to making whole lies out of half truths.
>
> —Christy Mathewson (baseball hall of fame pitcher who was paid to endorse Tuxedo pipe tobacco)

smokers has put Camels in competition with its biggest competitor for the female market, Virginia Slims, whose slogan "You've come a long way, baby," ironically reflects the fact that women, indeed, have come a long way—in catching up with male mortality rates for lung cancer.

Advertising audiences also are invited to make *faulty* or *invidious comparisons. Examples:* Pizza Hut ads that compared their delivery service with dingbat pizza parlors that don't deliver at all, ignoring their true competitors, such as Domino's Pizza, that do; Wisk ads that claim their product is more powerful than Tide, so you need to use less, making it seem that it costs less to use Wisk than Tide, which is not true (figure out why).

Some ads, though, use fallacious reasoning humorously and aren't meant to be taken seriously. A good example is this BMW ad: "Doctors say increased activity slows the aging process. Coincidentally, BMW drivers are ten years younger than other luxury car drivers." This humorous use of cause and effect was not an example of *questionable cause* because it was not intended to be taken literally. (But it nevertheless definitely was intended to manipulate prospective customers into buying a BMW.)

Advertisements Pound Home Slogans and Meaningless Jargon

In fact, ads run through the entire range of fallacies, challenging theorists to invent pigeonholes into which to put them all. How, for instance, should we categorize the fallacious reasoning that leads people to be swayed by endlessly repeated, mostly empty slogans? *Examples:* "Brut. Men are back." (Were they somewhere else?) "Because I'm Worth it." (L'Oréal) "The World's Greatest Newspaper" (that's the *Chicago Tribune,* in case Chicago area readers didn't recognize it—well, we should mention that the *Chicago Tribune* is one of the better newspapers around these days). "You can be sure of Shell." And so on, *ad* infinitum (heh, heh).

Slogans run the range from the modestly informative ("Miller Light: Great taste, less filling.") to the somewhat suggestive ("Chevrolet. Like a rock.") to the completely irrelevant ("Nike: Just do it."). In general, they work because they are repeated endlessly, so that they become ingrained in our minds. In the days before television, which is primarily a visual medium, singing commercials did the job on radio. There can be very few people over 70, for example, who could not at the drop of a hat sing the Rinso soap flakes

> The most brilliant propaganda must confine itself to a few points and repeat them over and over.
>
> —Adolf Hitler

jingle they heard belted out on radio countless times lo these many years ago: "Rinso white, Rinso bright; happy little washday song!"

Slogans that tout products as "the official" something or other are an interesting special case. In 2004, for example, Tylenol advertised itself as "The official supplier of pain relief products for the 2004 U.S. Olympic team" (accompanied by pictures of athletes with massive, rippling muscles, presumably injury prone). Puffs of this kind generally imply something that is false. The Tylenol slogan implied that Olympic athletes preferred this brand to others or that Tylenol was better than any other painkiller. But you can bet your life that if they were in real pain, they would take something stronger, like Vicodin. In fact, becoming official whatever merely means paying for the privilege of being identified with a name. Tylenol paid through the nose to be identified with the Olympic Games, as did other official Olympic sponsors, like Coca Cola, Chevrolet, and Budweiser. Another wrinkle on the "official" gambit is the naming of sports arenas and stadiums after companies that buy this privilege (Coors, Minute Maid, AT&T, and so on).

Ads Play on Weaknesses, Emotions, Prejudices, and Fears

Particular kinds of advertisements sell some products more easily than they do others. Those that play on weaknesses or fears are a case in point, one reason so many TV commercials are of this nature. *Examples:* The "ring around the collar" commercials; ads for mouthwashes, hair restorers, and hair colorers; "roach motels"; and so on. Some of these ads do have the virtue of being informative (Grecian Formula does darken gray hair), but in many cases the product doesn't do the job advertised (Listerine does very little if anything for bad breath, since most bad breath originates elsewhere; it does, though, kill some mouth bacteria). In many other cases, the advertised product doesn't do the job any better than competing products (Mylanta isn't any better at counteracting stomach acidity than Maalox, Gelusil, or several other brands; Energizer and Duracell batteries are equally good).

Ads Employ Sneaky Rhetoric

In particular, *weasel words* are quite common in advertising. When an ad says the product *"fights* bad breath," it's wise to assume it doesn't *cure* bad breath, because if it did, the ad would make this stronger, less weasely claim. Similar remarks apply to claims such as "*helps* control dandruff with regular use," "gets dishes *virtually* spotless," and so on.

We also need to watch out for sneaky uses of *comparative* and *evaluative* terms, like *good, better,* and (best of all) *best.* The term *best* at best translates into "tied for first with all other leading brands." The "lowest fare to Europe" may turn out to be the standard fare every airline charges. And when an ad says "No one sells ___ for less," you can be pretty sure others sell for the same price. And then there is that wonderful term, *free,* itself perfectly unsneaky, but so often used to lure the gullible (all of us in weak moments) into thinking they're getting something for nothing.

But these kinds of ads aren't as sneaky as the "official sweepstakes" notifications that arrive regularly in the mail. Their fine-print disclaimers have reached a high art, as the one received from *Time,* Inc., that featured very large type showing through a transparent window in the envelope stating:

**THE RESULTS ARE NOW IN: HOWARD KAHANE
HAS WON ONE OF OUR TWO $1,666,675.00 PRIZES!**

Above this, on one line and in very tiny and easily overlooked type, came the fine-print disclaimer:

> "Be it henceforth known that if you have and return the grand prize winning entry, we will be pleased to announce that . . . ."

All of which means that if H. K. happened to have been assigned the perhaps-one-chance-in-ten-million winning number, he would win the big bucks by returning the grand prize entry. (H. K. didn't waste time or a stamp finding out.) See the appendix for more on the topic of chances—probabilities—in general.

Deliberate deception: A Charles Schwab commercial shows a satisfied couple talking about their successful investments with the brokerage firm. Then a three-second statement appears on the screen with about ten lines of print, starting with the information that the people telling their story were real customers of Schwab. But only a speed reader could get to the end fast enough to read the sentence revealing that the customers were paid for their testimonials.

Here's another ad with fine print disclaimers—this time for a website.

"Today at 12:00 noon, GO.COM WILL LAUNCH THE WORLD'S FIRST ON LINE AUCTION SITE.*"

This deceptively clear claim is immediately contradicted in the footnote: "[The website is the first online] since eBay, amazon.com, yahoo, and a few others. But it is the first designed with better architecture, so it's more reliable . . . there's a better auction at go.com." In other words, it wasn't the first online auction site.

Ads Draw on Trendy Issues in the News

Issues that grip the country are fertile ground for advertisers, who use them to play on our fears and desires. For instance, mounting concerns over the obesity epidemic has inspired a glut of low-fat, low-sugar, low-salt, low-carb products. McDonald's is pushing McVeggie Burgers and McGriddles (cheese, eggs, and meat wrapped in pancakes). Kraft Foods is marketing a new version of Lunchables called Fun Fuels made with fruit, meat, grain, and dairy products. And Hershey's has launched sugar-free chocolates with slogans like "Your recommended daily allowance of indulgence."

Weight-loss ads aimed at fat-conscious consumers have been making such exaggerated claims lately that the Federal Trade Commission released a guide in 2003 to help consumers spot deceptive ads for phony weight-loss products. You'd think people would be skeptical of slogans like "lose weight without diet or exercise," but apparently not. P. T. Barnum got it right when he said there's a sucker born every minute.

Ads Play to Patriotism and Loyalty

If appeals to fears and prejudices can sell the product, why not patriotism and loyalty to one's country? At least that was what advertisers thought after September 11, when patriotic fervor was at its highest pitch since World War II. Everything from cars to the stock market to sports clubs was wrapped in the flag and sold to the public. Ford pledged to "Help America Move Forward" in zero financing ads, and GM used the controversial tagline "Keep America Rolling." The New York Stock Exchange urged Americans to invest in the market with the slogan "Let Freedom Ring," and the New York Sports Clubs offered reduced initiation fees under the tagline "Keep America Strong." Images of the flag popped up everywhere—on sheets and underwear, on napkins and

Boondocks © Aaron McGruder. Reprinted with permission of Universal Press Syndicate. All rights reserved.

All of us come from someplace else.

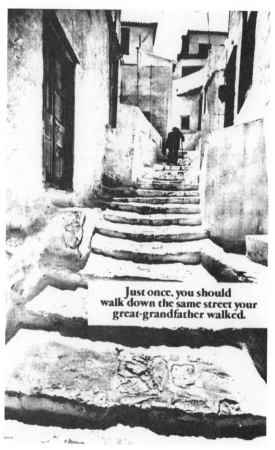

Just once, you should walk down the same street your great-grandfather walked.

Picture this if you will.

A man who's spent all his life in the United States gets on a plane, crosses a great ocean, lands.

He walks the same streets his family walked centuries ago.

He sees his name, which is rare in America, filling three pages in a phone book.

He speaks haltingly the language he wishes he had learned better as a child.

As America's airline to the world, Pan Am does a lot of things.

We help business travelers make meetings on the other side of the world. Our planes take goods to and from six continents. We take vacationers just about anywhere they want to go.

But nothing we do seems to have as much meaning as when we help somebody discover the second heritage that every American has.

America's airline to the world.

See your travel agent.

Courtesy of Pan American World Airways, Inc.

Advertising tends to concentrate on marginal needs, desires, and fears at the expense of many more important ones. Indeed, a frequently heard charge against advertising is that it increases the already strong tendency of people in industrial countries to become pre-occupied with buying and consuming goods. (Note the humorous bumper sticker WHEN THE GOING GETS TOUGH, THE TOUGH GO SHOPPING.) *Occasionally, however, an ad comes along that reminds us of what (for most of us) are much more important values, even though we tend to forget them in the hustle and bustle of everyday life. This Pan Am ad is one of those rare ads that tend to push us in the right direction. Yes! If we can afford it (and more of us could if we spent less on lesser needs), just once, we should walk down the same street our great-grandfather walked. (Pan Am went belly-up in the early 1990s, but for other reasons.)*

sweatshirts—but the trend was short lived. Consumers criticized many ads as tasteless, coming so soon after a national tragedy, and focus groups sent marketers the message that using patriotism to sell products was a turnoff.

Some ads were understandable, perhaps. Given the drastic drop in air travel after the terrorist attack, United Airlines had good reason to launch a major ad campaign. The documentary style ads featured interviews with United employees making patriotic comments like "We're Americans and this is not gonna beat us down" and "We took the blow but we're gonna get up." The ads received mixed reviews, and though they might have boosted United's image, they didn't sell tickets—air travel was down for two years after the attack.

Ads Whitewash Corporate Imagery

Whenever an ad sells a company's image instead of a product, you have got to wonder what is going on. With the popularity of environmental issues on the rise, corporations that have a major impact on the environment have sponsored an increasing number of "green" ads. DuPont's classic "seal slapping" ad captures the flavor of these eco-friendly spots. This one features a scenic shoreline with dolphins diving, penguins waddling, sea lions clapping (you get the idea)—all to the melodic strains of Beethoven's "Ode to Joy." Just visible on the horizon is an oil tanker. The voiceover tells us "recently DuPont announced that its energy unit would pioneer the use of new double-hulled tankers in order to safeguard the environment." Not long after the ad appeared—with its happy sea creatures cavorting in an eco-friendly environment—the EPA issued a report that DuPont was far and away the largest emitter of toxic waste.

More recently, GE launched an "eco imagination" campaign designed to remake the company's image as a leader in clean technology. The dancing elephant ad, a charmer that was top rated in viewer surveys, showed a computer-generated elephant dancing through a rainforest to "Singin' in the Rain." (Never mind that elephants don't live in rainforests.) The dancing elephant cavorts past a bunch of beaming monkeys, toucans, and flamingos—a bucolic scene intended to show us that GE's low-emission products benefit the environment. "Technology that's in step with nature," the voiceover intones. Judging from an Ad Track survey, this spot was one of the most engaging ads in 2005, and GE was well on its way to transforming its image.

Ubiquitous Ads and Sensory Overload

Marketers are nothing if not resourceful. What with conventional reading material and TV watching on the wane, they can no longer count on reaching consumers through established media like magazines, newspapers and TV. Instead they are taking a scatter-shot approach, plastering ads all over the place.[2] Microsoft advertised on tray tables in U.S. Airways planes; Geico, on subway turnstiles; Continental Airlines, on Chinese food cartons and pizza boxes; Perry Ellis, on shirt boxes and hanging bags at dry cleaners. And how about this for a mini-marketing gem: CBS was stamping the names of CBS

---

[2]Examples taken from "Anywhere the Eye Can See, It's Now Likely to See an Ad," *New York Times,* January 15, 2007.

television shows on supermarket eggs. Then there are the video screens that have appeared in taxicabs and elevators, ostensibly to provide news but heavily larded with ads. Ads are even projected on the sides of buildings, and old-fashioned billboards are being converted into digital screens that change messages throughout the day.

Given this marketing barrage, it is a wonder that consumers haven't reached a saturation point. According to Yankelovich, a marketing research firm, 30 years ago people in cities could see up to 2,000 ads a day. Now they see up to 5,000—that's 2½ times as many. In addition, consumers are regularly blitzed with spam e-mail and repetitive cell phone messages plugging the company's services. A growing number of people are offended by this onslaught, and that worries marketers—sort of—but not enough to deter them from trying even more ingenious ways to hawk their wares.

Puffery Is Legal, but Not Deceptive Advertising

Finally, it's worth noting that what is called "puffery"—generalized, vague, or exaggerated claims, particularly when asserted humorously—is legal. *Example:* The claim by BMW to be "The Ultimate Driving Machine." (Litigation does very occasionally arise concerning borderline cases.) However, ads can overstep legal boundaries and make fraudulent claims. The cigarette industry, in particular, has come under fire for deceptive advertising. For example, in spring 2003, Philip Morris was found guilty of consumer fraud in its ads for "light" cigarettes. Judge Nicholas Byron ruled that the company intentionally misled the public into thinking that Marlboro Lights and Cambridge Lights were "less harmful or safer than their regular counterparts" and ordered the company to pay $10.8 billion to the plaintiffs. This case is one of several lawsuits brought against cigarette companies in recent years.

EXERCISE 10-1

Here are several advertising snippets (usually including the main ploy). Evaluate each of them for honesty, cogency, and the like, and point out uses of the various kinds of gimmicks and devices (humor, jargon, etc.) discussed in the text.

1. Woman in a cigarette ad: "Until I find a real man, I'll settle for a real smoke."

*2. Burger King sign: "10 FREE French Fry Certificates for only $1.00."

3. Calvert Gin ad: "Dry, Drier, Driest, Crisp."

4. Ad for a car: "You can love it without getting your heart broken."

5. Mail-order ad: "Special collector's edition. Priceless recordings. $6.98 per album."

*6. Part of a Nike commercial: "You don't win silver; you lose gold."

7. Ad for Swiss Mocha: "Drift into a Chocolate Daydream."

8. Ad for presidential coins: "Every reader of this newspaper who beats the order deadline will still get one of the last never-circulated Golden Presidential Dollar Coins free with each sealed vault tube at just twenty-eight dollars plus shipping."

9. Budweiser commercial: A rooster very carefully crosses the road and then goes into a tavern where they serve Budweiser. A guy watching this then says to his buddy, "Well, I guess that answers that question." (Hint: This ad is a particular favorite of at least one of the authors of this text.)

*10. The principal part of a newspaper ad sponsored by the U.S. Council for Coconut Research/Information featuring a photo of Martin Agronsky: "The truth told by a famous U.S. television personality: Whoever says coconut oil's 'poisoning' America isn't supported by facts. . . . In fact, an on-going medical study in a Boston hospital has turned out some strong evidence that the 'fatty acids' of coconut oil could be beneficial to human health. America's intake of coconut oil fats is a lot less than what you think. The FDA [Food and Drug Administration] commissioner testified recently before the U.S. Congress that less than 1.5% of U.S. total fat intake is made up of coconut oil. . . ."

11. Newspaper ad for the Massachusetts State Lottery: "There's a good chance you could win the Numbers Game today. Just ask the 12,000 people who won yesterday. . . . The only thing that's hard to do is lose. When this many people win, how can you lose?"

12. Notice on the package of Elizabeth Arden Ceramide Time Complex Capsules: "Take your skin back in time to the future of a younger tomorrow."

EXERCISE 10-2

1. What is your opinion of the Nike commercial showing a woman struggling as she ran to the tape with the voiceover "If you don't lose consciousness in the end, you could have run faster. FASTER! Nike Air."

2. How about the following excerpts (paraphrased) from a *Wall Street Journal* commercial:

Twenty-five years ago, two very similar young men graduated from the same college and started work at the same company. Returning to college for their 25th reunion, they still were much alike—happily married, three children, and so on—but one was manager of a small department in the company, the other was the company's president.

The difference that made the difference was in what each of these two men knew and how they made use of that knowledge: one read the *Wall Street Journal;* the other did not.

*3. Here is a United Airlines TV commercial (used by permission of Leo Burnett Co.):

Ben (the boss, addressing his sales force): I got a phone call this morning from one of our oldest customers. He fired us. After 20 years. He fired us. He said he didn't know us anymore. I think I know why. We used to do business with a handshake—face to face. Now it's a phone call and a fax—get back to you later. With another fax probably. Well folks, something's gotta change. That's why we're gonna get out with a little face-to-face chat with every customer we have. *Salesman:* But Ben, that's gotta be over 200 cities.

Ben: I don't care. Edward, Ryan, Nicholas, ...

Voiceover: If you're the kind of business that still believes personal service deserves a lot more than lip service, . . . welcome to United. That's the way we've been doing business for over 60 years.

Salesman: Ben, where're you going?

Ben: To visit that old friend who fired us this morning.

Voiceover: United. Come fly the friendly skies.

Do you think this was a successful commercial? Why, or why not? Is this primarily a promise or an identification ad?

4. A letter from a travel company included this note on the envelope. "Lowest Fare Advertised on Holland America Guaranteed." Assume, as is likely, that this ad for Holland America (a large cruise ship company) is true. Is there something about this blurb that should make you suspect that the rates quoted are not the lowest you can get? Explain.

5. One of the classic ads in the Pepsi–Coke advertising competition is set some time in the distant future and shows a teacher taking his students to an archeological site containing artifacts from the late twentieth century. He explains the various objects while his students drink cans of Pepsi. One of them holds up a bedraggled Coke bottle and asks the teacher what it is, to which the teacher responds, after much puzzled thought, "I've no idea." A great commercial (why? what is its pulling power?), it brings to mind the way in which ordinary items from a time and place can reveal a great deal to discerning investigators (doing the archeological equivalent of reading between the lines).

   Advertisements, if you can believe Marshall McLuhan, contain a treasure trove of clues about our times. If you were an investigator who came across records containing most of today's advertisements a thousand years hence, what might you learn from them about life in the early twenty-first century? Explain.

EXERCISE 10-3

1. Create a magazine ad for a product: (1) Decide which product it will be, (2) decide on an intended audience for your ad, and (3) design the picture and the copy. Use the ad to make a sales pitch to the class. Then ask students why they would or wouldn't buy the product, based on your ad, and analyze the ad's appeal, or lack of same. (Doing this will make you better appreciate the creative ability of professionals in the advertising business.)

2. Compare two ads for the same or similar products in magazines with very different audiences (for instance, *Vogue* and *Time* magazine or *Sports Illustrated*). Explain how the intended audience influenced the ad design and sales pitch.

3. THE UPSIDE OF ADS

Although most ads hawk consumer goods, a few actually attempt to educate us or warn us against harmful activities. In recent years Partnership for a Drug-Free America has aired a series of ads aimed at combating drug use in this country. The ads, targeting young people as well as parents, focus on the harmful effects of drugs ranging from Ecstasy to marijuana to alcohol. For example, one set of TV spots focuses on embarrassing or disturbing moments that teen drug users experience as a result of their habit. One ad shows a girl trying to conceal a drug-induced nosebleed that starts suddenly in class. Another features a boy inadvertently dropping a drug packet on the counter of a fast-food restaurant. A more shocking series of ads appeals to the vanity of teens by running photographs of young adults who are long-term users in fashionable but grotesque poses that highlight the disfiguring effects of methamphetamines. For instance, under the caption "Body by Crystal Meth" a young man stands, hand on hips, revealing a skeletal body ravaged by drugs. Ads aimed at parents urge them to monitor their kids' activities and social life. They feature parents asking questions like "Where are you going after school?" or "What are your plans after soccer?" Companion ads show older, grateful teens who realize in hindsight that all those irritating questions their parents asked managed to deter them from using drugs. Clearly the message is that parents should be involved in their kids' lives by asking questions and by knowing what they do, whom they hang out with, and where they go. We can only hope that all the advertising devices and gimmicks used so effectively to market goods and services will be just as successful at discouraging drug use among teens.

4. MARKETING STRATEGIES

Although the advertising professionals are exceedingly good at their business, they are forced by increasing competition between advertisers, coupled with increased consumer sophistication, to do a good deal of market research. That is why, these days, there is an immense amount of research behind every successful advertising campaign. One way for consumers to defend themselves against the ad campaigns that result from sophisticated market research is to become familiar with methods advertisers use to market their products.

Eric Clark notes, in *The Want Makers*,[3] that "virtually nothing appears from a major advertiser or agency until it has been opinion-polled, test-marketed or copy-tested, submitted on the way to panels of consumers whose words have been turned into statistical tables or analyzed by psychologists." Most large agencies have research staffs of their own, in addition to using specialist agencies such as the A. C. Nielsen Company.

Types of research vary, depending on the method in favor at any given time, but roughly they can be divided into *qualitative research*—getting into people's heads to find out their thoughts and feelings—and *quantitative research*—gathering information by observation, experimentation, and surveys.

Qualitative research grew out of Freud's theory that unconscious motivations often influence behavior. The underlying assumption, already stressed here, is that people make many decisions irrationally and often are not even aware of their reasons for making them. So researchers try to figure out how people really feel about products, not just how one might suppose they would feel. For example, on the basis of interviews with 300 mothers about how they fed their babies, researchers concluded the mothers were more concerned that feedings should be convenient and enjoyable for *themselves* rather than

---

[3]Some of what follows is summarized from this fascinating book.

for their children, even though the mothers themselves said their baby's satisfaction was paramount. The resulting successful marketing ploy was merely to mention that babies would enjoy being fed the food but to stress that feeding time would be shortened.

Since all of us are motivated by unconscious desires at some time or other, these marketing techniques make it more difficult for us to make rational decisions about the products we buy (including political products, to be discussed shortly). We need to be more careful about what we buy and ask ourselves some commonsense questions before plunking down our money. Do we really need the product? Can we afford it? How does it compare with other similar products? Are we being conned—perhaps overly motivated—by advertising?

The quantitative approach to research has come a long way since the days when researchers asked people on the street what brand of soap or cereal they preferred. When you buy goods at most stores these days, the bar codes that are read at the checkout counter provide the retailer with a good deal of information concerning price, item purchased, and so on, that can be stored in computers; market researchers are now tapping into this information to find out what products people actually buy, not what they say they will buy. They are keeping track of the purchases made by carefully selected families, linking this information with further data concerning family income, number of children, and TV programs watched, including special test commercials. The result is that these marketing gurus can identify the ads that effectively sold the targeted products and plan large-scale ad campaigns accordingly. The currently popular "shopping cards" that claim to give discounts to customers on certain products are really intended to provide information on customer shopping habits that is analyzed and then sold to marketing companies. In many stores, sales clerks ask shoppers for their ZIP codes, which are fed into a marketing program (called PRIZM) that gathers consumer information. This program is advertised to marketers in *Advertising Age* as "the targeting tool that turns birds of a feather into sitting ducks." Perhaps an appropriate slogan these days would be that eternal vigilance is the price of economic solvency.

The object of all this research is not necessarily the low-income consumer but the more affluent. As Michael Schudson points out in *Advertising: The Uneasy Persuasion,*

Two electronic advertising ploys have raised a good bit of commotion because they raise serious political questions. The first is so-called dynamic pricing on e-commerce websites—setting different prices on items for different customers, depending on their personal "profile," based on electronically stored information concerning purchasing habits, and so on. (When accused of this practice, Amazon.com claimed its video sales price differences were completely random, simply a way to test the market.)

The other serious issue resulting from the electronic collection of information has to do with insurance policies, especially health insurance policies. Having access to a person's medical records, for example, could enable HMOs to deny coverage to those at great risk of serious illness, perhaps for genetic reasons.

It is unclear how these two problems will be worked out. What is clear is the threat the ability to electronically collect all sorts of information on virtually everyone poses, a new wrinkle indeed, but to a very old problem.

> *Luxury used to be for the happy few, but now it is hawked to the mass of con-*
> *sumers. Even ordinary products are hyped with inflated language to give them*
> *luxury status. James B. Twitchell comments on this trend in "Luxe Populi,"* San
> Francisco Chronicle, *May 20, 2007.*
>
> ---
>
> . . . the consumers of the new luxury have a sense of entitlement that transcends
> social class, a conviction that the finest things are their birthright. Never mind that
> they may have been born into a family whose ancestral estate is a tract house in
> the suburbs, near the mall, not paid for, and whose family crest was downloaded
> from the Internet. Ditto the signet ring design. Language reflects this hijacking.
> Words such as *gourmet, premium, boutique, chic, accessory* and *classic* have
> loosened from their elite moorings and now describe such top-of-category items
> as popcorn, hamburgers, discount brokers, shampoo, scarves, ice cream and
> trailer parks.

marketers are more interested in people with $100,000 to spend on nonessential goods
than those with $1,000. The consequence is that consumer choices are often top-heavy
in luxury items. Schudson argues that this tendency sometimes works to reduce the
spectrum of goods available to people with modest incomes. The example he gives is the
transformation of the automobile. "More and more extras become standard equipment
in automobiles and other products, and the low income consumer has no choice but to
go deeper into debt to pay for the simplest model, now weighted with superfluous 'standard' equipment." (In fairness, we need to note that used cars do cost less than new ones,
although prices for used, ah . . . , "pre-owned" cars, also reflect the fancy equipment—
electric windows and doors and the like—that they, too, are loaded with.)

There are psychological consequences to targeting the affluent as well. Fed a steady
diet of ads for upscale goods, low-income consumers begin to crave luxuries beyond
their wallets. How many people can afford a Rolex watch, a BMW X3, or diamonds
from Tiffany? But they can fantasize about luxury items in classy ads—and maybe then
max out their credit cards.

Even the best-targeted ads, however (fortunately?), often miss their mark because
people have become more adept at tuning them out. Increasingly sophisticated technology allows just about everyone to zap commercials with remote controls, or skip ads altogether with digital video recorders. We may not be outfoxing advertisers as much as
we think, though, when we fast-forward commercials to get to the main attraction. The
assumption has always been that ads have no effect when played at high speed, but
recent research suggests that they do, indeed, engage us. Experiments done by NBC
show that viewers are just as involved in speeded up commercials as they are when they
slow down and watch the program that follows. Not only that, but viewers who have
already seen an ad in slow time tend to register the same emotional response when they
speed through it again in fast time.[4]

---

[4]For more on this see "Engaging at Any Speed? Commercials Put to Test," by Louise Story, *New
York Times,* July 3, 2007.

So far, though, advertisers remain unconvinced and continue to devise insidious ways to offset audience apathy and devices used to block or skip commercials. Increasingly, characters on TV shows use brand-name products like Kleenex for crying women on *Days of Our Lives* or Apple computers on shows like *The Office* and *Heroes*. The virtual reality created by computer graphics makes digital product placement a no-brainer for advertisers. Like magic, Cheez-Its pop up on coffee tables or Starkist tuna on kitchen counters. More elaborate placement occurs when products are worked into the story line. Revlon paid millions for the writers of *All My Children* to incorporate the company name into the plotline of the soap opera that unfolded over several months. Hyundi bought a segment of the talk show *The Other Half,* featuring a Hyundi representative who gave tips on shopping for cars. Even *Playboy* magazine got into the act with a centerfold of a BMW on its June 2002 issue.[5] We can expect to see more "product placement" as conventional ads become less effective.

Advertisers also have to contend with the growing popularity of less well advertised generic products, and with the escalation of price wars that squeeze profit margins and advertising budgets. In response to this trend, advertisers regularly try new strategies. For the past decade, marketing money has shifted away from conventional media and into nonmedia sectors, such as sales promotions, public relations, direct mail, catalog marketing, and trade promotions. Think for instance of the avalanche of junk mail just about everybody gets these days. At least consumers inundated by telemarketing sales pitches can now block the calls by entering their names in the do-not-call registry.

Databased marketing is another of the current advertising concepts. As Stan Rapp and Thomas L. Collins point out in their book *Beyond Maxi Marketing,* advertisers are reducing their concentration on mass marketing in favor of more focused, less wasteful,

---

The Shopping Mall as Marketing Tool

Theatricality, illusion, pretense, manipulation, and artifice are the essence of the mall setting. The shopper must buy, . . . Every possible design tool is aimed at behavioral control, to make the shopper visit more often, stay longer, and buy more. Pathways are contrived to require her to walk past the maximum number of shopping outlets en route to the planned destination, tempting her to suspend judgment and yield to impulse. Attention-getting banners, vivid signs, dramatic lighting, seductive color schemes, lush plantings, upbeat music, and soothing sounds provide intense sensations, alternately stimulating and relaxing the visitor until she is freed from normal restraints and caught up in the mood of buying.

—From "America's Fantasy Urbanism:
The Waxing of the Mall and the Waning of
Civility," Carole Rifkind, an essay in
Dumbing Down

---

[5]See "Ads Gone Mad," in *Extra!,* September/October 2002, for ads that cross the line between commercials and content.

individualized marketing strategies, using precisely targeted database programs. For example, a Tennessee department store chain's database identified 1,400 customers who purchased clothes by high-fashion designers such as Anne Klein and Liz Claiborne only when they were on sale and then notified these customers when designer clothes went on sale, increasing two-day sale receipts on these items by 97 percent. Personalized marketing is much more likely to appeal to consumers than is mass marketing, making it harder to resist.

Drug manufacturers have come up with a new marketing ploy in recent years that has physicians and the FDA worried. Instead of advertising prescription drugs to doctors only, as has been the practice in the past, drug companies are marketing directly to consumers. Probably the most widely hyped product is Viagra, but all manner of drugs are hawked to the public for treating everything from depression to heart disease. It comes as no surprise that patients are now insisting that doctors prescribe the pills advertised on TV and are often unwilling to consider alternative treatments. One unfortunate consequence, noted in the *New England Journal of Medicine,* is that "demand by patients is the most common reason offered by physicians for inappropriate prescribing." Increasing concern about the adverse effects of advertising drugs has prompted the American Medical Association to study the potential problems of this type of advertising and the FDA to increase its surveillance of pharmaceutical ads.

Pharmaceutical advertising is bad enough as it is, but the problem is compounded when these ads feature doctors endorsing drugs. This happened when Dr Robert Jarvik, famous for pioneering work in artificial hearts, began appearing in television commercials for Lipitor, a Pfizer drug.[6] The ads showed him performing vigorous outdoor activities, like rowing a racing shell across a mountain lake, and plugging the product with taglines like, "When diet and exercise aren't enough, adding Lipitor significantly lowers cholesterol." To begin with, critics questioned his misleading credentials. Although Jarvik has a medical degree, he is not a cardiologist, nor is he licensed to practice medicine. Then there are his qualifications as an oarsman—which he is not. A stuntman did the sculling scenes. (As one colleague said, "He's about as much an outdoorsman as Woody Allen.") These misleading credentials had a congressional committee concerned about whether the ads were giving the public a false impression. It's no big deal when Brad Pitt hawks Heineken, but it is another matter when a reputable doctor with misleading credentials endorses a heavy-duty drug (let alone *any* doctor hawking products for drug companies). Apparently Pfizer got the message because they took Jarvik off the ad.

When all else fails, marketers can always change the look and shape of a product to seduce consumers into buying it. In days gone by, companies rarely changed their product packaging. Kleenex came in square or rectangular boxes, Pepsi redesigned its cans only ten times in 100 years.[7] But now that consumers have effective ways to bypass commercials, marketers are turning packages into three-dimensional ads that lure buyers to their products as they stroll down store aisles. Kleenex has come out with bright oval cartons, Coors Lite bottles turn blue when chilled, Pepsi is changing the graffiti-like

---

[6]See "For Jarvik Heart Pioneer, Drug Ads Raise Profile and Questions," by Stephanie Saul, *New York Times,* February 7, 2008.

[7]Examples are taken from "Product Packages Now Shout to Grab Your Fickle Attention," by Louise Story, *New York Times,* August 10, 2007.

design of its cans every few weeks (to attract the younger generation with its alarmingly short attention span), and Evian is packaging water in elegant, swan necked bottles. (The wildly successful marketing of bottled water is ironic, not to mention illogical, given the fact that most tap water in this country is as good or better than bottled water.) Future ploys include soda cans that emit a sweet-smelling spray when you pop the top and packages with tiny, embedded speakers that talk to you when you walk by. Talking boxes. Ah, the wonders of capitalism.

Advertising on the Internet

The days when the Internet was exclusively, or even primarily, noncommercial are now long-since over. A growing number of businesses are advertising their products on home pages on the World Wide Web. Users can click on to a commercial and read about and order the product in one fell swoop. Quick, easy, and tempting.

Because of mounting evidence that TV ads are less effective than they used to be, marketers are reaching a wider audience by integrating the Internet and television into their ad campaigns. One ploy is for networks to sell ad packages that combine Internet space with TV commercials. Some of the glossiest, most engaging Super Bowl ads run on ABC Sunday have been made available on websites like espn.com and nfl.com and video.google.com. (It's no wonder that advertisers want more bang for their buck when Super Bowl commercials cost $2.5 million for 30 seconds, as of 2006.)[8] Another ploy advertisers use to engage their audience is to take advantage of increasing consumer interest in user-generated content. Converse, the shoe manufacturer, came up with an ingenious campaign that transformed consumers into advertisers when it solicited homemade videos featuring Converse sneakers. The 1,500 entries from 20 countries were posted on conversegallery.com. What better way to sell a product than by converting consumers into advertisers.

Major players like Google and Yahoo have developed sophisticated ad systems that match ads with users and thus increase the likelihood that ads will be accessed. And some of these systems have analytic capabilities as well, giving marketers an idea of which campaigns are most successful. Google, in particular, with its huge database, has ramped up its advertising network to the point where it rakes in almost as much as do the four major broadcast networks combined. That's a lot of money—a projected $16 billion for 2008 alone.

Consumers are beginning to understand the privacy issues at stake when these sophisticated ad systems vacuum up information on Internet users. As early as 1999, *60 Minutes* ran a segment (November 19) on how advertising networks use tracking devices that allow them to record, *without our knowledge,* where we surf the Internet, thereby collecting data about our interests, shopping tastes, and even our medical concerns. With this information they develop a profile of us that enables them to personalize ads that come up on our screen. The more data we give them, the more complete their profile. To entice users to give personal information, Internet ad companies such as

---

[8]For more on this see two articles in the *New York Times:* "Commercials that Echo," by Stuart Elliott, February 2, 2006, and "TV and Top Marketers Discuss the State of the Medium," by Julie Bosman, March 24, 2006.

Double Click offer an array of personalized services. For instance, when we tell them our travel plans, they can let us know whether our plane is delayed or give us the weather forecast or provide an entertainment guide for the city we are visiting.

Perhaps the most questionable feature of this kind of practice is that the information we give Internet companies can be, and often is, shared with "offline" companies as well and can be obtained by employers or insurance companies doing background checks. So far there are no regulations governing the Internet. Savvy users give fake names and information to guard against invasion of privacy, but most people surfing the Net do not.

E-mail marketing has increased dramatically in recent years. In just two years (2001–2003) spam went from 8 percent to 45 percent of e-mail—two-thirds of which includes fraudulent offers, according to a Federal Trade Commission estimate. In December 2003, the president signed the CAN-SPAM Act banning commercial e-mail from using false headers and requiring U.S. businesses to include opt-out instructions. But this legislation is unlikely to rein in the spam stampede, since it is a worldwide phenomenon that is increasingly driven by Internet service providers abroad. Also, the new law overrides stricter state laws, like California's anti-spam legislation that was due to go into effect in 2004.

The creep of advertising into mobile phones has just begun, but a full-scale invasion is expected in the next few years. Mobile marketers are sending text ads to cell phone screens of people using web browsers on their phones, and banner ads are starting to pop up, prompting consumers to click on the ad for the sales pitch or call a hotel or restaurant with a click. Because mobile phones are location based, more ads are expected to be site specific, pitching the products of retailers in the area. It's too early to know whether consumers will tap into mobile-phone marketing or drop the wireless carrier promoting ads that are pushing into every corner of our lives.

On a more postive note, computers are becoming a kind of television set, allowing users to do things like switch from on-line programs to television, to films, to game playing. In a few places today, viewers using remote-control pads can play along with video quiz shows, select camera angles for sports events, and access detailed information about advertised products. These sophisticated telecomputers open up a whole new world for the advertising industry. Consumers can scroll through a mail-order catalog, order products instantaneously from the already-popular shopping channels, and access detailed information about the car they want to buy or the HMO they want to join. Which of these new marvels will turn out to be the wave of the future remains to be seen; billions are being spent by various competing parties intent on getting their feet in the doors they hope will be the right ones. But however these battles turn out, the danger is that lots of us will be pushed even more into the "consumer mode" and become even more likely to be talked into buying products it would be prudent for us to pass over.

EXERCISE 10-4

1. Find an ad that has strong emotional appeal for you and try to figure out why you find it so engaging. Once you have done so, decide whether you would purchase the product, and explain your decision. (Be honest. Think carefully about it. No off-the-top-of-the-head goody-goody.)

2. Go through a bunch of ads on some kind of product that interests you—cars, cosmetics, sports gear, whatever—and choose the one you would like to buy based on what you are told in these ads. Then do some research in *Consumer Reports, Consumers Digest,* or any one of several publications that specialize in product comparisons. On the basis of your research, decide whether you would still purchase the item you selected. Explain your decision.

3. Visit a shopping mall and examine the ploys used to seduce people into buying products. Consider subtle as well as obvious marketing devices and explain why you might be tempted to buy them.

4. Here is part of a comment made by John Kasson: "Advertising . . . has become . . . a way of telling us not just what we should buy but how we should live, how we should associate the advertised objects with ourselves."

   Is Kasson right? Or do ads primarily appeal to already-existing desires and lifestyles? It is obvious, for example, that we cannot have a desire to play computer games like Nintendo before they exist, but do most ads touting products merely tell us about new ways to satisfy old desires, or do they create new ones, or perhaps just strengthen existing desires so that we spend more on them than we should? Do ads, say, for designer jeans and other fashion clothes just reinforce existing preferences? (Defend your answer.)

5. In his book *Business Civilization in Decline,* Robert Heilbroner claims that advertising is "the single most value-destroying activity of a business civilization." Would you agree or disagree with this statement? Write an argument defending your position.

6. Imagine that you live in another country (or on another planet, for that matter) and know nothing about the United States except what you see in ads. What values and attitudes do you think Americans might have? Support your response by using ads as evidence.

7. As Internet use increases, marketing companies devise devious ways to reach potential customers, like targeting people's preferences by tracking their activities as they surf the Net. These surveillance techniques have raised ethical questions about web users' rights to privacy. Advertisers argue that people benefit from online targeting because they see more relevant ads, but privacy advocates worry that the increasing surveillance of web activities is an invasion of their right to privacy. Write an argument for or against government regulation of online advertising.

5. POLITICAL ADVERTISING

By now, just about everybody knows that political candidates and issues are marketed in pretty much the same way as breakfast foods and laundry detergents. This means that appeals to reason tend to be scarce, while devices designed to move emotions preempt the field.

In the very old days, only candidates for local office could reach more than a tiny fraction of their prospective constituents—via "whistle stop" campaigns in which they made speeches before small audiences and "pressed the flesh." Billboards, lawn signs, newspaper ads, posters, patriotic bunting, and that sort of thing were extremely important parts of any successful campaign.

But the average voter never heard the actual voices of candidates running for high office or, except for some presidential candidates, ever saw their pictures or photographs. Political parties and platforms thus loomed much larger than they do today. Charisma didn't travel very widely.

Things began to change early in the twentieth century with the introduction of electronic and other scientific devices, starting with methods for printing pictures in newspapers and continuing with the widespread ownership of radios. Franklin Roosevelt was the first president to fully understand and gain significant political advantage from the miracle of radio; his "fireside chats" were an immensely successful public relations instrument, and his voice was instantly recognized by virtually everyone in America in those days.

But the changes in political rhetoric and tactics that came after World War II dwarfed those that preceded it. A large increase in the number of primary elections reduced the power of political parties and party "bosses" and, much more important, television brought candidates and their pitches into living rooms across the nation. Political campaigns were changed forever (as was pretty much everything else—but remember the saying that "The more things change, the more they remain the same"). Within a few years, image makers, which means advertising experts, reigned supreme.

The first presidential candidate to make full and effective use of the new medium was Dwight D. Eisenhower. His successful 1952 campaign against Adlai Stevenson featured short television commercials like the following example, part of a series of TV spots in which General Eisenhower read from letters sent in by "citizens" asking questions that Eisenhower then "answered":

> *Citizen:* Mr. Eisenhower, what about the high cost of living?
> *General Eisenhower:* My wife, Mamie, worries about the same thing. I tell her it's our job to change that on November 14.[9]

No need for Eisenhower to tell viewers *how* he planned to change it.

Of course, Eisenhower conveyed an almost perfect image—war hero and father figure—and most people therefore strongly identified with him. War heroes, father figures, and candidates with charisma, John Kennedy being perhaps the best example, are very hard to beat. When Kennedy ran for office, his father, whose connections in Hollywood dated back to the 1920s, hired film professionals experienced in using effective film production techniques, to hype the candidate as a symbolic role model— a strong, courageous hero—and to capitalize on his undoubted glamorous appeal. Nowadays, candidates who project a less appealing image can, and frequently do, overcome their handicaps by hiring image makers to attractively tailor their campaigns *and their personalities.*

---

[9]David Ogilvy, in his classic book on advertising *Confessions of an Advertising Man* (New York: Atheneum, 1963). Ogilvy quotes Eisenhower as moaning between takes, "To think that an old soldier should come to this." Note that the device used is a promise to satisfy a strong desire (for lower prices) without providing a single reason for believing that the promise would be kept.

In the run-up to the 2008 election, Hillary Clinton's advisers softened the candidate's image to make her seem warmer and more relaxed than the strident image she projected in the years before the campaign. She wore pastel blouses under dark suits, softened her voice, made light-hearted jokes, and held "web chats" on her website, filmed in the homey atmosphere of her sun room. All this was part of the strategy to transform her image from the assertive woman who, a couple decades earlier, earned more money as a lawyer than her husband did as governor of Arkansas, and who said things like she didn't stay at home and bake cookies, and she wasn't "some woman standing behind my man like Tammy Wynette." An interesting footnote to this make-over is the double standard set for male and female candidates: John Kerry wasn't considered tough enough in the previous election nor was Barack Obama in 2008, but Hillary Clinton was too tough and had to be airbrushed into a kinder, gentler woman. Every time she played hardball with the opposition (and she frequently did), she was criticized.

Image makers have honed their craft in recent years. They have learned, for example, that negative ads attacking one's opponent can be dynamite. Mudslinging isn't new, of course. John Adams was labeled a closet monarchist, Thomas Jefferson was derided because he didn't enlist in 1775 (!), and Abe Lincoln was dubbed "Honest Ape." But television brought mudslinging to a far wider audience, and thus it was more effective. One of the first TV spots to use this technique to full effect—the 1964 "Daisy/Girl/Peace" spot—also is probably the most famous of all political TV commercials. It ran just once as a paid advertisement but received so much comment that it was broadcast several times as a news item. (It was once believed that this commercial was never run again

---

Negative campaigning has been honed to a fine art. Just abut every political campaign involves people who are opposition researchers, *a polite term for political hitmen (or women). Here is a description of the process by one such fellow who finally became so demoralized by the whole business that he dropped out and wrote a book about it.*

Step I: The political hitmen dig up the dirt.

Step II: The dirt is then given to the pollsters, who through sophisticated polling can determine which pieces of dirt are the most damaging in the minds of the voters.

Step III: The pollsters give their results to the media advertising folks, who put the most damaging two or three negative issues into the TV, radio, and direct-mail pieces that do their best to rip their political opponent into shreds.

—Steven Marks, *Confessions of a Political Hitman* (Naperville, Ill: Sourcebooks, Inc., 2007)

That final step only hints at the warped genius of ad writers who transform pages of research into 30- or 60-second spots that crucify the opposition in sound bites the public can easily grasp and often believe.

> Orthodontics and the hair dryer have become vital to the achievement of political power.
>
> —Len Deighton

because of a public outcry against it, but in fact the original plan was to run it just once and then to garner free repeat TV coverage, which is exactly what happened.)

The spot starts by showing a very young girl picking petals from a daisy while counting, "1, 2, 3, 4, 5, 7, 6, 6, 8, 9, 9," at which point there is the voiceover of a man counting, "10, 9, 8, 7, 6, 5, 4, 3, 2, 1, 0," followed by the blast of an atomic bomb on the screen and the voice of President Lyndon Johnson saying, "These are the stakes—to make a world in which all God's children can live—or to go into the dark. We must either love each other or we must die." Then another voiceover: "Vote President Johnson on November 3rd. The stakes are too high for you to stay home."

The point of this commercial was to picture Johnson's opponent, Republican Senator Barry Goldwater, as an extreme hawk all too willing to push the button, while Johnson is portrayed as a responsible "peace" candidate. Is it an accident that this best-known of all political spots also is one of the most vicious, inaccurate, and unfair?

This infamous ad sank into the quagmire of history, where it belonged, but ads using similar scare tactics have surfaced in recent campaigns. When Hillary Clinton was fighting for the Democratic nomination for president, her campaign ran an ad showing children sleeping peacefully in their beds with the ominous voiceover, "It's 3 A.M. and your children are safe and asleep. Who do you want answering the phone?" Clearly an attack on Barack Obama, the ad implied that he hadn't the foreign policy experience to deal with a call to the president in the dead of night announcing an imminent attack on the country. Obama was quick to respond. Within hours his team produced a commercial using some of the same scenes in the Clinton spot asking, "Shouldn't the president be the one—the only one—who had the judgment and courage to oppose the Iraq War from the start?"—a slam at Clinton for supporting the war when Obama stood strong against it. Because rapid response ads like this are effective, they have become increasingly common and thus perpetuate negative ad cycles that receive hundreds of thousands of hits on websites like YouTube within a few days after they have aired.

John McCain has been the target of some of the most vicious campaign smears in recent years, first when he was a candidate in the 2000 Republican primaries and then again in the 2008 presidential elections. In 2000, for example, he was accused of fathering an out-of-wedlock black daughter, Bridget—when, in fact, she was adopted from Mother Teresa's orphanage. The cumulative effect of the negative campaigning against McCain was to knock him out of the 2000 race early on. Unfortunately, there are no legal consequences for mudslinging, no matter how false the accusations. The Federal Trade Commission slaps fines on commercial advertisers who make false claims about a product, but not on political advertisers, who can say whatever they want about a candidate with impunity—and defend their slash-and-burn attacks as free speech.

Although (or maybe because) McCain suffered mightily from negative ads in 2000, he didn't hesitate to launch a blitz of misleading attack ads in 2008 against Barack Obama—who responded in kind. In these straw man attacks, the candidates distorted

> *Hitler's henchman, Joseph Goebbels, summed up the Nazi position on negative advertising: "The propaganda which produces the desired results is good and all other propaganda is bad. . . . Therefore, it is beside the point to say your propaganda is too crude, too mean, too brutal, or too unfair, for all this does not matter. Propaganda is always a means to an end."*

each other's positions by taking quotes out of context, by suggesting guilt by association, or by just plain lying. For example, the McCain campaign claimed Obama opposed nuclear energy (he didn't) and voted to raise taxes on families earning $42,000. (He voted on a nonbinding resolution for a $15 increase.) One vacuous ad derided his celebrity status by linking him to Paris Hilton and Britney Spears. Another claimed he made a veiled reference to Sarah Palin when he said, "You can put lipstick on a pig, but it's still a pig." Then there were the vitriolic, guilt-by-association robocalls claiming Obama "has worked closely with terrorist Bill Ayers, whose organizations bombed the U.S. Capitol, the Pentagon, a judge's home, and killed Americans."

The Obama campaign launched its own straw man attacks, most famously, the one claiming John McCain wanted to stay in Iraq for 100 years, taking out of context McCain's comment that he thought the troops should maintain a presence in volatile parts of the world for as long as it takes—not engage in actual combat for 100 years. Then there was the misleading ad that played to older voters claiming that McCain wanted to "cut [Social Security] benefits in half"—a distortion of his support for President Bush's failed plan to privatize Social Security. Another ad, aimed at the Latino community, quoted Rush Limbaugh calling Mexicans "stupid and unqualified," falsely implying that he was one of McCain's "Republican friends." On and on the negative ads went until the battleground states, in particular, were saturated with negativity, and voters finally seemed to say enough!

People who thought that Obama would—or even could—keep his promise to transcend traditional politics (with all the negative campaigning that implied) were wrong. And so were those who hoped that McCain, a victim of scurrilous ads in the past, would morph into a kinder, more positive campaigner. When it comes to advertising, it's politics as usual. To the credit of the media, many newspapers, magazines, and newscasts analyzed the most toxic ads throughout the campaign, exposing their distortions and lies.

Obvious political smears are the tip of the iceberg, though, in undermining political opponents. Less obvious techniques involve the visuals and the pacing. For example, an editor can make a candidate look less attractive by cropping the photo and going tighter on the face or by draining the color to black and white and reducing the action to slow

> You can fool some of the people all of the time, and those are the ones you need to concentrate on.
>
> —George W. Bush, quoting Robert Strauss
> (in a spoof) at the 2001 Gridiron Dinner

> Most people are eternally taken in by the myth and rhetoric of democracy. . . .
> What we have now is an increasingly uneducated public—especially in what
> used to be called civics—dealing with evermore complex issues with which they
> are unequipped to knowledgeably deal. . . . We have a population ripe for manip-
> ulation by powerful public relation firms and political consultants who are expert
> in sound bites and seductive imagery.
>
> —Gray Brechin, *Imperial San Francisco:*
> *Urban Power, Earthly Ruin*

motion. Editors have enormous power. They can—and do—manipulate every element
of an ad in ways so subtle that most viewers have no idea that they, themselves, are being manipulated.

Negative ads rejected by networks sometimes get more publicity than if they are
aired. A good case in point is the "Child's Pay" ad generated by MoveOn.org, showing
children doing adult work with the tagline "Guess who's going to pay off President
Bush's $1 trillion deficit?" When CBS rejected the ad for airing during the 2003 Super
Bowl, it got widespread publicity in the press. (The ad was later picked up by CNN.)
This tactic is used increasingly by groups with advocacy ads that will certainly be rejected. By issuing press releases and other protests to the media, these groups generate
free publicity for their causes.

Although voters have complained repeatedly about negative ads, the media continue
to run them—because they work. If this were the best of all worlds, people would study
the candidates' records and vote rationally on the basis of their credentials; instead, too
may people sit mesmerized in front of their television sets, passively absorbing the
sound bites they get from infotainment and its ubiquitous commercials—including negative political ads. It's no wonder campaigns resort to using these ads. They actually grab
the viewers' attention in ways that information about the candidates' records almost
never does. So when we complain about the onslaught of negative ads, let's remember
that political campaigns would never waste money on them if there weren't a receptive
audience ready to absorb their messages.

As must be evident by now, political campaigns are indistinguishable from advertising campaigns. In fact, one of the most successful factors in selling a product, brand
recognition, is just as effective in marketing a candidate, but in politics the brand name
is a recognizable family name of a politician whose father, uncle, or husband has
served in public office. Most recently there was George Bush, the father, then Bill
Clinton, then George Bush the son, then Hillary Clinton, the wife. Voters recognize
the family name and feel comfortable with it much as they do with brands like Ivory
soap or Campbell's soup. This tendency to favor candidates with dynastic names has
deep roots in American politics. Before the Bushes and the Clintons, the Kennedys
dominated the dynastic field, with John, the president, then Bobby and Teddy, the senators, and a raft of their offspring in Congress and state governments. Before them was
Teddy Roosevelt and his distant cousin Franklin Delano Roosevelt, and so on, all the
way back to John Adams, the second president, and his son John Quincy Adams, the
fourth president. It seems that voters often put more stock in the family names of

I'm not an old hand at politics. But I am now seasoned enough to have learned that the hardest thing about any political campaign is how to win without proving that you are unworthy of winning.

—Adlai Stevenson (1956)

What one candidate learned from two (failed) runs at the presidency.

prominent politicians than they do in the candidate's qualifications, a fact not lost on political advertisers.

Of course, most candidates don't bear the name of a famous forebear and have to market other attributes. One of the most important ploys in marketing candidates is image making, and one of the most effective formats for candidates to sharpen their image is presidential debates. The presidential debates provide candidates with the largest audiences they will be able to advertise to during a whole election campaign. (Nowadays, of course, a tradition has been established so that candidates pretty much are forced to debate or lose face.) Political debates are hardly a new idea—think of the famous debates between Abraham Lincoln and Stephen Douglas. But the first presidential debates, between Richard Nixon and John Kennedy, did not take place until 1960. (Interestingly, these debates are still the most vividly remembered.) Kennedy is generally seen as the winner because he exhibited "vigor" and youth and exuded great charisma, whereas Nixon appeared to be overcautious and a bit sneaky. (Nixon later complained that his makeup was incorrectly applied—a very important point.) The debates generally are credited with being the crucial factor in Kennedy's extremely narrow victory (we pass over the controversy concerning alleged chicanery in counting votes in Texas and Illinois), but not because his proposals and comments were any better than those of Nixon.

In all of the presidential debates so far, just as in the Nixon–Kennedy debates, it has been *image,* not reasoning or displays of intelligence or character, that has determined the winners. The 1988 debates between the first George Bush and Michael Dukakis illustrate this nicely. When Dukakis failed to respond with instant outrage to CNN commentator Bernard Shaw's famous question about what Dukakis would do if his wife were raped, his chances of winning the election pretty much flew out the window.

When neither candidate makes a gaffe and both seem well informed, the image or style they project is the deciding factor, as it was in the McCain/Obama debates. Barack Obama was judged the winner of all three debates (except on Fox News), not because he was more knowledgeable, but because he was cool, calm, and collected, no matter how provocative the attacks. Although John McCain took jabs at him for his (alleged) dubious political connections and wrongheaded economic policies, he failed to goad Obama into making any mistakes. Instead McCain seemed edgy, even angry at times, while Obama looked bemused and unflappable under attack. If anything, Obama was too controlled in all but the final debate, when he showed a little spark, but people responded to his measured responses and saw him as wise and presidential. His remarkable calm and confidence under intense pressure were some of the main reasons voters gave for electing him president. Image matters in the debates, no question, but for voters willing to look beyond the image, the debates do provide a good deal of substance, unlike campaign ads that hype the candidates but have no substance whatsoever.

Election Polls—A Special Case

Finally, no account of campaign rhetoric could be complete without mention of the role of polls in elections. No serious candidates for high office these days would open their mouths without having first tested the wind via polls. Whatever may be the case after they have won, when running for election, smart candidates make their pitches conform to what the polls indicate about voter sentiments and prejudices. During campaigns, at any rate, successful politicians generally are followers, not leaders. They waffle because they have to in order to get elected. It's always better to tell voters what they want to hear, not what the candidate genuinely intends to do if elected.

Of course, smart candidates also tailor their pitches to particular targeted audiences, often those who are undecided or already inclined to vote for them. Computer data on voter preferences make this information much more available than it was in the days when campaign aides thumbed through voter registration files to figure out likely supporters. Nowadays, software programs like Calipers Political Maptitude access files on census data, voter registration, and other pertinent records. Databases provide information on voters' magazine subscriptions, car purchases, charitable contributions, and consumer preferences that give both political parties the information to "microtarget" likely supporters and market their candidates and issues.[10] For example, direct-mail ads for health-care initiatives can be tailored to seniors and sent to AARP subscribers, issue advertising against tax cuts to the rich can be targeted to labor union members, and phone solicitations to boost voter turnout can be made to party supporters.

Polls tell candidates how to advertise; their media experts build campaigns in terms of what they learn from polls; blind advertising bit the dust a long time ago. In the 2008 campaign, for example, the polls gave advertisers information they needed to market their candidates to the small percentage of undecided voters who were considered so important in the campaign. To reach these voters, advertisers focused their efforts on ten or so swing states that could decide the election. As the campaigns heated up, some voters in these states got more than a dozen robocalls a day, that pounded away at poll-driven issues like the ailing economy, the failing housing market, and the Iraq War. But those who lived in the big states (like California, Texas, and New York) where the vote was predictable saw little if any advertising for the candidates.[11]

> *If politicians all told the truth, we'd be out of business.*
> —Talk show host Jay Leno (on *Larry King Live*)

---

[10]For more on this matter see "Where the Voters Are," by Holly Bailey, *Newsweek,* March 29, 2004.

[11]From an interview with Ken Goldstein, director of the Advertising Project at the University of Wisconsin, on the *Lehrer News Hour,* July 18, 2004.

Well, then, if virtually all political rhetoric is guided by expediency, why pay attention to it? If we can expect candidates to waffle, even to lie, why hear them out? The answer is that even waffling and lies can tell those of us who read between the lines a great deal about how candidates may perform if elected to office: Which sorts of lies they tell and what kinds of campaign promises they make tell us something about which groups and positions a candidate is likely to favor if elected. The promises made by Barack Obama, and his advocates during the presidential campaign were somewhat different from those made by John McCain and his advocates, because somewhat different constituencies were being appealed to.

Nevertheless, it is true in the political arena at least as much as anywhere else that actions speak louder than words. It has to be true that a candidate's past performance is almost always a better guide to future performance than is his or her political rhetoric. Smart viewers of the political scene always evaluate current political advertising in the light of past performance. So a sensible evaluation of political rhetoric requires us to bring to bear good background information (nothing new here). (The other key ingredient, aside from background information is, of course, the desire and attempt to be intellectually honest—to set aside prejudices of all kinds and come to fair, cogent evaluations.)

Noncampaign "Campaign" Rhetoric

Politicians don't just campaign via advertisements or after they have thrown their hats into the ring. Image building is a day-in, day-out task—indeed, in terms of time spent, perhaps a successful politician's principal task. Of course, for those holding high office, particularly for the leader of a nation, image building often coincides with ceremonial duties. At the start of the Gulf War, for example, the first President Bush was photographed going to church—symbolic of the seriousness of the step into war just taken—and evangelist Billy Graham was invited to spend the night with the Bush family in the White House. (Saddam Hussein prayed on camera nearly every day of that war in spite of being well known as a nonbeliever.) The second President Bush, who referred to the War on Terrorism as a crusade at one point, was photographed with all manner of religious figures from fundamentalist Christian delegates at the Southern Baptist convention to the pope in the Vatican. Candidates challenging incumbents don't have the opportunity to improve their images via ceremonial activities, one reason incumbents are hard to unseat.

Incumbents also have an advantage when it comes to garnering media coverage via press conferences. President Roosevelt was perhaps the first American president to exploit this kind of image-building opportunity, but the technique was perfected by President Kennedy, who, unlike Roosevelt, had television at his beck and call. Since Kennedy's time, presidential news conferences have generally been scheduled so as to gain the president free exposure on evening TV news programs. (President Carter arranged the Begin–Sadat Camp David agreement between Israel and Egypt so that the three leaders would sign on the dotted line and congratulate each other on television programs planned to have large national and international audiences.) Presidents are coached beforehand so that they have ready-made "answers" to all likely questions, and they rarely are forced into on-the-spot improvisations. (The same was true, of course, of the 2008 presidential and vice-presidential candidates' debates.)

Reprinted by permission of Paul Miller.

Typical politician at work.

Further Developments

The world does not stand still. New ways of doing things crop up now and then, mostly now these days.

Many years ago, virtually all political advertising was for candidates running for office. But with the advent of ballot initiatives and referendums—propositions put before voters for their direct decision—*issue advertising* entered the scene, and during the past few years it has become an extremely important kind of political advertising because voters in many states and localities now are regularly asked to decide all kinds of controversial issues. Interested parties now spend millions advertising their views on these measures. Philip Morris, for example, spent big bucks on a referendum measure that appeared to be antismoking but whose actual effect would have been to weaken existing antismoking legislation. (Unfortunately for Philip Morris, its originally concealed part in the campaign was revealed to the public, which then turned against the measure.) Another big change in political advertising stems from the increased ability of media experts to target specific audiences. This has enabled special interests to influence legislators indirectly by generating floods of letters and calls to their elected representatives.

Nowadays even wars are marketed to the public. The first Gulf War, generally thought to be the first war tailored for the mass media, was "branded" "Operation Desert Shield" much the way brand names are given to toothpaste or cereal. The second war, "Operation Iraqi Freedom," was promoted by state-of-the-art marketing techniques that launched the "conflict" (not the war) with "shock and awe" (instead of bombing), wrapped it in patriotism and morality (stressing good versus evil), and downplayed the ugly realities with euphemisms like "decapitation strategy " (for kill Saddam Hussein). War propaganda has a long history, of course, but current marketing savvy has raised it to new heights (or sunk it to new depths, depending on your point of view). We can only roll our eyes at the Alice-in-Wonderland approach to marketing wars displayed by Andrew Card (the second Bush's chief of staff) when he told the *New York Times* that the administration had waited until after Labor Day (2002) to make its case for military action in Iraq because "from a marketing point of view you don't introduce new products in August."

Some of the more important developments in political advertising are simply vastly increased and improved versions of methods employed for some time now. Campaigning on television shows such as *Larry King Live* is a case in point. Politicians have come to understand that TV and radio talk shows can be used for free and very effective exposure. Arnold Schwarzenegger, for example, outdid just about every candidate this way when he sold himself to voters almost exclusively on talk and entertainment shows. He kicked off his campaign by announcing his candidacy for governor of California on the Jay Leno show, then did an end run around the establishment media (newspapers and serious news programs) and plugged himself mainly on talk radio, entertainment shows, and televised daily events. His highly successful mass media blitz enabled him to create the image of a decisive, optimistic visionary without addressing detailed policies and programs that the establishment media usually demand.

The *interactive viewer opinion poll* has become increasingly popular in recent years. For example, a CNN phone-in poll instructed viewers that "If you think the economy is getting better, press one, then the pound sign. If you think the economy is getting weaker, press two and then the pound sign," and so on. Not exactly what could be considered a scientifically designed poll.

The great increase in negative telephone advertising that has occurred in the past few years is one of the more unfortunate recent developments in political advertising. The device itself is old, perhaps first being used on a large scale in 1946 when Richard Nixon first ran for Congress. A typical call in that telephone campaign went like this: "This is a friend of yours, but I can't tell you who I am. Did you know that Jerry Voorhis [Nixon's incumbent opponent] is a communist?" (Click.) Nothing much changes. Fast forward to the 2008 robocalls that accused Barack Obama of hanging out with terrorists and John McCain of voting to use unborn babies for medical research.

Political Ads on the Internet

Another development in political advertising, as in advertising in general, results from the dramatic increase in those who regularly surf the Net. Although television is still the mainstay for campaign advertising, the Internet is used more and more to target voters who visit websites in sync with the candidates' interests.[12] For example, in 2007 John McCain advertised on military.com, and Ron Paul campaigned on sites designed to attract libertarians.

---

[12]Examples taken from "Your Ad Here: Web Surprise Hits '08 Race," by Jim Rutenberg, *New York Times,* November 7, 2007.

But Internet campaigns are relatively new, and political strategists are learning the hard way how to promote them. When they use "ad networks" to target thousands of sites randomly, they sometimes land in hostile territory. "Mitt Romney for President—Join Team Mitt" appeared over 30,000 times for two days on gay.com, not exactly the ideal side for a candidate opposing same-sex marriage and homosexuals openly serving in the military. Banners for John McCain have mistakenly appeared on the liberal blog The Huffington Post, and ads for Rudy Giuliani on the another liberal blog, Daily Kos. Nonetheless, the benefits outweigh the dangers. The tremendous increase in the number of people who have access to computers has provided political advertisers with a cheap, quick way to marshal loyal troops for rallies and to raise money, generate talk show callers, and so on. Telephone solicitations and direct mailings are much more expensive and time-consuming than targeting websites.

Another development is that Internet users are generating their own ads. Until recently, political campaigns have controlled ads from the top down, but now that anyone can post ads on blogs or sites like YouTube; activists outside the structure can exert a powerful influence. The first such ad to make it big time in the 2008 presidential primary campaign was a remake of the classic 1984 ad introducing Apple Macintosh, but this one morphed into an attack on Hillary Clinton The remake (or "mash up" in computerese) shows a zombie-like audience seated in front of a wide screen on which Hillary Clinton, as Big Brother (or Sister), the ominous dictator in the novel *1984,* drones her message to the masses. From the back of the hall, a vigorous female athlete races down the aisle, swinging a sledge hammer that she hurls at the screen—obliterating Clinton. The Apple logo has morphed into an "O" and the name of "Barack Obama" appears beneath it, a symbol of the new generation. The implication is that vital young activists are ridding the country of the old guard that drones on and on, making empty promises. But beyond that is the real possibility that the average citizen can democratize the campaign process and have a greater impact on the political landscape than ever before. This ad, by the way, drew more than a million hits in less than a week.

The upshot of all the new ways to advertise is that the 30-second TV spots that played the major role in elections to high office during the previous 45 years or so have now become just one of several important devices used to influence the electorate (although still the most important). In 2008, tens of millions of Americans tuned in to at least one presidential debate, and at least that many heard candidates give their spiels on TV talk shows. What this electronic age has in store for us next is an interesting and exceedingly important question to which politicians and their media masters would very much like to know the answer. (So should we, so as to better defend ourselves against deceptive or emotively driven advertising.)

SUMMARY OF CHAPTER 10

1. Most ads can be divided into either of two groups. *Promise ads* promise to satisfy desires or allay fears. *Example:* Use Old Spice deodorant and get rid of body odor. *Identification ads* sell the product by getting us to identify with the product. *Example:* The Virginia Slims cigarette ads, "You've come a long way, baby," tailored to specific audiences.

2. Although ads provide us with useful information about products, often in an entertaining way, they also are designed to manipulate us via sophisticated ploys.
   a. They invite us to reason fallaciously. *Example:* Appeals to the authority of famous figures such as golf star Tiger Woods.
   b. They employ repetitive slogans and meaningless jargon. *Example:* "Nike: Just do it."
   c. They play on our weaknesses, prejudices, and fears. *Example:* The "ring around the collar" TV commercials.
   d. They use sneaky rhetoric, including fine-print disclaimers and weasel words. *Examples:* Using the word *free* when the product isn't free; weasely expressions like "fights bad breath."
   e. Ads draw on trendy issues. *Example:* The low-fat, low-sugar, low-salt, low-carb ads aimed at overweight Americans.
   f. They play on our patriotism, loyalty, and identification with members of our own group. *Example:* The ads wrapped in patriotism after September 11, 2001.
   g. They whitewash corporate imagery. *Example:* GE's "Singin' in the Rain" commercial designed to transform GE's image into an eco-friendly environment.

3. Although most ads hawk consumer goods, a few actually attempt to educate us and warn us against harmful activities. *Example:* The ads aimed at combating drug use in this country.

4. Old marketing techniques have been improved with new wrinkles, including new qualitative and quantitative procedures. *Example:* The Tennessee department store direct-mail ads based on in-store records of specific customer purchases.

   What the future holds is, of course, uncertain. *Example:* How will the latest Internet wrinkle, in which customers can see ads and immediately buy products with a few mouse clicks, ultimately play out?

5. Political candidates and issues are sold in pretty much the same way as any other products.
   a. In the age of television, elections are won or lost via exposure on the tube, whether in debates, paid 30-second TV spots, press conferences, or whatever. And it is *image,* not rationality, that often wins in this arena. *Examples:* The Daisy/Girl/Peace TV spot that portrayed Barry Goldwater as too trigger-happy to be trusted with the nuclear bomb button; Dukakis's "wimpy" response to Bernard Shaw's challenging question.

      It also should be noted that the campaign rhetoric of candidates running for high office generally is guided by the results of polls. It's always safer to tell voters what they want to hear, not what candidates intend to do if elected. That is why we can expect candidates to lie, exaggerate, or otherwise distort when necessary to curry the favor of voters. (But savvy voters still can learn from political rhetoric by reading between the lines and paying attention to past performance so as to figure out what candidates are likely to do if elected.)
   b. Politicians in a democracy "campaign" virtually all of the time, not just when actually running for office. They always have to be intent on projecting the

right *image* to the voters, and once in office, they have several standard ways of doing this. One is by performing the ceremonial duties of their office well; another is by holding press conferences.

c. Views on issues now are advertised just like candidates. The point is to influence voter preferences and thus legislation that is before Congress or state or local legislatures. *Examples:* Philip Morris's promotion of a referendum that would weaken existing antismoking laws.

d. The made-to-order TV spots that dominated campaigning during the past 45 years or so have received serious competition recently from TV talk shows that provide candidates with free exposure to mass audiences; prefabricated TV spots that save candidates tons of money; and interactive telephone polling of television audiences (with additional electronic campaigning marvels in the wings).

e. The Internet has become increasingly important in marketing politicians. Not only do campaigns advertise their candidates online, but Internet users generate their own ads, sometimes to huge audiences. *Example:* The remake of the Apple "Big Brother" ad targeting Hillary Clinton.

EXERCISE 10-5

Write two letters to one of your senators or representatives in Washington, D.C., in one taking a short, strong stand on an issue of importance to you, in the other taking an equally strong but different stand (completely opposite, if possible) on the same issue. Compare the two replies that you get. (Remember that you can't expect instantaneous replies.) Send each letter from a different address and use different names (because some members of Congress keep track on computers).

EXERCISE 10-6

Examine a political commercial for the visual effects, the pacing, and other nonverbal elements, and analyze how they either enhance a candidate's image or undermine it (in a negative ad).

EXERCISE 10-7

These days, the mass media (in particular, newspapers and magazines) spend a modest amount of time and effort covering and evaluating the political advertisements, especially TV spots, of candidates for high office. Look into some of this reporting; then (1) present and explain the content of at least two such analyses of advertisements for candidates in your state or locality; and (2) evaluate their accuracy and cogency.

EXERCISE 10-8

Recall Len Deighton's remark quoted on page 257 about straight teeth and blow-dried hair and consider what Andy Rooney had to say in his syndicated column (August 5, 1996) about what he called a candidate's "X-Factor"—what makes a person likeable.

Rooney noted that Eisenhower, Kennedy, and Reagan had it, whereas Johnson, Nixon, and Bush (the elder) did not, and he speculated that if Dole lost the 1996 election, it wouldn't be "because of any one stand he took on an issue. The loser will be the one who, for some unfathomable reason, appears least attractive [he meant in the sense of being likeable] to the American public. Never mind the issues."

Rooney meant to imply that the X-Factor goes much deeper than what can be manipulated by makeup artists. Do you agree? Is Rooney right that being liked by voters is frequently more important than differences over issues or past records in determining who wins elections? Do you think personality was crucial in the victory of George W. Bush over Al Gore and John Kerry? What about Barack Obama's over John McCain? Defend your opinions.

Exercise 10-9

Here is an excerpt from a syndicated political column by William Pfaff that appeared in newspapers around the country in March 1990 (still relevant today):

The Threat of Demagogic Oligarchy

Chicago—Pressure is mounting for campaign reform in American politics. Campaigning in cities like Chicago has always been rough, but now character assassination has become the privileged instrument of political ambition in national as well as local politics, excluding virtually all serious debate on issues. . . .

We are in fact witnessing the decline of American democracy towards a form of demagogic oligarchy. Individuals and groups with access to the vast sums now essential in American politics manipulate to their electoral advantage powerful images, some latently violent, some xenophobic.

. . . What prompts fear about what is happening in the United States is the general substitution of irrelevant emotional appeals for debate. More than half the population now fails to vote in national elections and there is a clear trend towards political alienation among those who do vote. Combine that with the mounting rates of illiteracy and general ignorance in the society and the substitution of manipulative oligarchy for representative democracy comes steadily closer.

For once there is a simple solution. It is possible, at a stroke, to solve the campaign money problem and deal a severe blow to demagogic image-manipulation. This solution is to prohibit political advertisements on television and radio. [Great Britain already does this.]

American political campaigns now are all but totally dominated by broadcast political advertising. The need to purchase time is responsible for the huge inflation of campaign costs in recent times. More than $250 million was spent on campaigns in the presidential year of 1988. Half a billion in current dollars will be spent during House and Senate campaigns in the 1990s. [The figures for 1992, 1994, and 1996 were much higher than for 1988 and 1990 and well over 1 billion for 2000, 2004, and 2008.]

The need for money to pay for advertising has made the single-issue political action committee the most powerful actor in American politics. It has made it all but impossible for an incumbent congressman or senator successfully to be challenged: the incumbent gets the PAC money because he can deliver what the PAC wants. Support for a challenger is speculation.

   . . . No other serious democracy tolerates this. Virtually nowhere else is paid campaign advertising permitted. Ours is a mad system, perversely American, jeopardizing democracy itself. Banning advertising will hurt only the broadcasters. They are a powerful lobby, and one that politicians rightly fear, but even broadcasters not obsessed with their private interest must recognize the gravity of the situation.[13]

1. Summarize the part of Pfaff's column that explains his view as to what the problem is.

2. State his proposal to solve this problem in your own words.

3. State whether you agree or disagree with him about there being the problem that he describes. Explain.

4. Critically evaluate his solution.

In this drawing, David Levine pictures the television-viewing audience as contented sheep. Do you agree?

When covering the Capitol, the first thing to remember is that every government is run by liars.

—I. F. Stone

Freedom of the press is guaranteed only to those who own one.

—A. J. Liebling

Has any reader found perfect accuracy in the newspaper account of any event of which he himself had inside knowledge?

—Edward Verrall Lucas

Journalists separate the wheat from the chaff . . . and then print the chaff.

—Adlai Stevenson

I really look with commiseration over the great body of my fellow citizens who, reading newspapers, live and die in the belief that they have known something of what has been passing in the world during their time.

—Harry S Truman

The Press, like the public, has room in its brain for only one story at a time.

—E. L. Doctorow

People who read tabloids deserve to be lied to.

—Jerry Seinfeld

If Abraham Lincoln wanted to make a point today, he would deliver the Gettysburg Sound Bite.

—Bob Greene

Chapter

11

MANAGING THE NEWS

The news media is going through a huge transformation now, comparable to what it went through with the advent of television. For the past several years, Project for Excellence in Journalism[1] has been tracking and analyzing significant trends and changes in the industry. Technological advances like the Internet have created new ways for people to access the news, and as a result, traditional news outlets are shrinking. Newspaper

---

[1]For a detailed analysis of emerging trends see "The State of the News Media; An Annual Report on American Journalism" (2007–2008), by Project for Excellence in Journalism, journalism.org.

circulation has spiraled downward, network news has lost about a million viewers each year for the past 25 years, cable news audiences dropped about 12 percent in 2006 alone, and in the same year even the number of users who go online for the news stopped growing. In fact, all media outlets except radio and the ethnic press have dropped in popularity.

The reasons for this are complex, and the outcomes are unclear so far. One important factor is the economics involved. For the past century, newspapers have been financed mainly by advertising, but with the growth of advertising on the Internet and the shift in classified ads to free sites like Craigslist, income from these sources is drying up. As a consequence, major investors are reluctant to finance newsrooms adequately, and large cuts in staff are inevitable. A good example is the downward spiral of the *Los Angeles Times*—one of the best newspapers in the country—whose newsroom has shrunk to half its size since its sale to the Tribune Company of Chicago in 2000, causing three top-flight editors in succession to lose their jobs for refusing to make further cuts. (Ironically, although Hollywood is in its back yard, it has only one movie reviewer left on the staff.) Even the *New York Times,* with its huge newsroom staff of over 1,300, cut 100 jobs in 2008.

These staff reductions, occurring in newsrooms across the country, have had a major impact on gathering the news. Since technology companies like Yahoo, AOL, and Google do little if any news gathering, the main source of the news is still the newsroom, which generates the stories that eventually appear on the Internet. Other news sources, like bloggers or "citizen journalists" (nonprofessionals), have neither the news gathering capacity nor usually the expertise of professional journalists. To counter this decline in income and drop in audiences, news outlets are groping for ways to reinvent themselves, some of which will be discussed in this chapter.

New trends in journalism require us to be even more vigilant in thinking critically about the way the news is managed and presented to the public.The good news is that there is more and better news out there than ever before in history. The bad news is that not all of the more is better. The trick is to know how to separate the wheat from the chaff and, thinking of the remark, above, by Adlai Stevenson, concentrating on the wheat. (Another bit of bad news is that masses of people pay more attention to news schlock than to news pearls.)

1. THE MEDIA AND THE POWER OF MONEY

In France, the expression is "Cherchez la femme" (find the woman). In America, at any rate, and perhaps in France and just about everywhere, a more apt expression would be "follow the money."

The Power of the People

Despite the decrease in popularity of media news, the chief sources of news for most people these days are still the mass media—ABC, CNN, Fox, *Time* magazine, the *Boston Globe,* and their cohorts. And the one overriding fact about these news sources is that they are businesses. They exist to make money. They sell a product and we buy it. Or we don't, in which case they go out of business. This means that we, the viewers of television programs, listeners to the radio, and readers of newspapers and magazines, have the most important say as to what sorts of news stories are reported in the mass media and how they are presented. That is why, for instance, the mass media so often play up relatively unimportant events while slighting more important ones—most people tend to be more interested in certain kinds of relatively trivial goings-on than in extremely important events. A case in point is the low priority often given to foreign news (unless, of course, the United States is involved, as in the Iraq War). Since the news is now driven by ratings and foreign news ranks low in public interest, foreign coverage has been slashed in the past decade by up to two-thirds, some media watchdogs estimate.

Item: During the week when the *New York Times* reported that al Qaeda was building a hub for terrorist operations in a mountainous tribal area of northern Pakistan, the mass media was obsessing over Britney Spear's sheared head, Jennifer Aniston's nose job, and the life and death of Anna Nicole Smith.

Large audiences also tend to be quite provincial, so the mass media concentrate on national affairs and home-grown celebrities, slighting news events from other countries.

Item: U.S. coverage of the 2008 Olympics in Beijing featured American athletes like Michael Phelps, while slighting those from other countries. Certainly Phelps deserved accolades for winning eight gold medals in swimming, a truly impressive world record. But the U.S. media paid scant attention to the string of gold medals (seven out of eight) won by China's superb diving team. (You can bet the Chinese media made much of it, though.) This kind of provincialism is common in all countries.

Similarly, because mass audiences are more interested in light-hearted material, human interest stories, and fantasy than in hardheaded reality, human interest also tends to crowd out more important matters.

As mentioned in Chapter 6, large numbers of people are superstitious or believe in pseudosciences of one kind or another, and we all are wishful thinkers to some degree. That is why many TV programs feature so many more pseudoscience programs than they do those concerning genuine science.

NBC and the Fox network are probably the worst TV networks when it comes to showing pseudoscientific and other fantasy junk programs. Fox, for example, pandered to audience interest in the supernatural with its April 2000 two-part series "Ghosts: Best Evidence Caught on Tape" and "UFOs: Best Evidence Caught on Tape." Even CNN gets into the act with *Larry King Live,* which often features psychics and other pseudoscientific offerings. King's uncritical presentation of spiritualists is particularly troubling because his impressive stature as a journalist gives credence to their claims.

Calvin and Hobbes © Watterson. Reprinted with permission of Universal Press Syndicate. All rights reserved.

> *Columnist Bob Herbert had this to say about Neil Postman's well-known 1985 warning that we were amusing ourselves to death.*
>
> ---
>
> More than 20 years later, the masses have nearly succeeded in drawing the curtains on anything that's not entertaining. No one can figure out what [to] do about Iraq or Al Qaeda. A great American cultural center like New Orleans was all but washed away, and no one knows how to put it back together. The ice caps are melting and Al Gore is traveling the land like the town crier, raising the alarm about global warming
>
> But none of that has *really* gotten the public's attention. None of it is amusing enough.
>
> —"From Anna to Britney to Zawahri,"
> *New York Times,* February 22, 2007

He regularly interviews political leaders and heads of state like Bill Clinton, Vladimir Putin, and George Bush on CNN—the network that bills itself as the "most trusted name in news." So, when mediums like John Edward and Sylvia Browne get the same kind of coverage, with little or no critical perspective to counter their claims, gullible viewers are more likely taken in by their paranormal shenanigans than if they appeared on an entertainment network like Sci Fi.[2]

It's also true that the mass media pander to the extremely short attention spans of so many people in their mass audiences.

Item: Shorter and shorter sound bites have become the mainstay of all network daily news programs. In 1968, sound bites lasted a mere 40 seconds on average. By 1988, they had shrunk to an average of 10 seconds. Nothing, absolutely nothing, of any consequence can be dealt with in 40 seconds, much less in 10. The current trend is even worse. News coverage of election campaigns from 1992–2004 used significantly more image bites than sound bites. Nowadays we watch candidates more than we listen to them. It is true, though, that the news on PBS is presented in modestly larger and somewhat more sophisticated chunks, but PBS audiences are minuscule compared to those of the major networks. (Some news programs on NPR—National Public Radio—tend to be a bit more detailed and sophisticated and are the best source of news on the radio or TV.)

The Power of Advertisers

The media are beholden not just to the people, as just mentioned, but also to advertisers. Advertising revenue is the most important source of income for virtually all newspapers and magazines and also the principal source for television stations and TV networks.

---

[2]For more on this see "King of the Paranormal," by Chris Mooney, *Skeptical Inquirer,* November/December 2003.

This Modern World by Tom Tomorrow. © 1991 Tom Tomorrow.
Reprinted by permission of Dan Perkins.

Exaggeration used to make a serious point about local news coverage on TV.

Since money translates into power, the media must cater to the interests of advertisers as well as to those of the general public. Commenting on this fact years ago, H. G. Wells, in his classic *Outline of History,* remarked:

> [T]hose fathers of America thought also that they had but to leave the Press free, and everyone would live in the light. They did not realize that a free press could develop a sort of constitutional venality due to its relations with advertisers, and that large newspaper proprietors could become buccaneers of opinion and insensate wreckers of good beginnings.

Wells would not be a bit surprised at the way things have been going on the tube.

But the main problem with advertising now is that it is drying up, as noted earlier in this chapter. Print journalism is particularly hard hit, now that advertising has shrunk, and classified ads—a big source of income in the past—have moved to free sites on the Internet. Online advertising on journalism sites has not lived up to its promise because marketers have learned that people surf the web for products and services much as they use the Yellow Pages, and so are less likely to be swayed by conventional ads that pop up on newspaper and magazines sites. Since over 90 percent of the revenue for the newspaper industry comes from print editions, not online sites, the industry is having a hard time staying solvent. Television news is the one medium that manages to support itself from advertising, despite decreasing audiences, because TV ads are still the most persuasive way to sell a product. So advertisers still make their power felt despite the downturn in the market.

However, the 30-second commercial doesn't have the appeal it used to, they are using more subtle ploys, like product placement and "news releases." One company, Citizens Bank, persuaded the venerable *Philadelphia Inquirer* to let it sponsor (that is, pay for) a column emblazoned with their green Citizens Bank banner. Although the *Inquirer's* editor had qualms about renting out editorial space to an advertiser, he promised that the newspaper staff would have "complete independent control" of the column. Well, maybe.

Another way the media caters to advertisers is by suppressing news that reflects badly on them or their products and by touting advertisers' products free as "new" items. When an editor for *The Pioneer Press* (publisher of many papers in suburban Chicago) ran a review critical of a restaurant that advertised in the *Press,* she was told by higher-ups that the paper was "not in the business of bashing business." A while later, a favorable review of the same restaurant was written by someone in the marketing division—not a journalist (*Extra!,* May/June 2004).

The Power of Government

Government has the right and often the power to regulate business activity. It thus can harass a news agency by being strict about the rules it sets up (it usually isn't) and the licenses it requires. The mere threat of government action has a "chilling" effect on the media. It is true, of course, that the U.S. Constitution guarantees freedom of the press as one of several freedoms necessary to make a representative government function. And various Supreme Court decisions provide added protection for the press. For instance, our laws protect journalists against libel suits, particularly by government workers, and against government censoring in advance anything the media want to report, except certain kinds of classified information. But more important, the media are free to advocate controversial, even dangerous ideas, like overthrowing the government—a freedom allowed in almost no other country.

Despite these legal protections, the government has ways of restricting the freedom of the press and has done so with increasing regularity since September 11, 2001. Just about every administration tries to muzzle the media in one way or another, and the Bush administration is no exception. William Bennett Turner, attorney and constitutional scholar, noted some of the ploys it used in the service of the "war" on terrorism.[3] Soon

---

[3]For more on this see Turner's informative article, "Assault on Press Freedom," *San Francisco Chronicle,* November 26, 2006.

after the attack on the World Trade Center, Attorney General John Ashcroft issued a directive to federal agencies that they could restrict access to government records under the Freedom of Information Act if an agency had any arguable basis for doing so. This ruling, in effect, often blocked journalists from getting information on controversial issues that they were previously entitled to. Another ploy the Justice Department used was to hold secret hearings on, for instance, the deportation of Muslim immigrants, which prevented the press from attending or even knowing that the meetings took place. Thus, under the guise of maintaining national security, the government also is able to keep all sorts of chicanery secret.

But government censorship doesn't end with classified information. Administrations can, and often do, suppress information that doesn't conform to their political agenda. For example, when Dr. Richard Carmona, the former surgeon general in the Bush administration, testified before a congressional oversight committee in 2007, he made the startling revelation that political appointees censored his speeches and prevented him from expressing his views on comprehensive sex education, emergency contraception, and the science on stem cell research—among other things. Two other former surgeon generals testified as well about the political interference of presidents they served under, but nothing approached the constraints placed on Dr. Carmona, who not only had to manipulate scientific information to suit the political landscape, but was ordered to mention President Bush's name three times on every page of his reports!

Governments have other ways of managing the news. One way is to censor material alleged to be obscene, which is not covered by the First Amendment. The problem comes in trying to determine legally what is obscene. The FCC sidesteps this issue by levying fines and revoking licenses, not by censoring material. In recent years the FCC has raised its fines considerably for obscenity and indecency. CBS was fined $550,000 after Janet Jackson's breast was famously bared during her halftime Super Bowl performance in 2004 with Justin Timberlake (who euphemistically called it a "wardrobe malfunction"). Later that year Clear Channel paid a whopping $1.7 million for indecency charges, mostly against Howard Stern for a graphic on-air exchange with a caller, and against deejay Ted Clem (Bubba the Love Sponge) for sexual material aired over a three-month period. With fines this hefty, the media quickly come into line. Clear Channel fired Clem, dropped Stern from all six channels that ran his show, and instituted a zero tolerance policy for indecent and obscene content.

Once in a while, common sense prevails, and the court overturns petty rulings against the media. For instance, the FCC threatened Fox Broadcasting with substantial fines when Nicole Richie let fly with a coarse comment at an awards ceremony aired by Fox. The agency made the unconvincing argument that "fleeting expletives" (FCC-talk for spur-or-the-moment obscenities) could not be separated from the sexual or excretory meaning. The court struck down this ruling, noting that the president and vice president had made similar slips of the lip that clearly had no such offensive meaning. In this instance, the media won out, but now that the Supreme Court has taken up the case, the decision may be reversed.

Government officials also can, and do, manipulate the news by playing favorites among reporters, leaking only to those news people who play ball in return. Since leaks are such a large source of media information (see the discussion of news-gathering practices a few pages forward), reporters have to think twice before crossing their government informants. Similarly, reporters have to be careful in press conferences not to ask embarrassing questions or follow-up questions; those who are too brash or persistent don't get called on in future. In the early days of the Iraq War, two reporters from the Knight Ridder chain wrote a series of articles expressing skepticism that weapons of mass destruction were the real reason for going to war. Their analyses never ran in the mainstream media, which was pro-war at that time, but *Editor and Publisher* (May 23, 2007) reported that the Pentagon spotted the articles and barred the reporters from the defense secretary's plane for "at least three years" because of their critical coverage.

Although many items leaked to the media are on target, the fact that their sources can be concealed gives government officials a good deal of power. They can rig stories to serve their own interest without being accountable. But if sensitive material is leaked that the government does not want released, it can, and often does, threaten reporters with criminal prosecution unless they reveal their sources. If reporters comply, however, they lose their credibility and their sources dry up, so they almost always refuse to cooperate. Since there is no federal shield law as of this writing that allows reporters to protect their sources (though some states have such laws), many reporters have been subpoenaed to reveal their sources before grand juries, and some have been convicted for failing to do so. The most famous recent case involved former *New York Times* reporter Judith Miller, who refused to identify her source in the "Scooter" Libby trial (for a story she never even published) and served three months in prison. With a jail threat hanging over their heads, reporters may well be deterred from using controversial, confidential sources.

Another way the government manages the news is by issuing prepackaged reports that can be slipped into 90-second slots in the local news. Presidents Clinton and Bush both used this ploy to get their messages out or to put a positive spin on the news, packaging it as though it came from traditional reporting. The Bush administration hyped all kinds of policies from regime change in Iraq to Medicare reform, often featuring government officials with scripted answers to scripted questions without any critical overview or comments. This covert propaganda, broadcast around the country without citing government as its source, is on the rise now that the news media are on the skids, and news staffs are shrinking.

A failed attempt to rig the news on a grand scale occurred during the Iraq War when the Pentagon developed the short-lived Office of Strategic Influence designed to modify views about the United States in other countries. As the *New York Times* reported (February 19, 2003), the idea was to develop plans ". . . to provide news items, possibly even false ones, to foreign media organizations as part of a new effort to influence public sentiment and policy makers in both friendly and unfriendly countries," according to military officials. This Orwellian attempt at disinformation came to an abrupt end before it got off the ground. Nonetheless, it is just one of many attempts to manage the news. The military and the State Department have long conducted various kinds of information warfare, ranging from factual press releases to outright lies.

Of course, no U.S. government agencies have censoring powers that are anywhere near those regularly exercised in quite a few foreign countries. In China, Myanmar (Burma), Liberia, and many other countries, newspapers rarely are allowed to criticize governmental policies or actions. (At the start of the October 2000 uprising in Yugoslavia that toppled the regime of dictator Slobodan Milosovic, TV viewers in foreign countries around the world were shown films of mass demonstrations and the burning of the Parliament Building in Belgrade, but at the same time state-controlled TV featured a classical music concert, as though nothing whatever was happening in

This Modern World by Tom Tomorrow. © 1991 Tom Tomorrow.
Reprinted by permission of Dan Perkins.

the streets a few blocks away, until protestors took over the Belgrade TV station and broadcast the news to the citizens of their own country.)

Worse still, reporters in dangerous countries are often threatened, even murdered, in the line of duty. In 2003, Daniel Pearl, a *Wall Street Journal* reporter, was kidnapped in Karachi by a group called the National Movement for the Restoration of Pakistan while he was working on a story about the Islamic military underground. Repeated efforts to rescue him failed and eventually his captors beheaded him, claiming, among other things, that he was an agent for the CIA and (later) for the Massad, the Israeli intelligence agency.[4]

From the start of the Iraq War to March 2008, 177 journalists and media support workers were killed on duty as a result of hostile action, according to the Committee to Protect Journalists (CPJ). During the same period 50 journalists were abducted, 12 of them murdered, and 5 were still in captivity. The CPJ website gives descriptions of each abduction and death, citing in grizzly detail the signs of torture (like body bruises and broken fingers), the gunshot wounds, and the beheadings. A quick look at this website is enough to deter any aspiring journalist from working as a foreign correspondent in hostile territory.[5]

---

[4]A riveting film, *A Mighty Heart,* follows Pearl's wife, Marianne, as she searches for her kidnapped husband.
[5]See "Iraq: Journalists in Danger" (www.cpj.org) for more data and grizzly details.

The Power of the Media

The media are not simply beholden to the three powerful groups just discussed. They themselves are a genuinely separate power faction. This is particularly true of the mass media: television, major newspapers and magazines, and so forth. Investigative reporters can, and sometimes do, unearth governmental chicanery as well as stories not in the best interests of advertisers, although we have gone to some pains to show why they often hesitate.

This doesn't mean that the media constitute a monolithic, organized group but, rather, that individual mass media organizations have a certain amount of power and that, taken as a whole, the mass media have great power and frequently common interests. Cases such as the *Washington Post* Watergate exposés, which set in motion events that drove Richard Nixon from office, are well known. Going back even further to the Vietnam War, the press turned the tide of public opinion when journalists began reporting that the chaos and destruction they witnessed on the battlefield was nothing like the official upbeat version. This may seem like ancient history, but it set an important precedent that continues to this day (with notable exceptions, like the media's failure to question the Bush administration's rationale for the Iraq War).[6]

During and after World War II, the press rarely questioned the judgment or truthfulness of our military leaders, but as the Vietnam War churned on, journalists became disillusioned with the war and its leaders when they saw what was really happening on the ground. They wrote about it forcefully and photographed it graphically. These reports were so upsetting that President Kennedy tried to persuade certain major newspapers to pull outspoken reporters out of Saigon. (Presidents Nixon and Johnson used similar tactics.) Future administrations learned from this experience that if they let journalists roam the battlefields unescorted, the news coverage might be very bad indeed, so they herded reporters into supervised "pools" during the Gulf War and embedded them in military units during the Iraq War.

But controlling access to the action in Iraq and imposing other official restraints didn't succeed in muzzling the media once they got over their initial patriotic fervor. Just as they had in Vietnam, reporters started filing gritty dispatches about car bombings, assassinations, rampant militias, and failed politics. And just as previous administrations had tried to control the press in Vietnam, the Bush administration fought back, excluding some reporters from official briefings, refusing others the chance to embed, classifying a mountain of material as top secret, and serving up its own optimistic version of the war. The media didn't cave in, however, and became probably the single most influential force in turning Americans against the war. For better or for worse, the media wields immense power in swaying public opinion.

Of course, one media giant's power has to compete with that of the others. CBS's power to determine what will be shown on its network programs is held in check by the identical power wielded by NBC, ABC, Fox, CNN, and the rest of its competitors, not to mention competitors in the print media, just as the power of one politician may be reduced by the power of others and by the power of the media. Vive le competition!

---

[6]For more on this see "A Skeptical Vietnam Voice Still Echoes in the Fog of Iraq," by Dexter Filkins, *New York Times,* April 25, 2007.

Comedy Central's Stephen Colbert skewered the media in this satiric send-up at the annual White House Correspondent's dinner (quoted in Extra! Update, *June 2006).*

Here's how it works: The president makes decisions. He's the decider. The press secretary announces those decisions, and you people of the press type those decisions down. Make, announce, type. Just put'em through a spell check and go home. Get to know your family again. Make love to your wife. Write that novel you got kicking around in your head. You know, the one about the intrepid Washington reporter with the courage to stand up to the administration. You know—fiction!

Needless to say, the press was not amused.

Every country has its own influential media, of course. A good case in point, given our current involvement in the Mideast, is the increasing importance of the media in the Arab world. Probably the most influential network in that area is Al-Jazeera, established in 1996 by the British-educated, progressive emir of Qatar. The network reaches over 35 million people and is reputed to have as much power as the *New York Times*. In an analysis of the network, two U.S. academics explained how the coverage of controversial issues in the Arab world revolutionized the way Arabs think about themselves and others.[7] Previously, the media were controlled either by Arab governments or by companies kowtowing to government interest. But Al-Jazeera changed all that. By featuring interviews and talk shows with open-air debates on provocative issues ranging from the role of secularism to human rights abuses under Arab regimes, the network has had a profound influence on the Middle East. Arab networks, in general, had a strong global impact during the Iraq War as well. Media around the world used footage from Al-Jazeera and other Arab stations that gave a much different perspective from the coverage by networks in the United States and other countries. As might be expected, the graphic footage of wounded soldiers and civilians, a staple of Al-Jazeera, has been highly controversial in this country and strongly criticized by the Bush administration.

The Power of Big Business

The days are long gone when most business in countries like the United States was conducted by individuals or small organizations. "Ma and pa" stores have given way to Wal-Marts and Safeways. Individual doctors hanging out their shingles have been replaced by group practices and HMOs. Most family farms have been replaced by huge agribusinesses. These days, virtually all industries are controlled by large corporations—in particular, by huge multinational conglomerates. Large corporations,

---

[7]*Al-Jazeera: How the Arab News Network Scooped the World,* by Mohammed El-Nawaway and Adel Iskandar (Boulder, Colo.: Westview Press, 2002).

individually and collectively, thus have great power, which they exercise almost exclusively in the interests of maximizing their own profits.

Corporate power affects the dissemination of news in two ways: first, by getting the viewpoints of big business reported favorably in the mass media; second, by preventing conflicting viewpoints from being reported or stressed. This censoring power of large corporations stems in part from their power as advertisers (a point already discussed). Large corporations, after all, are by far the largest advertisers in the mass media. But it also stems from the power money has in the political arena (a point to be discussed later). When the mass media cooperate with political power, they thus indirectly also cooperate with large corporate interests. Furthermore, the mass media themselves have become controlled in large part by very large media conglomerates, which often are parts of even larger corporate structures (a point also to be discussed shortly). In general, the interests of media conglomerates coincide with those of other large businesses—for example, in favoring lower wages for on-the-line employees—so that the mass media tend to have a built-in bias in favor of big business. (Interestingly, many conservative commentators regularly accuse the media of having a left-wing bias.)

The result is that news and opinion in the mass media tend to be skewed strongly to the interests of the rich rather than ordinary citizens or the poor. Ordinary people, of course, also have great power in determining how the mass media portray the world— they can switch channels or otherwise tune out. They also can go to non–mass media news and opinion sources (yes, these will be discussed shortly), but most people do not do so, one reason being that the average person does not understand how the news is slanted in the interests of those with great political power.[8] (Another reason is that large numbers of people—in particular, those in the lower half of the economic pecking order—tend to concentrate on their own personal lives and problems and to be inattentive when it comes to the important economic and political issues of the wider community, even though a good deal of what happens in their lives is seriously influenced by what happens in the broader social arena.)

However, when the economy slides into a recession—as it has recently—when people lose their jobs, foreclosures multiply, and retirement funds dwindle, the media pay attention, particularly in an election year. As the recession deepened in 2008, both John McCain and Barack Obama made the economy the centerpiece of their campaigns, larding their speeches with examples of ordinary people suffering in hard times. The media, of course, covered these speeches and added feature articles of their own, much as they did when Hurricane Katrina nearly wiped New Orleans off the map and decimated its residents. In times of disaster the economic plight of the average person does make the news, but not nearly as much as the plight of huge corporations that went bankrupt, like Lehman Brothers, or mega-banks that needed billions of taxpayer dollars to bail them out. When the economy returns to normal, the little guy and his financial woes disappear from the news again.

---

[8]The idea is widespread in America that there are no classes in the land of the free and the home of the brave. The truth in this idea is that in every generation some individuals move from lower into higher economic classes, even occasionally into the highest. The falsehood in this idea is that most of those born into rich families remain rich, and most of those born into average- or lower-income households never become rich. Class membership in large industrial democracies is not carved in stone in the way it was in the monarchies of old, but this surely does not mean that there are any truly classless societies on this planet, other than in tiny hunting-and-gathering groups.

Have you ever noticed that the heads of labor unions frequently are referred to as "union bosses" but that expressions like "big business bosses" or "the boss of XYZ corporation" are almost never used in the mass media? Big business bosses go under nice labels like "CEO" and "President."

Item: Most big city dailies have "business" sections that report the goings-on of large corporations and of the various financial markets—almost exclusively from the point of view of investors and other large money interests. But no daily newspapers have labor sections or report on business from the point of view of individual workers or, except on occasion, organized labor. Similarly, several business news programs are aired on TV during the day (when MSNBC is devoted almost exclusively to stock market goings-on), but no labor programs or programs regularly reporting from the point of view of ordinary workers. (But consider the fact that a majority of daytime TV audiences prefer to watch the soaps, sports news, and sitcom reruns. How then could a labor channel be a paying proposition?)

Item: When labor union stories are reported in the press they often have a negative slant. For example, a ten-year study of labor coverage (1991–2001) in the *Chicago Tribune,* conducted by Robert Bruno, of the University of Illinois, revealed that 77 percent of the descriptive language used to characterize labor was negative. In articles about labor disputes, 95.3 percent of the descriptors were negative and less than one story a year focused on unions improving working conditions. Interestingly, the most extensive coverage of labor relations was about player unions in the sports section, but more than three-quarters of these stories were negative in tone as well. The study concluded that the paper had an anti-union bias and that both the workers and their leaders were negatively characterized. The findings are a reflection of the fact that media sympathy for labor, once strong in big cities, has slowly evaporated. There may be a revival, though, now that the plight of the working class in a recession has hit the news.

One of the few labor disputes to make big news in recent years was the Writers Guild of America strike in 2007 against the powerful Alliance of Motion Picture and Television Producers. Union members held out for an increased share of lucrative DVD and digital revenues (which typically wind up in the pockets of the big stars, directors, and producers). Most strikes get minimal coverage, but this one got more publicity, partly because it had the glitzy appeal of a Hollywood drama. When movie stars like Ben Stiller and Robin Williams join the picket lines, they get the media's attention. And, of course, since journalists are writers too, they are more likely to sympathize with the cause.

Item: One segment of society given short shrift in the media is the poor people in our country.[9] One in eight Americans (37 million) live below the federal poverty line, defined in 2005 as roughly $20,000 a year for a family of four, and the poorest group is children, who number more than one in six. Yet the media coverage of poverty is a blip on the radar except during holidays and times of disaster (like Hurricane Katrina). A study conducted by the media watchdog FAIR revealed that the three major networks

---

[9]See "A Poverty of Coverage" and "The Poor Will Always Be With Us" in *Extra!* September/October 2007, for an excellent analysis of the problem.

(ABC, NBC, CBS) aired 58 stories about poverty over a 38-month period (from 2003–2006), a drop in the bucket compared to the 69 stories about Michael Jackson's legal problems during the same period. Journalists who were questioned about the low priority of poverty stories said it's not very compelling, and more to the point, not good for business. Advertisers don't like stories that are downers and put people off shopping. It is worth noting that during our recent major recession the media covered the plight of the working class, retirees, and other members of the middle class, but little mention was made of the very poor.

Power Tends to Cooperate with Power

Although the interests of big business and government often coincide with those of the media, sometimes they do not. Scandals may sell newspapers and increase TV news audiences, but they also tend to sink political careers. What is bad for Microsoft may be good for CNN. (But see the section at the end of this chapter on recent trends!)

In a majority of cases, however, it's better for the various power factions to cooperate rather than to fight. That is why, for instance, reporters covering the White House quickly learn which sorts of questions can be asked at presidential press conferences, how far follow-up queries can go, what sorts of editorial comments they can make in news reports, and the like. Journalists who don't play the game, who persist in challenging the standard self-serving replies to their questions, don't get called upon in the future. Columnists who tear into an administration in Washington with a great deal of gusto are less likely to receive leaks or other tidbits.

Talk show hosts with guests who bash the government suffer as well. For example, when Phil Donahue interviewed a number of antiwar, anti-Bush guests, his show was abruptly cancelled in February 2003. An internal NBC memo leaked later that month (on All Your TV website) revealed that the network was concerned that Donahue presented "a difficult public face for NBC in time of war" and that the show could be "a home for the liberal anti-war agenda at the same time that our competitors are waving the flag at every opportunity."[10]

Of course, when the interests of politicians or big business moguls happen to coincide with those of the masses, coverage of interesting or important events will be automatic, perhaps even large-scale.

> *Example:* This is especially true in time of war, particularly when the media and the government cooperate, as they did in the Iraq War. Partly in response to severe press restrictions during the Gulf War, the second George Bush's administration decided to "embed" reporters with the troops. They were sent to media boot camp, trained in military behavior, and shipped off to Iraq, where they were assigned to military units around the country. These embedded journalists gave up-close coverage of the war with plenty of human interest stories about men and women in battle for the folks back home. The interests of the media, the government, and the public converged in this riveting event. (An ongoing event that is newsworthy is the dream of everyone in the news business.)

---

[10]Quoted in "Dissent Unwelcome in Wartime," *Extra!*, May/June 2004.

It's true that, in practice, the system does not work in precisely this way every time. There is slippage due to inefficiency and to the fact that middle-class interest is worth more (to advertisers, for instance) than is that of the poor, coupled with the fact that it takes lots of audience interest to overcome serious political opposition. The media will generally buck political power only when buttressed by support from very large numbers of people or by competing powerful forces. But when all or most power blocks line up and the public is perceived to be receptive, the media will go for broke and public opinion will be moved.

News as Entertainment

For all the reasons discussed so far, the news has increasingly become a source of entertainment more than an information source. Because money is the bottom line, because vested interests like big business and government shape the news to their advantage, and because the public wants entertainment more than information, news items tend to morph into Hollywood action stories. A good example is the saga of Jessica Lynch that dominated human-interest stories during the Iraq War. True, her story was hard to beat, crafted as it was into a hair-raising thriller. Small town girl joins the Army, winds up in Iraq where she is injured in battle, suffers multiple fractures, and becomes a prisoner of war. Freed in a rescue mission eerily filmed by the military, she becomes a national hero, receives the Purple Heart, the Bronze Star, and the POW medal, and lands a million-dollar book deal. The public lapped up her story, despite the inconsistencies that surfaced. No, she really didn't empty her gun firing on Iraqi soldiers as was originally reported. Her gun was jammed and she fell on her knees in prayer. Her captors tried to return her to the Americans before the rescue mission, but were fired on by U.S. troops who mistook them for invaders. Her story unfolded in the media like a riveting sitcom, transforming her into a symbol of the war, which to her credit, she apparently found embarrassing and wrong-headed.

Years later, in her testimony before the House Oversight and Government Reform Committee in 2007, she said, "the story of little girl Rambo from the hills who went down fighting" was untrue. She never fired a shot. When the committee chair asked if she was aware that her rescue was put off a day so that arrangements could be made to videotape the event, she said she didn't hear about it until much later. "I'm still confused as to why they chose to lie and make me a legend," she said, "when the real heroics of my fellow soldiers that day were, in fact, legendary."[11] One reason, of course, was to hype battlefield heroism and play up the war. But another reason was that the American people wanted a hero—and they got one in Jessica Lynch, however manufactured the story was. Stories like this, played up by the media and skewed by vested interests, glamorized the war and overshadowed the day-to-day activities.

The war itself was filmed like a TV movie, starting with the buildup of tension for months in advance. Anticipation grew as we learned that journalists embedded with the troops would cover the war as it really was. Once the action began, we watched bombs bursting in air and cruse missiles toppling tall buildings. We saw victorious American troops marching across Iraq into Baghdad, and along the way journalists reported from

---

[11]Quoted in "Lynch Calls Tales of Her Heroics Lies," *San Francisco Chronicle,* April 23, 2007.

the battlefield, with gunfire in the background and troops on the attack. As Peter Arnett commented on NBC, "An amazing sight, just like an action movie, but this is real."[12]

The news as entertainment is just as prevalent in domestic politics as it is on the battlefield. The time is long gone when campaign coverage paid much attention to the candidates' positions on substantive matters. Too often the media slide past the issues in nanoseconds or reduce them to non sequiturs (see Chapter 4). Nowadays the name of the game is the horserace. Horserace journalism has the candidates galloping down the track to the finish line—to the roar of the media crowd. Every one wants to know who's going to win. Who has bit the dust? Will the losers gain on the pack and make a comeback? There is even Internet off track betting on which candidate will win the election. Campaigning has turned into a sport, and sports are entertainment. Is it realistic to expect the media to risk losing their audience by covering the issues in greater depth? Probably not.

2. News-Gathering Methods Are Designed to Save Money

The all-important fact about the mass media, as we have been at pains to point out, is that they are in business to make money, not lose it. When they regularly spend more money gathering the news than they take in, they go out of business. The result is that true investigative reporting tends to get slighted, because it is so very expensive in time, effort, and thus money. More "efficient" news-gathering techniques are used whenever possible, even though spending greater amounts of money might produce more accurate accounts, not to mention dredge up dirt the powerful are trying to hide. Media people generally do try to be careful in what they report, so as not to leave themselves open to libel charges, and (in most cases) because of a desire to adhere to professional ethics. But they rarely get to dig below the surface.

The principal way in which news is gathered is through established "beats." The major wire services, television networks, and a few top newspapers and magazines routinely assign reporters to cover the major news-developing institutions—the White House, Congress, and so on. At the local level, they cover city hall, the police, and the like. Roving reporters are assigned to cover breaking stories in business, medicine, and so on, by interviewing interested parties—representatives of large corporations giving press conferences, "experts" in relevant fields, union leaders.[13] In effect, then, *most news is given to reporters by government officials or by others who have or represent power or wealth.* The news thus is bound to reflect established interests much more than those of the general public, given that it is the rich and powerful who have the means to call press conferences, provide video footage, or issue fancy press releases.[14]

---

[12]Quoted in "That's Militainment," *Extra!*, June 2003, a well-researched analysis of press coverage of the Iraq War.

[13]Experts can be found on every side of virtually all issues. Which experts are consulted depends on the way in which a story is to be slanted, and that, of course, usually is determined by the various factors we have been considering in this chapter.

[14]An important exception to this rule is that ordinary people often are interviewed to impart "human interest" to stories that otherwise reflect the opinions and viewpoints of power or money. Another exception is the coverage of local news events such as fires—reporters actually go to the scene and interview those affected by the event.

"Hey, do you want to be on the news tonight or not? This is a sound bite, not the Gettysburg Address. Just say what you have to say, Senator, and get the hell off."

> *David Halberstam (one of the most respected journalists in recent years) on the importance of investigative reporting:*
>
> You have to keep digging, keep asking questions, because otherwise you'll be seduced or brainwashed into the idea that it's somehow a great privilege, an honor, to report the lies they've [those in power] been feeding you.
>
> — Quoted in "Working the Truth Beat," by Bob Herbert, *New York Times*, April 30, 2007

That is an important reason why *very few important news stories in the mass media result from true investigative reporting!* It's much easier, quicker, and cheaper to interview heads of government agencies or representatives of big business than it is to find out what actually is going on by tedious digging. (It's also safer; recall the discussion a while back about the power of government and why power tends to cooperate with power.)

Anyway, there is a bit of good news on the topic of true investigative reporting. In recent years, newspapers, and occasionally TV and radio programs, have been recycling items from non–mass media magazines and from the major newspapers (which have set up syndicates for this purpose to compete with feature syndicates). Reprinting someone else's investigative efforts is a good deal cheaper than digging on one's own. So items from *The Washington Monthly, The Atlantic, The New Republic, The National Review,* and other non–mass media publications, as well as from the *New York Times,* the *Washington Post,* and the *Los Angeles Times,* appear now and then in local rags and on network news programs.

3. Misdirection and Lack of Proportion

An important lesson to be learned from what has been said so far in this chapter is that the news, as presented to us by the mass media, tends to misdirect our attention away from important, underlying, day-to-day occurrences and trends in favor of "breaking news" (assassination of a foreign leader, Super Bowl coverage), "human interest" stories, particularly celebrity coverage, and what the powerful want to tell us.

It hasn't always been this way. In the years before the media mergers and increasing demands that news divisions show a profit, the coverage of celebrities was a small part of mainstream news. *Extra!* (October 1997) reports that Elvis Presley's death in 1977 was covered in 29 minutes over the following five weekdays. When John Lennon was killed in 1980, his murder received 59 minutes over the next five weekdays. But coverage of Princess Diana's death in 1997 totaled 197 minutes on nightly newscasts over a five-weekday period—almost two-thirds of all nightly news coverage in the first week of September 1997. And the sad saga of Britney Spears has had round-the-clock coverage in recent years. The media demand for her self-destructive antics was so great that a single exclusive photo could pull in about $10,000, plus thousands more in residuals (compared to $175–$700 for the average celebrity). Britney's real-life soap opera was a tabloid editor's dream, of course, but more troubling was the extensive coverage of her in mainstream media—a sad commentary on the media and their audiences.

A more serious misdirection occurs when the media sensationalize trivia and ignore substance. Take, for instance, the CNN debate in Nevada among presidential frontrunners in the Democratic Party. Although the candidates sometimes lapsed into the usual boilerplate rhetoric, they did have substantive discussions. But what captured the media's attention was a brief skirmish between Hillary Clinton and Barack Obama in which she accused him of serving on a legal team that represented a slum landlord, and he countered that she was a corporate lawyer for Wal-Mart. CNN played this "uniquely hostile exchange" in its entirety but virtually ignored the rest of the debate. The fact that CNN would devote 3 whole minutes—an eternity on TV news—to little more than a sharp, but hardly hostile exchange played up sensation and played down substance.

The mass media also tend to play into the average person's lack of a good sense of proportion. That is why, for example, the media often pay just as much attention to an economic issue concerning, say, $100 million as to one about $10 billion. (It's well known that a great many people are able to distinguish rightly between relatively small amounts—for instance, between $500 and $5,000—but tend to get hazy when the numbers get larger than the kind that directly relate to their own lives.) For example, when prescription drug benefits were added to the Medicare health program in 2004, most people easily grasped the amount involved for each person: Seniors would pay $35 a month, and after they met a $250 deductible, insurance would pay 75 percent of drug costs up to $2,280. But people's eyes tended to glaze over at the astronomical cost of the program—at least $400 billion by 2013 and possibly trillions by the time baby boomers retire. (Do you know how much a billion or a trillion is?)

Although satisfying the public's liking for human interest stories doesn't have to result in relatively trivial news getting a bigger play than more important items, in fact that is often the way it works. For instance, in 2007 the local media had a field day when two humpback whales lost their way along the California coast and wandered inland up the delta. Admittedly, this was a newsworthy story, but it went on for weeks as people fretted over the disoriented whales and worried that they would never find their way back to the coast again. The media covered the whales' journey inch by inch, up and down the Sacramento River, but gave relatively little coverage to environmentalists' efforts to cut the amount of mercury seeping into the San Francisco Bay, affecting the plants and making the fish inedible. The wandering whales were appealing to a large audience while the mercury pollution lacked pizzazz.

4. News Reporting: Theory and Practice

People don't often stand back and look carefully at what they're doing from a wider perspective; they don't often theorize about their activities. On the whole, media workers do so more than most, but their theories frequently are self-serving.

The Unusual Is News, the Everyday Is Not

Theory says that news is what is new—the unusual—not the commonplace. Yet what happens every day is generally more important than the unusual occurrences that make the headlines. For example, over the past 30 years or so, many kinds of bacteria slowly but steadily have been developing resistance to present-day antibiotics. Millions of people who would have been saved just a few years ago are dying, or being seriously

> *Pete Hamil, on the trend of journalists to degenerate into gossip hounds:*
>
> [Reporters in the 1950's] were conscious of their limitations; they knew that they never once had turned out an absolutely perfect newspaper, because the newspaper was put out by human beings. But in their separate ways, they tried very hard never to write anything that would bring the newspaper shame. They would be appalled at the slovenly way the word "tabloid" is now used. [*Tabloid* describes the shape of the page, not the content.] They didn't pay whores for stories. They didn't sniff around the private lives of politicians like agents from the vice squad. Even in large groups, on major stories, the photographers didn't behave like a writhing, snarling, mindless centipede, all legs and Leicas, falling upon some poor witness like an instrument of punishment. Somehow, they found ways to get the story without behaving like thugs or louts.
>
> —Excerpted from *News Is a Verb*
> by Pete Hamil (1998)

impaired, and everyone is at an increasing risk from diseases once thought to be virtually conquered by miracle drugs. (Tuberculosis is an example.) The media pretty much ignore this vitally important story or relegate it to newspaper back pages, except every once in a while, when a news magazine or TV news program runs a story that turns a few heads for a short time and then disappears—buried in the minds of media audiences under a mass of information about relatively trivial, or quickly unimportant, events. Yet without question, microscopic organisms—bacteria, viruses, and so on—constitute one of the two most serious threats to human life and health on this planet, the other being pollution and other swift environmental changes that threaten to unravel most, or at least an important part, of the ecological web on which human life depends and to result in immense suffering for millions of people. (A third serious threat—eliminating human life on Earth via a massive atomic war—has diminished considerably since the breakup of the Soviet Union in 1991, but worldwide terrorism and the threat of biological or chemical warfare and "dirty" bombs is taking its place.)

Part of the reason for this slanting of the news to cover what is new compared to more important everyday ongoing realities surely has to do with audience interest. The media provided mountains of coverage about Britney Spears, Lindsay Lohan, Paris Hilton, and others, but much less time on detailed reports of problems that more directly affect readers. For instance, there was very little coverage of a series of articles on HMOs in the prestigious *New England Journal of Medicine* (May 1998), stories that explained how some HMOs push cost-cutting procedures—often to the detriment of patients—and punish doctors who resist. The *Journal* showed how physicians who participate in HMO plans can earn significant fee increases by holding down hospital admissions, emergency room use, and referrals to specialists. These statistics certainly provide more valuable information to the average reader (who may be one of those patients denied adequate treatment) than facts about Britney's custody hearings for her children, but the media expended mountains more time on the dress and its evidence than it did on the serious problems with HMOs and what is euphemistically referred to as "managed care."

News Reporting Is Supposed to Be Objective, Not Subjective

Until well into the twentieth century American journalists covered the news from politically biased points of view, following the eighteenth- and nineteenth-century models that date back to the American Revolution. Alexander Hamilton took full advantage of the freedom of the press set forth in the Bill of Rights to expound his Federalist philosophy and attack his opponents in the Republican Party (not to be confused with the current political party). He, in turn, was vilified in opposition newspapers by such stalwarts as John Adams and James Madison. But in the early part of the twentieth century, journalism evolved into a more politically independent profession and attempted to report unbiased news, relegating opinion-based articles to the editorial pages. (Many European countries, though, still use the partisan model. In England, for example, the *Guardian* champions liberal causes, the *Times*, conservative ones.)

However, both conservatives and liberals claim that the other side dominates the news. In the 1970s to offset what conservatives believed was a liberal bias in the press, they launched magazines like the *National Review* and *Commentary* to get their message out and begin to influence news coverage. Later, conservative think tanks and television networks emerged, along with talk shows hosted by right wingers like Rush Limbaugh and Laura Ingraham. Liberals were slower to respond, maybe because the media did seem more liberal until the late 1970s. But gradually liberal think tanks sprang up, as did news programs, talk shows like *Air America,* and political comedy shows like *The Daily Show* and *The Colbert Report* that skewered the opposition on both sides and began to influence a more youthful audience than the more traditional programs did. In fact, one of the ways that the media bosses tried to bolster decreasing audiences was by injecting news programs like Keith Olbermann's countdown with a bias that would attract new viewers.

But even news coverage that strives to be unbiased cannot be completely objective. Reports of facts generally depend on somebody's judgment that they are facts. A reporter must reason to the facts, or at least report someone else's reasoning to the facts, just as one reasons to anything else. Facts are not like fruit on trees, to be plucked at one's leisure.

We just mentioned, for example, the fact that mutant bacteria are becoming an extremely serious health problem, but there is no single observation, or series of observations, that demonstrate this truth. Medical experts have to reason to this fact from what they observe (for example, that syphilis, tuberculosis, and malaria cases now often do not respond to previously effective antibiotics).

Similarly, the idea that media hands should not make value judgments is foolish. They *must* make value judgments, if only about which items are important enough to be featured, which should be mentioned only briefly, and which should be tossed into the round file (where most items that go over Associated Press wires end up). The point is that *editing,* one of the chief tasks performed by media workers, requires value judgments about the relative importance of events.

In any case, theory is one thing; practice, another. Practice is driven primarily by the various forces we have been at pains to describe and only to a small extent by abstract theory. The theory of objectivity serves as a convenient cover under which this can be done. Its cash value is that reporters are motivated to stay within the narrow,

Robert Caro, journalist and biographer, told this anecdote about the advice an editor gave him when he was assigned his first story on the paper. Caro was just a copy boy then, but because all the other reporters were busy, the editor asked him to cover a controversial development at City Hall. This brief piece of advice embodies the basic principles of good journalism.

"OK, here's what you do," the editor said, "You go down to City Hall and listen for a while until you think you know what's going on. After the meeting, talk to whoever is opposing this plan to find out why. Then you go to the developer to get his side of the story. If you're confused, go back to the opponents and ask more questions. Keep going back and forth until you've figured out the story. Got it?"

—Quoted in "Read All About It—But Where Exactly?" *San Francisco Chronicle,* June 17, 2007, a perceptive evaluation of the current state of journalism

middle-of-the-road social consensus when they make judgments or draw conclusions. So one effect of the theory of objectivity is to discourage the reporting of nonestablishment or nonconsensus points of view, satisfying instead the desires of media audiences, advertisers, and others who have great power. Objectivity turns into not rocking the boat.

It's also true, and worth noting, that journalists often confuse objectivity with its close relative—being evenhanded. It has become common practice, for example, for the major networks to present rebuttal from the "other side" when they carry major presidential addresses, so that both major parties get their say. Comments about the truth of whatever is at issue tend to get lost—they would be considered value judgments anyway and so would not satisfy the criteria of the theory of objective reporting.

Note, by the way, how the expression "other side" masks the fact that there are *many* sides to most issues and that the viewpoints championed by the two major political parties often run the range only from A to B. During the 2008 presidential campaign, for example, the mass media were more or less "evenhanded" in their coverage of Democratic and Republican candidates, but they did very little reporting concerning candidates of the Green, Reform, Libertarian, and other "minor" parties.

Even this attempt at evenhandedness is giving way to one-sided coverage on some TV news programs. Now that the public's interest in the news media is on the wane, cable TV outlets are experimenting with ways to build audience appeal by replacing conventional newscasts with opinion-based coverage. So on any given night we might tune into Lou Dobbs on CNN crusading for tougher immigration policies or Keith Olbermann on MSNBC attacking the president's Middle East policies—without bothering to present the opposite side. Fox News has done this for years, of course, but it is now more common on other cable news programs as well.

News Is Supposed to Be Separated from Analysis and In-Depth Reporting

The theory of objectivity requires that facts be reported separately from conclusions or evaluations (which are thought of as "subjective"). But this separation of news from analysis further aggravates a defect already in evidence in most media reporting: *the failure to tie what happens to any explanation as to why it happened and why it is important.*

For instance, in 1998, when Hurricane Mitch wreaked havoc in Honduras, Guatemala, and Nicaragua, the mass media reported horrendous destruction and a large number of deaths. But they failed to explain *why* the destruction was so great. To do that, they needed to explain how the Central American policies of the United Fruit Company and of the United States in the 1950s and 1960s led to intense deforestation that undermined the landscape. They failed to stress the important point that this deforestation, undertaken to replace local farmers with large-scale agriculture, was a major part of the cause of the massive flooding and landslides that resulted when Hurricane Mitch hit. See, for example, *Counterpunch,* November 1–15, 1998 — a left-wing non–mass media publication — or many good histories of Central America. Moral: To know what is really going on, you can't rely on the mass media.

Typically, when covering a story, a reporter consults those directly involved or affected by it. Writing, say, about civil service employee salaries, a reporter would very likely interview civil servants who, naturally, will say that their salaries are lower than for comparable jobs in industry, and critics who, having raised the issue, can be expected to say that the salaries in question are higher than in the nongovernment business world. In fact, this routine has been gone through several times in recent years. Most reporters, of course, have no idea which side is right — they don't know enough about the topic to make an intelligent judgment. They don't know, for example, whether civil service job specifications truly describe what happens on the job day to day. How could they, given that the topic they investigated the week before might have been water pollution in Pennsylvania, while next week's topic will be job flight to Mexico?

Although the theory of objective news reporting often tends to deter journalists from saying what they believe or even know to be true, as just described, it doesn't absolutely forbid the mixing of news with evaluation or analysis. In fact, reporters have a modest amount of freedom to spout off, at least when no toes of the powerful are being stepped on. Nevertheless, the impossibility of being experts on every topic they must investigate, coupled with the need to seem authoritative, whether they know what they are talking about or not, often produces rather mixed results. For example, the journalists embedded with the troops during the Iraq War reported a piece of the action as they experienced it, but they had no concept of the big picture. And since much reporting was instantaneous,

---

Thoughtfully written analysis is out, "live pops" are in. . . . Hire lookers, not writers. Do powder-puff, not probing, interviews. Stay away from controversial subjects. Kiss a ___, move with the mass, and for heaven and the ratings' sake don't make anybody mad. . . . Make nice, not news.

—Dan Rather (of CBS's *Evening News*)

aired on television or radio as it was happening, they had no time to sort through the information and give it context. As a result, the audience got a slice of the battle but little evaluation or analysis that would come from mature deliberation over time.

The Opinions of the "Right" Authorities Take Precedence

Since the reporters who gather the news are not usually experts in the fields they have to cover, they must, and do, seek out expert opinion. The trouble is that experts can be found on all sides of virtually every issue that is even mildly controversial. Which experts they consult thus becomes crucially important, and usually is determined by just a very few factors.

Perhaps the most important consideration is whether an expert's opinions might be unpopular either with the intended audience or with advertisers or other power groups. Experts with views that might raise too many hackles tend to be overlooked (or, sometimes, used as foils). Mainstream experts dominate the field. These days, for example, positions on race, gender differences, pollution problems, and so on, generally have to stay within bounds set by PC. There is, of course, still a great deal of racism in America, as in most other countries, but there also is an "official line" on the matter. Racism is definitely not PC.

During the 2008 presidential primaries, when racial attitudes were increasingly discussed, anyone who even hinted at racism was roundly criticized. The media shredded Bill Clinton for comparing Barack Obama's win in the South Carolina primary to Jesse Jackson's campaign in the South in 1984 and 1988 (implying that Obama would go no further than Jackson), and later they pounced on Hillary Clinton for citing evidence that "Senator Obama's support among working, hard-working Americans, white Americans is weakening again." Both of these comments, though mild, were perceived as racial slurs, and public sentiment turned against the Clintons—an ironic reversal considering that Bill Clinton had once been so supportive of blacks and appreciated by them that he was sometimes called the first black president. The experts called in to comment on Clinton's remarks and other racial issues were often black journalists and politicians who gave mainly white audiences insightful perspectives on how these issues were viewed in African American communities.

Even though TV reporters arriving on the scene of a breaking story generally know very little about what is taking place or about the topic that is at issue, they still must appear to be authoritative and not merely people reading someone else's news to us. That is why, for example, evening news anchors may turn up anywhere, reporting as someone "on the spot" and thus presumably knowledgeable about what is going on. The recent wars provided ample opportunity. During the early stages of the War in Afghanistan, Fox audiences were treated to a gun-toting Geraldo Rivera, reporting live from the battlefield claiming he'd kill Osama bin Laden if he had a chance. War wraps reporters in an aura of authority and makes them much more exciting than anchors who read the news.

Not all experts are trustworthy, however. When personal interest conflicts with public duty, ethical attitudes can disintegrate. This is exactly what happened when a group of high-ranking military officers were recruited by the Pentagon to sell the Iraq War to the American public. The *New York Times* ran a devastating, well-researched exposé of how these retired military experts became purveyors of Pentagon propaganda.[15] In dismal detail the article charted their activities from the run-up to the war through the 2008 surge. Dubbed "key influentials" by the Pentagon, these military analysts were well-decorated, authoritative commentators who framed the way the audience should interpret the war. They didn't simply give objective descriptions of warfare in the battle zones or explain the capabilities of military hardware; they passed on the administration's ideology and helped establish its priorities. True, many of them believed that the war was justified, and since they had devoted their lives to the military, were understandably reluctant to criticize it. Nonetheless, there were powerful incentives for them to play along. Some were defense lobbyists, others were involved with helping companies win military contracts, and still others were board members of military contractors. What their willing participation gave them was access to power and influence and the opportunity for lucrative business deals. Eventually the Pentagon recruited over 75 retired officers, although some became disenchanted over time, and others were only briefly involved. Most of them appeared on Fox News and to a lesser extent on NBC, CNN, and other stations.

Thus, viewers who thought they were getting an objective analysis of the war were really getting a sell job. When journalists in Iraq began filing reports about the rise of insurgencies, the shortage of armor, the corruption of Iraqi security forces, and so on, the counterforce was the military analysts, briefed with Pentagon talking points, who assured the public that all was well. And the Pentagon monitored their media appearances, taking them to task if they criticized the war effort even mildly.

Meanwhile, the networks not only remained in the dark about the extensive interaction between the Pentagon and the military analysts, but they didn't seem to know that some analysts had business relationships with the Pentagon that could create conflicts of interest. And so the public was hoodwinked.

For two years the *New York Times* battled with the Defense Department, finally suing it successfully to gain access to 8,000 pages of documents describing the interaction between the Pentagon and the military analysts. So the news finally came out that these so-called experts were little more than shills for the Pentagon. This story, by the way, is journalism at its best—a trenchant analysis of government corruption, well substantiated by evidence.

Self-Censorship

The theory that news reporting should be objective does not require that all of the news, even all of the very important news, be reported. During wartime, for example, national security takes precedence. When United States troops were poised to invade Afghanistan in 2001, the media knew a full day in advance the exact time that the strikes would begin, but virtually no major media organization reported this information in the news.

---

[15]See "Message Machine: Behind TV Analysts, Pentagon's Hidden Hand," by David Barstow, *New York Times,* April 20, 2008.

One of the most prevalent sources of "experts" is the think tanks that the media have used in recent years. It's a good idea to know the political orientation of these groups so that you can critically evaluate their analyses of the issues. Here are the most widely quoted think tanks (cited in Extra! *March/April 2008) and the ideological shift in network coverage over the years in the study.*

Citations of Think Tanks in Media

Think Tank	Political Orientation	2006	2007	% Change
1. Brookings Institution	Centrist	2,568	2,380	7
2. Council on Foreign Relations	Centrist	1,564	1,191	−24
3. American Enterprise Institute	Conservative	1,429	1,171	−18
4. Heritage Foundation	Conservative	1,390	1,168	−16
5. Center for Strategic and International Studies	Conservative	1,388	1,068	−23
6. RAND Corporation	Centrist	930	740	−20
7. Kaiser Family Foundation	Centrist	1,023	706	−31
8. Center for American Progress	Center-Left	687	673	−2
9. Cato Institute	Cons/Libertarian	776	640	−18
10. Urban Institute	Center-Left	472	558	18
11. Hoover Institution	Conservative	567	472	−17
12. Manhattan Institute	Conservative	493	425	−14
13. New America Foundation	Centrist	288	414	44
14. Economic Policy Institute	Progressive	733	353	−52
15. Woodrow Wilson International Center for Scholars	Centrist	245	348	42
16. Carter Center	Center-Left	347	341	−2
17. Carnegie Endowment	Centrist	356	287	19
18. Lexington Institute	Conservative	373	279	−25
19. Public Policy Institute of California	Centrist	517	274	−47
20. Center for Politics	Centrist	354	231	−35
21. Washington Institute for Near East Policy	Center Right	245	229	−7
22. Center on Budget and Policy Priorities	Progressive	420	222	−47
23. Inter-American Dialogue	Centrist	227	214	−11
24. Aspen Institute	Centrist	235	209	−11
25. Center for Economic and Policy Research	Progressive	210	197	−6

Number of Media Citations by Ideology	2006	%	2007	%
Conservative or Center-Right	6,661	37	5,462	37
Centrist	8,307	47	6,994	47
Progressive or Center-Left	2,869	16	2,344	16
Total	17,837	100	14,800	100

Source: Nexis database on major newspaper and radio and TV transcripts.
Note: Percentages may not add up to 100 due to rounding.

Last year, 300,000 Americans were arrested for smoking an herb that Queen Victoria used regularly for menstrual cramps.

It's a fact.

The herb, of course, is *cannabis sativa*. Otherwise known as marijuana, pot, grass, hemp, boo, mary-jane, ganja—the nicknames are legion.

So are the people who smoke it.

By all reckoning, it's fast becoming the new national pastime. Twenty-six million smokers, by some accounts— lots more by others. Whatever the estimate, a staggeringly high percentage of the population become potential criminals simply by being in possession of it. And the numbers are increasing.

For years, we've been told that marijuana leads to madness, sex-crimes, hard-drug usage and even occasional warts.

Pure Victorian poppycock.

In 1894, The Indian Hemp Commission reported marijuana to be relatively harmless. A fact that has been substantiated time and again in study after study.

Including, most recently, by the President's own Commission. This report stands as an indictment of the pot laws themselves.

And that's why more and more legislators are turning on to the fact that the present marijuana laws are as archaic as dear old Victoria's code of morality. And that they must be changed. Recently, the state of Oregon did, in fact, de-criminalize marijuana. Successfully.

Other states are beginning to move in that direction. They must be encouraged.

NORML has been and is educating the legislators, working in the courts and with the lawmakers to change the laws. We're doing our best but still, we need help. Yours.

Used with permission of NORML.

Ad censorship. NORML marijuana ad rejected by Time *and* Newsweek, *accepted by* Playboy.

Even in peacetime, the media sometimes voluntarily suppress news out of a sense of duty. Perhaps the most famous instance of this kind occurred during John Kennedy's time as president, when the *New York Times* decided not to print reliable information about the impending attack on Cuba by U.S.-trained forces intent on overthrowing Fidel Castro.[16]

Another important reason for media censorship has to do with the power of media audiences to switch channels or to not buy a newspaper. Television, in particular, has to be sensitive to its audience, because its product comes into living rooms with such immediacy (and children may be watching). The way in which Elvis Presley was allowed to appear on an Ed Sullivan TV show in 1956 constitutes a classic example; Elvis was shown only from the waist up so that TV audiences wouldn't be exposed to his pelvic gyrations. (That sounds silly today, but what may or may not be objectionable differs considerably from one time to another.) Another famous case occurred in 1952 when Lucille Ball became pregnant and the story line of the *I Love Lucy* show was adjusted accordingly: the TV Lucy could be said on camera to be "expecting" and *enceinte* (French for "pregnant"), but the word *pregnant* could not be used. Even in the 1950s, this sort of censorship seemed ridiculous to lots of people, but media moguls considered it to be a very serious matter; too many viewers were likely to be offended by use of the term *pregnant.*

Times change, of course, so that in the 1990s, when TV's Murphy Brown was allowed to be an unwed mother, only a slight fuss was made about referring to her as pregnant. But media self-censorship still is with us, as it always will be. It's just that standards and the topics subject to censorship change. Back in the 1950s a program about homosexuals would have been unthinkable—absolutely out of the question—so much so that the lack of such programs hardly could be considered to constitute self-censorship. Gays simply did not exist as far as television was concerned. But today they do, yet programs featuring gays sometimes are censored by one segment of the media or other. When Ellen DeGeneres's character "came out" on the sitcom *Ellen,* several stations refused to carry the episode.

But those who see self-censorhip as automatically evil might consider the right of individuals to privacy in their nonpublic life. Should detailed accounts of Clinton's sex life—even down to his "distinguishing mark"—have been broadcast in the media? At what point does one draw the line? A person in the public eye is still, after all, entitled to a private life. Anyway, things are not as bad here as in, say, England, where the press hounded Princess Diana up to her death and continues to cover every move of her sons Prince William and Prince Harry.

In days long gone, the media felt more constrained in its reporting of the private lives of important public figures. It was well known to some in the press, for example, that both before and after his marriage—as a congressman, senator, and president—John Kennedy was quite a lady's man. But the media, on the whole, chose not to divulge this feature of his private life. In those days, matters of this kind were usually passed over, even though they would have found an eager audience.

---

[16]The invasion turned into a fiasco that was terribly embarrassing to the Kennedy administration. Kennedy himself is alleged later to have had the chutzpah to take the *Times* to task for this self-censorship on grounds that publication of the story by the *Times* might have resulted in the aborting of that ill-fated venture!

There comes a point, though, when knowledge about a person's sex life may, in some cases, be relevant to character and thus to potential performance as a public figure. For example, when New York Governor Eliot Spitzer was caught with a prostitute in 2008, the media not only gave it immediate attention but followed it up with evidence that he had had a number of liaisons with prostitutes over the years. In light of the fact that Spitzer had prosecuted prostitution rings as attorney general and had been elected governor on a reform platform, his sexual hypocrisy was seen by the public as relevant to his political integrity, and he was pressured to resign

EXERCISE 11-1

In April 2007, two days after a psychotic student, Cho Seung Hui, went on a tragic rampage killing 33 people at Virginia Tech, NBC received a package in the mail from the killer that included an 1,800-word diatribe, along with photos and videos of himself making threats and waving guns and other weapons. NBC aired portions of the material on the *Nightly News* that were quickly picked up by other networks, newspapers, and the Internet. The ethical issues raised by releasing this footage were widely debated. Although NBC took care to edit out disturbing content, it was criticized in some quarters for its insensitive handling of the material and for doing precisely what the psychotic killer intended—getting his deranged message out to the public. But others argued for full disclosure and criticized the network's arbitrary editing.

Write an essay or debate the question whether NBC should have suppressed the material altogether or released all the footage uncensored. Or should it have done exactly what it did—aired an edited version?

5. DEVICES USED TO SLANT THE NEWS

So far, we have been considering why the media slant the news and how that affects story selection. Now let's take a brief look at a few of the many devices used to accomplish this task. (The examples are taken primarily from newspapers and magazines, but television and radio have their analogs.)

Stories Can Be Played Up or Down

Breaking news of immense interest, like the capture of Saddam Hussein, for instance, is always played up in the news. Photos of the haggard Hussein and his squalid hideout flashed across television screens and newspapers around the world within hours of his captivity. But not all news is that compelling. Often stories are played up because of audience interest or media bias. If the interest isn't there, the story may be buried by placing it on page 59 or by packing the undesirable material toward the end of an otherwise acceptable story. For example, hundreds of thousands of people sought refuge from the violence in the Darfur region of Sudan in 2003, yet few Americans knew about it. The Sudanese who fled into Chad when their villages were bombed and crops were burned to the ground got little international assistance and not much press coverage. The refugee crisis was voted one of the most underreported humanitarian stories in 2003 by Doctors Without Borders (Médecins Sans Frontières, winners of the 1999 Nobel Peace Prize). Much more attention is now being given to ongoing violence in

Calvin & Hobbes © Watterson. Reprinted with permission of Universal Press Syndicate. All rights reserved.

Darfur, but it was a long time in coming. American audiences tend to be relatively uninterested in much of Africa and most Far Eastern countries. Back pages are relatively unread, and readers tend not to get past the first few paragraphs of anything (including, alas, material in school textbooks, but that is another matter; if you've read this far, place an *X* at the end of this sentence). On TV, stories get buried by being run toward the end of a news program when attention may be wandering (although, interestingly, not usually at the very end) and by being cut to run for less than 10 or 15 seconds.

Of course, the most obvious way to bury the news is simply to ignore it. Bad news becomes no news when the media doesn't cover it. *Editor and Publisher,* an important trade magazine, noted that one of the least reported, major repercussions of the Iraq War was the massive displacement of Iraqi people. It raised the question whether coverage would improve after the report of the Iraqi Red Crescent (the Islamic equivalent of the American Red Cross) came out in the summer of 2007. The report indicated that the number of Iraqis displaced internally had gone up four times since January 2007, and eight times since the year before. Even worse was the unprecedented tragedy resulting from the rise in rape, armed gangs, theft, and drug addiction. But as *Extra!* (July/August 2007) pointed out, the only U.S. outlet to report the story was *Democracy Now!* The rest of the media ignored it. This, by the way, is only one of many times that the media have either downplayed or passed over news about the plight of the Iraqi people.

Other, less dramatic omissions occur as well. For instance, newspapers often inform readers about which movies are drawing the largest audiences, which records are selling best, and so on. But the *New York Times,* for obscure reasons of its own, routinely excludes religious books (Bibles and so forth) and "romance" (Harlequin) paperbacks from its lists of best-selling books, even though together these two kinds of publications account for a very large slice of the book market.

Misleading, Sensational, or Opinionated Headlines Can Be Used

Many more people read the headlines on stories than read the accounts that follow. So even if an account itself is accurate, a misleading or sensational headline (generally not written by whoever wrote the news report itself) distorts the news for many readers. For example, an MSNBC.com headline (June 21, 2007) implied that hordes of journalists were donating money to political campaigns.

Journalists Dole Out Cash to Politicians

But the article went on the explain that 143 journalists across the country — out of more than 100,000 newsroom employees — had contributed to campaigns over a four-year period from 2004 to 2008. Hardly a horde.

Here are two markedly different headlines for the same news item about a study posted on line (January 21, 2008) by the Center for Public Integrity, a research group concerned with ethics in government and public policy. The study cited 935 false statements made by the Bush administration over a two-year period following the September 11 attacks, which influenced the American public to support the Iraq War.

The *San Francisco Chronicle* sensationalized the item with this headline (January 23, 2008):

Hundreds of Lies Led to War, Study Says

The *New York Times* (same date) played it down to the point that readers would have had a hard time figuring out what the article was about:

Web Site Assembles U.S. Prewar Claims

Images Can Slant the News

Image has been important in American politics ever since George Washington refused the crown and declined a third term in office because he didn't want to create the wrong image. Abraham Lincoln played up his image as a rail-splitting back woodsman reared in a log cabin in the Illinois wilderness. But in those days news traveled slowly and photography was either nonexistent (in Washington's time) or in its infant stages (in Lincoln's). With the advent of television, visual images began to dominate the scene. Starting with John F. Kennedy and his photogenic family, the emphasis on visual imagery began to increase. Kennedy's impressive showing against Nixon in the presidential debates was due more to his handsome, debonair image than to the content of the debates. (People who listened to the debates rather than watched them on TV considered two out of three a draw.) Today image triumphs over content for most people.[17]

Now that photos can be transmitted instantaneously around the world, the power of imagery has enormous impact internationally as well as nationally. Knowing full well the effect of disturbing pictures on the public, the second Bush administration refused to allow coverage of the flag-draped coffins that were returned from Iraq to Powers Air Force Base. But provocative photos tend to slip through the cracks no matter how carefully they are guarded. (The coffin footage eventually surfaced.) The most notorious example was the graphic photos of U.S. soldiers abusing and humiliating Iraqi prisoners at Abu Ghraib. The *60 Minutes II* airing of this footage sent shock waves around the world. Americans were horrified, Iraqis were alienated, and the popularity of the Bush

---

[17]For more on this see "The Triumph of the Image," by Richard C. Wahl, in the *Columbia Review of Journalism,* November/December 2003.

administration plummeted in the polls. The Arab media were quick to respond. Although some of the coverage was evenhanded, media outlets opposed to U.S. intervention used the photos to inflame anti-American feelings. In the case of Abu Ghraib, the image was the story.

As the wars dragged on, the Department of Defense tightened regulations on publishing information of U.S. battlefield casualties, ruling that "names, videos, identifiable written and oral descriptions or identifiable photographs of wounded service members will not be released without service members prior consent."[18] Hardly likely, is it? Since U.S. news organizations depended on embedded reporters and photographers for coverage of the wars, they had to cooperate with the military or be denied access. But without these graphic photos, the public had no visual grasp of the ravages of war on our troops. It is worth noting, though, that the media raised almost no objections to the new regulations, and, in fact, did some self-censorship of war coverage in ways that skewed our perception. For instance, when they ran photos of dead or dying Afghans or Iraqis, they typically portrayed victims of attacks by their own countrymen, not by U.S. troops, thus revealing the damage Afghans and Iranians did to each other and not the harm we did. In an age when people rely more and more heavily on visual imagery for the news, it is no exaggeration to say that photos have far greater impact than the written word.

Follow-Up Stories Can Be Omitted or Played Down

Follow-up stories rarely make headlines, primarily for three reasons. The first is that they are more difficult to obtain than breaking news stories. It takes much less time and effort to record the fact that a bank has failed than to follow up details of an ensuing court case against its directors. The second is that the public (and media) conception of "news" is what is new, and follow-up stories are just more of the same, or just plain humdrum.

Breaking news is often sensationalized, but follow-up stories usually aren't sexy enough to grab the audience's interest, so the media ignore them. For example, the media tend to play up outrageous verdicts against big corporations like Philip Morris, McDonald's, and Firestone, but when these verdicts are overturned on appeal, they go unreported or are buried in the back pages. Molly Ivins in her syndicated column (August 27, 2001) cited a famous case in point, of an 81-year old woman who sued McDonald's after she spilled a cup of its coffee on herself and suffered third-degree burns. The big news was that the jury awarded her $2.9 million after learning that McDonald's ignored 700 similar cases over time. The underreported news was that the verdict was reduced to $480,000 on appeal, was later settled out of court for an undisclosed amount, and McDonald's no longer serves scalding hot coffee. The point here is not so much that juries make idiotic awards for frivolous lawsuits as was implied in the original story (after all, hundreds of people had been burned in the past by McDonald's coffee), but that civil litigation often works well in correcting wrongs—a lesson that didn't make the news.

Another reason for the paucity of follow-up stories is that most of us have short attention spans. Except for "ongoing" stories—wars providing the best examples—people

---

[18]Quoted in "From Self-Censorship to Official Censorship," by Pat Arnow, in *Extra!*, March/April 2007, an enlightening article on the muzzling of news coverage in the Iraq/Afghan wars.

tend to tire of any topic quickly (the truth behind Andy Warhol's remark "In the future, everyone will be famous for 15 minutes"). When bored, it's all too easy to flip the switch to another channel or to put down the newspaper and instead watch Oprah do her thing on the tube.

Well, no one can be in favor of boredom. The problem is that in the vast majority of cases it is the time-consuming details that make all the difference. Ten-second news sound bites aren't all that different from "Chevrolet—the heartbeat of America" or "Magnavox—smart, very smart." Short and easily remembered usually drives out long and complicated. That may well be the chief reason relevant background information and follow-up tend to be in short supply on TV news programs.

The public's lack of interest in or general weariness with the Iraq War may account for the scant attention the news paid to the second President Bush's announcement— six months after the onset of the war—that there was no evidence linking Saddam Hussein to the September 11 attack on the World Trade Center. Buried in the back pages of most newspapers, this was a belated follow-up story to the headline news months earlier that the administration wanted to wage war partly because it believed Hussein's government had links to al Qaeda and the terrorist network led by Osama bin Laden. Although Bush never claimed that Hussein was responsible for the attack, 70 percent of Americans inferred he probably was involved, based on their assumption that the administration was right about his links to al Qaeda. (As it turned out, the 9-11 Commission found no evidence of this connection either.) Unless they read deep in the paper or paid attention to 10-second sound bites, they may still be unaware of this important clarification.

Points of View Can Be Conveyed via Cartoons and Comic Strips

According to the old saying, a picture is worth a thousand words, which may account for the ability of cartoons and comic strips to effectively—graphically—make a point. In any case, it most certainly accounts for the large number of these handy little devices that have been reprinted in this particular textbook. A clever practitioner of the cartoonist's art can puncture prejudices and force us to open our eyes to unpleasant truths in a way that few others can match. The Tom Meyer cartoon on the next page, for example, forcefully brings home the point that the so-called "three strikes and you're out" laws— mandatory life sentences for those convicted of a third felony—don't really get at the nub of the crime problem, and it ironically suggests what needs to be done if we are to make a serious dent in that problem.

The *Doonesbury* strip, crafted by Garry Trudeau, deserves special mention here because it has been in the forefront of a minor trend on newspaper comic pages to feature strips that at least occasionally touch on social or political issues rather than just tickling the funny bone. A classic cartoon and a particular favorite of the authors of this text (one of whom is a UCLA alum) is the 1994 *Doonesbury* series that poked fun at the hiring of junk bond ex-con Michael Milken to teach a business course at UCLA. In one panel, Milken is pictured saying, "Who is Professor Milken, the genius who created a new world of financial instruments? Well, I'm many things, of course. But most of all, I'm a survivor. After a 98-count indictment and a 6-count plea bargain, I'm still here— and with $1 billion to show for it!" after which students repeat his code: "Greed works!

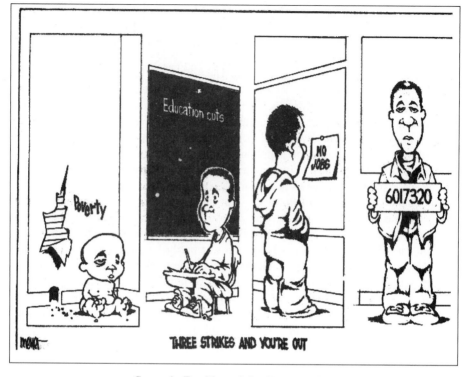

Cartoon by Tom Meyer. © *San Francisco Chronicle*. Reprinted by permission

Crime pays! Everybody does it!" In another strip, Milken states what must certainly be his actual opinion on the matter: that government attempts at regulation are a joke and government employees no match for "a true visionary and his defense team." Students are shown booing the student who has the temerity to ask a pertinent question: "As the key player of the greatest criminal conspiracy in the history of finance, do you think justice was served by your brief stay in a country club prison?" Interesting, isn't it, that this cartoon is just as relevant today as it was when it first appeared.

Unfortunately, this ability of comic strips to graphically make a point sometimes results in their being censored. *Doonesbury,* of course, bites the dust now and then. But even normally nonpolitical strips occasionally get the axe. For example, when a young boy in the *For Better or for Worse* comic strip summoned the courage to tell his parents that he was gay, the resulting furor came as a shock to the strip's creator, Lynn Johnston. The series of strips on this theme ran for just 10 days but was censored during that time in 40 papers, with 20 more canceling the strip outright. In Memphis, Tennessee, to cite just one city, about 2,000 readers canceled their subscriptions to the *Commercial Appeal* because that paper ran the strips they objected to. Johnston was flooded with mail, both pro and con, and stung by the anger and hate some letters exhibited. She wrote the series, she said, because several friends had died from AIDS, and one of her closest gay friends recently had been robbed and killed. "He was nothing more than a wonderful person and a good friend to me," she said. "My intent was to show that Lawrence [the gay boy in the strip] was different but that he's still the kid next door, still a member

Aaron McGruder's Boondocks *sometimes gets in trouble for its political satire.* Extra! *(December 2001) noted that this strip along with several others were pulled from some newspapers after September 11 because it was critical of U.S. foreign policy.*

of the community, someone who should be judged on his moral character, not his genetic code."[19]

In the United States, controversial cartoons may be censored or criticized, but they don't galvanize people into committing violent protests as they sometimes do in other countries. When a Danish newspaper printed cartoons caricaturing Muhammad a few years ago, a group of fundamentalist Muslim clerics urged Middle Eastern embassies to demand a meeting with the Danish prime minister. He refused, and the protests escalated into violence. Hundreds of Iraqis demanded an apology from the European Union, Palestinians stormed through European buildings in Gaza, burning German and Danish flags, and thousands of Syrians torched the Danish and Norwegian embassies in Damascus. No cartoon in this country has ever come close to inciting protests on that level.

6. TELEVISION, FILM, AND ELECTRONIC INFORMATION SOURCES

Although still a relative baby, television is by far the most important of the mass media. More households own television sets than bathtubs or showers. (Interesting fact: One family in four in the United States has three or more television sets.) TV gives us the closest thing we have to a way of bringing a whole diverse nation together. It is the town crier, certifier, authenticator, and grapevine of modern life. That's why political campaigns are fought, and won or lost, on it; the news is broadcast on it; and a nation's mood and tone are set by it.

It would be hard to overestimate the effects of television on everyday life. (One thinks, for a parallel, of the ways in which the automobile has transformed the world.) When film shot from a privately owned camcorder caught police in the act of beating up Rodney King, pictures of their brutality on TV news programs had a profound effect on

---

[19]See, for instance, the *San Francisco Examiner,* April 25, 1993.

the way in which police everywhere thenceforth carried out their duties. (Fear of being filmed in the act constitutes a powerful deterrent.) Similarly, the way in which the Los Angeles police department took it on the chin during the O. J. Simpson murder trial undoubtedly did much to improve police crime procedures everywhere. And more recently, footage of prisoner abuse at Abu Ghraib spiked an internal investigation that raised questions about the military flouting the Geneva Conventions.

All of the media, of course, have the power to force dramatic changes—to expose the bad and publicize the good. But television's power to expose and publicize is vastly greater and more immediate than all of the other mass media combined. Its power, therefore, is awesomely—indeed, frighteningly—greater. Consider, for example, what Americans know about Nazi Germany's extermination camps compared to what they know about Soviet labor camps. Only a few Americans know that many more civilians died in Soviet labor camps than were murdered in Nazi extermination camps. The names Auschwitz, Buchenwald, and Treblinka are familiar to us—well, to some of us—while extremely few Americans have heard, say, of Kolyma.

We also shouldn't forget the way in which news reporting has helped break down prejudices. It was a very important event indeed when the first woman, Barbara Walters, read the evening news to us on national TV and an equally important event when the first African American, Max Robinson, did so. In recent years, the number of TV commentators with diverse backgrounds has grown. When Barack Obama and Hillary Clinton vied for the Democratic presidential nomination, race and gender issues dominated campaign coverage as never before. To address these issues, cable news stations, particularly MSNBC and CNN, brought in seasoned minority analysts who hadn't had much exposure in the mainstream media. Although just about all major prime-time news programs are still hosted by white males (with the exception of Katie Couric on CBS), the infusion of women, blacks, and Hispanics brought fresh perspective to the issues and helped break down prejudice.

But perhaps the most graphic illustration of television's power to change the world is in its effect on the nature of war and associated diplomacy. It is a commonplace today that television shortened American involvement in the war in Vietnam through its living-room coverage, but insufficient notice has yet been taken of the way in which TV influenced the conduct of the Gulf War, the NATO bombing in Kosovo, and the Iraq War. The American government and its coalition allies were exceedingly careful to reduce the number of casualties, not just of their own forces but also of enemy civilians, in a way that (in the long history of warfare) has rarely, if ever before, been true. Compare that, for instance, with the American and British record of mass bombings of civilians in World War II, when television was not peeking over every general's shoulder.

Even sitcoms and the other prime-time entertainment programs sometimes have positive effects—in addition to providing entertainment—a case in point being their role in reducing ethnic and gender prejudice, one of the great improvements that has taken

Television is the first truly democratic culture—the first culture available to everybody and entirely governed by what people want. The most terrifying thing is what people do want.

—Clive Barker

place in the United States (and most other democratic nations) since World War II. African Americans are portrayed as middle-class workers, not just as janitors or (the very expression is odious) cotton pickers, and women as business executives, not just housewives.

But we don't want to go overboard here. Television generally caters to the tastes of mass audiences in ways that have nothing to do with breaking down audience prejudices. Think only of the fabulously successful *American Idol,* or the *Survivor* dramas, or programs as diverse as *Fringe* and *Dancing with the stars.*

Television Is the Best News Source for Many People

When we think of the mass media, it's important to remember that at least one third of American adults are or come close to being functionally illiterate. For them, and for many others, a picture is worth more than a thousand words. So for the mass of people, by default, television is the best news source. (Note, by the way, that it's much easier to become a couch potato and endlessly watch the tube than it is, say, to search the Internet for interesting material.)

But capturing and informing this kind of mass audience requires extremely tight editing (matched in print only by advertisements). The average attention span is short and comprehension, limited. TV does a better job than the other media in editing the news so that it can be understood, somewhat, by most Americans. However, a recent trend in cluttering the screen with multiple images tends to undermine otherwise concise editing. Even the most focused viewer gets distracted by split-screen pictures with headlines underneath and crawling commentary at the bottom.

The Internet

The good news, of course, is that the Internet provides another way to obtain useful information and opinion. It can be, and often is, more up-to-date than the best reference books; it allows people everywhere to read some of the best newspapers and magazines in the land; and it often is more readily available than books or other print media. The world of online journalism continues to expand. Just about all of the major media outlets have Internet access, including broadcast networks, cable networks, newspapers, and news magazines. In addition, Google News provides access to English-language news sites around the world. An outgrowth of the Google search engine, Google News draws on stories from 4,000 news sites, updating items on a second-by-second basis.

The Internet offers an unparalleled opportunity for the average person to express his or her views on blogs or on conventional news media sites that encourage audience participation. An increasing number of web-based sites are experimenting with news coverage from outside the profession. Global Voices Online, for example, mixes professional editors with volunteer "citizen reporters" from all over the world. In some respects the Internet is the new town crier, giving citizens a voice in the democratic process. Web users in the 2008 presidential elections, for instance, could send video-recorded questions to debate moderators through sites like YouTube,[20] livening up the sometimes colorless presidential debates with spontaneous questions. When the candidates actually saw people asking questions—people like a bald, breast cancer survivor without her wig or Darfur children in a refugee camp—they often responded authentically and scrapped their canned speeches.

For web users who want an in-depth look at the news, the Internet has the capability of offering extensive links to background sources like archived material and related stories, interviews, or photographs. In this way it provides much more information than a newspaper or magazine article. For instance, when the *Washington Post* ran a Pulitzer Prize-winning series on Dick Cheney in June 2007 ("Angler: The Cheney Vice Presidency"), the online version was studded with links to related sources. In a section that discussed the role Cheney played in stripping U.S.-held foreign terrorism suspects of access to any civilian or military court, links were given to the president's official military order on the treatment of terrorist suspects as well as the vice president's argument justifying the order. This deep background fleshed out the report on a very controversial issue in ways that the newspaper article could never do and gave web users a chance to examine related sources and judge for themselves the legality of the issue.

As the 2008 presidential campaign heated up, the Internet became an important source for campaign news. The Pew Research Center noted that the number of people who got news of the campaign from the Internet had nearly doubled (24 percent up from 13 percent) since the last election. Young people in particular turned increasingly to the Internet for political news (42 percent of those ages 18–29, compared to 20 percent in 2004), and a surprising number of them (37 percent of those 18–24) accessed campaign information on social networking sites like MySpace and SpaceBook. Although television is still the main source of campaign news, far fewer Americans say they got it from TV news programs than they did in 2000. (Alas, there was no data on those who got their information from comedy shows like *The Colbert Report* because these shows were not airing new episodes during the writers' strike when the poll was taken.)

The downside to the Internet is that it spawns so much more schlock than even the TV networks do. It takes a rather sophisticated web browser to separate the wheat from the chaff. Of course, this is always a problem; the point is that it becomes more urgent to be able to do this well when surfing the web. (Instructors regularly tear their hair out when students turn in papers based on second-rate Internet sources.) The Internet is now inundated with bloggers and citizen reporters, and though they sometimes have more expertise in a particular field than career journalists, they often express strong biases that professionals try to avoid in straight news reporting.

---

[20]"The State of the News Media:" 2008 at journalism.org gives an extensive evaluation of digital journalism.

Other problems are looming on the horizon. Project Censored has listed the debate over the future of the Internet as the most significant underreported news story in 2007.[21] The issue involves "network neutrality," an equal access principle that Internet users should have the right to view or post any lawful content they want and use any application or device on the Internet. It also advocates equal access for an equal price, preventing network providers from blocking or slowing access or charging higher rates for rival Internet provider services (ISPs). Phone and cable companies like AT&T and Comcast have been battling it out with consumers and ISPs in Congress and in courts of law over whether restrictions or limitations can be imposed by network providers. The question in a nutshell is whether these companies should be allowed to regulate themselves or should abide by government regulations that protect Internet neutrality.

Until recently ISPs had free access to cable lines under the "common carriage" agreement. But in 2005 the Supreme Court ruled that cable corporations were not required to share their cable lines with rival ISPs, and the FCC did the same with digital subscriber line (DSL) services. So within a few months, the Net neutrality protections were undone. Congress is currently considering a bipartisan bill, the Internet Freedom Preservation Act, that will restore Net neutrality protections in effect before July 2005. But as of now Internet users may well have their options limited to cable

---

Todd Oppenheimer, a seasoned journalist, on the limitations of "citizen journalists" who report news on the Internet:

. . . it's one thing (a good idea) to use citizen journalists for material from the field, such as on-the-scene accounts from a Hurricane Katrina, or soldier diaries from the trenches of Iraq. It's quite another (a bad idea) to expect amateurs to figure out who is telling the truth about Iraq, or which priests have committed pedophilia. Stories in this later category obviously require skill in a host of exacting tasks, such as interviewing evasive sources, understanding how and where bureaucracies hide evidence and writing a narrative that is compelling yet properly sourced.

. . . In every field, standards are devised and continually refined by the profession's senior members. These masters earn their wisdom through years of challenging, often painful experiences. Their duty is to pass on their lessons to up-and-comers, who should serve some demanding period of apprenticeship. This is how every profession achieves its high ideals. In the media's case, those standards involve strong writing, fairness and independence, thoroughness and accuracy, ethics and astute judgment.

> —From "Read All About It—But Where Exactly?" *San Francisco Chronicle,* October 17, 2007; an insightful article about the current state of journalism

---

[21]See projectcensored.org, "Top 25 Censored Stories for 2007," and a host of websites for Net neutrality like aclu.org and commoncause.org, or against it like the AT&T-sponsored Hands Off the Internet website.

or phone companies' ISPs, which would have the option of blocking access to ISPs or filtering information as they see fit. Unfortunately this very important issue is getting almost no coverage in the media.

7. THE NON–MASS MEDIA TO THE RESCUE

The mass media are a reasonably good source of information about breaking stories — speeches made by important officials, fluctuations in the Dow, bills passed by Congress (but not about a bill's value or who benefits and who is harmed!), and so on. Television does these stories rather well, at least when it can get good visuals. But for detailed, sophisticated, in-depth accounts, and for analysis that doesn't just parrot what powerful people are saying, the non–mass media are indispensable.

The commercial networks do feature several rather good investigative, in-depth programs—namely, *60 Minutes, Nightline,* and *20/20.* But PBS, the Public Broadcasting Service, is the best everyday television news source—best, without doubt, for in-depth reporting and analysis. Indeed, in most ways, PBS is perhaps the brightest spot on the television spectrum. But those viewers who are on the cable, which means an ever-increasing majority, also can click to the Discovery Channel, Arts and Entertainment, C-Span, and, of course, CNN, which still gives its viewers a good deal more news and analysis than the major networks. Those people on cable can now choose among two NBC news channels and a Fox News channel, in addition to others just mentioned, and for coverage in the sciences, *Nova* (PBS) does an excellent job of reporting interesting developments. (Lots of young people prefer instead to watch channels like MTV, alas.)

Nevertheless, TV still easily is eclipsed by the few good daily newspapers and especially by small-circulation magazines and journals. The mass media, even the big-city newspapers, generally focus on what is current, in the air, neglecting the underlying forces that ultimately determine what will be big news at a later date. For example, in January 1999, the mass media finally got onto the story of corruption in the International Olympic Committee (they shake down cities competing for the games) and even occasionally got into the shady pasts of the IOC heads and how they may be on the take. But readers of several non–mass media publications (e.g., *The Nation*) read about this long before it appeared in the mass media. Moral: If you really care what's going on in the world, you either won't find out from the mass media, or if you do, you'll get late and incomplete news. *Time, Newsweek,* and *U.S. News & World Report* do a bit of digging under the surface, but they tend to sensationalize what is going on and to be flighty, blowing with the winds of public opinion. Yet it is precisely the underlying forces that are the bread and butter of small-circulation periodicals, some of which deal with these matters very well indeed.

In addition, they often cover important stories that slide under the radar. For example *Extra!,* a media watchdog that evaluates news coverage, reported on the mass media's failure to cover adequately the starting testimony on wiretapping by former Deputy General James Comey in May 2007.[22] The story is not only gripping but reveals a disturbing behind-the-scenes attempt to ambush the Justice Department. When U.S. Attorney General John Ashcroft was hospitalized for gall bladder surgery in 2004,

---

[22] "Illegal Yes—But Not Newsworthy," by Peter Hart, *Extra! Update,* June 2007.

Comey, as acting attorney general, refused to sign an extension of the controversial wire-tapping program partly because it was considered illegal by the Justice Department's legal counsel. In a scene right out of a film noir, the White House chief of staff at the time, Andrew Card, and counsel Alberto Gonzales hurried to Ashcroft's bedside to persuade the very sick man to overturn Comey's ruling. Meanwhile Comey and FBI Director Robert Mueller got wind of the ambush and rushed to the hospital to intervene. But Ashcroft rallied his strength, rose to the occasion, and dramatically quashed the attempt. The media could have had a field day with this sensational, important story, but they didn't. Although the *New York Times* and *Newsweek* mentioned it in 2006, Comey's testimony before the Senate Judiciary Committee a year later got little notice except from a *Washington Post* editorial critical of the president for proceeding with a program that the Justice Department itself considered illegal. As *Extra!* points out, this significant scandal never even appeared in most of the mass media. This is the type of revelation that the non–mass media bring to our attention. (See an annotated list of publications at the end of the book for examples and for some thoughts by the authors of this text concerning some of these important information sources.)

Finding out what is really going on, however, isn't so much a matter of mass versus non–mass media as it is of learning how to be selective—learning how to separate pearls from schlock. Those interested in science, for example, would do well to avoid newsstand magazines that pander to the appetite so many people have for stories about ESP and other matters on the edge of legitimate science and that try to sensationalize science to increase sales. (Will stories about "close encounters of the third kind" ever go away?)

The point is that the non–mass media contain lots more pearls per square inch and are, on the whole, a good deal more sophisticated in their discussions of what is going on in the world than are newspapers, TV, and even mass-sales books. Best-selling books—for instance those concerning politics, economics, and the like—often are shallow or sensationalist.

Of particular note are the self-serving memoirs of "distinguished statesmen," such as Henry Kissinger, that are often little more than bald-faced attempts to rewrite history in their favor. Presidential memoirs, supposedly written by former presidents, are perhaps the most self-serving of these tomes. *Example:* Ronald Reagan's *An American Life* (Simon & Schuster, 1990), apparently written by Robert Lindsey (whom Reagan credits by saying "Robert Lindsey, a talented writer, was with me every step of the way"). Also, Bill Clinton's, *My Life* (Knopf, 2004), written in longhand by Clinton himself, he claimed, played up his triumphs and played down his failures (as do most presidential memoirs), though he did take full blame for the Monica Lewinsky affair.

We should note, by the way, that National Public Radio (NPR) does a better job of presenting the news and analysis than does any television channel or most other radio outlets. Some examples of their regular programs are *All Things Considered, Talk of the Nation, BBC World News, Fresh Air, Science Friday,* and *As It Happens,* an excellent Canadian news program broadcast widely in the United States. There is even at least one major network entertainment program, *Law and Order,* that provides a good deal of information about how the legal system really works, as opposed to how it is supposed to work (more will be said in the next chapter about the great gulf between theory and practice) in addition to straight entertainment.

Finally, a word or two more about newspapers and magazines. The best newspapers in the United States, overall, probably are the *New York Times* (unfortunately sans comic strips, which means no *Doonesbury*), the *Los Angeles Times,* and the *Washington Post.* Even so, most large metropolitan areas have at least one reasonably good newspaper that is a better source of information than any of the major networks or cable news channels, for that matter.

8. RECENT DEVELOPMENTS

During the past 30 years or so, dramatic changes have been taking place in the news business. Perhaps the most important of these is the ever-increasing concentration of media ownership, and thus power, in fewer and fewer hands.

The first and much smaller concentration of media power occurred way back in the late nineteenth century with the development of newspaper chains—the most important, perhaps, being the one put together by William Randolph Hearst and fictionalized in the movie classic *Citizen Kane.* The power of these early media magnates is illustrated in that film by a scene in which a journalist sent to Cuba in 1898 reports back that there is no sign of war in Cuba, only to be told that Kane (Hearst) would supply the war. (The scene is a takeoff on what is held by some to be true: that the United States' involvement in the Spanish-American War was in large part due to the Hearst publications' sensationalistic journalism. More likely, though, it was just one of many factors leading to that one-sided, unprovoked, war.)

The power of the Hearst media empire was illustrated again in 1941 when Hearst forced RKO, the producer of *Citizen Kane,* not to show that film in its theaters nationwide. The threat was to refuse ads listing any RKO theater offerings in Hearst's many newspapers around the country, which would have caused RKO a tremendous financial loss.

This blacklisting of *Citizen Kane* nicely illustrates the great censorship potential of concentrated media power. But back in those days, all big cities had more than one newspaper so that no small group or individuals could effectively control the newspaper business. (It was not until the 1950s that television usurped the role of newspapers as the principal news source for a growing majority of people in the United States and Canada.)

Today's media conglomerates are a good deal more worrisome than were the newspaper chains of old, because they concentrate power into an extremely few hands in all of the major news media—television, radio, mass-circulation magazines and newspapers. Independent newspapers still exist in some cities and towns, but their number

---

The founders of this country believed a free and rambunctious press was essential to the protection of our freedoms. They couldn't envision the rise of giant megamedia conglomerates whose interests converge with state power to produce a conspiracy against the people. I think they would be aghast at how this union of media and government has produced the very kind of Imperial power against which they rebelled.

—Bill Moyers, on media and democracy,
www.media.reform.net, November 25, 2003

shrinks every year, and most big cities now are down to just one daily paper, usually owned by a large and powerful chain. So today, a single individual may control quite a few TV outlets as well as newspapers and magazines, as does, for example, Rupert Murdoch (the Fox TV network, the New York *Post,* and many other newspapers, including the prestigious *London Times,* and magazines worldwide).

This problem was compounded when the FCC voted to ease restrictions on media ownership in June 2003. This decision allows companies to own even more TV and radio stations, as well as cross-own newspapers and radio and TV stations in the same market (previously banned by the FCC). The measure has prompted widespread opposition from groups as diverse as the Christian Coalition, the National Rifle Association, and the National Organization for Women. In response to these massive protests, the Senate voted to overturn the FCC's new rules allowing TV networks to own stations that reach as much as 45 percent of the country's market. It reduced the percentage to the previous cap of 35, but the cap was later revised upward to 39 percent under pressure from the White House.

Equally frightening is the fact that the giant media empires have multiple business interests outside the news media world that provide enormous opportunity for product sales and promotion. The ruling principle of these megacorporations is the bottom line, not the best possible dissemination of news. Here is a list of some of the holdings of four of these huge media giants:

- **Time Warner** owns or controls the Turner Broadcasting System (CNN, TNT, TBS, and other networks), HBO, Warner Brothers Studios and Television, Warner Books, Little Brown and Company, and dozens of online services. It has over 50 magazines, including *Time, Fortune, Sports Illustrated, Money,* and *People,* and though it dropped AOL from its corporate name, it still has holdings like AOL Instant Messenger and AOL Movie Fone. If that isn't enough, add to the list Netscape Communications, the Atlanta Braves, and a bunch of theme parks.

- **Walt Disney** owns ABC (*ABC Network News, Prime Time Live, 20/20,* TV stations serving a quarter of U.S. households, and over 65 radio stations), Fox Family Worldwide, Walt Disney Pictures, Miramax Films, Hyperion Books, Disney Publishing Worldwide, and the Walt Disney Internet Group. Then, of course, there are Disneyland, Disneyworld, and a host of other theme parks, plus more than 400 Disney stores selling Disney products. It owns a nice slice of ESPN, A&E, and the Walt Disney Internet Group.

- **General Electric** has primary interests elsewhere but is heavily invested in the media. It owns 80 percent of NBC (Vivendi controls 20 percent), including *NBC Network News, Dateline NBC,* the *Today* show, and cable networks (CNBC, MSNBC, Bravo, and USA). It owns Universal Studios and the Telemundo Communications Group, an investment group that includes Sony and Liberty Media. Big as they are, the media investments are just part of GE's vast empire. GE manufactures aircraft engines, power generators, and a wide array of consumer products. It owns an important insurance division and is involved in industrial, transportation, and power systems.

- **News Corporation** is Rupert Murdoch's international conglomerate with lots of U.S. holdings: Fox broadcasting and dozens of television stations, DBS and cable holdings, 20th Century Fox, the *New York Post, Wall Street Journal,* and London *Times,* as well as a few dozen newspapers and book companies in the United States, Great Britain, and Australia. And on top of all that, a percentage of the Los Angeles Kings and the Los Angeles Lakers.

Then there are the gigantic newspaper and media service corporations such as The New York Times Co., The Washington Post Co., The Dow/Jones Wall Street Journal, The Tribune Co., Knight Ridder, and Gannett—groups that control an ever-larger portion of the newspaper business in America.

Well, then, why should the rest of us care about this concentration of media power into fewer and fewer hands? Doesn't size, after all, yield efficiency? Aren't large news companies better able to afford large staffs of reporters gathering news items around the world? The answer to both of these questions may well be yes. But three other nagging questions immediately arise. Will being *able to afford* larger staffs automatically translate in practice into larger staffs? Will greater efficiency generally translate into better news reporting or simply into greater profits? Will media moguls resist the temptation to further their own interests, including the interests of their own nonnews subsidiaries, at the expense of news quality and fair evaluation? The answer to all of these questions, unfortunately, seems to be *no.*

Item: The *Washington Post* ran an advertising supplement for General Motors (GM) that publicized the company's environmental credentials. The problem was that it was filled with articles by *Post* reporters and thus gave the impression of a partnership between the *Post* and GM, blurring the line between news stories and advertising.[23]

Item: Since media consolidation leads to news staff reductions, local news, including emergencies, may well go unreported. A notorious example (cited in *The Public I,* November 2003) occurred in Minot, North Dakota, where Clear Channel, by far the biggest player in the Midwest radio industry, owned six of the eight commercial stations in the area. The public was never warned of a chemical spill in January 2002 because emergency workers were unable to find a living person at any station to broadcast the news.

Since megacorporations are profit driven and risk averse, one consequence of their dominating the industry is that the quality of programming has gone down in recent years, so instead of getting high-caliber, innovative sitcoms like the Mary Tyler Moore productions in the 1970s, for example, we get reality TV—cheap thrills that cost a fraction of a good sitcom to produce. Even more important, though, is that big media have the ability to limit the free exchange of ideas and thus undermine democracy. Because they are able to control the news, they can (and do) limit the range of information and debate from diverse sources, slant the news to their advantage, and kill stories that threaten their own interests.[24]

Item: When the lead singer of the Dixie Chicks, Natalee Maines, criticized President Bush during a London concert, Cumulus Media ordered its 50 country music stations not to play the group's songs for a month. Her comment, "We're ashamed the president of the United States is from Texas," was made the summer of 2003, soon after the U.S. invasion of Iraq.

Item: When *Frontline* showed a documentary "Hand of God," their PBS affiliate in Brownsville, Texas, KMBH, claimed it didn't get the video feed in time to air the program in January 2007. But critics, knowing the station was owned by the Roman Catholic diocese of Brownsville, suspected the real reason was that the documentary dealt with child molestations by Catholic priests.

Another disturbing issue closely connected to the concentration of media power in a few companies is the cozy relationship between media giants and corporate America. Project Censored did a study of media interlocks with big corporations and found that all 118 board members of the ten largest media companies sat on boards of 288 national and international corporations.[25] Not only that, but eight out of ten of these media companies had board memberships in common with each other. The *Washington Post* and NBC, for instance, both had board members with seats on J.P. Morgan and Coca-Cola.

These interlocking connections raise obvious conflicts of interest. How likely is a network or newspaper to play down or ignore news stories harmful to companies with close ties? Very likely. And how tempting would it be to play up the products and images of these companies? Tempting, indeed. Take, for example, an NBC *Today* show

---

[23]This item and the *Frontline* example are from "Fear & Favor 2007," by Janine Jackson and Peter Hart, *Extra!,* March/April 2008. It's a goldmine of examples of how power shapes the news.
[24]For more on this see Ted Turner's article "My Beef with Big Media," in *The Washington Monthly,* July–August 2004. Turner focuses in particular on the way big media increasingly shut out independent entrepreneurs with diverse points of view but not enough cash or clout to compete with the big guys.
[25]For a full discussion and list of overlaps between media giants and corporations see "Big Media Interlocks with Corporate America," by Peter Phillips, projectcensored.org.

(April 30, 2007) that featured Matt Lauer making glowing comments about Boeing aircraft in a segment shot at their Everett, Washington, factory. His "full disclosure" that Boeing is owned by NBC's parent company, General Electric, was a blip on the screen compared to the footage given to the favorable coverage of Boeing's 777s. Viewers were assured that the planes would make flying more comfortable, safer, and cost effective and would boost the U.S. economy. Not only that, employees loved making this "great product." The sign-off, "If it ain't Boeing, we ain't going," added the final touch. With news stories like this, "why bother with commercials."[26]

All is not lost, though. There are quite a few positive developments on TV, one of which is Oprah Winfrey's use of her TV pulpit to convince audiences that reading books can be both fun and informative. When Oprah selects a book for discussion on her program, it usually rises quickly onto best-seller lists. People write to her about how they have started reading and love it. Hooray for Oprah Winfrey! (On the negative side, Winfrey engages in some of the shoddy news practices that are routine on TV and radio talk shows—for example, concerning health news.)

Which brings us to the Internet, interactive television, and the other electronic wonders. Of course, no one can be sure how these new media will work out with respect to the news and other kinds of information. Bill Gates, for example, predicted that people would regularly watch TV programs on their computer screens. TV sets now are available that can do some of the simple things done by computers. HDTV (high-definition TV) has arrived. Most computers these days are programmed to handle CD-ROMs containing whole dictionaries, almanacs, encyclopedias, and the like. Billions are being wagered one way or another in the attempt to get in on the ground floor of the new ways in which the electronic marvel industry is going to change our lives.

Perhaps the biggest threat to current news dissemination on these new electronic media has to do with advertising and the Internet. Newspapers get most of their revenue from ads, including classified ads. If a good deal of this advertising revenue is diverted to the Internet, newspapers will suffer greatly, and many, perhaps most, could go out of business. (The flip side of this is that advertising on the Internet, so far, has not been as successful as it still is on the relatively old-fashioned TV outlets, but it is rapidly catching up.)

It also has been argued that the Internet is going to increase the division in large, industrial countries between the resources available to the rich as compared to the poor. Public libraries, for example, traditionally (well, for the past 100 years or so) have been free sources of all kinds of information, but the Internet seems to be headed more and more toward information provided at a price that may seriously limit access by the poor.

Nevertheless, many viewers on the scene see the Internet as a wonderful democratizing force, counteracting the concentration of media power now taking place. Increasingly the Internet provides news coverage from major publications, like the *New York Times,* and from online magazines. In addition, it provides information that may be slighted by mainstream news outlets. A case in point is the Internet coverage of the political conventions in the 2008 presidential campaign. When broadcast networks cut back on airtime for the conventions, the Internet filled the gap with around-the-clock coverage that included polls, live chats, and interactive events. When used this way, the Internet provides

---

[26]Example from "Fear & Favor 2007," *Extra!,* March/April 2008.

a megaphone for ordinary people, allowing all of us to tell the world what is on our minds. (Whether the world will be tuned in is another matter.) Correspondence via e-mail also has great promise as an information source. But so far, the now-traditional media (television, radio, newspapers, periodicals, libraries) still remain the principal news source for the majority of people, though that is changing now.

SUMMARY OF CHAPTER 11

1. The mass media are businesses intent on making money. So they have to satisfy their audiences, advertisers, and governments.

They cater to their audiences by simplifying the news to make it more easily understood—by breaking news items into small sound bites that stay within the average attention span in length and by arranging coverage of news so as to conform to audience interests and prejudices. *Example:* The 2008 Olympic Games featuring U.S. athletes but paying scant attention to those from other countries.

The media cater to advertisers by suppressing news that reflects badly on them or their products and by touting advertisers' products free as "news" items. *Example:* The *Pioneer Press* quashing a review critical of a restaurant that advertised in the paper.

The media also has to take account of the power of government to harass them by rescinding licenses, restricting access to government records, censoring information that doesn't conform to their political agenda, playing favorites in the dissemination of news, and fining networks for broadcasting indecent material. *Example:* The half-million-dollar fine slapped on CBS for airing Janet Jackson's indecent exposure during her halftime Super Bowl performance. The media often give in to this power of government by treading more carefully in criticizing government actions. *Example:* Reporters at press conferences who are careful not to ask overly pointed follow-up questions. Another way the government manages the news is by inserting into newscasts prepackaged reports that get their message out or put a positive spin on the news. (Note that the power of government to censor is much greater in many other countries than in the United States and in some other industrial democracies.)

But the mass media have a good deal of power of their own, stemming from their ability to expose and publicize whatever they care to. *Famous example:* The *Washington Post*'s dogged exposé of the Watergate scandal that forced President Nixon to resign in disgrace.

The business world—in particular, very large corporations—have a large say in the dissemination of news. They often use this power, first, to suppress stories unfavorable to their own narrow interests and, second, to get favorable stories included in media presentations. This power of big business stems from its power as advertisers (to withdraw advertising), from its ability to influence politicians and governments (principally through "campaign contributions") and from its ownership of a good deal of the mass media.

Of course, in practice the media tend to try to satisfy all of the various power factions and not to needlessly throw their weight around. It almost always is more profitable to cooperate with power than to fight it. *Example:* Politicians and the media cooperating to produce sound bites: The pols get exposure and the media get cheap footage to show on the evening news. Unfortunately, the news has increasingly become a source of entertainment more than information, playing up human interest stories like the saga of Jessica Lynch at the expense of hard news.

Since the bottom line is, as they say, the bottom line, news-gathering methods tend to be designed to save money, which means that regular beats are set up to gather the news from those able to regularly supply it (the rich and/or powerful and the government). True investigative reporting is very costly and thus relatively less common than a mere gathering of the news from other sources. *Example:* The regular attendance at presidential press conferences as compared to the amount of journalistic digging below the surface.

2. For reasons already mentioned, the media tend to misdirect audience attention away from important, underlying issues and events to human interest stories. In doing this, they tend to take advantage of the average person's lack of a good sense of proportion. *Example:* Playing up celebrity scandals and playing down or ignoring serious issues.

3. What happens every day is not new and is therefore not usually considered to be newsworthy by the mass media. *Example:* The ongoing and extremely serious threat posed by bacteria and viruses that tends to get only sporadic coverage.

The media's theory of objectivity, to which lip service is widely paid, requires that news stories be separated from speculations, judgments, evaluations, and the like, which are considered to be subjective. But this theory is off the mark. Facts don't just lie around waiting to be picked up; reporters must reason to the facts. Similarly, decisions as to what will be covered and what will not depend in part on value judgments, so that news and evaluations cannot be completely separated.

In practice, however, the theory of objectivity simply keeps the media from straying too far in their judgments and evaluations from the mainstream social consensus. *Example:* Their attempts to be objective by being "evenhanded" merely result in our hearing what the Democrats have to say as compared to the Republicans.

Because the theory of objectivity says that news reporting must be separated from judgments, speculation, and background information, the mass media tend to be short on explanations as to why things happen as they do. Of course, reporters cannot be expected to be experts on every topic they cover. But they still want to appear to be authoritative—to appear to know what they are talking about whether they do or don't. *Example:* Geraldo Rivera reporting from Afghanistan.

The media generally want to play it safe when featuring expert opinion. They want to satisfy all relevant power factions, if possible. So they tend to consult establishment figures, including media bigwigs, and not to annoy their audiences. The result often is silly pontificating. *Example:* The political correctness of almost all political discussion on TV.

Note that the media sometimes act as self-censors, either out of patriotic intent (as in wartime), or in order to placate their audiences or advertisers, or to avoid the possibility of libel. *Example:* Showing Elvis Presley doing his stuff only from the waist up on the old Ed Sullivan TV show.

4. The media need to slant the news can be accomplished in quite a few different ways: playing a story up or down, using a misleading or sensational headline, omitting or playing down follow-up stories, using (or not using) emotive language, using suggestive photos and other imagery, and using cartoons to convey a point of view. *Example:* Underreporting the massive displacement of the Iraqi people during the Iraq War.

5. The most important mass medium these days is television, which serves as town crier, certifier, and grapevine. It is the chief medium on which political contests are fought and news about major events such as wars is disseminated. No other medium comes close to television in the size of its audience or the immediacy of its offerings.

   The result is that the television industry has greater power than the other media and indeed can and does influence the course of events in the world on which it reports. *Example:* The way in which TV coverage of the Iraq War influenced the public to support it early on and turn against it as coverage became negative.

   Even prime-time television entertainment sometimes has positive features. *Example:* It has helped to break down prejudices against ethnic and religious groups and women—portraying blacks and women in important jobs in the business community. Note also the positive effects of employing African Americans and women on TV news programs. (TV also is superior in explaining the news to ordinary people on the street.)

6. The Internet offers an unparalleled opportunity to obtain useful information and to participate in public discourse. But because of all the schlock on the web, we have to be vigilant in thinking critically about the way the news is reported or managed. *Example:* "Citizen reporters" or bloggers expressing strong bias or misrepresenting the news.

7. Although the mass media are a modestly good source of breaking news, smaller-scale outlets are much better at analysis, at supplying background information, and at investigative reporting.

   PBS is a relatively good source of news, generally better than most mass media outlets, in particular in providing background information and analysis. But lots of small-circulation magazines are significantly better than PBS and CNN, being crafted so as to appeal to more sophisticated audiences. *Example:* The *Washington Monthly* coverage of politics.

   But the point is selectivity, not mass versus non–mass media. This is true not only with respect to television, newspapers, radio, and magazines, but also to books. Popular books tend to be lighter weight than some that are less popular, because mass audiences tend to be rather unsophisticated. *Example: Discover* and *Omni* magazines, which hoke up science in the attempt to make it interesting to a mass audience. (Note that presidential memoirs and those of other high government officials tend to be particularly shoddy products. *Example:* President Reagan's rearrangement of facts called *An American Life.*)

8. The intense concentration of media power in the hands of giant conglomerates is one of the more ominous recent developments in the media business. *Example:* Walt Disney owning ABC, dozens of radio stations, hundreds of Disney stores,

and so forth. Although size theoretically can yield efficiency and better news coverage, in general it hasn't worked that way so far.

EXERCISE 11-2

When Barack Obama was campaigning for the presidential nomination, CBS News.com received so many ugly remarks about the senator that the network decided to block all comments on its stories about him out of concern for the latent racism and the safety of the candidate. (Obama had been assigned Secret Service protection the previous week.) But CBS allowed comments on stories about all the other candidates. The network was criticized for denying him the publicity and for suppressing useful discussion about the candidate. Do you think CBS made the right decision?

EXERCISE 11-3

1. Evaluate the coverage in your local newspaper of a particular event or issue of national importance, with respect to (1) objectivity, (2) original versus secondhand reporting, (3) use of headlines, (4) establishment or mainstream point of view compared to minority opinions, and (5) any other matters discussed in this chapter.

2. Do the same for a recent issue of *Time, Newsweek, U.S. News & World Report,* or one of the online magazines such as *Salon.*

3. Do the same for an ABC, NBC, or CBS national evening news program.

4. Get a recent copy of *The Economist,* a British news magazine that widely circulates in the United States and Canada. Select a story in it about a particular event, and compare how it is handled with the way it is dealt with in one of the major American news magazines.

5. Compare news reporting on the BBC world news program carried on National Public Radio (NPR) with news reporting on any network TV or radio station. Which is better, and why?

6. Watch several episodes of *Grey's Anatomy* or *House* and explain how doctors and the medical industry are portrayed. Be sure to explain how their portrayal is similar to and different (if it is) from the real medical world. Do you think these programs influence how viewers tend to see doctors and medical care?

7. How are the elderly and teenagers portrayed on network TV programs, both in news stories and, especially, in popular entertainment programs? Back up your conclusions with details. How about women as compared to men?

8. Check the front page of a single issue of your local newspaper and determine as best you can the sources of their stories. (In the case of wire stories—Associated Press, Reuters, and the like—try to determine their sources.) How many of these stories are based primarily on a single handout or speech, how many were compiled from several such sources, and how many from reporters going out and finding for themselves what is going on?

9. Read through a single issue of three non—mass media magazines, one liberal (for instance, *The Nation*), one conservative (say, *The National Review*), and one libertarian (for example, *Reason*). Are their points of view evident? How do you think they compare to mass media magazines such as *Time* or *Newsweek* or to network national TV news programs?

10. How do you think the news would be presented to us if the federal government controlled and managed the mass media? Be specific and defend your answer with some thoughtful analysis.

11. Suppose that you owned a local television station or newspaper, or a whole television network. Would you report the news any differently from the way that the outlets in your area do now? If so, how, and why? If not, why not? (Assume that, while rich, you can't withstand losses forever. And be realistic, not goody-goody.)

12. Many more women are working in the mass media today than in the old days, but fewer women than men rise to the top. Do you think the fact that men hold so many of the top positions in the mass media and thus make most of the important policy decisions seriously influences work conditions and news content in ways that would be different if women were equally represented in news media high management? If so, how? If not, why not?

13. For the energetic: Go to the library or the Internet and dig through back issues of some mass media publication and evaluate its coverage over time of some important, underlying, or long-term national issue or problem (for example, under- and unemployment, crime, pollution). Defend your evaluation.

14. Also for the energetic: Write your own news story about a personal event that truthfully makes you look bad. Write it as though it were to appear in your local or school newspaper, including headlines and the rest. Now rewrite the story to show your part in it in the best light possible without actually lying. Compare the two. Was this little exercise educational? (Answer: Very definitely, if you did it well.)

15. Examine the photographs accompanying a news story and explain how they slant the news.

16. The thrust of the discussion about the recent intense concentration of media power into fewer and fewer hands was that on the whole this is bad for the effective dissemination of the news. We noted, for example, that the chief concern of these large corporations is the bottom line, not the best presentation of the news. But isn't it possible, perhaps even likely, that these megacorporations will find that the highest profits are obtained by best satisfying their audiences, thus putting all of us (collectively) into the driver's seat—being given the sort of news coverage we most prefer? And if so, isn't that all to the good? So why worry about the concentration of media power that has been taking place lately?

By Handelsman, from *The New Yorker*. Reprinted by permission of Tribune Media Services.

"Do your owners treat you well? Mine are very kind."

This New Yorker *drawing depicts what many critics claim is the principal problem with the political process in industrial democracies like the United States today—politicians are beholden to fat-cat contributors who provide most of the cash required to campaign successfully for high office. (By the way, what do you think are the chances that a social studies text containing this cartoon would be adopted by your school?)*

Not to know what has happened before one was born is always to be a child.

—Cicero

A high school teacher, after all, is a person deputized by the rest of us to explain to the young what sort of world they are living in and to defend, if possible, the part their elders are playing in it.

—Emile Capouya

A child educated only at school is an uneducated child.

—George Santayana

The less people know about how sausages and laws are made, the better they'll sleep at night.

— Otto von Bismarck

Germany has taught me that an uncritical view of the national past generated an equally subservient acceptance of the present.

—Hans Schmitt (who grew up in Nazi Germany)

If a nation expects to be ignorant and free, . . . it expects what never was and never will be.

—Thomas Jefferson

Chapter

12

TEXTBOOKS: MANAGING WORLDVIEWS

Public schools are one of the earliest sources of information about the world that most of us are exposed to. So it is important to have a good idea about how accurate what we have been told while growing up might be.

One way to get an idea about this is to examine typical textbooks used in public school classrooms. Most teachers, after all, tend to coordinate classroom instruction with textbook content. This is particularly true in history courses, where the textbook is often the backbone of the curriculum. Since most history teachers in middle and high school haven't majored or minored in the subject, they tend to rely heavily on the content of the textbook. In some countries, like Japan and Singapore, where teachers are usually experts in history, they can supplement national curriculum guides with their own materials and can instruct students from their knowledge of the field.But since many teachers in the United States get their information from the same source as their students, it is critical to evaluate the quality of the average history textbook in this country. So let's discuss, first, the ways in which history texts tell high school students about the history of the United States.

1. HIGH SCHOOL HISTORY TEXTBOOKS

Textbooks don't stay the same for very long. Ups and downs in quality and content are bound to occur every so often.

The Good News

The good news is that since about 1960, the quality of high school history textbooks has improved in many significant ways. The first of these improvements was in the portrayal of African Americans. Blacks had been close to invisible in texts published before that time. They were mentioned, of course, with respect to slavery and its elimination via the Emancipation Proclamation, and reference generally was made to two "token" Negroes, Booker T. Washington and George Washington Carver. But by some time in the 1970s, virtually all history and civics texts had been revised to include more, and fairer, material about African Americans and their place in American history and everyday affairs.

Improved treatment of other minority groups and of women quickly (as these things go) followed, reflecting changing attitudes and roles in the body politic. In older textbooks no mention was made of the atrocities committed by European explorers against Native Americans or of their later subjugation by the government. Today, virtually every high school history textbook mentions the "Trail of Tears" (the forced move of the Cherokee Indians from their homeland in the South to the Oklahoma territory), the illegal incarceration of loyal Japanese citizens in concentration camps during World War II, and so on.[1]

Coupled with the improved treatment of minority groups has come a moderately large step toward objectivity in the portrayal of the darker side of American history.

> He that reads and grows no wiser seldom suspects his own deficiency, but complains of hard words and obscure sentences, and asks why books are written which cannot be understood.
>
> —Samuel Johnson

---

[1] Interestingly, hardly any texts mention homosexuals (about 5 percent of the population?), and, while Jews are referred to, anti-Semitism in this country rarely is discussed except in connection with the Ku Klux Klan. Some books do mention the discrimination against the Irish that was common in times past, but never with more than a line or two. (The paucity of textbooks that talk about homosexuals has made the selection of texts quite difficult in the very few places—the most prominent being San Francisco—where gays have a certain amount of political clout.)

Imperialistic interference in the affairs of other countries—for example, of the so-called "banana republics"[2] of Central and South America—sometimes is hinted at (although the nasty details are never gone into in any depth).

The Bad News

Oh, yes—the bad news.

History Texts Are Dull and Overly Long   Public high school history books, as virtually all junior and senior high school textbooks, are exceedingly dull and full of misleading verbiage, so that only the brightest and most diligent students who do a good amount of reading between the lines are apt to learn much from them about the true history of their country. Very little in these texts is likely to raise student interest in these matters. Part of the problem is that textbooks cover far too much material, compressing it in brief passages that squeeze out the juicy details, lobotomize the personalities, and suck the life out of the stories. Most of the better-selling high school history textbooks run to more than 1,000 pages (and weigh 7½ pounds) with endless "learning aids," exercise questions, special features, and gorgeous graphics but no riveting accounts of dramatic events in American history that capture a student's imagination.

Students are snowed by an avalanche of facts ladled out one after another in a monotonous style devoid of what English teachers call "voice" or "tone"—not surprising since almost all these books are written by multiple authors. The groupthink that results weakens their views, blurs their differences, and reduces the text to a dull mass of information, not to mention trivia. Names that even professional historians would not always be able to identify—for example, of some of the failed early nineteenth-century vice-presidential candidates—pile up one after the other as details concerning the election of 1816, the

---

Overly long books, overstuffed with facts, facts, facts, are not just dull, dull, dull. They're also heavy, heavy, heavy, often weighing more than six pounds. Students now carry these books home with them in backpacks, homework assignments being a regular feature of today's educational system (as opposed to the one in effect when the authors of this text attended high school—we're talking ancient history here).

The result is that backaches and strained back muscles have become all too common these days among public school students. One third of the students in a study by researchers at Simmons College in Boston said that their backs hurt so much that they had missed whole school days, or had missed physical education classes, or had needed to visit their doctor.

So the overstuffed texts in use today not only fail to increase student comprehension but also harm student health.*

*See, for instance, "Weighty Backpacks Straining Schoolkids," *San Francisco Chronicle*, February 14, 2001, p. 1.

---

[2] The expression derives from the way in which the United Fruit Company dominated the political affairs of many of these countries for many years.

election of 1820, the election of 1824 . . . are described. Interesting topics have the guts wrung out of them. Even accounts of the good features of the American social system tend to fall flat.

That detailed facts spewed out one after another don't easily become part of the working knowledge of students is supported by all sorts of surveys (in which, for instance, students identified J. Edgar Hoover as a nineteenth-century president, Jefferson Davis as a guitar player, and Socrates as an Indian chief). But students also don't seem to grasp the general, or approximate, kinds of knowledge that are more important than most precise facts. It's more important, for example, that students know the approximate size and population of their country rather than precise statistics on this matter, and the evidence indicates that the ideas of most students concerning these important matters are either way off the mark or nonexistent.

Evidence of this is apparent in the results of periodic general knowledge polls. For instance, in a 2000 survey of seniors at prestigious colleges around the country (Amherst, Duke, Harvard, Grinnell, and some others), more students named Civil War General Ulysses S. Grant as the commander of the Continental Army in the final battle of the Revolutionary War than selected George Washington. Only one in five correctly identified the source of the famous and wonderful phrase "Government of the people, by the people, and for the people." (And who did utter that immortal line, and when?)

History Texts Have Been Dumbed Down   Another part of the bad news is that in the past several years a great many textbooks have been dumbed down with respect to vocabulary and sentence construction, although a few more linguistically sophisticated texts still are available. Dumbed-down texts shortchange students in several ways. One is the failure to stretch the already low student reading abilities that have led some educators to prefer the dumbed-down texts. Another results from the difficulty in presenting any complicated material using just simplified linguistic structures, forcing authors to oversimplify inherently complicated material.

One of the really annoying features of today's texts is the inane questions they sometimes ask students ("What evidence does this photo give of the depth of their poverty?"— under a photo that clearly shows the extreme poverty of the people pictured) or the allegedly "critical thinking" sidebars ("What kind of president do you think Americans were looking for after Watergate and the Nixon resignation?"). Not much critical thinking is needed the answer these make-work questions.

History Texts Have Gone Overboard on Multiculturalism   Still another part of the bad news is that history textbooks in recent years have reflected a general tendency to carry good, worthwhile improvements too far. If minorities and women were once seriously neglected in public school history texts, they now receive attention that distorts the history of the United States. History texts, in current lingo, have become *politically correct* and *multicultural*. (Recall the discussion in Chapter 1 concerning these trends.)

Noted historians and scholars who review textbooks have criticized this trend in both U.S. and world history texts.[3] For example, in one widely used U.S. history textbook,

---

[3]See *A Consumer's Guide to High School History Textbooks,* published by the Thomas B. Fordham Institute 2004—an excellent source for textbook reviews. The books discussed here are two of a dozen reviewed by a panel of historians.

Native American cultures are discussed in ten pages, the West African backgrounds of slaves get six pages, but the European background of white settlers rate no more than five pages—a gross distortion of actual fact.[4] The same book makes pretty much equal mention of immigrants from Europe, Asia, the West Indies, and Mexico a century ago, but has no discussion of the significant Jewish immigration in that same period.

Similar distortions occur in world histories. In an effort to avoid ethnocentrism, they pay the same attention and respect to all cultures, past and present, promoting a cultural relativism that misleads students into thinking that all cultures are equally important. Further, they tend to harshly criticize shortcomings in Western cultures but ignore or skirt them in other cultures. For example, one popular history text is critical of sexist attitudes in the medieval Catholic Church but not of discrimination against women in Islamic societies.[5] In fact, since September 11, 2001, textbooks have handled the Islamic culture with kid gloves. No mention is made of the brutal treatment of hundreds of thousands of "comfort" women and sex slaves in Korea, China, the Philippines, and Taiwan. In an effort to avoid offending people from any one culture, textbooks like these distort history by suppressing evidence.

American History Is Distorted   But arguably the most serious defect in today's history and social studies textbooks is that they still tend to distort American history and how the social/political system actually works in the United States, even if less so than in the past. Although those who ultimately decide what sorts of textbooks will be adopted surely do not intend to adopt books that stray too far from the truth, they also always have in mind the need to make students into loyal, proud citizens when they take their places in adult life, and they are influenced by the opinions and prejudices of those who have political power (a point to be discussed later).

United States History Is Sanitized   History texts "clean up" our past so as to maintain student pride in America. As much as possible, our leaders are pictured as better than human, all dressed up and minus their flaws (except, of course, for a very few Benedict Arnolds whose transgressions can't be papered over). Take the way in which Theodore Roosevelt, affectionately referred to as Teddy (the teddy bear was named after him), is spruced up in virtually all public school texts. Typically, he is portrayed as an energetic, hard-driving, exuberant, brave, trust-busting conservationist, reformer, and progressive, who was against monopolistic big business—a great man deserving of his place on Mount Rushmore.[6]

And perhaps he was. But no textbooks the authors of this text have ever seen, or even heard of, tell students about another side of good old Teddy. They don't describe him as a bloodthirsty bigot who, though unusually brave, reveled in the slaughter he personally engaged in and witnessed during the Spanish-American War; a man who expressed pleasure after 30 men had been shot to death in the Civil War draft riots ("an admirable

---

[4]*The Americans* (McDougal Littel, 2003).
[5]*Connections to Today* (Prentice Hall, 2003).
[6]But Roosevelt's role in the machinations that went on before construction of the Panama Canal, now seen as definitely not politically correct, sometimes are mentioned as a minus, whereas his role in the building of the canal previously was cited as one of his more glorious achievements. ("The more things stay the same, the more they change."—Harold Gordon)

> The soul of historical research is debate, but that sense of uncertainty and contingency seldom finds its way into textbooks. By its nature, the textbook must pretend that its condensation of events and its presentation of their meaning are correct. In reality, every textbook has a point of view, despite a façade of neutrality; the authors and editors select some interpretations and reject others, choose certain events as important and ignore others as unimportant. Even when they insert sidebars with point and counterpoint on a few issues, they give the false impression that all other issues are settled when they are not. The pretense of objectivity and authority is, at bottom, just that: a pretense.
>
> —Diane Ravitch
> *The Language Police*

object lesson to the remainder"); a man who justified slaughtering Indians on the grounds that their lives were only "a few degrees less meaningful, squalid, and ferocious than that of the wild beasts," and who said that "All the great masterful races have been fighting races. . . . No triumph of peace is quite so great as the supreme triumph of war." Not exactly a teddy bear, this Teddy Roosevelt. (History texts also falsely pump up the part played by Roosevelt's Rough Riders in the famous charge up San Juan Hill in Cuba during the Spanish-American War at the expense of the black American soldiers, who did the most effective fighting.)

Embarrassing Facts and Topics Are Omitted or Played Down   Although outright lying is frowned upon, the writers of public school textbooks have other devices at their disposal enabling them to satisfy the various kinds of social and political demands made on them. The most commonly employed of these devices is the complete omission of embarrassing historical events or facts. For example, most of the CIA "dirty tricks" and other sorts of interferences in the internal affairs of several foreign countries over the years—for instance, in Chile—get passed over. (Interestingly, the "Irangate" scandal that occurred during President Reagan's administration usually is mentioned.) Similarly, although all textbooks expend dozens of pages on World War II, most omit reference to the terrible firestorm bombing of Tokyo that killed more people than either of the atomic bombs we dropped on Japan, and they frequently fail to mention the deliberate policy of the American and British air forces to bomb German civilians, mostly women and children, as a way of breaking down German will to continue fighting.[7]

---

[7]Absolutely no texts provide anything like an accurate depiction of the nature of these cataclysmic bombings of German cities and of Tokyo (although there are hints—tiny hints—about the horror of the atomic bombings of Hiroshima and Nagasaki). Only a very few even mention the infamous firestorming of Dresden in which about 50,000 to 100,000 civilians were killed, an extremely ugly blot on the American and British escutcheons because Dresden had next to no military importance, and in any case the war was all but won when the thousands of bombers turned that once architectural gem into an inferno. An accurate count of the dead was impossible because all that was left of many people were heaps of ashes or a layer of gelatin covering the floors of cellar air raid shelters. See, for instance, *Target: Hitler's Oil,* by R. C. Nesbit (Kimber, 1985), or *Brute Force: Allied Strategy and Tactics in the Second World War,* by John Ellis (Viking, 1990).

It's interesting to compare how Native Americans are portrayed in public school textbooks with how historians picture them. Here, for instance, are excerpts from an account of Indian atrocities committed during the French and Indian War, discussed in a review in the New York Review of Books *(May 11, 2000) of a book about that war by historian Fred Anderson:**

Indians at war followed cultural conventions that eighteenth-century Europeans could not, at least openly, condone. Indians gave no quarter and did not expect any. . . . [W]hen they were enticed into large-scale actions of British and French military operations, they still carried the expectation that victory meant the right to do what they wished with prisoners of whatever age or sex. What they wished was to torture and kill some of them, maybe eat a few, and to adopt some of the rest into their own depleted ranks, procedures that continued to horrify and mystify Europeans.

The review quotes Anderson:

The only rewards that the Indians—whether Christian or heathen—had expected were plunder trophies to prove their prowess in battle, and captives to adopt or sacrifice as replacements for dead warriors or perhaps to hold for ransom. When it became clear that the man whom they called "Father" [French General Montcalm] intended to do what no real father would and deprive them of the reward they had earned, most of the warriors decided merely to take what they have come for and then to leave.

The review continues:

The immediate result was "the massacre of Fort William Henry," familiar to all readers of *The Last of the Mohicans.* Despite all efforts to restrain them, Montcalm's Indians killed close to two hundred of the garrison, troops and civilians alike, and carried off more than three hundred captives, at least one of whom was ritually boiled and eaten just outside Montreal.

Nothing like this ever appears in today's politically correct public school textbooks.

*The Crucible of War: The Seven Years War and the Fate of the Empire in British North America, 1754–1766 (Knopf, 2000).

Embarrassing events also sometimes are papered over by carefully controlled emphasis, especially by simply expending relatively little space on a topic. For example, most history textbooks these days, unlike those of times past, do tell readers about the war that occurred between American troops and Philippine guerrillas intent on gaining independence after the United States annexed the Philippine Islands at the end of the Spanish-American War, but they do so quickly, thus masking the extreme nastiness of the way in which the Filipinos were subjugated. The war with Spain gets relatively lots of space in most texts; the war against Filipino patriots extremely little, even though many more deaths and much greater destruction resulted from the war to force the Philippine people to knuckle under than from the war against Spain (itself quite a blot on the American escutcheon).

These devices are very hard for uninformed or unsophisticated readers to see through, particularly because we all want very much to believe in the greatness of our own society and tend to see national warts only after a good deal of experience has forced us to do so.

As might be expected, the role of the United States in foreign wars such as World War II is puffed up and cleansed. But it might also be supposed that the suffering and dying of American fighting troops would be explained in a way that would let students understand the extent of their sacrifices and the terror they endured, as they did, for instance, on June 6, 1944 (D-Day), when several thousand American troops lost their lives on the beaches of Normandy, in France. After all, this would show how brave and self-sacrificing American troops have been. But telling students about this would require explaining what modern warfare really is like: about what it means to advance into

---

A Typical High School History Textbooks

This textbook, America: Pathways to the Present, *contains 1,187 huge, double-columned 8½ by 12-inch pages, chock full of teaching devices (graphs, critical thinking questions, and so on)*. As might be imagined, this text is also chock full of facts about American history ladled out one after another in a deadly flat tone of voice. Here, for example, is a short excerpt from this book's account of the presidential election of 1880:*

As the 1880 presidential election approached, the Republican party was split into three factions. The Stalwarts, followers of Senator Conklin, defended the spoils system. The Half-breeds, who followed Maine senator James G. Blaine, hoped to reform the spoils system while remaining loyal to the party. Independents opposed the spoils system altogether. James A. Garfield, a congressman from Ohio, won the party's presidential nomination. Garfield was linked to the Half-breeds. To balance the ticket, the Republicans chose as their vice-presidential candidate Chester A. Arthur, the New York Stalwart whom Hayes had fired two years earlier.

In the 1880 election Garfield won a narrow victory over the Democratic candidate, General Winfield S. Hancock . . . [*ad infinitum*].

Fascinating. But how many students ever remember even the tiniest bit of this dreary account?

*This textbook, *America: Pathways to the Present,* by Andrew R. L. Cayton, Elisabeth Israels Perry, and Allan M. Winkler (Prentice Hall, 2000), is reviewed in *The Textbook Letter* (March/April 1999), the premier journal dealing with junior and senior high school textbooks.

> Who controls the past controls the future; who controls the present controls the past.
>
> —George Orwell (*1984*)

concentrated machine gun fire that is certain to mow down most of those who find themselves in this terrible and terrifying circumstance; about flying on bombing missions with the knowledge that sooner or later most bombers in your unit are likely to be shot down and their occupants killed;[8] about suddenly being covered with the splattered brains of a buddy who has just been hit by an unseen sniper; about the last moments of men drowning on submarines; about incinerated tank crews or the soldiers blasted into thousands of tiny pieces by enemy shelling. (Back in high school did you notice the total omission of pictures of dead American soldiers in history textbooks or of anything that graphically conveys the true horror of modern warfare?)

Violence in current wars is whitewashed in the same way. For example, in the 2007 edition of *The Americans* (an 11th-grade history cited earlier), no pictures of dead soldiers appear in the two-page account of the Iraq War, and no mention is made of the death toll, particularly of Iraqis. In fact, the only deaths cited are attributed to "insurgents or rebels engaged in acts of violence that killed thousands, including many Americans." Deaths caused by Americans are not discussed. The entire account glosses over the real reasons for the war and the ploys used to sell it to the American people, yet 11th graders—some of whom would soon go off to war—weren't considered old enough to process this information.

Before passing on to other matters, perhaps we should point out that the worst distortions of American history occur in grade school texts and that as students move up in grade level, textbooks become less goody-goody and quite a bit more accurate. The idea, which certainly is not without merit, seems to be that tiny tots are not ready for unvarnished truth and need to be gently introduced into the "facts of life" over time. What we have stressed here is that even in high school, students are provided a dolled-up version of reality, an account that fails to square with the true history of the United States. (Similar remarks apply to the social studies—civics, government, politics—texts about to be discussed.)

2. SOCIAL STUDIES (CIVICS) TEXTBOOKS MINIMIZE THE GREAT GULF BETWEEN THEORY AND PRACTICE

In the constant struggle for power and wealth that goes on in every country, national ideals, customs, and laws get violated. Thus, a great gulf always exists between the official story about how a system is supposed to work and actual, everyday practice. It is extremely important that we know the extent of this gulf if we are to have even a modestly good idea about what is likely to be in store for us as we go through life. We need

---

[8] That is one of the important points made in the well-known and excellent novel *Catch-22* by Joseph Heller.

Drawing by David Levine. Copyright © 1969 NYREV, Inc. Reprinted
by permission of Kathy Hayes Associates, agent for David Levine.

Hamburger Hill

*David Levine's drawing of Hamburger Hill (a hill in Vietnam on which many
soldiers lost their lives) pictures two American presidents as jolly mass murderers.
Would the Texas State Textbook Committee give its approval to a book containing
this caricature?*

to know, for example, what our chances are of getting justice if we have to go into court,
how far we can trust the leaders of our nation to consider our economic and other interests, and to what extent elected officials are influenced by lobbyists to do what is in their,
but not necessarily our or the nation's, best interests.

In the old days, civics texts restricted themselves almost entirely to descriptions,
detailed and quite accurate, as to the theory of American government and social practices,

more or less ignoring everyday reality. A typical text went on for pages about the "checks and balances" of government, provided minute details concerning the Constitution, the various departments and bureaus of the federal government, and so on, but hardly ever discussed the ways in which the system fails in actual practice to operate as it is supposed to.

Today's textbooks, unlike those in the past, often atleast hint at everyday reality. In most social studies textbooks, for example, even the better ones, the issue of bribery via "lobbying" and corruption in general are sanitized. Here, for instance, is how one venerable text that has been much improved in recent years discusses lobbying:

> The typical lobbyist of today is a far cry from those of an earlier day—and from many of the fictitious ones still found on television and in novels and the movies. The once fairly common practice of bribery and the heavy-handed use of unethical practices are almost unknown. Most present-day lobbyists work in the open, and their major techniques come under the heading of friendliness, persuasion, and helpfulness.
>
> Lobbyists are ready to do such things as buy lunches and dinners, provide information, write speeches, and prepare bills in proper form. The lunches and dinners are good, the information usually quite accurate, the speeches forceful, and the bills well drawn [!]. Most lobbyists know that if they behaved otherwise—gave false information, for example—they would damage, if not destroy, their credibility and so their overall effectiveness. . . .
>
> Lobbying abuses do occur now and then, of course. False or misleading testimony, bribery, and other unethical pressures are not common, but they do exist.[9]

Obviously, textbook accounts of this nature don't come close to revealing the way in which legislators are bought by the rich and powerful. (Notice then-Senator Bob Dole's unusually candid comment, quoted by Edward Sorel in his drawing reproduced on p. •••: "When these political action committees give money, they expect something in return other than good government.") But most of today's public school textbooks do at least hint at something close to the truth, and this is a great improvement over the way in which the topic of graft was discussed in times past. Students carefully reading between the lines now may be able to get at least a vague idea as to how the system works in practice.

3. TEXTBOOKS AND INDOCTRINATION

The obvious question to ask is why public school textbooks are written in the way just described. There is no easy answer to this question, but one thing is clear: The ultimate purpose of public schools is to educate the young to fit into adult society. This means, first, giving them the knowledge they will need to be productive citizens and, second,

---

[9]*Magruder's American Government,* by William A. McClenaghan (Prentice Hall, 1995.) This book has been a popular one since 1917. The quotes here are from a four-page account of lobbying that almost in its entirety is a whitewash of the topic. Still, anyone who wants to see how much better today's texts are than those of even 20 or 30 years ago would do well to look at earlier editions of this work.

Dependence Day, 1993

EDWARD SOREL

This July 4, Senator Dole has a special reason for celebrating. The American political system has been good to him. According to reports filed with the Federal Elec-tion Commission, his campaign receipts for 1991-92 totaled $2,362,936—almost all from special interests. His agribusiness contributors include Philip Morris, Dow Chemical, John Deere, Kellogg, General Mills, Archer Daniels Midland and Farmland Industries. (Dole is a senior Republican on the Agriculture, Nutrition and Forestry Committee.)

Finance and real estate interests also contribute. These include Equitable Life, Goldman Sachs, American Express, Glendale Federal Savings and Loan, PaineWeb-ber, First Boston, Chemical Bank, Mutual of Omaha and Prudential Insurance, among others. (Dole is *the* senior Republican on the Finance Committee.)

Senator Dole insists that his interventions on behalf of his contributors are perfectly legal, and while being interviewed by *The Wall Street Journal* was surprisingly frank about how Congress operates: "When these political action committees give money, they expect something in return other than good government."

Drawing by Edward Sorel from *The Nation,* July 1993. Reprinted by permission of Edward Sorel.

This drawing (with comment) by Edward Sorel, whose excellent work frequently graces the pages of The New Yorker, The Nation, *and* Atlantic Monthly *magazines, nicely illustrates the point that lobbying in the United States today is quite different from, and a good deal more insidious than, the lobbying described in public school textbooks.*

inculcating in them the values, attitudes, and practices that will make them good citizens. Education thus inevitably involves a certain amount of indoctrination.[10]

Applying these thoughts to public school textbooks yields some tentative conclusions as to their likely content, conclusions that are borne out by examining these works. The first is that history and social studies texts are bound to distort their material. The history of every nation has its dark spots as well as bright, and no system works the way it is supposed to. Public school history and civics texts therefore inevitably distort their subject matter so as to make "Our Great Nation" appear better than it really is. No society wants disaffected citizens. Embarrassing matters have to be papered over somehow or other; exactly how depends on social and political factors that change from time to time. Today, these factors are more favorable for providing students with greater accuracy and less indoctrination than ever before. (But not all is sweetness and light by any means, as we shall see shortly.)

The second tentative conclusion is that noncontroversial topics, such as mathematics, will be presented in a much more straightforward way than are history and social studies texts, with indoctrination at a minimum. Society wants just about everybody to be able to do arithmetic.

Finally, a third tentative conclusion is that controversial or touchy topics will be approached gingerly, papered over, or simply not discussed at all. Examples include the effects of campaign contributions on the performance of elected officials; so-called *regressive* taxes—indeed, most controversial economic issues; and social justice or its lack. As remarked on before, all of these tentative conclusions turn out to be accurate.

An unexpected new trend in education may modify the indoctrination built into American textbooks and, for that matter, the schoolbooks of other countries as well. Education, like big business, is going global. For example, a Swiss-based secondary school program developed by the International Baccalaureate Organization is being used in hundreds of schools throughout the world, and curricula for elementary and middle schools are in the works. Since publishers will be selling to an international community with potentially far more consumers than any single country could provide, textbooks will be much less likely to favor the bias of any one nation. It's worth keeping an eye on this trend.

4. Textbooks and Politics

When discussing the mass media in the previous chapter, we pointed out how the various interested parties—media owners, governments, big business, readers, and viewers—exert their power both in the political and the business arenas. The textbook arena also is the scene of power encounters, although, as should become evident, the various strengths and roles of the players are modestly different from what they are in the mass media. The players in the textbook political arena are voters, in particular, parents of schoolchildren

---

[10]Although the primary intent of the adults who write and adopt public school textbooks is indeed to educate the young of their society, human nature being what it is, they also have other motives: to defend their own collective contribution to the history of their nation and to deny or play down their collective mistakes and misadventures. It's always difficult to notice how this creeps into the content and tone of the works of one's own group, but it becomes more evident when we examine those of other societies.

and organized groups of interested individuals; teachers, educators, and other scholars; and textbook manufacturers. Governments, of course, particularly on the state and local levels, have a large say in the matter, but they more or less act in response to guidance and pressure from the interested parties and in particular to voter demands.

There is nothing new in the fact that politics plays an important role in determining textbook content. It has always played a big role in the field of education. Even the idea of universal literacy was once fought over in the political arena. Until well into the nineteenth century, education in Europe and America was confined to the upper classes, with very few exceptions. Indeed, the dominant upper-class worldview held that the masses of people were easier to control if they remained ignorant. (It also self-servingly held that the lower classes were too loutish to be able to learn to read and write with any facility.) The push for universal literacy began only with the nineteenth-century growth in the size and political power of the middle classes. Textbooks, in fact, themselves are an invention, more or less, of nineteenth-century educators. In Shakespeare's day, for instance, studying the great classical writings and other treatises constituted a relatively large part of grammar school education.

Nineteenth-century textbooks had just as strong a political orientation as those used in schools today. For half a century after the Civil War, southern states insisted on a sympathetic account of their part in the war, whereas northern states demanded inclusion of the South's treason, so publishers came up with the two different versions of the war for their respective clients. After the First World War, patriotic groups like the American Legion and Veterans of Foreign Wars criticized textbooks that failed to arouse patriotic fervor, and ethnic groups insisted that their heroes be included in history books, much as ethnic and women's organizations do today. Then as now, textbook publishers complied.[11]

How Textbooks Are Selected

In the United States today, textbooks are selected and purchased on the local level. School boards either select the texts to be used or provide teachers and school principals with lists of approved books from which to select. In practice, of course, local boards follow the advice of teachers, except when under political pressure or higher-level direction of the kinds about to be described. Teachers, quite naturally, are influenced in their selection of texts by what they were taught in schools of education and thus by dominant members of their disciplines. (Similar remarks apply to the way things work in most democratic countries, including Canada and most of the European democracies.)

School boards, elected by the public or appointed by elected officials, tend to be rather vulnerable not only to the advice of teacher and educational theorists but also to lobbying by politically active groups. These groups thus indirectly influence textbook publishers intent on satisfying the requirements of local and state boards. This is perhaps the most important reason for the textbook revisions in the treatment of class, gender, and race briefly described a while back. Publishers today wouldn't dream of using a title like *Man and His Changing World*, to cite a 1930s example, any more then they would

---

[11]For more history on textbook bias see Chapters 3 and 4 in *The Language Police*, by Diane Ravitch.

illustrate a textbook exclusively with pictures of white, middle-class males. Minority groups with increasing political power are insisting that textbooks reflect more accurately the historical and cultural experiences and contributions of nonwhites, of women, and of other minority groups. Women's rights organizations have successfully reduced the use of sexist language in textbooks, and the hotly debated traditional canon of Western literature has been broadened to include a wider selection of multicultural writers. All of these changes have been politically driven.[12]

Another skirmish currently being fought on the textbook battlefield concerns the liberal versus conservative interpretation of traditional values. In 1995, for instance, the decision to use textbooks depicting nontraditional families (including homosexual parents) in certain San Francisco public schools sparked a controversy that threatened government funding. There also still is a good deal of infighting going on over the issue of evolution versus creationism (more about that later). And the controversial issue of birth control has motivated some textbook writers either to skirt the subject or to take a moral position on it. For example, in a review of the high school text *Global Science*, Max G. Rodel noted that the excellent discussion of birth control in the previous edition had all but disappeared in the 2000 edition. It was replaced by a chapter called "The Case for Abstinence for Young People."[13] Revisions like this reflect the tenor of the times.

Nor should we overlook political fights over ideological issues concerning the quality and standards maintained in textbooks. Over the past two decades, the American school system has been intensively scrutinized and extensively criticized. Textbooks have come under fire, in particular, for being dumbed down in both content and linguistic sophistication. Educators are under pressure to raise textbook standards, to standardize content, and to link material to an increasing number of state and national achievement tests.

In times now long gone, funds spent by local boards in America came exclusively from local taxes—chiefly property taxes—and each district controlled its own choice of textbooks. Nowadays, a great deal of school money comes from state coffers, and even from the federal government, with the inevitable consequence that school boards are restricted from above as to their textbook choices. Political power concerning education thus has been dispersed from being almost exclusively local, to spreading to entire states and even, to a lesser extent, to the nation as a whole. Nearly half of the states in America now have state textbook adoption committees that screen publisher offerings—in particular, those concerning basic or sensitive topics and books intended for the first six school grades. Local boards in states with textbook committees must choose books from lists approved for adoption within their state. Inevitably, politicking on the state (and to a much lesser extent) national levels increasingly shapes the content of the textbooks from which local boards must choose.

---

[12]Of course, as in most cases of this kind, success usually depends on a readiness to change on the part of many ordinary citizens, the point being that perhaps organized groups can succeed only to the extent that the times are ripe, even though, without organized political pressure, little change might take place. In any case, organized political agitation surely was (and is) an important cause of widespread changes in attitude concerning minorities and women.

[13]See the July/August 2000 *Textbook Letter* for what is a generally favorable review of *Global Science: Energy, Resources, Environment,* Kendall/Hunt Publishing, 2000.

The Power of Big Business

All of this means, by the way, that big business has less power in determining textbook content than it does in shaping the news offered by the mass media. But textbook publishing companies still exert a good deal of power in the textbook arena. State and local boards, after all, are forced to choose from the books offered to them by textbook publishers (whose number grows smaller every year because of the same market-driven forces that have been shrinking the number of mass media outlets). But publishers, in their turn, are guided by the demands of state and local agencies, especially of textbook committees in two key states: California and Texas. (Pressure groups are particularly strong in Texas. And when you consider that one adoption alone—the 2003 social studies texts for all grades—amounted to $345 million, you can understand the clout that state has.)[14] That is why the power that publishers derive from their role as commodity supplier is not as large as one might suppose.[15] A textbook that makes neither the California nor the Texas list is going to have a hard time hanging around long enough to find a sufficiently large constituency in other states, and so the major publishers pretty much have been forced to tailor their offerings accordingly. (The very few low-budget books intended for use in a single state or locality are obvious exceptions.) Furthermore, because local boards also generally specify a pool of potential texts from which individual schools in their districts must select, publishers also have had to take these boards' preferences into account. The requirements of big city school boards (remember the extent to which the United States has become an urban society) thus are an important influence on textbook publishers.

But the large textbook conglomerates, just like other large corporations, can and do influence the marketplace for their products in another way—namely, by lobbying. (Ironically, one of the important defects of social studies textbooks is that they must pussyfoot around controversial issues such as the effect of lobbying on the political process.) In 1996, for example, after intense lobbying by publishers, the California State Board of Education voted six to one to approve three new series of math textbooks for use in California schools even though they had been given very low scores by a special review committee of math instructors. Eliminated from the approved list, and thus ineligible for adoption in any California public school, was the rigorous math series developed by the University of Chicago and adopted by many prestigious private schools (including, interestingly, Sidwell Friends Academy, the school attended by Chelsea Clinton and now, the Obama girls).

How Authors Influence Textbook Content

Authors and experts in the various fields also inevitably have a say as to textbook content. Although under the thumb of political and market forces of the kind just discussed, authors do generally have scruples concerning truth telling and do tend to be constrained

---

[14]A state committee in California approves all books used in kindergarten through the eighth grade; in Texas, through grade 12. But California does lay down requirements that all texts used in every grade must meet.

[15]If the idea that the supplier of a commodity has great power in determining the nature of those goods is foreign to you, think only of the way in which Microsoft, by gaining a controlling portion of the computer software market, has been able to influence the computer revolution.

Here is part of what Texas textbook laws stipulate concerning the selection of texts to be used in Texas public schools:

Illustrations and written materials shall avoid bias toward any particular group or individual and should present a wide range of goal choices. Particular care should be taken in the treatment of ethnic groups, roles of men and women, and the dignity of workers, and respect for the work ethic. [Textbooks] shall present examples of men and women participating in a variety of roles and activities and shall further present the economic, political, social, and cultural contributions of both men and women, past and present. . . . Traditional and contemporary roles of men, women, boys, and girls shall be included. . . .

Textbook content shall promote citizenship and understanding of the essentials and benefits of the free enterprise system, emphasize patriotism and respect for recognized authority, and promote respect for individual rights. [They shall not] include selections or works which encourage or condone civil disorder, social strife, or disregard of the law, [nor shall they] contain material which serves to undermine authority . . . or which would cause embarrassing situations or interference in the learning atmosphere of the classroom. . . . [They] shall not encourage life styles deviating from generally accepted standards of society.

But Texas State Board of Education members find ways of stretching definitions. In an article about the board's annual battle over textbook bias, the Christian Science Monitor (July 22, 2003) cited two examples: "The state board rejected an environmental science book last year in part because it put the U.S. and the free enterprise system in a bad light as significant players in global warming. And, earlier this year, a history text was withdrawn by the publisher after board members objected to references of rampant prostitution in the 1800s."

by professional standards. They aren't inclined to stray from the straight and narrow (as they see it!) any more than they are forced to do so. (There no doubt are rotten apples in this barrel, just as in every other, and let's pass over the charge occasionally heard that some authors of public school history and social studies texts do not have a realistic grasp of their subject matter.) But they rarely, if ever, have a genuinely free hand to "write it as they see it." (We also should mention the disgraceful fact that the authors listed on some public school textbooks sometimes have had little or nothing to do with the actual writing of their books.)

Although content is the most important element of textbooks, the clarity, the style, and the author's ability to engage the reader's interest go a long way in making the material palatable. It's little wonder that students' eyes glaze over when the style is turgid, the presentation dull, and the writing unclear. Too often books written by committees fall into this category. Once in a while, though, a textbook comes along that is not only packed with information but is interesting as well. One such book is *Environmental Science: The Way the World Works* (Prentice Hall, 2000), a science book for high school honors courses. In a very positive review of this book, *The Textbook Letter* made particular note

The Weekly Reader *and Channel One are not alone in this field. Here are excerpts from an article in the August 2000 issue of* The Hightower Lowdown *describing a more recent entry:*

The ZapMe! Corporation, an Internet provider that's backed by such giants as Microsoft and Dell Computer, has contracts with 6,000 schools and, on the surface, the contracts look great. The company provides computers, Internet access, maintenance, and support services free of charge. What the company gets in return, however, is an agreement that their computers will constantly flash ads at the bottom of the screen, for the four hours a day the students are supposed to be online[!]. Plus the schools must agree to hand out sponsors' promotional materials for the kids to take home. Plus ZapMe! tracks where the students go on the Web and delivers that as demographic information to its sponsors—with no control over how the information is used or to whom it can be sold.

The point, of course, is to sell students products in ways that resemble those discussed in the advertising chapter in this book. As noted earlier, in Chapter 10, math texts engage in a special kind of product advertising, asking students questions like, "How many square inches of label are on a box of Kellogg's Cocoa Frosted Flakes?" and "If a package of M&Ms includes 56 pieces and 16 are brown, what fraction of the total are brown?" But now that California, the largest textbook-adopting state, has passed a statute outlawing this sort of practice in taxpayer-financed textbooks adopted for use in California public schools, this type of plugola may be a thing of the past. No publisher wants to lose that vast market for their products.

of its narrative flair and engaging style.[16] Instead of plunging into scientific explanations, each chapter begins with a descriptive scene that sparks the reader's interest in what will follow. For instance, one chapter starts with the description of a dense fog that settled over the town of Donora, Pennsylvania, for five days in 1944. The reader's natural tendency is to wonder why there was such a dense fog and to read on for the answer. Similar techniques are used in fiction to draw the reader into the action of the story. How much more interesting textbooks would be if they used some of these narrative devices.

But Students Have Little Influence on Textbook Content

Oh, yes, students also have an indirect say in textbook content, particularly as to style and level of difficulty. Unliked books, or those that are too difficult, tend to be unread books. Teachers want the textbooks they select to be read—indeed, to be studied. Anyway, that's why, in the case of public school textbooks, the term *indoctrination* isn't

---

[16]See "This Is a Fine Textbook, All in All, and I Recommend It," by Max Rodel, *The Textbook Letter,* September–October 2004.

far off the mark. In the case of the mass media, the ultimate users of the commodity wield great power (as should be evident from the discussion in the last chapter). In the case of public school textbooks, the ultimate users, students, have relatively little say. (But then, most mass media audiences consist of "responsible" adults, while public school textbook audiences are considered to be "just children" or, extrapolating from other currently popular lingo, just "preadults.")

5. CENSORSHIP

It's very difficult to determine in particular cases whether books have been censored, but the earlier discussion about the ways in which local and state boards influence textbook content should make it clear that censorship does occur. Government agencies, from the federal government down to local school boards, do in fact force changes in the content of public school texts (and also nonprint materials). Authors definitely are not free to write the books that they might prefer to; at least they cannot do so with any serious hope of having their efforts published and adopted. Textbook writers these days try very hard to tailor their works so as to be politically correct (more will be said about this shortly), just as, you will recall, do writers in the mass media.

The Controversy Concerning the Teaching of Evolution: An Instructive Example

All even remotely controversial topics are subject to censorship, or at least to serious attempts at censorship. The theory of evolution is an especially interesting case because, perhaps more than any other scientific theory, it goes against the grain of many deeply held religious beliefs.

Starting in 1859 with the publication of Charles Darwin's great work *On the Origin of Species,* the theory of evolution has been challenged and denied countless times and for several different reasons. But the most important of these reasons has always been that evolution theory runs counter to literal interpretations of the Old Testament. In a famous 1925 court case, commonly referred to as the "Scopes Monkey Trial," John Scopes was convicted of violating a Tennessee law against the teaching of the theory of evolution in public school classrooms. In more recent times, however, courts have systematically struck down laws like the old Tennessee statute, notably in 1968 when the U.S. Supreme Court declared unconstitutional an Arkansas law that banned the teaching of evolution.

After the 1968 Supreme Court decision, religious fundamentalists invented the theory they call "creation science" in an attempt to make their biblical view at least be taught alongside that of evolution theory in science classes. Creationists believe in the Genesis explanation of God as the architect of the universe and the creator of each species on Earth. They reject the theory of evolution and try to discredit it in the classroom. But in 1987, after several lower court decisions, the U.S. Supreme Court declared creation science to be religious advocacy, not science, and thus not to be taught as science in public school science classes. Although this has dealt a blow to those advocating creationism as science, it has not stopped attempts at state and local levels to flout the law; in fact, creationism is still espoused in some schools where community sentiment is highly in favor of this being done, and evolution theory is slighted in many others because of that

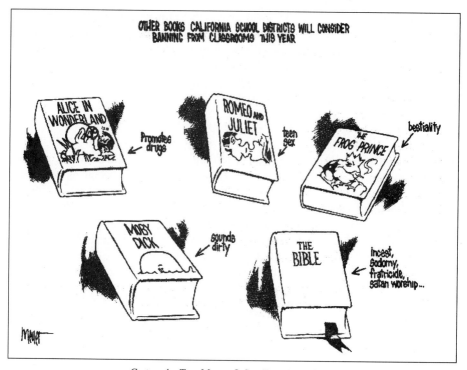

Cartoon by Tom Meyer. © *San Francisco Chronicle*. Reprinted by permission.

pressure. However, because of the Supreme Court's ruling, fundamentalists now often avoid the terms *creation* and *creation science,* instead employing the euphemism *intelligent design.* Intelligent design holds that life is too complex to be explained by the theory of evolution and therefore must have been created by a higher power as part of a purposeful design, but that power may or may not be the biblical God.

Fundamentalists continue to attempt to picture evolution as just one theory (as the name "theory of evolution" implies to those who don't understand scientific lingo) and to get the biblical account in Genesis taught alongside it. In fairness, it needs to be said that at least some advocates of creation science or intelligent design believe it to be scientific—so, for that matter did the second President Bush, who endorsed the teaching of intelligent design even though it put him at odds with scientific thinking.

Nevertheless, the relative failure of religious fundamentalists in their attempt to counter the teaching of evolution and to get intelligent design taught in science classes has not reduced their efforts. Indeed, in recent years pressure on state and local school boards and on individual schools has increased, no doubt due to the increase in enthusiasm for fundamentalist religion in the United States (as in many other countries).[17]

---

[17]Note, however, that other sorts of books espousing the creationist viewpoint sometimes are used in public schools, especially in states such as Louisiana and Texas, where fundamentalist interpretations of the Bible are widely accepted. Also of interest is the fact that the influence of fundamentalist Jewish and Muslim groups on public school education has been comparatively slight because these groups constitute only a tiny minority in America today.

Evolution is often discounted as "just a theory," and, in fact, the concept was extremely controversial in the past. But with the continued gathering of substantiated evidence for 150 years, it has finally been validated. Here is an explanation of why scientists today would accept evolution not merely as a theory, but as an overarching set of principles or laws. *

In the physical sciences there are many observations or facts that have given rise to generalizations. . . . The statements of facts and their convenient generalization to laws are expressed in terms of macroscopically observable and weighable quantities. The overarching explanation for these laws is achieved in atomic theory, which is expressed in terms of invisible atoms and molecules. No one thinks that atomic theory is "just a theory," for it possesses extraordinary explanatory power and provides the context in which many of the conveniences of our civilization depend. Thus we proceed from many observations or facts to their generalization in terms of laws, both levels macroscopic, to a theory expressed in terms of invisible entities.

If we now apply this scheme to biology, we see that the concept of evolution is at the law level, as it summarizes the results of a large number of observations or facts about organisms. The analogous theory is natural selection or other means by which evolution is achieved. Unknown nearly 150 years ago to Darwin, explanations of macroscopic evolution in terms of microscopic genes and molecular sequences of nucleic bases in DNA are known to us. Placing the concept of evolution at the law level clarifies its status; it is not a theory.

*Taken from "Neither Intelligent nor Designed," by Bruce and Frances Martin, *Skeptical Inquirer,* November/December 2003.

Americans remain astonishingly resistant to accepting evolution as a bedrock idea of science. For years they have been evenly divided on the issue, with 45 percent rejecting it and 10 percent undecided. People in other industrial countries are far more likely to accept the theory—80 percent overall, with a high of 95 percent in Japan.[18]

In the United States, though, court battles continue to rage. In 2005 public schools in Dover, Pennsylvania, required science teachers to make students aware that the theory of intelligent design is an alternative to the theory of evolution. The teachers refused to comply, and parents filed a lawsuit challenging the board's decision on the grounds that it violated the constitutional separation of church and state. After a contentious, six-week trial, the U.S. district judge ruled that it is unconstitutional to teach intelligent design as an alternative to evolution in a public school science classroom.[19] But feelings

---

[18]See "Evolution Takes a Back Seat in U.S. Classes," by Cornelia Dean, *New York Times,* February 1, 2005.

[19]For a more complete discussion on the trial and judicial opinion see *NOVA,* "Judgment Day: Intelligent Design on Trial," www.pbs.org, and "Exploring Constitutional Law," www.law.umkc .edu.

continue to run high on this issue, and court decisions never seem to settle the matter. There is always another skirmish around the corner.

Kansas, long a battleground for creationists and evolutionists, went at it again in fall 2005, when the board of education rewrote public school testing standards to include language supported by intelligent design advocates. But the conservative board lost control in the 2006 primary elections when the balance of power swung back to those who opposed the new quasi-religious standards. The victory was slim though. Half the people in Kansas thought evolution should be taught alongside intelligent design, according to a 2005 poll taken by six news organizations. And Kansas is not alone. In recent years, legislators in Georgia and Alabama have introduced bills that allow teachers to challenge Darwin in science classes, and 20 other states are battling over the issue on a local level.

Before going on to other matters, it is worth noting that a significant number of high school science teachers do not have a satisfactory grasp of their subject matter, as many studies have shown, and that many teachers believe in creationism and would like to teach it. What is equally troubling is that some teachers who accept Darwin's theory as a scientific law are afraid to teach it for fear of getting into trouble with school administrators and fundamentalist parents. Or they find ways to present evolution obliquely by discussing it without actually mentioning the word or by assigning a chapter on the subject without discussing it in class. Teachers are only human after all, and like the rest of us they sometimes cave in to intimidation.

It is worth noting that Darwin himself did not believe that his theory of evolution was antithetical to belief in the existence of a creator. In fact, the last sentence in his classic book *On the Origins of Species* affirms such a belief:

> There is a grandeur in this view of life, with its several powers, having been originally breathed by the Creator into a few forms or into one; and that, whilst this planet has gone cycling on according to the fixed law of gravity, from so simple a beginning endless forms most beautiful and wonderful have been, and are being evolved.

It is difficult to be sure why the very well-organized fundamentalists are not winning more battles than they do, but one reason has to be the pressure exerted by an aroused scientific community, worried that a generation of scientific illiterates will be raised in the United States. Eminent scientists, for example, testified in the court cases mentioned before that creation science is not a science and convinced courts to hold that this is the case. Nevertheless, fundamentalists have not given up the fight by any means and, indeed, have had success at the local level in many places where large numbers of parents do not want students to be taught that evolution theory is a fact. Ah, well, at least we don't convict scientists on the charge of heresy any longer, as the Inquisition did to Galileo for his "heretical" belief that the Earth went around the sun.

Interestingly, religious fundamentalists are largely responsible for one of the improvements in recent public school textbooks—namely, the very modestly improved treatment of the topic of religion in American life. After World War II, and up to just a few years ago, religion tended to get mentioned only in the colonial period, except for accounts of the Mormons' great trek west in the nineteenth century and the inauguration of the first (and so far only) Catholic president, John F. Kennedy, in 1960. Most of the newer texts today provide much more information than that about the role religion has played in American life, even if their accounts still have a bit of the flavor of a token gesture.

Although the majority of biology textbooks in use today in public schools in America hold the line, more or less, against fundamentalist censorship demands, they do so in different ways. In some cases they teach evolution theory as a very well-confirmed scientific theory and simply ignore creationism entirely. That is the way the problem is handled, for instance, in one of the best biology textbooks.* In other texts, creationism is briefly mentioned and then dismissed, as illustrated by this excerpt from a rather good, although "linguistically simplified" text:†

When [H.M.S.] *Beagle* sailed from England [in 1831, Charles] Darwin, like most people of his time, believed in creationism. . . . According to creationists, God designed each kind of animal and plant to match its particular habitat. Thus, places with similar environments have similar kinds of plants and animals. Moreover, creationists believe that species are unchanging.

During his journey Darwin often left the ship to collect specimens of animals, plants, and fossils. His observations led him to doubt creationism and its assumption of unchanging species.

This text then describes some of Darwin's findings, including those concerning the famous finches on the Galápagos Islands, findings that provided Darwin with very good evidence for what became his theory of evolution and natural selection.

Another way in which biology texts respond to religious challenges to evolution theory is illustrated by this excerpt from a somewhat better-than-average high school biology textbook, in which "creation science" is dealt with in a section titled Pseudoscience:‡

"Creation science" is not science because its working assumptions cannot be examined by scientific methods. The word *creation* is associated with religion and a supreme being. It is, therefore, a matter of faith—not of scientific investigation. Furthermore, creationists resist modifying their model even when observations fail to support it. These characteristics do not exclude creationism from a place in the school curriculum. Rather, they strongly suggest that creationism should be taught as a religious belief and not as a scientific theory.

* *Modern Biology,* by Albert Towle (Holt, Rinehart & Winston, 1999).
† *Biology: Visualizing Life,* by George B. Johnson (Holt, Rinehart & Winston, 1994).
‡ *Biological Science: A Molecular Approach,* 6th edition (Heath, 1996). The revision is by a team of seven writers from Colorado College, Colorado Springs.

Publisher Self-Censorship

Given what has been said so far, it shouldn't come as a surprise that publishers have become exceedingly cautious in the editing of public school textbooks or that they try very hard not to offend powerful special-interest groups. This is especially true with respect to grade school textbooks, as might be expected, because most parents want their children apprised of the harsher realities of life rather slowly. (Few see anything wrong in telling tiny tots that there is a Santa Claus or a tooth fairy.)

This caution on the part of publishers sometimes has rather ludicrous consequences. For example, a West Coast publisher asked one of its illustrators to remove the stem from a picture of a plum because it cast a shadow that might be construed as phallic. Harcourt Brace, a very large textbook publisher, once had an artist remove a mother's apron from a drawing picturing a typical eighteenth-century family scene because the apron was seen to be "demeaning to women." (Never mind that the portrayal was accurate.) Some publishers no longer allow udders on drawings of cows or flies on the trousers of little boys.

In the old days, when Dick and Jane reigned supreme, the world was portrayed as having a gardenlike quality. Slums did not exist, nasty people were restricted to fairy tales, almost everyone was white, and women were primarily pictured as housewives and mothers. The pressures on publishers were different, so the product was different. Textbook publishers inevitably try to make their products be as politically correct as possible; what changes over time is what counts as politically correct.

Currently the most significant source of self-censorship is the bias guidelines issued by every educational publisher. They all conduct bias and sensitivity reviews that regulate the way textbook authors discuss ethnic and minority groups, including women, the disabled, and the elderly, and they respond to both liberal and conservative pressure groups. In one sense, this is understandable, given the strong impetus to eliminate discrimination since the 1960s, but guidelines have gone way beyond their original intent, as Diane Ravitch points out in *The Language Police* (2003), an excellent analysis of test and textbook bias. Here are a few examples she cites to give you the flavor of constraints placed on authors. (These are drawn from the Scott Foresman-Addison Wesley and McGraw-Hill guidelines.)[20]

Writers must include women in equal numbers with men in both the text and illustrations (despite the fact that men have dominated Western culture up to and including much of the twentieth century—like it or not). But they must avoid such stereotypes as passive, weak, gentle, illogical, short, or emotional women and active, strong, brave, logical, tall, or unemotional men. Sexist terms like *sissy, tomboy, lady, hen-pecked husband,* and *forefathers* are out. Disabled people must never be referred to as "the disabled" but as "people with disabilities." The blind and the deaf should be called "people

---

In The Mad, Mad World of Textbook Adoption, *Chester Finn, Jr., and Diane Ravitch have this to say about the Alice-In-Wonderland world of textbook guidelines:*

Textbooks are now judged not by their style, content, or effectiveness, but by the way they live up to absurd sensitivity guidelines. Do literary anthologies have more male than female story characters? Do textbooks portray stereotypes such as female nurses or male mechanics? Do history textbooks suggest that religious strife has been a cause of conflict in human history? Do they mention junk food, magic, or prayer; suggest that the old are wise or the young are vigorous; or leave out any ethnic, racial, or religious group, no matter how small? If they do, that is grounds to have a textbook rejected.

---

[20]See Chapter 12 of *The Language Police* for a full account of these bias and sensitivity reviews.

who are blind" and "people who are deaf," and midgets and dwarfs are "people of small stature." But it's just as bad to call someone "normal" or "able-bodied"; the correct term, instead, is "a person without disabilities" or "a person who is nondisabled"!

The discussion of ethnic and racial groups is closely monitored as well. Writers must present "a fair and balanced representation" of racial, ethnic, and gender groups in text and illustrations. Here is a random sampling. Authors cannot refer to "primitive cultures" because there are no primitive cultures. African tribes have been replaced by ethnic groups, and they don't live in huts but in little houses. Illustrators must not draw African Americans in loud colors or prints, straw hats, and white suits—or in middle-class clothes. They can't show these people in tenements and bright cars or in "dull, white picket-fence neighborhoods." Given these constraints, one wonders how African Americans *can* be depicted, or for that matter, why anyone would want to write a text-book to begin with (except, of course, the intrepid authors of this text).

Even science textbooks are skewed by politically correct bias. In *Life Science,* a middle school biology textbook, Navajo physicist Fred Begay rates a half-page discussion on his study of Navajo medicine, but no mention is made of Nobel Laureates James Watson, Maurice H. F. Wilkins, or Francis Crick—the co-discoverers of DNA. In *Discovery Works,* a fifth-grade science textbook, students wade through three pages of Algonquin Indian myths about season changes before they find out that the tilt and rotation of the Earth affect climate change—not the migration of crows. In distortions like these, the scientifically sound sinks under the weight of the politically correct.[21]

Nontextbooks Also Often Are Censored

Books that are not explicitly textbooks often are subjected to censorship. The censor in most of these cases is the local school board, but state boards have been getting into the act in recent years.

Almost any kind of book may be censored, but most that are contain passages alleged to be obscene, racially or ethnically biased, slighting or demeaning of women, or they provide a favorable portrayal of a lifestyle claimed to be immoral. A Tennessee county school board, for example, removed the old standby *Drums Along the Mohawk* from an assigned list because it contained words judged to be obscene, such as *hell* and *damn.* Shakespeare's *The Merchant of Venice* is sometimes censored because Jewish groups object to its portrayal of Shylock, and a New Hampshire school banned *Twelfth Night* because it violated a school board ruling that prohibited alternative lifestyle instruction. (Viola, the heroine, is disguised as a boy who inadvertently becomes romantically entangled with another woman, Olivia.)

A bit sillier was the removal from California's annual English exam list for tenth graders of the short story "Am I Blue," by Pulitzer Prize–winning author Alice Walker—removed primarily because it was "anti-meat-eating." But perhaps silliest of all, surely the most ironic, is the fact that one of the most frequently censored books is *The Adventures of Huckleberry Finn.* Sam Clemens would have been amused, but not surprised. The Clemens classic has two groups on its back: fundamentalists and others offended by its portrayal of religion and by the way Huck flouts conventional morality, and African Americans offended by its portrayal of Negroes and by the racist language

---

[21]Examples taken from "A Textbook Case of Junk Science," by Pamela R. Winnick, *Weekly Standard,* May 9, 2005.

The number of books and magazines censored out of public school classrooms and libraries runs into the thousands every year. Here are a few striking examples: *

Of Mice and Men (John Steinbeck)
The Sun Also Rises (Ernest Hemingway)
The Catcher in the Rye (J. D. Salinger)
The Grapes of Wrath (John Steinbeck)
Look Homeward Angel (Thomas Wolfe)
The Invisible Man (Ralph Ellison)
Native Son (Richard Wright)
Brave New World (Aldous Huxley)
Slaughterhouse Five (Kurt Vonnegut, Jr.)
To Kill a Mockingbird (Harper Lee)
The Naked Ape (Desmond Morris)
I Know Why the Caged Bird Sings (Maya Angelou)
Ms. magazine
(The *American Heritage Dictionary* was banned because it includes "gutter words" like *ball, nut,* and *tail* and cites certain uses of the term *bed* as a transitive verb.)

Oh, yes. Perhaps in an attempt to prove that George Orwell is the Nostradamus of the twentieth century, lots of school districts have banned use of . . . 1984.

*See the American Library Association's *Newsletter on Intellectual Freedom.*

it puts into the mouths of bigoted slave owners. Irony of ironies: One of the schools that has censored *Huck Finn* turns out to be Mark Twain Intermediate School in Fairfax County, Virginia. Censoring *Huck Finn* is ironic, of course, because Clemens intended his great work to expose the evils of slavery—precisely what civil rights groups today want every American to remember.

It would be provincial, however, to conclude that public school book censoring is a uniquely American phenomenon. On the contrary, this sort of censorship, like most other kinds, is less frequent and less severe in the United States than in most, perhaps all, other countries. Every nation dolls up its past, for the same reasons that we do so in the United States, and many censor on religious grounds or out of a sense of propriety. In Germany, starting after World War II and continuing to a lesser extent until the mid-1990s, history texts have understandably played down the atrocities committed by Germans during that most horrible of all wars—so far!—and teachers still sometimes engage in their own kind of censorship by simply never quite finding sufficient time to cover that period in German history adequately. Similar remarks, incidentally, apply more or less to the teaching of Japanese history in Japan. And Soviet texts didn't bother to mention the millions killed by the Soviets during Stalin's reigns of terror or the smaller but still extremely large number of people worked to death in Siberia even after his death.

Needless to say, authoritarian regimes have absolute control over the education of their young. Before Saddam Hussein was ousted, schoolbooks in Iraq were vehicles for

> [W]hen American scholars talk about . . . Soviet texts which blatantly indoctri-
> nate, they are called brainwashing. When our own texts are biased, prejudiced,
> one-sided and unfair, it is called "transmitting a favorable view of our democracy."
> —S. Samuel Shermis

Baathist party propaganda. History books traced the dictator's ancestry back to a cousin of the prophet Muhammad and compared him to great leaders of the past. His quotes were sprinkled throughout math texts, and his name was incorporated into English primers in birthday greetings and songs to Father Saddam. Iraqi teachers are now at work deleting this garbage from their schoolbooks.

Although the censoring of books outside public schools' walls (and also most schools that are religiously sponsored) always has been, and still is, much less common than it is within these walls, it does occur, and this obviously limits what students as well as adults can read. Favorite targets are books with sexual content and those affecting national security.

In the long history of censorship, however, all sorts of books have been banned. Way back in 1526, the first English translation of the New Testament was banned and printed copies burned; in Spain, a similar fate awaited the first translation into Spanish. Indeed, the Bible may be the most censored book in history. For decades, *Lysistrata, Canterbury Tales, Decameron, Moll Flanders,* and versions of the *Arabian Nights* were banned from U.S. mails under the Federal Anti-Obscenity Act (the Comstock Law of 1873), and *Fanny Hill,* the story of a prostitute told with explicit sexual descriptions, has been suppressed on and off since its publication in 1749. D. H. Lawrence's *Lady Chatterley's Lover* was in and out of obscenity trials until the 1960s, and James Joyce's *Ulysses,* voted the best novel of the twentieth century by the Modern Library, was banned in this country for 11 years (1922–1933) because of its obscenities.

In the 1980s censorship focused more on sex and swear words, but as we moved into the new millennium, the emphasis switched to witchcraft and wizardry. For several years the Harry Potter series headed the American Library Association's list of most challenged (that is, banned) books. Although most readers enjoy as fantasy the tales of sorcerers and magic spells, some take them literally as corrupting forces of evil; others are concerned about the clash between Christianity and witchcraft, still others by the depiction of family dysfunction and violence. In 2003, the Alice series (*Alice in Agony, Simply Alice, Alice the Brave,* and so on) topped the Harry Potter series, criticized for the usual reasons—too sexually explicit and too many swear words. But that series was bumped to third place in 2006 by *And Tango Makes Three,* a story about two male penguins who parented an egg from a mixed-sex penguin couple. (You can guess why that one was censored.) If fairy tales were as popular now as the Alice and Harry Potter series, they'd probably be banned too. (In fact, they have been cleaned up over the years—for example, in Grimm's version of "Cinderella," her mean stepsisters were brutally punished at the end when pigeons plucked out their eyes in the wedding procession. How many kids hear that version today?)[22]

---

[22]See Banned Books Online for further examples; digital.library.upenn.edu/banned-books.htm.

Exercise 12-1

A school superintendent from Burlingame, California, stopped eighth-grade classes from reading *Kaffir Boy,* by Mark Mathabane, when a parent complained that her child was disturbed by the subject matter. The award-winning memoir describes the author's experience growing up in South Africa when blacks had no civil rights and were brutally treated. (The word *kaffir* is a highly offensive racial slur.) The controversial section includes two paragraphs describing grown men preparing to rape young boys in exchange for giving them all the food they could eat, a powerful incentive since the boys lived in poverty and were desperate for food. In the memoir Mathabane ran away, and as a consequence, the other boys shunned him. The point of the story, he explained, was to show that "resisting peer pressure is one of the toughest things for young people to do," and he was concerned that "it's a lesson that seems to be lost on people who want to censor my book." But given the graphic nature of the paragraphs in question, the superintendent considered it inappropriate for eighth graders. (Story reported in "Burlingame Schools Pull 8th-Grade Book from Class," by Nanette Asimov, *San Francisco Chronicle,* April 12, 2007.)

What would you do if you were the parent of a 13-year-old eighth grader? Would you want the book censored or not? Or would you take the middle road and allow the book to be taught as long the controversial section was deleted? Write an argument defending your position.

6. Textbooks Fail to Give Students Genuine Understanding

From what has been said so far, it should be clear that public school textbooks fail to give students a true understanding of the history and workings of their society. They, and schools in general, fail to orient students in space and time—fail to help them understand how life is different from place to place and, in particular, from one time to another. These failures are due primarily to defects in style and content of the kinds we have been at pains to describe—defects, we have suggested, that result from the various forces at work shaping the finished products, in particular, conflicting pressures from interested social groups.

But it is important to understand that these defects do not result from something peculiar to the American system. The textbooks of any democratic society are bound to reflect the different opinions and interests of its citizens. To have it otherwise would be to surrender control of this important part of our lives to others, as is the case in most authoritarian societies around the world. While fighting to make textbooks better than they are today, we should not forget how much they have improved since, say, the authors of this college text went to school (eons ago, when dinosaurs still roamed the Earth).

One final comment. The praise that has been somewhat begrudgingly given to today's public school textbooks [23] in this chapter should not cloud the fact that the writers of this

---

[23] The history and social studies books used in private schools are, with rare exceptions, quite similar to those discussed here, except for some of the textbooks used in schools run by organized churches. Of course, in some of the very best private schools, original sources—books intended for adult readers—are more in evidence than are texts designed explicitly for schoolroom use. (Yes, the schools attended by the offspring of the rich are indeed better than the ones the rest of us are subjected to.)

If you're still wondering whether all that much progress has occurred in textbook quality in recent years, this snippet from a really bad textbook still in circulation as late as 1970 should provide a bit of evidence:

As you ride up beside the Negroes in the field they stop working long enough to look up, tip their hats and say, "Good morning, Master John." You like the friendly way they speak and smile; they show bright rows of white teeth. "How's it coming, Sam?" your father asks one of the old Negroes. "Fine, Marse Tom, jes fine. We got more cotton than we can pick." Then Sam chuckles to himself and goes back to picking as fast as he can.

—Mentioned in *The New Republic* (July 25, 1970);
the book's title is best omitted here.

If that sort of writing doesn't make every current textbook look wonderfully good, nothing will.

college text do not care for the large doses of indoctrination they contain. This text was written in a completely different spirit. A student who accepts its contents uncritically, without thinking carefully about the subjects discussed, has missed its main point, which is that in important or controversial matters, free men and women must become their own experts, or at least must be able to judge for themselves the opinions and advice of those who call themselves experts. The success of a free society depends on an informed and thinking electorate, not on an indoctrinated one.

7. POSTSCRIPT ON COLLEGE TEXTS

The question naturally arises about college textbooks: Do they distort American history and practice as do public school texts? Do science texts fudge in their portrayal of evolution theory? If the forces at work are the same with respect to college as public school texts, we should expect the results to be roughly the same (taking into account the greater maturity of college students). If they aren't, we should expect the finished products to be different. What do our worldviews tell us about this question?

Note first that the publishers of college texts have exactly the same motives as those who produce public school textbooks. In fact, most publishers in one field also publish in the other. Second, most college texts are adopted by the teachers who will use them in their own classes (or, in the case of courses having several sections, by group faculty decisions), not by school boards or state agencies. (Students buy them but can't choose which ones to buy.)

The reason for this important difference is the history and the current funding of higher education in the United States as compared to primary and secondary education. Primary and secondary school traditions are largely "homegrown" and intended for a mass audience. Public school teachers have always had their rights to academic freedom infringed upon by local school boards or, more accurately, never had such rights. Teachers who express controversial opinions in the classroom have little legal protection and may be fired if school administrators consider their opinions inappropriate. Although individual cases have been appealed, so far the federal courts have ruled consistently that teachers do not have free speech rights in grade school or high school classrooms.

American colleges and universities evolved on the model of their European counterparts (chiefly in Germany and England), which were intended for an elite clientele. Professors, at least, were granted a great deal of academic freedom. (They were, of course, more constrained under monarchical systems, and professorial freedoms were nonexistent during the Nazi period in Germany and, to a lesser extent, during the Fascist period in Italy.) The result of transplanting this tradition to the United States, the freest Western society, has been academic freedom for almost all faculty members; thus, college teachers have always had the privilege of selecting the books they and their students will use.[24] It follows, then, as night follows day, that college textbook publishers will try to produce books that please college teachers—their potential adopters.

College teachers, however, do not operate in a vacuum. They, too, have an audience to consider—their students—and many students, unfortunately, are not as well prepared to do college work as typical students were, say, 40 years ago. (This obviously tends to be less true of students in "elite" colleges and universities.) A recent federal study done by the National Center for Education Statistics found that only 31 percent of college graduates are able to read and understand complex prose passages—almost 10 percent less than college grads in 1992. One reason for this fact is that a larger proportion of young people go to college today than in times past, when only brighter students (and a few who were merely rich) went to college. Other reasons, not fully understood yet, are that students read less now, watch more TV, and learn to read and write on computers, which involve a different kind of literacy. But a contributing factor, often overlooked, is that more and more students have become victims of the dumbing down of grade school and high school texts mentioned a while back and find it difficult to comprehend some of the more high-powered college texts. They are more easily intimidated by thick books or those written in past centuries in a dense or a different style. College teachers, being human, often react (consciously or unconsciously) to the problem this raises by selecting textbooks and works of literature that are relatively brief and more easily understood. Reading lists have been shortened; books perceived as "weighty tomes" tend to get neglected in introductory courses.[25]

Anyway, college texts, wherever they may rest on an absolute scale, are genuinely unlike their public school counterparts. College teachers want widely differing textbook

---

[24]More precisely, almost all *tenured* faculty members. Nontenured faculty still have to worry about offending those who determine who will be rehired and who "terminated." This benefit of the tenure system often is overlooked but is of great importance. (Nontenured faculty also usually are paid a good deal less than the tenured variety. But that is a topic for another time, another class.)
[25]There also is the fact that what is "in" at one time may well become "out" at another; textbook selection tends to reflect these changes, especially the dramatic changes in course offerings. Thirty-five years ago, for example, there were no courses in critical reasoning. Most schools required courses in formal logic, usually taught in philosophy or math departments, and these obviously did deal with the principles of good conclusion drawing. Critical reasoning was taught by English department instructors primarily in the context of the writing of argumentative essays. That is why there was only one true critical reasoning textbook (Monroe Beardsley's *Thinking Straight,* mentioned in Chapter 7) in common use prior to *Logic and Contemporary Rhetoric*'s appearance on the scene in 1971.

content and levels of difficulty, creating a market in which all sorts of views and qualities find a constituency. College texts even tend to be less dull than their lower-level counterparts, a happy note on which to end this particular—immensely interesting, entertaining, and completely unbiased—college textbook.

SUMMARY OF CHAPTER 12

Public school textbooks in America have improved a great deal in the past 30 years or so.

1. History and social studies texts are more accurate in their portrayal of minorities and women and in the way in which they deal with the dark side of the social system and history of the United States. But textbooks still are written in a dull, one-fact-after-another style that makes true understanding, and also retention of specific facts, quite difficult. They also have reflected the general dumbing down that has occurred in public schools and colleges during the past several years.

2. History texts tend to bombard students with almost endless lists of forgettable facts that tend to bury important information. They also distort reality so as to satisfy the various interested pressure groups and to mold students into good, loyal citizens. They portray American presidents and heroes in a one-sided manner (for instance, not mentioning the vicious, bloodthirsty side of President Theodore Roosevelt). They also exaggerate the American role in world affairs (as in World War II) and play down the nasty side of U.S. history. *Example:* Putting down the Filipino attempt to gain independence.

3. Although today's social studies texts are light-years better than those of even 30 years ago, they still say relatively little about the large gulf between theory—how the American social system is supposed to work—and practice—how it actually works in everyday life. For example, they don't tell students about the preferential treatment often given to the rich and powerful (how they are sent to cushy jails when they are convicted of crimes, for instance) and play down the corruption that is common in government. *Example:* At best only hinting at the extent to which governments are corrupted by lobbying and by campaign contributions.

4. The ultimate purpose of public schools is to educate the young to fit into the adult world. Textbooks are intended to provide students with the knowledge they will need to be productive citizens and to inculcate the values, customs, and attitudes of the society as a whole. (That is why it is accurate to speak of indoctrination.)

   We can expect, then, that noncontroversial topics will be presented in a more or less straightforward manner, while topics that are controversial, or sensitive—in particular, those connected to the history and social practices of society—will tend to pull punches and portray matters in the best light possible.

5. Just as in the case of the mass media, politics enters into the textbook business. Because they are a commodity, textbooks are written so as to satisfy potential buyers, which means primarily local school boards, state agencies, and the professional educators who are empowered to make selections. Political considerations enter in at every level—local, state, and national.

Although the details change from time to time, there is nothing new in this intrusion of politics into the educational arena. Even the very idea of public school education is political, there being no public schools whatsoever in the United States until some time in the nineteenth century.

Big business, of course, has some power over textbook content, but less than it does, say, concerning how the news is presented in the mass media. But it does have some power, including power derived from its ability to lobby state legislatures and local school boards.

The most important of the state agencies concerned with textbook selection are those of California and Texas.

6. Pressure groups have been rather successful—indeed, sometimes oversuccessful—with respect to their demands that textbooks be politically correct by increasing coverage of minorities, women, and religion in American history and life, leading publishers to tailor their products to fit expected pressure group preferences. Many of these demands have been incorporated into bias guidelines that are the most significant source of self-censorship for educational publishers. But attempts to have discussions of creation science or intelligent design included in biology texts, either alone or alongside evolution theory, on the whole have not been successful.

   It should be noted that nontextbooks also sometimes are censored by public schools, including classic works of literature (by such writers as Ernest Hemingway, Mark Twain, and more recently J. K. Rowling for the Harry Potter series) as well as dictionaries listing four-letter words.

7. The result is that textbooks fail to provide students with genuine understanding or even, because of their dull styles and piling on of facts, knowledge of particular facts that is retained for any length of time. They do, however, reflect what organized groups and professional educators want students to read, which is as it should be in a democratic society.

8. But college texts, having a different sort of clientele, are different. (Vive la difference.)

EXERCISE 12-2

Look through a high school or college textbook for examples of the following types of hidden bias:

1. Pictures in the text that either reflect a bias (like photos dominated by Caucasians) or portray multiracial groups but devote little discussion to them in the text.

2. Gender, ethnic, or racial stereotypes like women described as caregivers or men as strong, successful professionals.

3. Exclusion of groups such as Latinos or people with disabilities or members of non-Christian religions.

4. Sexist or slanted language that subtly conveys a bias.

Describe the examples you found and explain the biases they reveal.

EXERCISE 12-3

1. Here is a famous quote by Northrop Frye: "Censorship is to dissent (and democracy) what lynching is to justice." Evaluate this quote, in particular, discussing the charge that it contains a fallacy.

2. Now here is a (fortunately) much less famous quote by Mel Gabler, of Educational Research Analysis (a pressure group that has had success, particularly in Texas): "When a student reads in a math book that there are no absolutes, suddenly every value he's been taught is destroyed. And the next thing you know, the student turns to crime and drugs."
   a. What is Gabler's (unstated) point? What is he advocating, and why?
   b. Evaluate his argument, again considering the charge that his reasoning is fallacious.

3. The Alabama State Education Department requires that the following disclaimer be included in all biology texts used in Alabama public schools that include an account of evolution and evolutionary theory:

   This textbook discusses evolution, a controversial theory some scientists present as a scientific explanation for the origin of living things, such as plants, animals, and humans. No one was present when life first appeared on the earth; therefore any statement about life's origins should be considered as theory, not fact.

   Critically evaluate this disclaimer.

EXERCISE 12-4

1. At what point in their educational careers do you think students are ready to be taught the biological facts concerning human sex and reproduction? Or do you think these topics should not be broached in public schools? Defend your answers.

2. It has been forcefully argued that very young children are tender shoots who need to find out the bad features of their society (as of life in general) rather gradually, so that it would be wrong to tell them too quickly that quite a few presidents (including such "heroes" as Franklin Roosevelt and John Kennedy) had mistresses, or that America's history is filled with nasty deeds and steeped in blood and conquest. The point of these arguments is that we don't want to destroy the pride and loyalty of the young, and we don't want to make future citizens into cynics.
   a. Do you agree or disagree with this line of reasoning? Defend your answer.
   b. Does it tend to undercut one of the themes of this chapter—that less indoctrination means better education?
   c. At what age, if ever, should students be given a completely accurate and balanced account of these matters?
   d. It has been argued that, in a society such as exists today in the United States, where several religions flourish and there is no single moral code accepted by all, public schools should not attempt to teach students about alleged values, customs, or traditions of the culture. What is your opinion on this question and, of course, why do you think so?

*3. Does the term *creation science* ring a bell with respect to a topic discussed in Chapter 7? Explain.

4. Recall how the Boston Massacre was described in your history textbooks back in high school. Then look up that event in a first-rate history book and describe the differences. (Hint: If there are no differences, either your high school history text was the best ever published, or your memory is poor or your new source is not a first-rate book.)

5. Evaluate the following argument:

> Because evolution cannot be reproduced in the laboratory, it should not be taught as though it is the only theory believed by sane individuals concerning the origins of life on Earth.

EXERCISE 12-5

Here is Lewis Lapham in *Harper's* magazine essay (August 2000) explaining why he believes that today's public schools are as poor as he thinks they are:

> Why . . . do the public schools continue to decay . . . [?] Possibly because the condition of the public schools is neither an accident nor a mistake. The schools as presently constituted serve the interests of a society content to define education as a means of indoctrination and a way of teaching people to know their place. We have one set of schools for the children of the elite, another for children less fortunately born, and why disrupt the seating arrangement with a noisy shuffling of chairs? Serious reform of the public schools would beg too many questions about racial prejudice, the class system, the division of the nation's spoils. A too-well-educated public might prove more trouble than it's worth, and so we mask our tacit approval of an intellectually inferior result with the declarations of a morally superior purpose. . . .

What do you think of some of Lapham's claims, for instance, that we have a two-tiered school system, that issues concerning racial prejudice and our class system (is there one?) intrude, and that there is tacit approval of the intellectually inferior result?

EXERCISE 12-6

Here is a short excerpt from a video, *Fueling America's Future,* produced by the Shell Oil Company and distributed to many high schools:

[Two young people of about high school age are driving through the countryside.]

FEMALE: Oh, what a beautiful day, . . . Hear the sounds, smell the smells.
MALE: Ah, birds, flowers, newly mowed grass.
FEMALE: I'm talking about the sound of an internal combustion engine! The smell of the open road!
MALE: But what about the wonders of nature?
FEMALE: What about the wonders of cars and trucks? Planes and gasoline?
MALE: What are you talking about?

FEMALE: That's how we travel. See the sights. Live where we want. Work where we want.

MALE: What about nature?

FEMALE: It takes gasoline to power the vehicles that get us to nature. And gasoline comes from nature.

MALE: Gasoline comes from nature?

FEMALE: Sure! . . . [F]rom the sea! Millions of years ago, . . . billions of tiny sea creatures and plants lived there, and when they died, their remains sank to the bottom of the sea floor. . . .

MALE: Right. Scientists think that the earth's crust buckled and shifted and got all mangled and turned all that sea life into petroleum products. . . .

FEMALE: [I]n 1908, horseless carriages started to be mass produced. That's what they called cars.

MALE: . . . Because they didn't need horses to pull them?

FEMALE: Right. But they did need . . .

MALE: Gasoline. . . .

FEMALE: Right. . . . This person looks at a horse and a carriage, thinks about it, and invents the impossible—a car with an engine to run it, instead of a horse!

MALE: *Now that is amazing.*

FEMALE: Hey, it's the spirit of America! . . . doing something that can't be done! Thinking and trying and figuring until you can do the impossible. . . .

MALE: But with all those cars, we also got smog.

FEMALE: Well, that's why the spirit of America went to work again. New gas nozzles introduced in 1976 take 120 tons of smog out of the air every day! . . .

1. In your opinion, how accurate is this snippet from the Shell Oil video? Why do you think so?

2. Do you think this video is appropriate for use in high school classrooms? Why, or why not? (Isn't it appropriate to teach sutdents about where gas and oil come from and how they are a natural product whose use enables us to take drives through the countryside?)

*EXERCISE FOR THE ENTIRE TEXT

This text, like all others, is based on certain presuppositions (only some made explicit) and no doubt contains fallacious reasoning, in spite of the authors' best efforts to reason cogently. So, as the final exercise, write a brief critique of this textbook with respect to (1) its major presuppositions (that is, the worldviews of the authors as stated or implied in the text); (2) possible fallacious arguments; (3) biased selections of material; and (4) rhetorical devices used to persuade readers to accept the authors' opinions on this or that. (Be sure to defend your findings, including examples to back up your claims.)

"It'll stop, Joey. It always has before."

A youthful inductionist at work.

The object of reasoning is to find out,
from the consideration of what we
already know, something else which we
do not know.

　　　—Charles Sanders Peirce

A simple person believes every word he
hears; a clever one understands the
need for proof.

　　　—Proverbs 14:15

APPENDIX: MORE ON COGENT REASONING

1. MORE ON CAUSE AND EFFECT

In Chapter 1, we said a few words about how inductive reasoning is used to discover causal relationships—to discover how one thing causes another. But just as in the case of most interesting concepts, that of causation is really a cluster of related concepts, mostly with blurred edges. When we call one thing the cause of another, we can mean simply the *sufficient condition* for bringing it about. In this sense, the cause of Marie Antoinette's death was being guillotined—having one's head cut off certainly suffices to bring about death.

On the other hand, we often mean by the cause of a thing or event whatever is a *necessary condition* for bringing it about. Striking a match on a rough surface (thus heating it) can be thought of, for example, as a necessary condition of the lighting of a match, even though it is only part of what must be true for the effect—the lighting of the match—to occur. It is a necessary condition, but not a sufficient condition: Matches also need to be dry and struck in the presence of oxygen if they are to light. Being in the presence of oxygen and being dry and being heated together constitute both the necessary and the sufficient conditions for a match to light.

The point here is that, even though striking a match (heating it) cannot alone cause a match to light, we still in everyday life talk as though striking a match is what makes it light. It usually makes perfectly good sense to say, for instance, that the match lit because it was struck on a rough surface (which heats the match to the required temperature), even though a match struck on a rough surface in a vacuum will not light (because of a lack of oxygen). But we would not say, for example, that it lit because it was in the presence of oxygen. The difference, roughly speaking, is *human agency*—in everyday life, it's easy to make a match light by striking it (heating it), but we can't usually make it light by providing oxygen. (For one thing, the oxygen already is there; for another, the match still won't light because ordinary air temperatures are too low.)

Also of interest is the fact that we sometimes need to distinguish between *proximate causes* and those that are more *remote*. Suppose that a truck jackknifes on an icy highway, blocking three of four lanes, and that an auto, call it auto A, has to swerve into the unblocked lane and that another auto, B, then crashes into auto A. The ice on the road would be said to be the proximate cause of the truck's jackknifing but a much more remote cause of the accident between autos A and B.

The difference between proximate and remote causes can be important in everyday life, in particular in legal cases. Clearly, auto A's swerving into the last unblocked lane is a proximate cause of the crash between A and B, yet the driver of A may well not be held responsible, since his need to go into that lane was caused by more remote events. The guilty party more likely will be held to be the driver of the truck for driving without sufficient care on an icy highway.

This example brings to mind the fact that, in everyday life, a given effect can be explained in terms of more than one cause. Which one we select usually depends on our particular interest in that effect. In assessing blame, say, in the case of a knife murder, we don't care about the neural and muscular causes of the murderer's arm movement, but we do care very much about his having consciously willed to do the act. A biologist, on the other hand, might be very interested indeed in neural firings in the guilty party's body, and in a court of law might well testify to neural and muscular causes of the knife blow. So it makes sense to say either that the willing caused the event or that the neural firings and muscle contractions did so.[1]

2. SCIENTIFIC METHOD

Scientific method is just common sense writ large, sharpened, fine-tuned, and applied (in the best cases) with creative persistence and patience. There is nothing mysterious or impenetrable about how scientists go about justifying their hypotheses.

Common sense requires that beliefs about the nature of the world be justified, more or less, by cogent arguments, as discussed in earlier chapters. Scientists have no other way, no magic formulas or wands, for coming to justified beliefs about the nature of the world. Science's "secret" lies in the persistent accumulation of knowledge by thousands (now literally millions) of practitioners who have required of each other the elimination so far as is possible of the shoddy, wishful thinking that peppers everyday reasoning. The rules of the scientific game force scientists to reject unjustified theories[2] and to give up their most cherished ideas when experience shows that they are false (or unsupported by good evidence).

Typical scientific theories result from a complicated mixture of deductive and inductive arguments, but the key arguments are inductive. Good scientists try to find *patterns* in what they have observed so far, in particular in their scientific experiments,[3] and

---

[1] For more on causation and related matters, see Alan Hausman, Howard Kahane, and Paul Tidman, *Logic and Philosophy,* 10th edition (Wadsworth, 2007).

[2] Scientists use the terms *theory* and *hypothesis* in at least two ways. In one sense, both of these terms refer to untested speculations or to insufficiently confirmed patterns. In another, they refer to well-established, well-confirmed, and accepted patterns. The second sense is synonymous with the expressions "scientific law" and "law of nature."

[3] A scientific experiment is just a kind of deliberately arranged experience. Instead of waiting for an event to happen, scientists arrange for it to happen, perhaps in their laboratories. For instance, they may mix two chemicals in the laboratory that rarely, if ever, are found mixed in nature, to see the result. But whether an event is "found" in the laboratory or found in "nature" is irrelevant to scientific procedure.

project these patterns via inductive reasonings to larger slices of reality. In everyday life, common sense reasons by inductions from past experiences that sugar sweetens, vinegar sours, bread nourishes, and drought kills crops. Scientists, using the same commonsense methods, but much more persistently and stringently, conclude that copper conducts electricity, cigarette smoking causes cancer, the Earth's path around the sun is an ellipse, and radioactive substances have half-lives. (They also, of course, use viewing instruments they have learned to construct by means of inductive reasoning—telescopes, microscopes, X-ray machines, and so on—that we ordinarily don't have at our disposal in daily life.)

So science is just the accumulated knowledge gained by huge numbers of individuals observing nature, proposing theories (patterns) that explain what has been observed, and testing by additional observations to confirm their theories (hypotheses). When scientists claim to have discovered a new pattern, others will try to duplicate their findings; when they succeed, a theory tends to be accepted into the scientific canon; when they cannot successfully duplicate the findings, a theory will be discarded, or at least modified so as to take account of what has been learned by the failure to confirm. It is this that distinguishes science from pseudoscience: A scientific theory predicts what will be experienced under certain conditions; if it is not experienced, the theory must be rejected or revised to conform to what has been discovered. Those who believe in pseudosciences—for example, extrasensory perception—cling to theories that are disconfirmed by experience and that do not make successful predictions about what will be experienced in the future.

Speaking of pseudoscience brings to mind the fact that a truly scientific theory must conform not just to evidence directly supporting it but also indirectly to all scientific theories whatsoever. Pseudosciences, on the other hand, never conform to the whole body of scientific knowledge or even, sometimes, to ordinary everyday thoughts. Creation science, for example, asserts that all human beings except for Noah and his family perished about 5,000 or so years ago in the biblical flood. This means that all of the human genetic variety we see today—all racial differences—must have evolved in just a few thousand years from the common Noah family stock, and this contradicts everything we know about how human beings, or any mammals, evolve and propagate. So anyone who accepts creation science on this point must reject virtually everything known about genetics, along with a great deal of the rest of modern biology.

Note, by the way, that failure to confirm a proposed scientific theory does not mean that the attempt to do so was of no value. On the contrary, failure can be very revealing; indeed, it often is more enlightening than success. For example, the failure of experiments conducted in the 1880s to prove the existence of an "ether," believed in those days by scientists to be the medium through which light (and other electromagnetic waves) traveled through space, led to a crisis in Newtonian physics that was finally resolved by Einstein's special theory of relativity. So, in a sense, one of the most important scientific advances of the twentieth century grew out of the failure to confirm a previously widely accepted scientific theory.

Students often misunderstand this aspect of scientific investigation. They often object, for example, to biological research done on animals because what works with respect to other animals frequently does not do so in the case of human beings; students often see this as proof that animals were made to suffer with no offsetting increase in knowledge about how human diseases can be conquered. They don't understand that failures of this kind may lead investigators away from a wrong path and on to a right one. (They also often overlook the many cases in which, say, drugs that work well on close mammalian relatives also do so when tried on human beings.) Note, by the way, that those who champion pseudosciences generally do not learn from failures to confirm their theories; they tend simply to sweep this sort of counterevidence under the nearest metaphorical rug.

Pseudoscientists also tend to ignore ways in which their theories run counter to simple facts and ideas about how things work that we all hold in everyday life. Creation science, for example, fails to take account of what we all know about the abundance of species in today's world. There are thousands of mammal species, thousands of bird species, thousands of amphibian and reptilian species, and millions of insect species, all of which could not have fitted into one ark that even today's technology might with great effort construct. So even forgetting that lions can't be expected to lie down with lambs; forgetting that the ark would have had to be stocked with an incredible amount and variety of food and water so animals would not starve or dehydrate; forgetting that literally millions of plant species would have had to be collected; forgetting the physical impossibility of Noah and his family going around the world to collect all of these animals and plants and food; forgetting about bacteria and viruses; and forgetting fussy details about getting rid of huge amounts of fecal material, it should be clear that the creation science story violates not just dozens of extremely well-confirmed, high-powered scientific theories but also all kinds of everyday ideas about how the world works, *while predicting nothing about what sorts of (earthly!) experiences the future may hold for us!* The scientific theory of evolution, on the other hand, is consistent with every other well-confirmed scientific theory and has predicted all sorts of things that have been and continue to be discovered to be true, including how and where fossils might be found, and so on.

Finally, let's take a look at a rather simple and truly scientific theory—the "sea-of-air" hypothesis—and at how scientists test and confirm their hypotheses. The theory was proposed by the seventeenth-century mathematician and physicist Evangelista Torricelli, a disciple of Galileo. It was well known then that water can be pumped from a well only from a maximum of about a depth of 34 feet (without the aid of auxiliary power); Torricelli proposed to explain this and other facts by his theory that a sea of air surrounds the surface of the Earth and presses down on it because of the force of gravity, just as water presses down on something at the bottom of the ocean. Pumps thus can raise water from a well (at most) to a height of about 34 feet, Torricelli theorized, because of this *air pressure.*

Torricelli's theory can be, and was, confirmed by performing several different sorts of experiments. For instance, if the limit that water can be pumped from a well is about 34 feet, and if mercury is about 14 times heavier than water (it is), then if the sea-of-air theory is correct, it follows that air pressure will hold up a column of mercury only $\frac{1}{14}$ as high as a column of water. So we can confirm the sea-of-air hypothesis by constructing a mercury device (we call these things *barometers*) and finding that this is the case. Torricelli's followers also confirmed his theory by testing at higher-than-sea-level elevations where, according to the sea-of-air theory, a column of mercury should be held up a lesser amount than at sea level, because there is less air pressing down on the mercury. (We now use this fact in other ways—for instance, in measuring fluctuations in air pressure at a given elevation, part of the knowledge needed to predict changes in the weather.) Notice, by the way, that had the results of experiments not conformed to Torricelli's theory, his hypothesis would not have been accepted by the scientific community.

The point of all this is twofold. First, scientific method is not some mysterious entity; and second, although in practice it leads to extremely complicated experiments and arguments, the basic underlying patterns of scientific inquiry are rather simple. We also should mention that it is the incredibly diverse evidence that supports scientific theories that is the reason why they are so reliable and why we should not reject what science has to say on any subject without having *extremely good reasons* for doing so.

3. CALCULATING PROBABILITIES AND FAIR ODDS

Billions of dollars are legally wagered on games of chance each year in the United States, and billions more are wagered illegally. The popularity of Atlantic City, Reno, and Las Vegas testifies to the fact that many millions of people in America gamble every year. Yet most who gamble have no idea how to calculate fair odds, one reason almost all gamblers lose in the long run. (Another reason, of course, is that the odds on all legal gambling games, including in particular slot machines and state lotteries, are rigged against the player—the odds *always* favor the house.)

Legitimate, fair odds depend on the *likelihood* (*probability* or *chances*) that a given outcome will occur. For example, when you flip a symmetrical coin, the chances are *one out of two,* or ½, that the coin will land heads up because there are two possibilities, and both are equally likely. *Fair odds* on heads thus should be even money—one to one—and someone who bets a dollar and wins should win a dollar. (Note, though, that very few coins are absolutely symmetrical. They tend to be very slightly heavier on one side or the other. Also notice that the dice at places like Las Vegas are specially made to be as close to asymmetrical as possible. Just any old pair of dice will not do, because of possible numbers "bias" favoring some numbers over others.)

Most games of chance are designed to present players with a specific number of equally likely alternatives, or combinations of alternatives, on which they must wager. To find the *probability* of combinations of outcomes, simply divide the number of favorable outcomes by the total number of possible outcomes, favorable or unfavorable. (Remember, though, that this works only in cases in which all individual outcomes are equally likely and outcomes are *independent* of each other—a matter to be discussed soon.)

Suppose we want to calculate the chances of getting a 7 on the next toss of an honest (symmetrical) pair of dice. There are exactly 36 possible outcomes on each toss, of which exactly 6 add up to 7 (namely, the combinations 1 and 6, 2 and 5, 3 and 4, 4 and 3, 5 and 2, and 6 and 1). So the probability of getting a 7 on a given toss equals $\frac{6}{36}$, or ⅙. Out of six tosses, the average wagerer will win once and lose five times. That is why fair odds on 7 in a dice game are 5 to 1 and why someone who wins a dollar bet should win $5.

At a casino, someone who bets a dollar is required to place it on the table, so that, if winners were paid fair odds, they would get back $6—their own dollar plus $5 in winnings. But no casino in history has ever paid fair odds. Gambling establishments are in business to make money, not to run fair games of chance!

At Las Vegas and other places where gambling is legal, perhaps the best odds for average players are at the dice tables. Slot machines provide the worst odds (except for wagers on sporting events or horse races). Yet the slots are without doubt the most popular way to lose money at every legal gambling casino. But state lotteries very likely offer players (one is tempted to say "suckers"!) the worst odds of any legal popular games of chance, since they pay back in winnings only from one-half to at best two-thirds of what they take in.[4]

Anyway, probabilities being what they are, when the odds are less than fair, virtually everyone who gambles must lose in the long run. But people being as so many of us are, all sorts of foolish theories have gained wide currency among those who like to gamble. The most foolish theory, of course, is that there is something called luck and that in certain situations luck is on our side—an idea that was discussed earlier.

But there are also two other, more sophisticated theories that should be mentioned. One is the belief that doubling a bet after a losing play, say, at the dice table, assures victory in the long run even when the odds are stacked against you. After all, you must win sooner or later, thereby recouping all losses plus a nice profit.

Alas, there is no gambling Santa Claus. First, the odds are against you on every play; doubling the bet cannot change that fact. Second, unless you are a Bill Gates or a Warren Buffett, the house always has a very much larger pile of reserve cash than you do and therefore can withstand a greater run of losses. In the battle between house and gambler, the gambler thus almost always gets wiped out first by a streak of bad luck. (There are old stories and even a song about "the man who broke the bank at Monte Carlo," but if it ever happened, it wasn't in living memory.)

According to a variation of the double-the-bet gambit, a bet made after previous losses should cover just what has been lost so far plus just a small amount extra—say, the amount of the first bet—so that if you bet $2 on the first play and lose, the second play is for $4, the third for $8, and so on until you win, at which point you start over with a $2 bet. This method certainly increases the average number of plays until a gambler will get wiped out, but it still can't change the inevitable failure lurking in the distance. This method also has the disadvantage that, even if you beat the odds and end up a winner, you've just won the tiny amount of your initial wager. (A friend of the authors of this text tried this system at Las Vegas several years ago—at $10 a pop—and actually lasted over 2 hours before losing her bankroll.)

The other cute fallacy that gamblers fall for is to believe that the less often, say, a 7 has shown up lately at the dice table, the more likely it is that it will show up on the next toss of the dice. The odds, gamblers are fond of saying, have to "even out." Wait until 7 has not shown up for a specified number of tosses, say, ten in a row, and then bet heavily on 7.

The trouble with this system is that each toss of the dice is *independent* of every other toss, which means that what happens on one toss is independent of what happens on any other. The point is that the dice don't know (or care!) what has shown up on previous

---

[4] That is why playing a state lottery amounts to paying a voluntary state tax. Thomas Jefferson, among other illustrious figures, favored lotteries for that very reason. Ordinary taxes are compulsory; lottery "taxes" are completely voluntary. Good point. Of course, human nature being what it is, plenty of people who regularly toss money away on state lotteries complain bitterly about having to pay state sales and income taxes.

tosses. The conditions that determine the odds on any given toss determine them to be the same for all tosses, no matter how previous tosses turned out. The dice, after all, are still the same symmetrical devices obeying the same laws of physics on every toss.

True critical reasoners, of course, don't need to know anything about correct odds to be sure that systems like this don't work. The house is in business to win; if they let you play, you can bet your system is no good.[5]

Although the theory about how to calculate fair odds in general is quite complicated, there are a few simple rules that cover most common cases. Using the lowercase letter a to stand for a first event or outcome and b for a second, and P as shorthand for probability, here are four such rules:

Restricted conjunction rule:

If two events are *independent* of each other (the occurrence of one has no effect on the occurrence of the other), then the probability of both occurring is equal to the probability of the first times the probability of the second. In symbols, this reads:

$P(a \& b) = P(a) \times P(b)$.

For example, the probability of getting two 7s in a row with a fair pair of dice is equal to the probability of first getting a 7 ($\frac{1}{6}$) times the probability of 7 on the second toss ($\frac{1}{6}$), and thus is $\frac{1}{6} \times \frac{1}{6} = \frac{1}{36}$.

General conjunction rule:

$P(a \& b) = P(a) \times P(b,$ given that a occurs$)$.

For instance, the probability of drawing two spades in a row out of an at-first-complete deck of cards is equal to the probability of drawing the first spade ($\frac{13}{52}$, because 13 of the 52 cards in a deck are spades) times the probability of drawing a second one, given that the first spade is not replaced in the deck ($\frac{12}{51}$), and thus is $\frac{13}{52} \times \frac{12}{51} = \frac{1}{17}$.

Restricted disjunction rule:

If a and b are mutually exclusive events (an outcome cannot be both a and b), then

$P(a$ or $b) = P(a) + P(b)$.

For example, the probability of drawing a spade or a heart on a given draw is equal to the probability of drawing a spade ($\frac{1}{4}$) plus the probability of drawing a heart ($\frac{1}{4}$), and

---

[5]There have been very few exceptions to this rule. One occurred many years ago when card-counting systems were devised for blackjack that changed the odds so that they were in favor of adept card counters. At first, casinos refused to let card counters play—they actually kept lists—but then they simply increased the size of blackjack decks or used mechanical devices spewing out an endless series of cards, thereby ruining the card-counting game. (The card counters proved to be not much of a problem, because extremely few players were sufficiently adept at keeping track of cards played, and anyway, the idea that there is a way to beat the odds is good for business.) Another exception also occurred many years ago when college students discovered the tiny bias of a particular Las Vegas casino roulette wheel by patient observation over several days. They were allowed to win several thousand dollars, because of the great publicity, before the house ruined the game simply by changing the wheel.

thus is $\frac{1}{4} + \frac{1}{4} = \frac{1}{2}$. (Drawing a spade and drawing a heart are mutually exclusive because no card can be both a spade and a heart.)

General disjunction rule:

$P(a \text{ or } b) = P(a) + P(b) - P(a \& b)$.

For instance, the probability of getting at least one head in two tosses equals the probability of getting a head on the first toss ($\frac{1}{2}$) plus the probability of doing so on the second toss ($\frac{1}{2}$) minus the probability of getting heads on both tosses ($\frac{1}{4}$), and thus is $\frac{1}{2} + \frac{1}{2} - \frac{1}{4} = \frac{3}{4}$. (Note that we can't just say it is equal to $\frac{1}{2} + \frac{1}{2}$.)

It should be obvious, by the way, that the probability of a contradiction equals zero and of a tautology (logical truth), one.

EXERCISE A-1

*1. What is the probability of getting either 2 or 12 on a given toss of an honest pair of dice?

2. How about one or the other in two tosses?

3. What is the probability of getting a red jack, queen, or king with an ordinary deck of cards on one random draw?

*4. If a state lottery paid fair odds, how much should a $2 wager pay a winner who picked the correct five-digit number?

5. Can we use the general disjunction rule in cases in which the events are mutually exclusive, as in the spade/heart example just mentioned? Explain your answer, and give an example.

EXERCISE A-2

Here is a "system" promoted in a book on gambling.[6] (A tiny part of the system has been omitted here.) Explain why it doesn't work (hard question, but well worth figuring out).

There is only one way to show a profit. Bet light on your losses and heavy on your wins.

Bet minimums when you're losing.

You recoup losses by betting house money against the house, not your own. When you win with a minimum bet, let the winnings ride and manage to come up with a few more wins. . . .

Bet heavy when you're winning.

Following a win with your minimum bet, bet the original minimum plus the amount you won. On a third win, drag [keep?] the minimum and bet the rest.

---

[6]Clement McQuaid, editor, *Gambler's Digest: The World's Greatest Gambling Book,* 2nd edition (Iola, Wisc.: DBI Books, 1981).

You now have a one-minimum-bet profit on the round, regardless of what happens. . . . As soon as you lose, go back to the minimum bet. . . .

Always make your heavy bets with the other fellow's money, not your own.

The worst thing you can do betting house money against the house on a bet is break even on that particular wager. Actually, you've lost money on the round—but it was money that you got from the other fellow, not part of your original venture money. . . .

Don't limit your winnings.

Always ride out a winning streak, pushing your skill to the hilt. . . .

Quit on a losing streak, not a winning streak.

While the law of mathematical probability averages out, it doesn't operate in a set pattern. Wins and losses go in streaks more often than they alternate. If you've had a good winning streak and a loss follows it, bet minimums long enough to see whether or not another winning streak is coming up. If it isn't, quit while you're still ahead.

ANSWERS TO
STARRED EXERCISE ITEMS

These answers certainly are not presented as revealed truth. They represent the authors' thoughts on the matter, which it is hoped will prove useful to the reader.

Exercise 1-1 (pp. 3–4)

4. *Premise:* We are sinners all.
   Implied premise: All sinners should forbear to judge (others).
   Conclusion: We all should forbear to judge (others).

6. *Premise:* Since 18-year-olds are legally allowed to vote,
   Premise: Since they can be drafted into war,
   Conclusion: Eighteen-year-olds should be allowed to drink alcoholic beverages.

Exercise 1-2 (pp. 4–6)

1. *Premise:* If we keep burning so much coal and oil, the greenhouse effect will continue to get worse.
   Premise: But it will be a disaster if it happens.
   Conclusion: So we've got to reduce our dependency on those fossil fuels.

4. No argument. Just a narrative of summer activities.

9. *Premise:* We all think ourselves so abundantly provided with good sense that we don't desire any more.
   Implied premise: If everyone is satisfied with the amount of good sense he has, then good sense must be equally distributed.
   Conclusion: Good sense is equally distributed.

   (The bit about it being the most equally distributed item is, we can assume, a rhetorical flourish. By the way, do you suppose Descartes was being a bit ironic?)

Exercise 1-5 (p. 21)

3. $10.9 billion is a drop in the bucket these days for military expenditures. The United States spends a great many times more than that every year on the military.

Exercise 2-3 (p. 36)

4. Disjunctive syllogisms have the form

A or B

Not A

B

   If we replace the As by the *sentence* "Snow is white" and the Bs by the *sentence* "Snow is pink," we get the following argument:

Snow is white or snow is pink.

Snow isn't white. (Not snow is white.)

Snow is pink.

   The term *or* in this disjunctive syllogism serves as a *sentence connective* (grammarians would say it serves as a coordinating conjunction); it connects whole sentences. In this case it connects the sentences "Snow is white" and "Snow is pink." "Snow is white or snow is pink" is said to be a *compound sentence* composed of the two *atomic sentences* "Snow is white" and "Snow is pink," joined together by the sentence connective *or*.

   Contrast this with the following syllogistic form and argument:

All *S* are *M*.   All sinners are betrayers.

All *M* are *P*.   All betrayers are untrustworthy.

All *S* are *P*.   All sinners are untrustworthy.

   In this case, we replace the *S*s, *M*s, and *P*s not by the whole sentences but by parts of sentences—namely, sentence *subjects* or sentence *predicates*. The term *are* serves not as a sentence connective but rather as a *verb* (the verb *to be*); it connects the subject of a sentence with its predicate. In the case, say, of the atomic sentence "All sinners are betrayers," the verb *are* connects the subject *sinners* with the predicate *betrayer* to form the atomic sentence "All sinners are betrayers." (The term *all* serves as a *quantifier*, indicating how many sinners, but that is another story, discussed in formal logic texts.)

Exercise 2-4 (p. 38)

3. *Contingent.* It certainly is not a contradiction, and it also is not a tautology because there is no law of logic that forbids one from running for both president and vice president in the same election. (Is there a legal law of the land?)

Exercise 3-1 (pp. 66–70)

1. *Appeal to authority.* Doctors are specialists in medicine. They don't necessarily know anything more about moral issues than anyone else. Anyway, don't we all need to make up our own minds about moral matters?

2. *Inconsistency.* Clinton clearly made a blanket statement about taking nuclear weapons off the table in the 2006 interview but flip-flopped when she criticized Obama for making a similar statement.

17. *Suppressed evidence.* Most of us are in our own home a lot more than we are in these other places. The rape rate per unit of time is much greater in the other places mentioned by Dr. Brothers than in one's own home.

25. *Inconsistency.* Doesn't the phrase "heritable disposition" mean a disposition caused by a genetic inheritance?

Exercise 4-1 (pp. 86–90)

4. *Irrelevant reasons.*

6. *Slippery slope.*

14. *Equivocation.* You don't have to make the past or future present in thought. What you make present, the "it," is thoughts about the past or present. The term *it* is used equivocally, the first use denoting the past or present and the second the thought of the past or present.

24. *Equivocation.* To imagine our own death is to visualize what it would be like to experience it. In this sense we can and do imagine our own death. Freud changes the meaning of *imagine* so that to imagine it we would have to not visualize it, which, of course, is impossible.

Exercise 5-1 (pp. 112–113)

5. Students taught this way could be, and very likely are, different from "average" students in having more concerned parents (than average), more affluent parents, homes in which books and the like form a larger part of life, and so on. We already have good reason to believe that "booked" households produce children who, on average, score higher than average.The point is bringing background beliefs to bear. You may have specific, relevant background beliefs, as above, or just general ones that should lead you to have some doubts about the implication of the stat—that home teaching is better than public schools.

Exercise 5-2 (pp. 113–116)

13. *Questionable cause.* Lewinsky's peccadilloes had nothing to do with the decrease in crime or the robust economy in 1998.

20. If LaPierre intended his analogy to prove anything, then he was guilty of the fallacy questionable analogy. But since he then provided reasons for believing gun bans do not reduce crime rates, we have to assume he meant his analogy to be illustrative, not demonstrative.

22. *Questionable statistics.* We can roughly estimate what is spent on illegal drugs, say, give or take $10 billion, but precise figures have to be unknown since they are illegal, therefore unrecorded actions people want to keep secret.

Exercise 5-3 (pp. 116–120)

1. *Questionable analogy.* Here's an example for which some background information is essential. (Precise figures aren't necessary.) On a trip to Saturn, the *Titan 4, Cassini,* carried 72.3 pounds of plutonium—the most carcinogenic substance known to man—with far greater radioactivity than was in the Chernobyl reactor at the time of its meltdown. The failure rate of *Titan 4* is 1 in 12.5. If *Cassini* disintegrated at its closest point (500 miles) in encircling the Earth, scientists estimate that millions of people would die—vastly more than the fatalities in a car crash. It's also worth noting that the chances of having an accident when driving a car are very much less than 1 in 12.5.

2. *Suppressed evidence.* In a nation where most people live in cities, where pigs cannot be kept, forbidding the sale of pork, bacon, and such is tantamount to forbidding the eating of these items. *Inconsistency.* So Rabbi Shapira came close to being inconsistent when he claimed that the ultrareligious Jews in Israel want the sale but not the eating of these kinds of meat to be forbidden, since the one is tantamount to the other.

8. *Questionable statistics.* Having extolled scientists for their generally correct handling of statistics, here is a case where they goofed. The problem isn't that a rough statistic did not follow from their evidence but rather that precise ones such as 968.1 billion tons of carbon stored 18,000 years ago did not. Note, for instance, that they estimated how much carbon dioxide was locked within plants, and so on.

11. *Suppressed evidence.* (1) Superstition is more accurately defined, in part, as belief without good evidence or in the face of contrary evidence. (So the article changed the meaning of the term *superstition,* and some readers may have been guilty of falling for the fallacy equivocation.) (2) Some of the greatest scientists may have been superstitious, Isaac Newton being perhaps the best candidate. But the parts of their beliefs that became incorporated in science were not superstitions, Newton again furnishing perhaps the best example. (3) In addition, a great deal of what scientists once accepted, *on good evidence,* they now reject, or have modified or sharpened, because of better evidence (for example, the rejected ether theory). Rejecting or modifying well-supported theories because of better evidence in favor of more accurate theories is the heart of science and is definitely not superstition.

15. No fallacy. His analogies are apt.

21. *Hasty conclusion.* The evidence cited certainly is relevant to the question and favorable to Peirce's claim that the ads caused a rise in teen smoking, but it is not conclusive. Many other factors were at work (was there a similar increase in the use of other harmful drugs such as alcohol or marijuana?) and need to be evaluated along with the ads. *Questionable statement.* Why isn't banning cigarette ads a First Amendment issue? It's true that we don't think a ban on ads for illegal substances would violate the First Amendment prohibition on censorship of speech, but, on the other hand, we wouldn't be inclined to agree that nothing can be advertised that causes serious illnesses (for instance, high-fat foods).

22. *Hasty conclusion.* There certainly are plenty of good background reasons for concluding that raising the speed limit will increase traffic fatalities. But we can't automatically credit the 55-mph speed limit with reducing fatalities. (For one thing, that limit was generally flouted anyway; for another, cars have been made safer, and perhaps drivers on average are more sober.) Still, it would have been a good guess, based on background beliefs, that increases in speed would result in increases in fatalities. (Experience so far is mixed as to whether in fact the new higher maximum speed limits have resulted in increased highway deaths.)

24. *Questionable analogy.* The issue is not the similar sizes of California and Iraq, but the populations. There are 35 million Californians but only 140,000 U.S. soldiers in Iraq. California homicides would amount to 125,000 if people in that state were actually killed at the same rate as our soldiers were dying in Iraq.

Exercise 5-4 (pp. 120–121)

Questionable cause/Hasty conclusion. To begin with, if we subtract the U.S.'s figures, the stats look much different (suggesting the criminal population in the United States is high for other reasons). Also, Ireland, with 88 percent church attendance, has a lower jail rate than four of the six low-church nations and lower than the average. This raises all kinds of questions. Are the Irish secret sinners? Are their police incompetent? How many criminals are behind bars in the United States because they committed victimless crimes (such as smoking dope) or because of race prejudice?

In any case, the statistics cited completely fail to support the implication that churchgoing leads to criminal behavior, nor do any other statistics known to the authors of this text.

Exercise 7-2 (pp. 177–178)

3. *Translation:* Printed on paper that is at least 10 percent recycled, with a minimum of 40 percent new material.

   Is there something sneaky about this? Yes, indeed. Starting out with the statement "Printed on recycled paper" leads one to suspect that the item is printed on 100 percent recycled paper, thus playing to those who like to use recycled materials. The bit about post- and preconsumer materials is bound to be confusing to most of these people, who will then rely on the (misleading) first statement—the one they can understand. At the same time, the manufacturer is protected from fraud by the statements about pre- and postconsumer materials.

6. What the good admiral said in militaryese was that navy teams had gone around the country trying to find ways to get naval installations to spend more money. (It was close to the end of the fiscal year, and the navy had not used up its appropriation for that year. Yes, bureaucracies, with very few exceptions, do work this way.)

Exercise 7-4 (p. 179)

2. Actually, two of the sayings might be challenged. Charles Beardsley's quote may be thought to be doublespeak, and the Chinese proverb clearly does use the pronoun *he* when people in general are meant. But Beardsley deliberately employed "pompous prolixity" in order to rail against that very kind of language. And it makes not a great deal of sense to change ancient sayings (or should we commit to flames the King James version of the Bible with its sexist sayings, such as "Let him who is without sin cast the first stone"?).

   Confucius's precept does exaggerate the slipperiness of the slope he describes. But it is slippery!

Exercise 8-1 (pp. 186–187)

3. *Thesis:* None of the historical or anecdotal parts of the Bible are the word of God.
   Reason (premise): What I've seen (or know?) needs no revelation.
   Conclusion: Revelation is that which reveals what we don't know (haven't seen) before.
   Reason: Revelation is that which reveals what we don't know (haven't seen) before.
   Conclusion: Revelation can't tell us about earthly things men could witness.
   Reason: Revelation can't tell us about earthly things men could witness.
   Conclusion (thesis): None of the historical or anecdotal parts of the Bible count as revelation. (Paine assumed an equation between revelation and the word of God.)

Exercise 9-4 (pp. 221–223)

2. It is very difficult to construct margin notes or a summary for material such as these excerpts from *Mein Kampf,* because confusion and ambiguities abound. Nevertheless, here is a reasonably accurate summary (omitting Hitler's anthropomorphization of laws of nature):

   1. It is a law of nature that animals mate only with members of their own species.

   2. Breeding higher with lower within a species produces a medium that will lose out eventually to the higher.

   3. If a law of nature did not exist forbidding breeding higher to lower, still higher could not develop.

4. The struggle for food and mates results in a higher development of a species.

5. Just as mating stronger with weaker *individuals* goes against nature, so does mating higher with lower races.

6. Proof: Aryans in North America remained pure and became masters of the continent; Latins in Central and South America mixed with the natives and produced an inferior culture, of which they are not complete masters. (This isn't exactly what Hitler says, but it is what he means. Remember that a good deal of Latin America was still in a colonial status in the 1920s when Hitler wrote his tome.)

Exercise 10-1 (pp. 244–245)

2. Clearly there's a contradiction here. Certificates that cost $1 aren't free.

6. This Nike commercial wins the *Logic and Contemporary Rhetoric* "Most Offensive Commercial of the Decade" Award for telling those who have just proved to be the second best at an activity (perhaps by the tiniest margin) among the several billion people on the planet that they are losers, instead of crediting them with their great accomplishment. (The underlying offensive message is captured by Vince Lombardi's famous remark, "Winning isn't everything; it's the only thing." Compare that to "It isn't whether you win or lose but how you play the game.")

10. *Appeal to authority.* Agronsky is no authority on the subject. *Straw man.* No one claims coconut oils are "poisoning" America. *Suppressed evidence.* (1) While some fats are healthier than others, coconut oil is low on the healthy list. (2) It is total amount of fat intake that is most important. (3) No single fat source supplies more than a small portion of total intake of fat, so that "only" 1.5 percent coming from coconut oil proves nothing. The point is that it's prudent to reduce one's total amount of fat intake well below the national average and to reduce intake of some kinds of fat—coconut oil being a prime example—more than others. (4) If true that the fatty acids in coconut oil are beneficial, that would be a good reason to prefer this oil to others—say, when cooking. But this claim is generally not accepted by the medical profession. On the contrary, it is fats such as olive oil that seem to be the most beneficial.

Exercise 10-2 (pp. 245–246)

3. This commercial points to a profitable use of air travel—to foster face-to-face business relationships. That is why this has been an extremely successful ad—it reminds business executives of the value of catering to customers in person. But the commercial gives no reason to fly United instead of other airlines. (The implied reason that United flies to more than 200 locations is not a good reason for choosing United. For one thing, some other airlines fly to that many cities; and for another, what difference does it make if you intend, say, to fly to Chicago, whether the airline you choose also flies to 199 other cities or just to half that many?) *Jargon-type slogan.* "United. Come fly the friendly skies." *Identification.* Casting the right actors for TV commercials is crucial, and this ad does it beautifully. Ben is someone most people in business will identify with.

Exercise 12-4 (pp. 355–356)

3. The topic is the one discussed in Chapter 7 entitled "Those Who Control the Definitions"—defining oneself into victory. Those who favor teaching the biblical account of creation in science classes were trying to define themselves into victory by calling the biblical account "creation science," very much like businesses do who call employees "subcontractors."

Exercise for the Entire Text (p. 357)

You didn't really expect an answer to this one, did you? (If you did, go back to page 1 of Chapter 1 and start reading—carefully this time.)

Exercise A-1 (p. 366)

1. Since it isn't possible to get both 2 and 12 on a given toss, we can use the restricted disjunction rule. And given that the probability of getting a 2 = $\frac{1}{36}$ and of a 12 = $\frac{1}{36}$, the probability of getting 2 or 12 = $\frac{1}{36}$ + $\frac{1}{36}$ = $\frac{2}{36}$ = $\frac{1}{18}$.

4. There are 100,000 five-digit numbers, each one equally likely to be picked. Thus, the odds on any given number are 100,000 to 1. So a winning $2 bet should pay $200,000 plus the $2 wagered. (None do. But note that in lottery cases of this kind, how much is paid to winners usually depends on how many people pick the correct number and whether there was a winner of previous plays. When there is no winner for several plays and the pot becomes very large, the number of people who play increases dramatically [people are not always rational!], so that, even though the amount of prize money increases, the probability that there will be several winners increases, thus dividing each winner's share. Of course, when the odds against winning anything are 100,000 to 1, the chances of winning are so miniscule that it is a waste of time to play. It almost never makes sense to wager at such poor odds, even if they are statistically in your favor; doing so loses you the opportunity to profit in some more likely ways. Human irrationality makes most of us see things differently, but that's just one of the tendencies that a good rational thinker fights against.)

BIBLIOGRAPHY

Asterisks indicate works mentioned in the text.

Cogent Reasoning

Carroll, Lewis. *Symbolic Logic and the Game of Logic*. New York: Dover, 1958.

Dewey, John. *How We Think*. Lexington, Mass.: Heath, 1910.

*Hausman, Alan, Kahane, Howard, and Tidman, Paul. *Logic and Philosophy,* 10th ed. Belmont, Calif.: Wadsworth, 2006.

Kahane, Howard. "The Proper Subject Matter for Critical Thinking Courses." *Argumentation* 3 (1989).

Lemmon, E. J. *Beginning Logic,* rev. G. N. D. Barry. Indianapolis, Ind.: Hackett, 1978. (A strictly formal logic text.)

Fallacious Reasoning

*Bentham, Jeremy. *The Handbook of Political Fallacies*. New York: Harper Torchbooks, 1962. (A reprint of a classic nineteenth-century tract.)

Broad, C. D. "Some Fallacies in Political Thinking." *Philosophy* 29 (April 1950). (Interesting article by an important twentieth-century philosopher.)

*Cerf, Christopher, and Navasky, Victor. *The Experts Speak: The Definitive Compendium of Authoritative Misinformation*. New York: Pantheon, 1984.

*Dixon, Paul. *The Official Rules*. New York: Delacorte, 1978.

Ekman, Paul. *Telling Lies: Clues to Deceit in the Marketplace, Politics, and Marriage*. New York: Norton, 1992. (Fascinating book that will help readers to perceive when they are being lied to.)

Hamblin, C. L. *Fallacies*. Newport News, Va.: Vale, 1986. (A reprint with new preface of the definitive history of fallacy theory.)

Huff, Darrell. *How to Lie with Statistics*. New York: Norton, 1954.

*Jackson, Brooks, and Jameson, Kathleen Hall. *Unspun, Finding Facts in a World of Disinformation*. New York: Random House, 2007.

*Kahane, Howard. "The Nature and Classification of Fallacies." In *Informal Logic: The First International Symposium,* eds. J. Anthony Blair and Ralph H. Johnson. Inverness, Calif.: Edgepress, 1980.

Miller, James Nathan. "Ronald Reagan and the Techniques of Deception." *Atlantic Monthly* (February 1984). (Nice illustration of how statistics can be misused for political advantage.)

Morgan, Chris, and Langford, David. *Facts and Fallacies: A Book of Definitive Mistakes and Misguided Predictions.* Exeter, England: Webb & Bower, 1981. (One of several excellent books illustrating expert feet of clay.)

Morgenstern, Oscar. "Qui Numerare Incipit Errare Incipit." *Fortune* (October 1963). (Still one of the best explanations of how government statistics on business and such can be and are manipulated for political purposes.)

*"Real World Macro: A Macroeconomics Reader from Dollars and Sense." 1996. (How statistics can be manipulated, in particular by the federal government.)

Smith, H. B. *How the Mind Falls into Error.* N.p.: Darby, 1980. (Reprint of the 1923 edition.)

Thouless, Robert H. *Straight and Crooked Thinking.* New York: Simon & Schuster, 1932.

Wheeler, Michael. *Lies, Damn Lies, and Statistics: The Manipulation of Public Opinion in America.* New York: Dell Laurel, 1977.

Impediments to Cogent Reasoning

Bartholomew, Robert E., and Goode, Erich. "Mass Delusions and Hysterias: Highlights from the Past Millennium." *Skeptical Inquirer* (May/June 2000). (Fascinating article on human irrationality during the just-completed thousand years. Great companion to the Charles MacKay book listed later.)

*Bentham, Jeremy. *The Handbook of Political Fallacies.* New York: Harper Torchbooks, 1962. (A reprint of a classic nineteenth-century tract.)

*French, Christopher C., Fowler, Mandy, McCarthy, Katy, and Peers, Debbie. "Belief in Astrology: A Test of the Barnum Effect." *Skeptical Inquirer* (Winter 1991).

Gardner, Martin. *Science: Good, Bad, and Bogus.* Buffalo, N.Y.: Prometheus, 1981. (Debunking of pseudoscience.)

———. *Fads and Fallacies in the Name of Science.* New York: Dover, 1957. (The classic debunking of pseudoscience.)

*Gilovich, Thomas. *How We Know What Isn't So.* New York: Free Press, 1991.

*Goffman, Erving. *The Presentation of Self in Everyday Life.* New York: Anchor, 1959. (A classic.)

*Goleman, Daniel. *Vital Lies, Simple Truths.* New York: Simon & Schuster, 1985. (The best understandable explanation of recent scientific ideas about self-deception, its biological functions, and the unconscious.)

MacKay, Charles. *Memoirs of Extraordinary Popular Delusions and the Madness of Crowds.* New York: Harmony, 1980. (Reprint of 1841 edition, with foreword by Andrew Tobias. An excellent account of several disasters—the Crusades, the seventeenth-century Dutch tulip madness, the South Sea Bubble—driven by mass hysteria.)

Nickell, Joe. *Inquest on the Shroud of Turin.* Buffalo, N.Y.: Prometheus, 1982. (An example of sanity on a foolishness-provoking topic.)

Nisbet, Robert. *Prejudices.* Cambridge, Mass.: Harvard University Press, 1986.

Peirce, Charles Sanders. "The Fixation of Belief." *Popular Science Monthly* (1877). (A classic article by America's premier philosopher.)

Sagan, Carl. *The Demon-Haunted World.* New York: Random House, 1996. (A protest by an eminent astronomer against superstition and the uncritical acceptance of pseudoscientific claims.)

Shermer, Michael. *Why People Believe Weird Things: Pseudoscience, Superstition, and Other Confusions of Our Time.* New York: Freeman, 1997.

Twain, Mark. *Mark Twain on the Damned Human Race,* ed. Janet Smith. New York: Hill & Wang, 1962. (The great American humorist on all sorts of human foibles. If you think of Sam Clemens as just a writer of stories, you should read this book. For one thing, it will make evident to you how ridiculous it is to censor *Huckleberry Finn* on grounds of racism.)

Vyse, Stuart A. *Believing in Magic: The Psychology of Superstition.* New York: Oxford University Press, 1997.

Language

*American Philosophical Association (APA). *Guidelines for Non-Sexist Use of Language*. (Publication of the APA, available from their national office in Washington, D.C.)

*Carroll, Lewis. *Alice's Adventures in Wonderland*. New York: New American Library, 1960. (Reprint. The Reverend Dodgson, by the way, was a first-rate logician.)

"Guidelines for Equal Treatment of the Sexes in McGraw-Hill Book Company Publications." (Eleven-page, in-house statement of policy that has been generally adopted in the publishing business.)

Hall, Edward T. *The Silent Language*. New York: Doubleday, 1973.

*Jacoby, Susan. *The Age of American Unreason*. New York: Pantheon Press, 2008.

*Lakoff, George. *Don't Think of an Elephant*. White River Junction, VT.: Chelsea Green Publishing Co., 2004.

*———. *Moral Politics: How Liberals and Conservatives Think*. Chicago: University of Chicago Press, 2002.

Lutz, William. "Notes toward a Description of Doublespeak." *Quarterly Review of Doublespeak* (January 1987).

*———. *Doublespeak Defined*. New York: HarperCollins Publishers, Inc., 1999.

*Orwell, George. *Nineteen Eighty-Four*. New York: New American Library, 1949. (Shows how language control helps control thoughts and thus behavior.)

*———. "Politics and the English Language." Reprinted in *A Collection of Works by George Orwell*. New York: Harcourt Brace, 1946.

Postman, Neil. *Amusing Ourselves to Death: Public Discourse in the Age of Show Business*. New York: Penguin, 1986.

Solomon, Norman. *The Power of Babble: The Politician's Dictionary of Buzzwords and Doubletalk for Every Occasion*. New York: Bantam Doubleday Dell, 1992.

Evaluating and Constructing Extended Arguments

Cavender, Nancy, and Weiss, Len. *Thinking/Writing*. Belmont, Calif.: Wadsworth, 1987.

Flew, Antony. *Thinking Straight*. Buffalo, N.Y.: Prometheus, 1977.

Lanham, Richard. *Revising Prose*. New York: Scribner's, 1979. (A good guide to clear writing.)

St. Aubyn, Giles. *The Art of Argument*. Buchanan, N.Y.: Emerson, 1962. (A beautifully written little book on argument.)

Writing Cogent (and Persuasive) Essays

*Hayes, John R., and Flower, Linda S. "Writing as Problem Solving." *Visible Language* 14: 396–398.

*Kahane, Howard. *Contract Ethics: Evolutionary Biology and the Moral Sentiments*. Lanham, Md.: Rowman & Littlefield, 1995. (Helpful in bringing value judgments to bear when evaluating arguments.)

Advertising

Baker, Samm Sinclair. *The Permissible Lie*. Cleveland, Ohio: World, 1968.

*Beiler, David. *The Classics of Political Television Advertising: A Viewer's Guide*. Washington, D.C.: Campaigns and Elections, 1986. (Companion guide to a 60-minute videocassette containing some of the great TV campaign spots. Great fun and educational, too.)

Benn, Alec. *The 27 Most Common Mistakes in Advertising*. New York: AMACOM, 1978.

*Clark, Eric. *The Want Makers*. New York: Viking, 1988.

*Collins, Thomas L. *Beyond Maximarketing*. New York: McGraw-Hill, 1994.

Faucheux, Ron. "How to Win in '94." *Campaigns and Elections* (September 1993). (Interesting to compare with how campaigns were run in 1994.)

*Feldstein, Mark. "Mail Fraud on Capitol Hill." *Washington Monthly* (October 1979).

Glatzer, Robert. *The New Advertising: The Great Campaigns from Avis to Volkswagen*. New York: Citadel, 1970.

Hopkins, Claude. *Scientific Advertising*. New York: Crown, 1966. (Reprint of one of the classics on advertising.)

Iyengar, Shanto, and Ansolabehere, Stephen. *Going Negative: How Political Advertisements Shrink and Polarize the Electorate*. New York: Free Press, 1996.

Jamieson, Kathleen Hall. *Dirty Politics: Deception, Distraction, and Democracy*. Oxford University Press, 1992. (How campaigns dominated by 30- and 10-second TV spots fail to provide voters with adequate information.)

————. *Packaging the Presidency: A History and Criticism of Presidential Campaign Advertising*, 2d ed. New York: Oxford University Press, 1992.

*Kilbourne, Jean. *Deadly Persuasion: Why Women and Girls Must Fight the Addictive Power of Advertising*. New York: Simon & Schuster, 1999.

*Lemann, Nicholas. "Barney Frank's Mother and 500 Postmen." *Harper's* (April 1983).

*Marks, Steven. *Confessions of a Political Hitman*. Naperville, IL: Sourcebooks Inc., 2007.

McGinnis, Joe. *The Selling of the President 1968*. New York: Trident, 1969. (Still the best inside account of a presidential campaign—Nixon's successful run for the presidency.)

*Ogilvy, David. *Confessions of an Advertising Man*. New York: Atheneum, 1963.

Preston, Ivan. *The Great American Blowup: Puffery in Advertising and Selling*. Madison: University of Wisconsin Press, 1975. (Interesting account of what legally counts as mere puffery rather than false advertising.)

Rowsome, Frank, Jr. *They Laughed When I Sat Down*. New York: Bonanza, 1959. (Perhaps still the most interesting book on the history of advertising.)

*Sabatim, Karry J., and Simpson, Glenn R. "When Push Comes to Poll." *Washington Monthly* (June 1996).

Savan, Leslie. *The Sponsored Life: Ads, TV and American Culture*. Philadelphia: Temple University Press, 1995.

Stauber, John, and Rampton, Sheldon. *Toxic Sludge Is Good for You: Lies, Damn Lies, and the Public Relations Industry*. Monroe, Me.: Common Courage Press, 1995.

*Washburn, Katharine, and Thornton, John, eds. *Dumbing Down: The Strip-mining of American Culture*. New York: Norton, 1996.

In addition to the books already listed, several excellent videocassettes are available from Campaigns and Elections, Washington, D.C., including the June 1986 *The Classics of Political Advertising* (with an accompanying booklet by David Beiler); *Prime Time Politics*, a 1989 cassette primarily concerned with the 1988 elections; and *The 25 Funniest Political TV Commercials* (actually, not all that funny, but instructive). There also are several other modestly interesting videocassettes available, including *30-Second Seduction*, a 1985 cassette by Consumer Reports.

Managing the News

Bagdikian, Ben. *The Media Monopoly*, 4th ed. Boston: Beacon, 1992.

Bennett, James. "The Flack Pack: How Press Conferences Turn Serious Journalists into Shills." *Washington Monthly* (November 1991).

Cohen, Jeff, and Solomon, Norman. *Adventures in Medialand: Behind the News, Beyond the Pundits*. Monroe, Me.: Common Courage Press, 1993.

Cohen, Richard. "Making Trends Meet." *Washington Post Magazine,* September 28, 1986. (How *Time* and *Newsweek* exaggerate and invent trends and fashions.)

Crossen, Cynthia. *Tainted Truth: The Manipulation of Fact in America.* New York: Simon & Schuster, 1994.

Croteau, David, and Hoynes, William. *By Invitation Only: How the Media Limits Political Debate.* Monroe, Me.: Common Courage Press, 1997.

Day, James. *The Vanishing Vision: The Inside Story of Public Television.* Berkeley: University of California Press, 1995. (A good account of how and why public television [PBS] succeeds in some ways and comes short in others.)

*El-Nawawy, Mohammed, and Iskandar Faraq, Adel. *Al-Jazeera: How the Arab Network Scooped the World.* Boulder, CO: Westeview Press, 2002.

Fallows, James. *Breaking the News: How the Media Undermine American Democracy.* New York: Pantheon, 1996. (Important book by the now [1997] editor of *U.S. News & World Report.*)

Faludi, Susan. *Backlash: The Undeclared War Against American Women.* New York: Bantam, 1991.

Fineman, Howard. "The Power of Talk." *Newsweek,* February 8, 1993. (How "call-in democracy"—TV and radio talk shows—are influencing elections and the legislative process.)

Hansell, Saul, and Harmon, Amy. "Caveat Emptor on the Web." *New York Times,* February 26, 1999.

Hausman, Carl. *Lies We Live By: Defeating Double-Talk and Deception in Advertising, Politics and the Media.* New York: Routledge, 2000. (One of the best books on these related topics.)

Hess, Stephen. "Television's Self-Fulfilling News." *Washington Post,* National Weekly Edition, October 30–November 5, 1989. (How TV shops around for expert opinion that conforms to the view they want to air.)

Hitt, Jack. "Warning: CIA Censors at Work." *Columbia Journalism Review* (July/August 1984).

*Jensen, Carl, and Project Censored. *Censored: The News That Didn't Make the News—and Why.* New York: Seven Stories Press, 1996. (A [hopefully] yearly publication about censored news stories.)

*Knightly, Phillip. *The First Casualty.* New York: Harcourt Brace Jovanovich, 1975. (The first casualty in war is, of course, truth.)

Levine, Richard M. "Polish Government versus the Workers: Why TV Is the Prized Weapon." *TV Guide* (November 7, 1981). (An illustration of how important TV has become for politics everywhere.)

Lieberman, David. "Fake News." *TV Guide* (February 22, 1992). (How video press releases, created by public relations firms, are surreptitiously slipped into TV news programs.)

McChesney, Robert. *Corporate Media and the Threat to Democracy.* New York: Seven Stories Press, 1997. (Interesting critique of corporate media power, plus some suggestions for improving the fairness and accuracy of the mass media.)

Miller, John J. "MLK, Inc." (How the Martin Luther King family is making big bucks by charging high permission fees to reprint from King's "I Have a Dream" speech and other writings, thereby inadvertently acting as censors.)

Perkins, Ray, Jr. *Logic and Mr. Limbaugh.* Chicago: Open Court, 1995. (A nifty account of how Rush Limbaugh mangles truth and logic.)

*Perry, David L. "No Way to Celebrate." *Columbia Journalism Review* (July/August 1990). (On how increasingly large jury awards in libel cases are putting a chill on investigative reporting.)

Smiley, Xan. "Misunderstanding Africa." *Atlantic Monthly* (September 1982). (How government intimidation and interference mangles news from Africa. An old article, but not that much has changed.)

Waters, Frank. *The Earp Brothers of Tombstone.* Lincoln: University of Nebraska Press, 1976. (The most accurate account of the exploits of the famous "Wild West" Earp brothers, Wyatt and Virgil, including a reasonably accurate account of the so-called "gunfight" at the O.K. Corral. A good antidote to the baloney the media dish out on this and other aspects of western U.S. history.)

*Zepezauer, Mark, and Naiman, Arthur. *Take the Rich off Welfare.* Tucson, Ariz.: Odonian, 1996.

In addition to the books just listed, there are several excellent videocassettes on managing the news, perhaps the most revealing being *Fear and Favor in the Newsroom,* distributed by California Newsreels, dramatically illustrating how corporate power influences news coverage.

Textbooks: Managing Worldviews

American Indian Historical Society. *Textbooks and the American Indian.* San Francisco: Indian Historical Press, 1970. (Shows how textbooks in those days—pre-1970—covered up the horrible treatment of Native Americans by European invaders.)

Barzun, Jacques. "The Wasteland of American Education." *New York Review of Books,* November 5, 1981. (Still very relevant.)

Black, Hillel. *The American Schoolbook.* New York: Morrow, 1967.

Chubb, John E. *Politics, Markets, and America's Schools.* Brookings Institution, 1990.

Cockborn, Alexander, and St. Clair, Jeffrey. *Al Gore: A User's Manual.* New York: Verso, 2000.

DelFattore, Joan. *What Johnny Shouldn't Read.* New Haven, Conn: Yale University Press, 1992.

*Elson, Ruth M. *Guardians of Tradition: American Schoolbooks of the 19th Century.* Lincoln: University of Nebraska Press, 1964.

*Finn, Jr., Chester E., and Ravitch, Diane. *The Mad, Mad World of Textbook Adoption.* Washington: Thomas B. Fordham Institute, 2004.

*Fussell, Paul. *Wartime: Understanding and Behavior in the Second World War.* New York: Oxford University Press, 1989.

Henry, Jules. *On Sham, Vulnerability, and Other Forms of Self-Destruction.* (Unfortunately out of print.)

"History/Social Science Framework for California Public Schools, Kindergarten Through Grade Twelve." (The basic document governing California schools.)

Kasarda, John D. "The Jobs-Skills Mismatch." *New Perspectives Quarterly* (Fall 1990). (The economy needs highly educated workers; schools produce "low achievers.")

Loewen, James W. *Lies Across America: What Our Historic Sites Get Wrong.* New York: New Press, 1999.

———. *Lies My Teacher Told Me: Everything Your History Textbook Got Wrong.* New York: New Press, 1995. (Terrific book explaining how and why public school textbooks distort history the way they do. Probably the best book on the topic ever written.)

Lynch, Michael W. "Rampaging Toward Choice." *Reason.* (Libertarian slant on the issue of school vouchers and charter schools.)

*Nelson, Jack, and Roberts, Gene. *The Censors and the Schools.* Boston: Little, Brown, 1963. (The best book on the topic up to 1963.)

Paulos, John Allen. *Innumeracy: Mathematical Illiteracy and Its Consequences.* New York: Hill & Wang, 1988.

Raloff, Janet. "Errant Texts." *Science News,* March 17, 2001. (Very good article on the poor quality of public school science textbooks.)

*Ravitch, Diane. *The Language Police: How Pressure Groups Restrict What Students Learn.* New York: Knopf, 2003.

Schrank, Jeffrey. *Understanding Mass Media,* 2d ed. Skokie, Ill.: National Textbook, 1986. (One of the best public school social science texts.)

*Shenkman, Richard. *Legends, Lies and Cherished Myths of American History.* New York: Morrow, 1988.

Stotsky, Sandra. *Losing Our Language: How Multicultural Classroom Instruction Is Undermining Our Children's Ability to Read, Write, and Reason.* New York: Free Press, 1999.

Washburn, Katharine, and Thornton, John. *Dumbing Down: Essays on the Strip-mining of American Culture.* New York: Norton, 1996. (Several fascinating essays on how the dumbing down of American public schools is harming society.)

Zinn, Howard. *A People's History of the United States.* New York: Harper & Row, 1980. (Perhaps the easiest-to-understand antidote to the history learned via public school history texts.)

Selected List of Periodicals

One of the themes of this text is that good reasoning requires reasonably accurate background beliefs, and one of the best ways to acquire a good stock of general information and theory is by reading some of the literally thousands of periodicals—magazines and journals—that are readily available these days. Here is a selected list of (primarily) non–mass media periodicals, the majority concerned mostly with social/political issues, the media, or science, which the authors of this text happen to dip into at least now and then. (The comments represent our opinions and are not to be taken as some sort of revealed truth.) Most of these publications have websites. For a complete list of magazine reviews see *Magazines for Libraries,* ed. Cheryl LaGuardia, available in the reference section of most college libraries.

American Heritage. Perhaps the most interesting history magazine, covering a broad range of topics in American history, some by well-known authors of historical pieces. Most articles are well illustrated, and the writing style is engaging. It now appears in e-journal only, however, and is not available in print.

American Spectator. A wild-swinging, right-wing publication that has as its mission "to provide its unique view of American conservative politics, with a keen sense of irreverence." The writing is often humorous, particularly in regular pieces like "Enemy of the Week."

Amnesty International. Magazine publication of Amnesty International, reporting on government torture around the world. (Reading this publication makes one appreciate living in a democratic society.) *Examples:* Fall 2008 articles, "Outsourcing Intelligence" and "The 60th Anniversary of the Universal Declaration of Human Rights."

Atlantic Monthly. One of the best general magazines with some excellent articles and fiction. It always covers foreign affairs and the Washington scene, plus a wide variety of articles on everything from Internet dating to soldiering in Gaza. *Examples:* "The Wars of John McCain" and "Is Pornography Adultery?" in the October 2008 issue.

Black Enterprise. A business magazine oriented toward African Americans in the business world whose mission has always been centered on "closing the black wealth gap and financially empowering African Americans." It regularly covers such topics as family finances, money management, business opportunities, and home ownership.

BusinessWeek. A good business magazine, written for those in business on a level that the general reader can appreciate and understand. In addition to a wide range of business articles, it covers social issues and lifestyles as well. Editorials are generally moderate in their position.

Columbia Journalism Review. One of the best journalism publications, full of interesting, newsworthy articles as well as articles on the field of journalism and a particularly good book review section. *Example:* The cover story of the November–December 2008 issue: "Overload, Journalism's Battle for Relevance in an Age of Too Much Information."

Congressional Digest. A monthly publication providing impartial coverage of the pros and cons on controversial issues before Congress, as well as legislative and judicial background information. *Example:* The September 2008 issue debating the pros and cons of domestic oil drilling, particularly off shore.

Consumer Reports. Publication of Consumers Union, an unbiased, nonprofit organization; a very good source of information about consumer products. All products it tests are purchased, no free samples are accepted, and no revenue comes from outside advertising—all of which make for objective dependable reviews.

Discover. Perhaps the best of a bad lot of mass media popular science magazines. Articles cover research from all science disciplines, profiles well-known scientists, reviews books, and reports on other science related issues. *Examples:* The October 2008 issue with articles on energy ("Anything into Ethanol"), food ("Growing a Better Burger"), and voting ("Technology that Makes Certain Your Ballot Gets Counted").

The Economist. A very informative British newsweekly, well respected internationally for articles on business and economics, world politics, science, technology, and the arts. *Examples:* Articles in the November 8, 2008, issue on the American election ("Great Expectations"), derivatives ("Giving Credit Where Credit is Due"), and climate change ("Green, Easy, and Wrong").

Editor and Publisher. Important trade magazine and a good source of information about how those in the business see things. Its newsy articles are aimed at industry leaders.

Environment Nutrition. A very good publication on diet, nutrition, and health that covers a wide range of topics, including food safety, nutrition comparison charts, herbal remedies, and best buys in brand-name foods. It is edited by a team of doctors, nurses, academics, and other health professionals.

Extra! The best magazine on the media, the main publication of FAIR (Fairness and Accuracy in Reporting). *Examples:* Articles in the September–October 2008 issue, "The Myth of Pro-Obama Media Bias" and "Spinning the Surge: Iraq and the Election."

Free Inquiry. Secular humanist publication that defends the importance of free inquiry in all areas of human endeavor. *Examples:* Articles on controversial topics like "The Republican War on Science" and "The Best Antidote for Religious Fanaticism."

Harper's. Very good general monthly, with some of the best writing on politics and culture in the country. The Harper's Index is famous for its illuminating statistics and facts about a wide variety of subjects. *Examples:* October 2008 article, "Bleak Houses," on the ruins of the mortgage crisis and a letter from Bombay, "Bollywood Shuffle."

Harvard Health Letter. An eight-page newsletter containing reasonably reliable medical information. The editorial board is staffed with doctors in different specialties, but the writing is geared to the general public.

Index an Censorship. A chronicle of censorship around the world that acts as a political forum with an international outlook. *Example:* The September 2008 issue examining extremism as one of the most common triggers for censorship since 9/11.

In These Times. Left-wing, socialist publication. Analyzes social, environmental, and economic justice in popular movements and discusses politics that shape our lives.

Mother Jones. Successor to *Ramparts:* radical left viewpoint, with occasionally very good exposes. Investigates politicians, corporations, and governments, sometimes irreverently, and champions environmentalism. *Examples:* September–October 2008 articles, "Will the Next Prez Give the Power Back?" and "Why Did the Press Let the President Lie?"

The Nation. Long-established left-wing magazine, very much improved under the current editor and now very good indeed. It covers politics extensively, as well as economics and the arts, and has a searchable index of items in every issue from 1865 to the present. *Examples:* November 10, 2008, articles, "Obamalina," "Protect This Election," and "The GOP's Blame-ACORN Game."

National Geographic. The long-established special-topic magazine. Tends to make the world look somewhat better than it is, but nevertheless has interesting articles, with very good, sometimes stunning, visuals about interesting places around the world. *Examples:* November 2008 articles, "Elephant Seal Sojourn," "In Mexico, a People Apart," and "Light Pollution."

National Review. Perhaps the most interesting conservative magazine. It covers mainly current political issues, with a long cover story for each issue as well as columns, book reviews, and political cartoons. *Examples:* Articles in the September 29, 2008, issue: "Palin Fire" and "Biden's Baggage."

Natural History. A publication of the American Museum of Natural History. An attractive magazine with good nature photography, featuring articles written by scientists or naturalists for a general audience.

Nature Conservancy. Magazine sent to contributors to the Nature Conservancy, an organization that purchases land in the attempt to preserve natural habitats. *Examples:* in autumn 2008 issue, "Flora and Fauna Coral" and "Mediterranean SOS."

New Internationalist. Excellent, very left-wing publication intent on reporting issues of world poverty and inequality and the unjust relationship between the powerful and the powerless. *Examples:* the November 2008 issue devoted to Afghanistan—"Afghanistan on the Edge," "Beyond the Burka," and "Theater of Justice."

New Republic. Long-established liberal (sort of) political magazine. *Examples:* September 2008 articles, "The Case Against Sarah Palin" and "Obama Versus McCain, the Money Map."

Newsletter on Intellectual Freedom. American Library Association newsletter containing lists of censored books.

Newsweek. Mass media, general news weekly. Trendy, good for summarizing a week's happenings, but generally fails to scratch the surface. *Examples:* October 8, 2008, articles, "Sarah Palin's Just-Folks Problem," "Will Folk Remedies Cure a Cold," and "Capitalism's Not Dead Yet."

New Yorker. A very good general magazine, with funny cartoons (several reprinted in this textbook), great photos, plus information on goings-on in New York City. *Examples:* in the October 27, 2008, issue, "The Insiders, Sarah Palin's Elite Washington Friends," "Method Man, Marlon Brando's Dilemma," and film reviews of *W.* and *Changeling*.

New York Review of Books. Very good left-wing publication with excellent, indeed sometimes superb, lengthy reviews and articles. *Examples:* November 20, 2008, articles, "Obama and Sweet Potato Pie," "Science: The Coming Century," and a review of the book *Angler: The Cheney Vice Presidency.* Also David Levine's great caricatures.

Nutrition Action Health Letter. Publication of the Center for Science in the Public Interest. An excellent source of information about food and health. Each issue tends to focus on topics in the news. *Examples:* October 2008 articles, "Germ Warfare" and "Food Additive Loopholes."

Politico.com. New (2007) online magazine covering national political news (about congress, the 2008 election, lobbying, etc.). Run by two former *Washington Post* staffers, it has brought some big-name journalists on board and is a publication worth watching. *Examples:* Articles from November 2008, "Conservatives Mull Their Political Future," "How to Get an Obama Staff Job," and "Prop. 8 Wins Supreme Court Review."

Reason. Perhaps the most interesting of the libertarian (pro free enterprise, con big government) publications. *Examples:* Articles in the December 2008 issue, "Back to the Barricades," "Free Markets Are Under Attack Again," and "The Spin We Love to Hate."

Salon.com. Online magazine with a liberal slant that focuses on U.S. politics but covers a range of issues from technological advances to book, music, and film reviews. *Examples:* November 2008 articles, "Sex and Power in the Age of Obama," "Democratic Leadership: No Bailout for Detroit," and "Trust Obama on Clinton."

Science News. Very good weekly, packed with information about what is new in science. *Examples:* Articles in October 11, 2008, issue, "Nurture Alone Can Lead to Depression," "Oldest Known Rocks Uncovered," and "Fatty Acid Makes Rats Happy."

Scientific American. Excellent science monthly, often difficult going for lay readers, but worth the effort. *Examples:* The September 2008 special issue on privacy with articles on "Brave New World Wiretapping," "Keeping Your Genes Private," and "Beyond Fingerprinting."

Skeptical Inquirer. Publication of the Committee for the Scientific Investigation of Claims of the Paranormal—the best periodical on pseudoscience. *Examples:* Articles in the September–October 2008 issue, "The Bipolar Bamboozle," "The Myth of Nibriu and the End of the World in 2012," and "Lighthouse Specters."

Slate. A liberal online magazine of news, culture, and politics—plus *Doonesbury* cartoons. *Examples:* November 2008 articles, "Barack to Reality," "What's the Best Way to Pack a Court," and "The Conservative Crack-up," a debate on the future of the GOP.

Textbook Letter. The best source of information about the quality of new public school textbooks.

Time. Mass media general news weekly. Trendy, generally fails to scratch the surface. *Examples:* October 28, 2008, articles, "The Obama Surge," "The Meltdown Goes Global," and "The Limits of Race."

TV Guide. Lists each week's TV offerings, plus sometimes interesting articles on TV programs and personalities.

Utne Reader. Reprints "the best of the alterative press" and is perhaps itself the best of the magazines that reprint material from other magazines. *Examples:* Articles in the September–October 2008 issue, "Green All the Lawyers," "In Praise of Economic Pain," and "Taking Sex Ed to School."

U.S. News & World Report. A mass media general newsweekly that is tilted a bit to the right. *Examples:* October 3, 2008, articles, "Negative Campaigning, Is it Good or Bad for the Country," "Election 2008, Swing State Showdown," and "The Environment: The Race for the Arctic."

Washington Monthly. Neo-liberal. Our favorite magazine on how our political system works and might be improved. *Examples:* Articles in August–September 2008 issue, "Freedom's Long March," "Iraq Bottom," and "Setup on K Street."

Washington Post National Weekly. A compendium of articles, columns, and cartoons from the *Washington Post. Examples:* Articles in the September, 29, 2008, issue, "Bush Veterans Run the McCain Campaign," "Finances: Retirement? Dream On . . . ," and "Medicine: Surgery Without an Incision."

Wired. Nerds' online magazine on computing, the Internet, and other areas of science and technology. *Examples:* November 2, 2008, articles, "A Photo Essay of Classic Instruction Manuals" and "Cairo Activists Use Facebook to Rattle Regime."

Women's Health Watch. A very good Harvard University health letter for women. *Examples:* October 2008 articles, "Strengthening Core Muscles" and "Viagra for Antidepressant-Related Sexual Problems."

World. A weekly newsmagazine reporting from a right-wing Christian perspective. *Examples:* November 2008 articles, "No Retreat, Conservative Reaction to GOP Defeat" and "In a Day of Hardship Remember Nothing is Too Hard for God."

GLOSSARY

ad hominem   An attack on one's opponent rather than one's opponent's argument.

affirming the consequent   Arguing in a way that has the following invalid form (also called *asserting the consequent*):

1. If *A* then *B*.
2. *B*.
∴3. *A*.

analogical reasoning   Reasoning from the similarity of two things in several relevant respects to their similarity in another.

appeal to authority   Accepting the word of an authority, alleged or genuine, when we should not.

appeal to ignorance   Believing that something is true because there is no good evidence that it is false.

argument   One or more statements (premises) offered in support of another statement (a conclusion).

background belief   A belief that is brought to bear in evaluating an argument's cogency.

begging the question   Assuming as a premise some form of the very point that is at issue—the conclusion we intend to prove.

biased statistics   Fallaciously reasoning from a sample that is insufficiently representative of the population from which it is drawn.

categorical proposition   A proposition (statement) that asserts or denies a relationship between a *subject class* and a *predicate class*.

cause   (of an event) Something necessary to bring about a particular result, or part of what is sufficient to bring it about.

claim   The argument's conclusion.

cogent reasoning   Valid reasoning from justified (warranted) premises that include all likely relevant information.

cognitive meaning   The part of the meaning of a word or expression that refers to things, events, or properties of one kind or another.

common practice   The fallacy in which a wrong is justified on the grounds that lots or most others do that sort of thing.

comparison of alternatives   Arguing for a course of action by showing that likely alternatives are less desirable.

composition   The fallacy in which it is argued that a particular item must have a certain property because all or most of its parts have it.

concatenated reasoning   Reasoning that employs several inductions and deductions, concluding to a pattern that fits what has been observed so far.

conclusion   What the premises of an argument are claimed to prove.

contingent statement   A statement that is neither necessarily true (a tautology, logical truth) nor necessarily false (inconsistent, a contradiction).

contradiction   A statement that is necessarily false (inconsistent, a contradiction), or a group of statements that taken together are inconsistent.

culture lag   The tendency of practices and beliefs to persist long after whatever conditions made them useful or sensible have disappeared.

deductively valid   An argument the truth of whose premises guarantees the truth of its conclusion, so that if its premises are true, then its conclusion must be true also.

deductively invalid   Any argument that does not have a deductively valid form.

delusion   A strong belief held despite strong evidence invalidating it.

denial   Denying the existence of painful situations, thoughts, or feelings or reinterpreting them to make them seem less threatening.

denying the antecedent   Arguing in a way that has the following invalid form:
1. If A then B.
2. Not A.
∴3. Not B.

dilemma   An argument that presents two alternative courses of action, both claimed to be bad.

disjunctive syllogism   A deductively valid argument having the following form:
1. A or B.
2. Not A.
∴3. B.

division   The fallacy in which it is assumed that all (or some) of the parts of an item have a particular property because the item as a whole has that property.

either-or fallacy   Mistakenly reasoning from two alternatives, one claimed to be bad (to be avoided), so that we ought to choose the other alternative in particular when there is at least another viable alternative.

emotive meaning   The positive or negative overtones of a word or expression.

equivocation   Use of a term in a passage to mean one thing in one place and something else in another.

essay   A passage (usually consisting of at least several paragraphs) that argues for a conclusion.

evading the issue   A fallacy in which a question at issue is avoided (usually) while appearing not to.

fallacious reasoning   Reasoning that is not cogent, because it suppresses relevant evidence, contains a questionable premise, or is invalid.

false charge of fallacy   Wrongly accusing others of a fallacy.

false dilemma   A dilemma that can be shown to be false because either one of its premises is false or there is a third alternative.

faulty comparison   A questionable analogy.

form   (of an argument) Its logical or grammatical structure.

guilt by association   Judging someone guilty solely on the basis of the company that person keeps.

hasty conclusion   The fallacious drawing of a conclusion from relevant but insufficient evidence.

herd instinct   The tendency to keep our beliefs, and thus our actions, within the bounds of what society as a whole will accept.

higher-level inductions   Very general inductions that can be used to evaluate those that are less general.

hypothetical syllogism   A deductively valid argument having the following form:
1. If *A* then *B*.
2. If *B* then *C*.
∴3. If *A* then *C*.

identification advertisement   An ad aimed to motivate its intended audience to identify either with a particular product or with the product's manufacturer or distributor.

inconsistent   Contradictory.

indirect proof   An argument in which the opposite of a desired conclusion is assumed as a premise, leading to a conclusion that is false, contradictory, or patently absurd, justifying acceptance of the desired conclusion.

induction   Reasoning that a pattern of some sort experienced so far will continue into the future.

induction by enumeration   An inductively valid argument moving from a premise stating that all so far examined *A*s are *B*s to the conclusion that all *A*s whatsoever are *B*s.

inductively valid   Correctly reasoning that a pattern experienced so far will continue into the future.

irony   Locutions that literally say one thing although their intended meaning is something else, usually opposite to its literal meaning.

irrelevant reason   A broad fallacy category containing several narrower fallacies in which a premise of an argument is irrelevant to its conclusion.

logical truth   A statement that is necessarily (logically) true; a statement that can be proved to be true by logic alone.

loyalty   Unwavering allegiance to one's group.

major term   The predicate of the conclusion of a syllogism.

margin note and summary method   A method for evaluating an extended passage by constructing a summary of that passage and evaluating the summary.

middle term   The term that occurs once in each premise of a syllogism but not in its conclusion.

minor term   The subject of the conclusion of a syllogism.

modus ponens   A deductively valid argument having the following form:
1. If *A* then *B*.
2. *A*.
∴3. *B*.

modus tollens   A deductively valid argument having the following form:
1. If *A* then *B*.
2. Not *B*.
∴3. Not *A*.

mood   (of a syllogism) The classification of a syllogism depending on the kinds of propositions (A, E, I, or O) it contains.

obfuscate   To be so confused or opaque as to be difficult to understand.

particular affirmative proposition   A proposition having the form "Some *A*s are *B*s"; an I proposition.

particular negative proposition   A proposition having the form "Some *A*s are not *B*s"; an O proposition.

partisan mind-set   An attitude of strong, often biased, allegiance to a faction, cause, or person that results in viewing everything in terms of "us" versus "them."

philosophy   The most important of one's background beliefs (including those about morality, God, the "meaning of life," etc.), usually but not always very general; one's worldview.

plagiarism   Verbatim, or close to it, use of someone else's writings without acknowledging the source, making it appear to be one's own material.

predicate class   The items referred to by the predicate of a categorical proposition.

prejudice   Thinking ill of others without sufficient warrant, particularly members of a specific group, race, or religion.

premise   A reason offered in support of an argument's conclusion.

pro and con argument   An argument that considers reasons in favor of and against a thesis or conclusion.

procrastination   Putting off for tomorrow what common sense tells us needs to be done today.

promise advertisement   An ad that promises to satisfy desires or allay fears.

provincialism   A limited perspective shaped by the ideas, interests, and kinds of behavior favored by the groups with which we identify.

pseudoscientific theories   Theories that are without scientific foundation.

questionable analogy   Reasoning by an analogy that is not apt, not justified.

questionable cause   Labeling *A* as the cause of *B* on evidence that is insufficient, negative, or unrepresentative, or is in serious conflict with well-established high-level theories.

questionable premise   Accepting a less than believable premise or other statement.

quibble   To attempt to take advantage of the failure of one's opponent to cross every *t* and dot every *i*, to spell out what should be taken for granted.

rationalization   A psychological ploy we use to justify our actions or beliefs, however wrong, by coming up with self-satisfying but incorrect reasons to explain them.

reasoning   Inferring from what we already know or believe to something else; the conclusion reached by reasoning.

reasons   Statements (premises) offered in support or acceptance of another statement (conclusion).

reductio ad absurdum proof   An argument in which the contradictory of a desired conclusion is assumed as a premise, leading to a conclusion that is false, contradictory, or patently absurd, justifying acceptance of the desired conclusion.

refutation to counterargument   An attempt to refute one's opponent's arguments against one's own position.

scapegoat   One who is blamed for the ills of the world.

self-deception   Consciously believing at a deeper level what we know to be dubious.

slanting   A form of misrepresentation in which a true statement is made to suggest something else (usually either known to be false or not known to be true). Also, the careful selection of facts so as to imply something else (usually something false).

slippery slope argument   Objecting to a course of action on the grounds that once it is taken, another, and then perhaps still others, is bound to be taken; or arguing that whatever would justify taking the first step would justify the others, where, given that the last step is not justified, then neither is the first.

slippery slope fallacy   Arguing that a slope is slippery without providing good reasons for thinking that it is.

small sample   Drawing conclusions about a population on the basis of a sample that is too small to be a reliable measure of that population.

statistical induction   An induction that moves from the premise that a certain percentage of a sample has a particular property to the conclusion that the whole population from which it is drawn has the same percentage of that property.

stereotype   A conventional oversimplification, often negative, of characteristics that describe a specific group of people.

straw man   A fallacious form of reasoning in which an opponent's position, or a competitor's product, is misrepresented or a weaker opponent is attacked rather than stronger ones.

subject class   The items referred to by the subject of a categorical proposition.

superstition   An irrational belief, based on biased evidence or on small or unrepresentative samples, that ignores logical evidence to the contrary.

suppressed evidence   The fallacy in which evidence contrary to one's position is neglected (overlooked).

suppression Avoiding thoughts that are stressful by either not thinking about them or by thinking nonstressful thoughts.

syllogism An argument containing exactly three categorical propositions, two of them premises, one a conclusion.

tautology A statement that is logically, or necessarily, true or so devoid of content as to be practically empty.

thesis The conclusion of an extended argumentative passage; its conclusion.

tokenism Mistaking a token gesture for the real thing, or accepting a token gesture in lieu of something more substantive.

tone The attitudes or feelings expressed by a passage.

traditional wisdom Accepting an unsuitable practice because doing so follows a traditional or accepted way of doing things.

two wrongs make a right Justifying a wrong by pointing to a similar wrong done by others, usually by one's accuser.

universal affirmative proposition A proposition having the form "All *S* are *P*"; an *A* proposition.

universal negative proposition A proposition having the form "No *S* are *P*"; an E proposition.

unrepresentative sample Fallaciously reasoning from a sample that is insufficiently representative of the population from which it is drawn.

valid A criterion of cogent reasoning requiring that the premises of an argument genuinely support its conclusion, either deductively or inductively.

warranted premise A premise that is believable given one's background beliefs and other evidence.

weasel word A word that appears to make little or no change in a passage while in fact sucking out most of its content.

wishful thinking Believing what we would like to be true, no matter what the evidence.

worldview The most important of one's background beliefs (including those about morality, God, the "meaning of life," etc.), usually but not always very general; one's philosophy.

INDEXES

Subject Index

Name Index

Media Index

K

King Features Syndicate, 34
Knight Ridder, 278, 314

L

Larry King Live, 90, 115,
    264, 273–274
Law and Order, 311
Lehrer News Hour, 261
Literary Digest, 107
Little Brown and
    Company, 314
London Times, 291, 313, 314
Los Angeles Times, 120, 173,
    268–269, 272, 288, 312

M

*Marin Independent
    Journal,* 115
Masterpiece Theater!, 39
McGraw-Hill, 346
Meet the Press, 89
Miramax Films, 314
Money, 314
MSNBC, 283, 292, 301,
    306, 314
MSNBC.com, 301
Murphy Brown, 298
MySpace, 308

N

The Nation, 21, 55, 310,
    321, 334
The National Review, 229,
    288, 291, 321
NBC, 234, 273, 280, 284,
    286, 295, 299, 310, 314,
    316, 320
NBC Network News, 314
New Corporation, 314
*New England Journal of
    Medicine,* 96, 251,
    290–291
The New Republic, 68,
    288, 351
*Newsletter on Intellectual
    Freedom* (American
    Library Association),
    348

Newsweek, 20, 261, 297, 310,
    311, 320, 321
The New Yorker, 215,
    234, 322
The New Yorker Collection,
    2, 46, 72, 202, 287
New York Post, 313, 314
*New York Review of
    Books,* 329
New York Times, 24, 62, 66,
    67, 75, 85, 86, 88, 99,
    113, 117, 155, 157, 161,
    162, 170, 187, 193–194,
    198, 243, 249, 251, 252,
    264, 272, 274, 278, 280,
    288, 295, 298, 301,
    311–312, 314, 316,
    343, 381
New York Times Magazine,
    90, 170
Nightline, 310
Nightly News
    (NBC), 299
Nova, 310
NPR (National Public
    Radio), 274,
    311, 320
*Nutrition Action Health
    Letter,* 112
NYREV, Inc., 270, 332

O

Omni magazine, 319

P

Pacific Sun, 90
PBS (Public Broadcasting
    Service), 39, 274, 310,
    315, 319, 343
People, 314
Philadelphia Inquirer,
    89–90, 276
The Pioneer Press,
    276, 317
Prime Time Live, 314
The Progressive, 121
Project Censored, 309
*Public Citizen's Health
    Letter,* 121
The Public I, 315

Q

*Quarterly Review of
    Doublespeak,* 155
Quill magazine, 119–120

R

Reason, 321
Reuters, 320

S

San Francisco Chronicle, 60,
    69, 86, 102, 106, 114,
    118, 133, 160, 162,
    201–203, 223–224,
    225, 230, 249, 276,
    285, 292, 301, 309,
    325, 342, 350
San Francisco Examiner,
    118, 199, 305
Science Friday, 311
Science News, 79–80,
    103, 117
Scientific American,
    120, 138
Scott Foresman-Addison
    Wesley, 346
*Secular Humanist
    Bulletin,* 142
60 Minutes, 67, 252, 310
60 Minutes II, 301–302, 310
Skeptical Inquirer, 141,
    274, 343
SpaceBook, 308
Sports Illustrated, 175, 314
Survivor, 307

T

Talk of the Nation, 311
TBS, 314
Telemundo Communications
    Group, 314
The Textbook Letter, 337,
    339–340
This Week, 86
Time magazine, 21, 67, 69,
    104, 114, 272, 297, 310,
    314, 320, 321
Time Warner, 314
TNT, 314

CREDITS

This page constitutes an extension of the copyright page. We have made every effort to trace the ownership of all copyrighted material and to secure permission from copyright holders. In the event of any question arising as to the use of any material, we will be pleased to make the necessary corrections in future printings. Thanks are due to the following authors, publishers, and agents for permission to use the material indicated.

Chapter Opener 1. xiv: © The New Yorker Collection 1987 James Stevenson from cartoonbank.com. All rights reserved. **12:** Calvin and Hobbes © 1992 Watterson. Reprinted with permission of Universal Press Syndicate. All rights reserved. **14:** Doonesbury © 1997 G. B. Trudeau. Reprinted with permission of Universal Press Syndicate. All rights reserved.

Chapter 2. 30: Peanuts © United Feature Syndicate, Inc. **34:** Beetle Bailey © King Features Syndicate.

Chapter 3. 46: © The New Yorker Collection 1975 George Booth from cartoonbank.com. All rights reserved. **53:** Cartoon by Tom Meyer. © San Francisco Chronicle. Reprinted by permission. **54:** Mike Peters EDTCTN (New) © King Features Syndicate **56:** Reprinted by permission of Tribune Media Services. **63:** Doonesbury © 1973 G. B. Trudeau. Reprinted with permission of Universal Press Syndicate. All rights reserved.

Chapter 4. 72: © The New Yorker Collection 1974 Henry Martin from cartoonbank.com. All rights reserved. **80:** © Dan Wasserman, The Boston Globe, Tribune Media Services.

Chapter 5. 92: Doonesbury © 1975 G. B. Trudeau. Reprinted with permission of Universal Press Syndicate. All rights reserved.

Chapter 6. 122: Calvin and Hobbes © 1993 Watterson. Reprinted with permission of Universal Press Syndicate. All rights reserved. **146:** Luann: © GEC Inc./Dist. by United Feature Syndicate, Inc.

Chapter 7. 150: Toles © 1989 The Buffalo News. Reprinted with permission of Universal Press Syndicate. All rights reserved. **156:** Toles © The Buffalo News. Reprinted with permission of Universal Press Syndicate. All rights reserved. **160:** Farley by Phil Frank. San Francisco Chronicle, April 22, 1998. © Phil Frank. Used by permission. **168:** © 1996 Don Wright, Inc. **171:** © 1996 Signe Wilkinson. Used with the permission of Signe Wilkinson and the Washington Post Writers Group in conjunction with the Cartoonist Group. All rights reserved. **175:** Calvin and Hobbes © 1993 Watterson. Reprinted with permission of Universal Press Syndicate. All rights reserved.